Revelation Revealed

Revelation Revealed

Understanding the Book of Revelation

NICK PEROS

WIPF & STOCK · Eugene, Oregon

REVELATION REVEALED
Understanding the Book of Revelation

Copyright © 2022 Nick Peros. All rights reserved. Except for brief quotations in critical publications or reviews, no part of this book may be reproduced in any manner without prior written permission from the publisher. Write: Permissions, Wipf and Stock Publishers, 199 W. 8th Ave., Suite 3, Eugene, OR 97401.

Wipf & Stock
An Imprint of Wipf and Stock Publishers
199 W. 8th Ave., Suite 3
Eugene, OR 97401

www.wipfandstock.com

PAPERBACK ISBN: 978-1-6667-3542-0
HARDCOVER ISBN: 978-1-6667-9248-5
EBOOK ISBN: 978-1-6667-9249-2

MARCH 3, 2022 8:11 AM

Scripture quotations marked NIV are taken from the Holy Bible, New International Version®, NIV®. Copyright © 1973, 1978, 1984, 2011 by Biblica, Inc.™ Used by permission of Zondervan. All rights reserved worldwide. www.zondervan.com

Scripture quotations marked NKJV are taken from the New King James Version®. Copyright © 1982 by Thomas Nelson. Used by permission. All rights reserved.

Scripture quotations marked NASB are taken from the New American Standard Bible®, NRSV®. Copyright © 1960, 1962, 1963, 1968, 1971, 1972, 1973, 1975, 1977, 1995 by The Lockman Foundation Used by permission. www.Lockman.org

Scripture quotations marked RSV are taken from Revised Standard Version of the Bible. Copyright © 1946, 1952, and 1971 National Council of the Churches of Christ in the United States of America. Used by permission. All rights reserved worldwide.

Scripture quotations marked ESV are taken from The ESV® Bible (The Holy Bible, English Standard Version®). Copyright © 2001 by Crossway, a publishing ministry of Good News Publishers. Used by permission. All rights reserved.

Scripture quotations marked YLT are taken from Young's Literal Translation, public domain.

Scripture quotations marked ASV are taken from American Standard Version, public domain.

Scripture quotations marked GB are taken from Geneva Bible, public domain.

Contents

Introduction | vii

1 Beasts | 1
2 The Prostitute, Babylon, the Sea | 11
3 The Rapture | 31
4 Israel and Judah | 53
5 Breakdown and Timelines of Revelation | 71
6 Introduction—Revelation 1 | 91
7 The Seven Letters—Revelation 2 and 3 | 102
8 Prelude to Judgment—Revelation 4 and 5 | 120
9 The Seven Seals | 134
10 The Great Tribulation—The Trumpets and the Bowls | 166
11 The Days of Noah | 191
12 The Nephilim | 212
13 The Nature of the Beast | 236
14 The Rule of the Beast | 259
15 The Mark of the Beast | 293

16	THE TWO WITNESSES AND THE 144,000	307
17	THE GREAT TRIBULATION	321
18	SEAL 6—THE FALL OF BABYLON THE GREAT	331
19	SEAL 7—THE RESURRECTION OF BELIEVERS	345
20	SEAL 7—THE SECOND COMING	351
21	JUDGMENT AND THE KINGDOM	359
22	THE NEW JERUSALEM	374
23	THE BOOK OF REVELATION–A SUMMARY	385

Introduction

THE BOOK OF REVELATION is perhaps the most unique book of the Bible. It is the only book that tells us we are blessed if we read its words aloud (Rev 1:3), and yet also warns us that we are cursed if we add to, or take away from, its words (Rev 22:18–19). It is the only New Testament book that is all prophecy, and it is steeped in symbolism. It is often approached with trepidation since it describes terrible events to come upon the Earth, and at times it seems almost impenetrable due to its extensive imagery.

However, as with any book of the Bible, it is very much understandable, and we can unlock its meaning by referring to the Bible itself. One of the fundamental keys in helping to understand Revelation is understanding its key imagery and symbols. Some of this key imagery includes beasts, the Prostitute, Babylon, horns, the sea. It is important to understand that when God uses imagery and symbols in the Bible, he is consistent in his use and meaning of those symbols—when he uses an image or symbol in an initial context, then the meaning of that image or symbol remains constant throughout the rest of the Bible.

For example, the beasts described in Revelation 13 and 17 can only be understood by referring to Daniel 7 and 2. By looking at both Daniel 7 and 2 we can come to understand exactly what those beasts mean, for God explains it for us in Daniel. Likewise, in order to understand the image or symbol of the Prostitute, we must look to see how that symbol was originally, and consistently, used by God throughout Scripture, for it is a common image throughout the Bible. By using Scripture itself as our guide, we can come to a clear understanding of these symbols.

Revelation is a prophecy of the events that lead to the Second Coming, the return of Jesus Christ. Some, though, believe the events of Revelation have already been fulfilled in ancient times (preterism)—this is based on trying to identify certain aspects of Revelation in the historical context.

It is true that there are parallels between some of the events of Revelation and history. For example, the number of the name of the Roman emperor Nero is 666. Also, the seven churches of Revelation 2 and 3 were actual churches upon the Earth in John's day. However, those historical parallels are just that—parallels, they are not the fulfillment of future events. So yes, the number of the name of the Roman emperor Nero is 666, but that does not mean that Nero is the fulfillment of the prophecies of the Beast; rather, by being a historical parallel, then, by understanding key elements about Nero, it allows us to understand some of the key elements of the future Beast. Likewise, the seven churches of Revelation 2 and 3 are not the fulfillment of prophesied events; rather, by being a historical parallel, the issues faced by those seven churches are themselves an illustration of the issues that will be faced by the future church, which will be present on Earth in the days that precede the Second Coming. As historical parallels, those ancient events are themselves only a picture of future events, acting, in their own way, as a further symbolic imagery of the events to come.

However, in regard to preterism, although biblical prophecy can often be working on multiple levels simultaneously, speaking to the day in which it was written while also having a much broader scope and context for a fuller future fulfillment, there is no question that the events of Revelation are yet to happen, for the Second Coming of Jesus Christ is not a symbolic event, but a real happening, and it is an event yet to happen. Likewise, the events that precede his Second Coming are yet to unfold, for we are told by Jesus himself that the events of those days will be the worst events ever upon the Earth, never to be equalled again, telling us that if he does not return to stop those terrible events, there would be no life left upon the Earth (Matt 24:21–22). No such thing has yet occurred upon the Earth, and so these events are yet to happen.

In addition to helping unlock the *meaning* of the symbols and imagery of Revelation, Scripture itself is fundamental in helping us unlock the *sequence* of events in Revelation. It is impossible to understand the sequence of events in Revelation without referring to Matthew 24:3–31. In Matthew 24:3–31, Jesus himself describes for us the Seven Seals of Revelation (Rev 6; 8:1–5; 19:11–21). We know from Revelation itself that only Jesus Christ has the authority to open the Seven Seals (Rev 5)—any angel can blow the Trumpets of Revelation, any angel can pour the Bowls of Revelation, but only Jesus Christ himself can open the Seven Seals. From Matthew 24, we learn that the Seven Seals of Revelation are the *entirety* of the judgment of Revelation, spanning a period of forty years, with the entire seven-year rule of the Beast, the persecution of the church and the Great Tribulation, all happening during Seal 5—Jesus himself makes that clear in Matthew 24. Matthew 24 is the foundational key to understanding the big-picture timeline of Revelation.

One of the things that makes Revelation particularly confusing is trying to understand the various timelines. It is a great help to first recognize that Revelation can be divided into four clear sections—chapter 1 is the introduction; chapters 2–3 are the letters to the angels of seven churches; chapters 4–18 are the details of the Beast's rule, the persecution of the church and the Great Tribulation; chapters 19–22 describe the Second Coming and beyond.

Within these four clear sections, it is important to recognize that the events described are not always chronological. Chapters 1–3 are chronological and chronologically precede chapters 4–18, but it is in the events of chapters 4–18 that confusion arises. It becomes clear, upon close study of Scripture, that there are three different

INTRODUCTION

timelines described in chapters 4–18. The first timeline is the overall, big-picture timeline of the Seven Seals, spanning forty years. The second timeline is the timeline of the Great Tribulation and the events immediately preceding the Second Coming, spanning three and a half years—this is the timeline of the Seven Trumpets, with those Trumpets all occurring during Seals 5, 6, and 7. The third timeline is the final five months of the Great Tribulation in more detail, as well as the thirty days following the Great Tribulation—this is the timeline of the Seven Bowls, all of which occur during Trumpets 5 and 6.

In addition, throughout chapters 4–18, there is a further going back and forth in time, which is why certain very major events are repeated in the text and, seemingly, happen twice.

For example, in Revelation 6:14 we are told that every island and mountain has moved, but we are also told again, in 16:20, that every island and mountain has moved; in 6:17 we are told that the day of wrath has come, and we are told again in 11:18 that the wrath has come; in 9:14 we are told of events at the Euphrates River concerning armies and military movements, and in 16:12 we are told again of events at the Euphrates River concerning armies and military movements; in 14:8 we are told that Babylon has fallen, and we are told again in 18:2 that Babylon has fallen; we are told in 14:20 that the winepress of God's wrath is now trodden, and we are told again in 19:15 that the winepress of God's wrath is now trodden; we are told in 11:15–18 that the Second Coming will now happen, and we are told again in 19:11–21 that the Second Coming will now happen.

Is it possible that each of these events are happening twice? Does Babylon fall twice? Does Jesus have two Second Comings? Does the Euphrates dry up to make way for military maneuvers twice? No, each of these events happen only once, and the reason they appear twice in Revelation is because in one instance the event is described as part of the bigger Trumpet timeline, while in the other instance that same event is described in the more detailed Bowl timeline. The Trumpets are just details of events mostly during Seal 5, and the Bowls are just further details of the events of Trumpets 5 and 6. Once we understand the going back and forth in time, and the three different timelines that are described, we can begin to have a much clearer grasp and understanding of Revelation.

Another key point to understand in regard to the events of Revelation is the nature of Israel and the Jews. One very common misconception that leads to many problems in understanding the prophecies of the days of Revelation is to confuse Israel with the Jews.

During the reign of King Rehoboam, Solomon's son, the one nation Israel split into two nations, with one nation becoming the Northern Kingdom and with the other nation becoming the Southern Kingdom. The Northern Kingdom, comprised of ten tribes and with Samaria as its capital, continued to be called Israel, while the Southern Kingdom, comprised of only three tribes and whose capital was Jerusalem, took the name Judah. The word "Jew" comes from the name Judah, and only the people of the three tribes of the nation Judah are Jews. Since the days of King Rehoboam, during whose reign that split of Israel occurred, the distinction between Israel and Judah is a distinction that God keeps throughout all prophecy, and this is foundational to understanding some of the meaning of Revelation—only three tribes of Israel are Jews, while all the other tribes of Israel are, to the world, Gentiles.

Another factor that causes confusion in understanding Revelation is a teaching known as the Rapture. The Rapture is a teaching that was invented only in the 1830s by John Darby, and popularized by Scofield only from 1909 with the publication of his Scofield Reference Bible. In the two-thousand-year history of the church, the Rapture teaching did not exist for 95 percent of the church's entire existence—the church has never believed nor taught such a teaching; it is a new teaching, and it is important to understand that the Rapture teaching, in every version, variation or form, is unbiblical, having no scriptural support whatsoever. However, when the Rapture teaching is invoked, it begins to make Revelation almost impossible to understand. The Rapture teaching has been described as Satan's favorite teaching, as it ensures that the church will not be prepared for what is to come, and yet the preparation of the church for the events that will come is so vitally important that Revelation begins with seven letters from Jesus to the angels of seven churches, telling the church to be prepared, to get ready for what is about to come, to persevere, and that if they persevere, they will inherit rewards, and the rewards that are described are the rewards that Jesus gives after his Second Coming.

The time period of Revelation, the days and events preceding and leading up to the Second Coming, are the most prophesied events in the Bible—there is more prophecy about those days and events than there is about anything else in the Bible. It is clear that those days and events are of great importance to God, and so it is important to pursue a clear understanding of Revelation. To begin to understand Revelation, we must begin by understanding some of the fundamental imagery and symbolism of Revelation—the imagery of beasts, horns, the sea, Babylon, and the Prostitute.

1

Beasts

Symbolism and imagery are at the very heart of the book of Revelation, and one of the key symbols used throughout Revelation is the image of a beast. The first detailed use of the beast symbol is in Revelation 13:1–4, and then again in 13:11–13 and 17:3, as follows:

> The dragon stood on the shore of the sea. And I saw a beast coming out of the sea. It had ten horns and seven heads, with ten crowns on its horns, and on each head a blasphemous name. The beast I saw resembled a leopard, but had feet like those of a bear and a mouth like that of a lion. The dragon gave the beast his power and his throne and great authority. One of the heads of the beast seemed to have had a fatal wound, but the fatal wound had been healed. The whole world was filled with wonder and followed the beast. People worshiped the dragon because he had given authority to the beast, and they also worshiped the beast and asked, "Who is like the beast? Who can wage war against it?" (13:1–4 NIV)

> Then I saw a second beast, coming out of the earth. It had two horns like a lamb, but it spoke like a dragon. It exercised all the authority of the first beast on its behalf, and made the earth and its inhabitants worship the first beast, whose fatal wound had been healed. And it performed great signs, even causing fire to come down from heaven to the earth in full view of the people. (13:11–13 NIV)

> Then the angel carried me away in the Spirit into a wilderness. There I saw a woman sitting on a scarlet beast that was covered with blasphemous names and had seven heads and ten horns. (17:3 NIV)

The beasts described in these passages are not natural beasts; they are not animals. It is clear that there is substantial symbolism in these beasts. The first beast, described in 13:1–4, is presented as a strange hybrid of three different beasts—a leopard, a bear, and a lion—and it is described as rising out of the sea. In addition, that beast is described as having seven heads and ten horns and as having the power, throne, and authority of the dragon. It is also described as having blasphemous names upon each of its seven heads and as having crowns upon its ten horns.

The second beast (13:11–13) is described only as coming out of the earth and as having two horns like a lamb, but speaking like a dragon.

The third beast (17:3) is the same beast of 13:1–4, but now there is an added element to the picture, an additional symbol, the image of a woman sitting on the beast and, seemingly, riding it.

How are we to understand the symbolism of these beasts? There is nothing in the context of those chapters, nor in the entirety of the book of Revelation, that helps explain the symbolism of the beasts. However, when we read Daniel 7, and then also Daniel 2, we encounter these exact same beasts, and in the book of Daniel the meaning of those beasts is explained for us.

DANIEL 7

> Four great beasts, each different from the others, came up *out of the sea*. The first was like a *lion*, and it had the wings of an eagle. I watched until its wings were torn off and it was lifted from the ground so that it stood on two feet like a human being, and the mind of a human was given to it.
>
> And there before me was a second beast, which looked like a *bear*. It was raised up on one of its sides, and it had three ribs in its mouth between its teeth. It was told, "Get up and eat your fill of flesh!"
>
> After that, I looked, and there before me was another beast, one that looked like a *leopard*. And on its back it had four wings like those of a bird. This beast had *four heads*, and it was given authority to rule.
>
> After that, in my vision at night I looked, and there before me was *a fourth beast*—terrifying and frightening and very powerful. It had large iron teeth; it crushed and devoured its victims and trampled underfoot whatever was left. It was different from all the former beasts, and it had *ten horns*. (Dan 7:3–8 NIV)

In Daniel 7 we encounter the same beasts as are represented in Revelation 13—a lion, a bear, and a leopard, with the leopard described as having four heads. Like the beast in Revelation 13, these four beasts also rise out of the sea. In addition, we encounter another very different and very strange beast, a fourth beast, described as "terrifying and frightening," as having iron teeth and as devouring its victims; like the beast of Revelation 13, that fourth beast is also described as having ten horns.

In regard to the number of heads of the four beasts in Daniel 7, the lion, the bear, and the beast with ten horns each have one head, three heads in total, while the leopard is described as having four heads. The four heads of the leopard, when combined with the one head each of the lion, the bear, and the fourth beast with ten horns, give a total of seven heads. When we combine the four beasts of Daniel 7, we have a lion-bear-leopard beast with seven heads and ten horns, rising out of the sea, exactly as the beast of Revelation 13. The beast of Revelation 13 is the combination of Daniel's four beasts.

What is the meaning of the beasts of Daniel 7? What do they represent? The meaning of those beasts is explained for us in the book of Daniel.

THE MEANING OF THE BEASTS

Daniel 7 continues and gives us the meaning of the beasts in the vision.

> I, Daniel, was troubled in spirit, and the visions that passed through my mind disturbed me. I approached one of those standing there and asked him the meaning of all this.
>
> So he told me and gave me the interpretation of these things: "The *four great beasts are four kings* that will rise from the earth. But the holy people of the Most High will receive the kingdom and will possess it forever—yes, for ever and ever."
>
> Then I wanted to know *the meaning of the fourth beast*, which was different from all the others and most terrifying, with its iron teeth and bronze claws—the beast that crushed and devoured its victims and trampled underfoot whatever was left. I also wanted to know about the *ten horns on its head* and about the *other horn that came up*, before which three of them fell—the horn that looked more imposing than the others and that had eyes and a mouth that spoke boastfully. As I watched, this horn was waging war against the holy people and defeating them, until the Ancient of Days came and pronounced judgment in favor of the holy people of the Most High, and the time came when they possessed the kingdom.
>
> He gave me this explanation: "*The fourth beast is a fourth kingdom that will appear on earth*. It will be different from all the other kingdoms and will devour the whole earth, trampling it down and crushing it. The *ten horns are ten kings* who will come from this kingdom. After them *another king will arise*, different from the earlier ones; he will subdue three kings. He will speak against the Most High and oppress his holy people and try to change the set times and the laws. The holy people will be delivered into his hands for a time, times and half a time." (Dan 7:15–25 NIV, italics added)

In Daniel 7:15–25, the meaning of the beasts of Daniel's vision is made clear. Each of the four beasts represents a *king* and a great *kingdom* to come upon the Earth, and these four great kingdoms are also understood as being four great *empires*. We are also told that the ten horns represent ten *kings*, and that an eleventh little horn will arise, and that little horn also represents a king. Based on Daniel 7, we know that the beast of Revelation 13, comprised of a lion, a bear, a leopard with four heads, and with a total of seven heads and ten horns, and rising out of the sea, is the combination of the four beasts of Daniel 7. As a result, since the meaning of the four beasts in Daniel is explained for us, we can therefore also know the meaning of the beast in Revelation 13. Since the beasts of Daniel 7 represent both great kingdoms and the kings who rule those kingdoms, likewise the beast of Revelation 13 represents a combination of the same *kingdoms* of Daniel 7 into one *new*, yet-to-come kingdom. Also, the ten horns of the Revelation 13 beast, like the ten horns of the beast in Daniel 7, represent an additional ten kings. Therefore, we can understand that the beast of Revelation 13 is a great, yet-to-come global kingdom, or empire.

THE SEVEN HEADS

In regard to the distribution of the seven heads in the Revelation 13 beast, we can understand that as follows:

In Daniel 7, it is the *leopard* that has the *four heads*, and all ten horns are *only* on the head of the fourth beast. Likewise, since the Revelation 13 beast is the combination of the four beasts of Daniel 7, we can understand the seven heads of the Revelation 13 beast in that same way, with four of the seven heads belonging to the leopard, and with the ten horns all being on only one of the beast's heads, rather than being distributed among all seven heads. Although Revelation 13 specifically names the lion, bear, and leopard in its description of the beast that rises from the sea, we can also understand that Daniel's fourth beast, the terrifying beast having teeth of iron, as certainly being part of the combined beast of Revelation 13, being that part which is the head with ten horns.

As a result, we can know that the strange, symbolic beast of Revelation 13 is in fact the combination of the four beasts of Daniel 7—the combination of the lion, the bear, the four-headed leopard, and the terrifying beast of iron with ten horns. We also know that since Daniel's four beasts represent four great kingdoms, the combination beast of Revelation 13 must also represent a great kingdom, or empire, that is itself, somehow, the combination of the previous four kingdoms that preceded it. Since the ten horns of Daniel 7 are clearly explained as being additional kings, that is, ten kings that are *in addition* to the kings and kingdoms represented by the four beasts, likewise the ten horns on the beast of Revelation 13 must also be additional kings, that is, ten kings that are in addition to the yet-to-come global empire and its global king.

Since the four beasts of Daniel 7 represent four kingdoms, then what are the four kingdoms that Daniel's beasts represent? In order to understand which kingdoms are represented by the four beasts of Daniel 7, we turn to Daniel 2.

DANIEL 2

Daniel 2 outlines a dream that was dreamt by the Babylonian king Nebuchadnezzar, and which was interpreted by Daniel and explained by him. Here is the passage in Daniel 2 that outlines the dream and the interpretation:

> The king asked Daniel (also called Belteshazzar), "Are you able to tell me what I saw in my dream and interpret it?"
>
> Daniel replied, "No wise man, enchanter, magician or diviner can explain to the king the mystery he has asked about, but there is a God in heaven who reveals mysteries. He has shown King Nebuchadnezzar what will happen in days to come. Your dream and the visions that passed through your mind as you were lying in bed are these:
>
> "As Your Majesty was lying there, *your mind turned to things to come*, and the revealer of mysteries showed you *what is going to happen*. As for me, this mystery has been revealed to me, not because I have greater wisdom than anyone else alive, but so that Your Majesty may know the interpretation and that you may understand what went through your mind.
>
> "Your Majesty looked, and *there before you stood a large statue—an enormous, dazzling statue, awesome in appearance*. The *head of the statue* was made of *pure gold*, its *chest and arms* of *silver*, its *belly and thighs* of *bronze*, its *legs* of *iron*, its *feet partly of iron and partly of baked clay*. While you were watching, *a rock was cut out, but not by human hands*. It *struck the statue on its feet of iron and clay and smashed them*. Then the iron, the clay, the bronze, the silver and the gold were all broken to pieces and became like chaff on a threshing floor in the summer. The wind swept them away without leaving a trace. But *the rock that struck the statue became a huge mountain and filled the whole earth*.
>
> "This was the dream, and now we will interpret it to the king. Your Majesty, you are the king of kings. The God of heaven has given you dominion and power and might and glory; in your hands he has placed all mankind and the beasts of the field and the birds in the sky. Wherever they live, he has made you ruler over them all. *You are that head of gold.*
>
> "*After you, another kingdom will arise*, inferior to yours. *Next*, a *third kingdom, one of bronze, will rule over the whole earth*. Finally, there will be *a fourth kingdom, strong as iron*—for iron breaks and smashes everything—and as iron breaks things to pieces, so it will crush and break all the others. *Just as you saw that the feet and toes were partly of baked clay and partly of iron, so this will be a divided kingdom*; yet it will have some of the strength of iron in it, even as you saw iron mixed with clay. *As the toes were partly iron and partly clay, so this kingdom will be partly strong and partly brittle. And just as you saw the iron mixed with baked clay, so the people will be a mixture and will not remain united, any more than iron mixes with clay.*
>
> "*In the time of those kings*, the God of heaven *will set up a kingdom that will never be destroyed*, nor will it be left to another people. It will crush all

those kingdoms and bring them to an end, but it will itself endure forever. This is the meaning of the vision of the rock cut out of a mountain, but not by human hands—a rock that broke the iron, the bronze, the clay, the silver and the gold to pieces.

"The great God has shown the king what will take place in the future. The dream is true and its interpretation is trustworthy." (Dan 2:26-45 NIV, italics added)

Daniel 2 tells us that in King Nebuchadnezzar's dream there was a large statue, divided into four parts—the statue had a head of gold, a chest and arms of silver, a belly and thighs of bronze, and legs of iron, with its ten toes being a combination of iron and clay. Daniel tells us that the head of gold is King Nebuchadnezzar; that is to say, it is his kingdom, Babylon.

After the head of gold, there is the chest and arms of silver, representing another kingdom that will succeed the kingdom of Babylon as a world power, and, being a kingdom of silver rather than a kingdom of gold, the kingdom that succeeds Babylon will be an inferior kingdom.

After the kingdom of silver, a third kingdom will arise, being described as a kingdom of bronze, and it too will be a great world power.

Finally, a fourth kingdom will arise, a kingdom of iron, succeeding the kingdom of bronze, a kingdom that will break and smash everything. That fourth kingdom will also have weakness in it, and that weakness is represented by the ten toes of iron and clay. Daniel tells us that all of this will happen in the future; it will happen in days to come, in the days *after* Nebuchadnezzar's Babylon.

How are we to identify the four kingdoms represented in Nebuchadnezzar's dream? Daniel gives us a concrete place to start—he tells us, very clearly, that the head of gold, the first part of the statue, is King Nebuchadnezzar and his kingdom of Babylon; that is our starting point in identifying the other kingdoms represented in the statue.

PARALLELS BETWEEN DANIEL 7 AND DANIEL 2

When we examine and compare Daniel 7 and Daniel 2, we see some very clear and striking parallels.

There are four beasts outlined in Daniel 7—ordered as lion, bear, leopard, and beast of iron. We are told that each of these four beasts represents a kingdom. There are four parts to the statue of Nebuchadnezzar's dream—a head of gold, chest and arms of silver, belly and thighs of bronze, and legs and toes of iron, with clay mixed with iron for the toes—and we are told that each section of the statue represents a kingdom.

The fourth beast of Daniel 7 is a very different and terrifying beast, and it has ten horns and is described as having iron teeth and as "devouring" all the Earth (7:23).

The fourth section of the statue in Daniel 2 is made of iron, very different than the precious metals of gold, silver, and bronze, which comprise the rest of the statue, and that statue section of iron has ten toes, and is described as a kingdom that will "break and smash everything" (2:40).

There is also a further parallel between the fourth section of the statue and the fourth beast—the material that comprises the fourth section of the statue, iron, is the same material that comprises some of the fourth beast, with its teeth of iron. The kingdom represented by the fourth section of the statue, the kingdom of iron, is described as a kingdom that will "break and smash everything," while the terrifying fourth beast of Daniel 7, with teeth of iron, is described as "devouring" all the Earth.

The parallels between the four sections of the statue and the four beasts are striking, and especially so with the fourth section of the statue and the fourth beast. In fact, we can understand that the four sections of the statue in Daniel 2, the four kingdoms, are parallel and analogous to the four beasts of Daniel 7, also four kingdoms. As a result, we can equate the first part of the statue in Daniel 2, the head of gold, with the first beast of Daniel 7, the lion; we can equate the second part of the statue of Daniel 2, the chest and arms of silver, with the second beast of Daniel 7, the bear; we can equate the third part of the statue of Daniel 2, the belly and thighs of bronze, with the third beast of Daniel 7, the four-headed leopard; and we can equate the fourth part of the statue of Daniel 2, the legs of iron, with the fourth beast, the terrifying iron beast of Daniel 7, and we can equate the ten iron-clay toes of the statue's iron legs with the ten horns of the fourth beast of Daniel 7.

In regard to identifying the kingdoms represented by the statue of Daniel 2, and therefore also represented by the four beasts of Daniel 7, we know the following. The first section of the statue, the head of gold, is King Nebuchadnezzar and his kingdom, Babylon, and since we know that the first section of the statue, the head of gold, is equivalent to the first beast of Daniel 7, we can therefore understand that the first beast of Daniel 7, the lion, is also the kingdom of Babylon. With that as our starting point, we can then identify the kingdoms of the remaining parts of the statue, and thereby the remaining beast kingdoms, from history.

THE KINGDOMS OF THE STATUE AND THE BEASTS

Historically, if we begin with Nebuchadnezzar's kingdom of Babylon (the Neo-Babylonian Empire, 626–539 BC), the kingdom that succeeded the Babylonian Empire, was the Medo-Persian Empire (539 BC–331 BC). The Medo-Persian Empire itself was then conquered by, and succeeded by, Alexander the Great and his empire. Alexander the Great was a Macedonian king who was tutored by Aristotle and, although he himself was Macedonian, he brought and spread Greek culture throughout the world by way of his vast empire. As a result, Alexander's empire is described as a Greek empire

(331–323 BC). The next great empire after Alexander's empire was the Roman Empire (241 BC–476 AD).

Alexander's empire bears a closer look, since the details of his empire are directly tied in with the beast of Daniel 7, the four-headed leopard.

Alexander the Great is considered the greatest conqueror in history, having fought some of the most significant battles in world history, and who alone among the great conquerors of history never lost a battle. Alexander was unstoppable, single-handedly building a vast empire that was bigger than the entire Roman Empire at its greatest extent, and doing so in only thirteen years, eventually having an empire that stretched from Greece to India and to Egypt. Alexander died young, at only thirty-three years of age, with no real successor, and upon his death his vast empire was split among his four generals—Ptolemy, Seleucus, Lysimachus, and Antigonus.

Alexander the Great's defeat of the Medo-Persian Empire is prophesied in Daniel 8:1–22. In that passage, Alexander is represented as a goat (once again, a kingdom represented by a beast) with a very large horn (once again, a king represented by a horn, and here it is a very large horn, representing Alexander's great position), going to battle and smashing a two-horned ram. The angel in 8:19–22 explains that the goat with the great horn is the king of Greece, and the ram with two horns is Media-Persia (the ram being a beast representing the Medo-Persian Kingdom, with one horn of the ram representing Media and one horn representing Persia). Daniel 8:22 also specifically tells us that when the great horn upon the goat (the king of Greece, Alexander) was broken (i.e., when Alexander died), it was replaced by four smaller horns (the division of Alexander's empire among his four generals). The four smaller horns of 8:1–22, representing the division of Alexander the Great's empire into four territories, each with its own ruler, is an exact parallel to the four-headed leopard of Daniel 7. The four-headed leopard represents the divided empire of Alexander the Great, a vast empire that, upon his death, was divided into four regions, divided amongst his four top generals.

Based on the four sections of the statue of Daniel 2 being a parallel to the four beasts of Daniel 7, and based on Daniel 2 telling us that the first part of the statue, the head of gold, is the kingdom of Babylon, then, from that and from the record of history, we can know that the four beasts of Daniel 7 represent, in order, Nebuchadnezzar's Babylon (lion), the Medo-Persian Empire (bear), Alexander the Great's empire (four-headed leopard), and the Roman Empire (beast of iron).

THE BEASTS ALSO REPRESENT KINGS

We are told that the beasts of Daniel 7, in addition to representing kingdoms, also represent the *kings* who ruled those empires (7:17). How can the symbol of a beast represent *both* a kingdom *and* its king? We can understand it as follows.

Each of the empires represented by the beasts of Daniel 7—Babylon, Medo-Persia, Greece, Rome—was ruled by an absolute ruler, one whose word and will was law. As an absolute ruler of the kingdom, this makes the king *synonymous* with the kingdom—in effect, as an absolute ruler, the king and his kingdom were one and the same. Since the king and his kingdom were one and the same, the beasts of Daniel, in representing the kingdom, also represent the absolute ruler of that kingdom. As a result, the beasts of Daniel 7 represent *both* the kingdom *and* the king, where the king is an absolute ruler of the kingdom.

THE TEN TOES AND THE TEN HORNS

How do we understand the feet and the ten toes of the statue in Daniel 2, which are themselves synonymous with the ten horns of the fourth beast of Daniel 7?

Many understand the feet and ten toes of the statue in Daniel 2 as a fifth section of the statue, a final, fifth empire, yet to come. Daniel specifically tells us that the ten toes of the statue are ten kings, and that in the time of "those kings" (2:44, the ten toe-kings), that is, during the time that those ten kings will rule, God will set up his kingdom on Earth, a kingdom that will never be destroyed. The kingdom that God will set up on Earth and that will never be destroyed is the coming kingdom of Jesus Christ, which is instituted on Earth upon his Second Coming. The Second Coming, and the kingdom that follows it, is yet to happen and it is, in fact, the climax of the events of Revelation.

Since Daniel tells us that God will set up his kingdom on Earth "in the time of those kings" (Dan 2:44); that is, God will set up his kingdom on Earth during the reign of those yet-to-come ten kings, and since God's kingdom is to be set up on Earth only after the Second Coming, this is strong affirmation that the ten toes of Daniel 2, and the ten kings that they represent, will be ruling on Earth *just prior* to the Second Coming. This affirms that the ten toes, the ten kings, are a yet-to-come future, fifth empire.

As a result, since we can understand the ten toes of the Daniel 2 statue as being synonymous with the ten horns of Daniel 7's fourth beast, and since the ten horns of Daniel's fourth beast are synonymous with the ten horns of the Revelation 13 beast, we can then understand the ten toes of the Daniel 2 statue as being synonymous with the ten horns of the Revelation 13 beast.

With this understanding of the symbolism of beasts as explained for us in Daniel, we can understand the Revelation 13 beast as follows. The beast of Revelation 13, which rises out of the sea, represents a coming global empire upon the Earth, an empire that will be on Earth prior to the Second Coming, an empire that will be ruled by an absolute ruler. The ten horns of that same beast will be part of that coming empire; they will be ten other kings ruling that empire, but their rule will be subservient to the overall beast who will be the absolute ruler of the empire. All of this is a yet-to-come final, fifth empire.

HORNS

In the prophecies of the book of Daniel, reference is often made to horns. Horns are specifically referenced in Daniel 7 and 8:1–22. In Daniel 7 we are told of the ten horns upon the head of the terrifying fourth beast, and we are also told of an eleventh horn that comes up afterwards. In 8:1–22 we are told of the great horn upon a goat, and the two horns upon a ram. What do these horns represent?

Daniel 7:24 specifically explains that the ten horns of the terrifying fourth beast are in fact ten *kings*, and that the eleventh horn that comes up afterwards is also a *king*. In 8:20, we are told that the two horns upon the ram are the two *kings* of Medo-Persia, and in 8:21 we are told that the great horn upon the goat is the first *king* of Greece. As a result, we can clearly understand that the symbolism of horns is that a horn represents a king, a ruler.

In examining the book of Daniel, we gain a clear understanding of the biblical symbolism of beasts and horns. The prophetic symbol of a beast represents a great kingdom, a world power. It also represents the king who rules that kingdom as an absolute ruler. The prophetic symbol of horns represents other individual kings and rulers.

Once we establish the symbolic meaning of beasts and horns as used in prophecy, whose meaning is clearly explained for us in the Bible at the time that those symbols are first used in prophecy, we can then apply that understanding to that same symbol when it occurs again in later prophecy. The symbolic meaning of beasts and horns, when used in prophecy, remains consistent throughout the entirety of Scripture, and we can therefore apply that same understanding of beasts and horns to the beasts of Revelation. As a result, we can understand the beasts of Revelation as representing great kingdoms, as well as representing the absolute-ruler kings of those kingdoms, while the additional horns represent other individual kings.

2

The Prostitute, Babylon, the Sea

THE PROSTITUTE

In Revelation 17 we encounter one of the other very key symbols in the book of Revelation, the Prostitute. The symbol of the Prostitute is, in fact, combined with a secondary symbol, the symbol of Babylon. That symbol, the combined symbol of the Prostitute and Babylon, is then further combined with the beast of Revelation 13. The Prostitute/Babylon symbol is a major part of Revelation—two entire chapters, chapters 17 and 18, are devoted to describing the Prostitute/Babylon, and other chapters make reference to the Prostitute/Babylon. To understand the symbolism of the Prostitute, and of Babylon, we need to examine each image, one at a time, beginning with the image of the Prostitute.

We first encounter a detailed description of the Prostitute in Revelation 17.

> One of the seven angels who had the seven bowls came and said to me, "Come, I will show you the punishment of the great prostitute, who sits by many waters. With her the kings of the earth committed adultery, and the inhabitants of the earth were intoxicated with the wine of her adulteries." Then the angel carried me away in the Spirit into a wilderness. There I saw a woman sitting on a scarlet beast that was covered with blasphemous names and had seven heads and ten horns. The woman was dressed in purple and scarlet, and was glittering with gold, precious stones and pearls. She held a golden cup in her hand, filled with abominable things and the filth of her adulteries. The name written on her forehead was a mystery:
>
>
>
> BABYLON THE GREAT
>
> THE MOTHER OF PROSTITUTES
>
> AND OF THE ABOMINATIONS OF THE EARTH.
>
>

I saw that the woman was drunk with the blood of God's holy people, the blood of those who bore testimony to Jesus. (Rev 17:1–6 NIV)

What is the meaning of the Prostitute symbol? In fact, the symbol of the Prostitute is used frequently throughout the Old Testament and, by examining its usage throughout the Bible, we can come to understand its meaning in Revelation.

THE MEANING OF THE PROSTITUTE

A common teaching as to the meaning of the prostitute symbol is that it represents false religion, or a false religious system. However, in the Bible, the prostitute never represents either false religion or a false religious system; rather, the symbol of the prostitute always represents a *nation*, and not just any nation, but a very specific kind of nation. The specific kind of nation represented by the prostitute is a nation that, from its very inception as a nation, was born as a nation *unto God*, but then later *turns away from him*. Since that nation came into existence as a nation unto God, as God's nation, then the act of turning away from him, that act of unfaithfulness, makes that nation a prostitute—it is the nation's forsaking of God that is the act of prostitution. The only way a nation could forsake God or turn away from him is if that nation first *belonged* to God.

Throughout recorded history, up to the 1500s, there is only one nation that fits the definition of a nation coming into existence as a nation unto God, as being his nation, as belonging to him from its inception as a nation, and that is the nation Israel (which later, during the reign of Solomon's son, King Rehoboam, split into the two nations of Israel and Judah, so both Israel and Judah, as the two divisions of the one Israel, fit that definition). No nation of Europe, Asia, or Africa came into being as a nation unto God; rather, they all came into existence as pagan nations and only *later* came to be Christian nations—of all the nations of Europe, Asia, and Africa, only Israel/Judah *came into being* as a nation unto God, a nation belonging to God from its very inception as a nation.

However, since the 1500s, with the discovery of the New World and with the birth of the nations of the New World, all of those New World nations, that is, all of the nations of North America, South and Central America, and Australia, were founded by Christian mother countries and, as such, were founded, from their inception, as Christian nations. As a result of being founded, from their inception, as Christian nations, *all* the nations of the New World *also* came into existence, from their inception, as nations unto God, as his nations. Until the birth of the nations of the New World, only Israel/Judah was a nation born unto God from its inception. As a result, in the Old Testament, only Israel/Judah is ever called a "prostitute."

> And the Lord said to Moses: "You are going to rest with your ancestors, and these people will soon prostitute themselves to the foreign gods of the land

they are entering. They will forsake me and break the covenant I made with them." (Deut 31:16 NIV)

Gideon made the gold into an ephod, which he placed in Ophrah, his town. All Israel prostituted themselves by worshiping it there, and it became a snare to Gideon and his family. (Judg 8:27 NIV)

No sooner had Gideon died than the Israelites again prostituted themselves to the Baals. They set up Baal-Berith as their god. (Judg 8:33 NIV)

But they were unfaithful to the God of their ancestors and prostituted themselves to the gods of the peoples of the land, whom God had destroyed before them. (1 Chr 5:25 NIV)

He had also built high places on the hills of Judah and had caused the people of Jerusalem to prostitute themselves and had led Judah astray. (2 Chr 21:11 NIV)

How the faithful city has become a harlot!
It was full of justice;
Righteousness lodged in it,
But now murderers. (Isa 1:21 NKJV)

For of old I have broken your yoke and burst your bonds;
And you said, "I will not transgress,"
When on every high hill and under every green tree
You lay down, playing the harlot. (Jer 2:20 NKJV)

They say, "If a man divorces his wife,
And she goes from him
And becomes another man's,
May he return to her again?"
Would not that land be greatly polluted?
But you have played the harlot with many lovers;
Yet return to Me," says the Lord. (Jer 3:1 NKJV)

Therefore, you prostitute [Jerusalem], hear the word of the Lord! (Ezek 16:35 NIV)

The word of the Lord came to me: "Son of man, there were two women, daughters of the same mother. They became prostitutes in Egypt, engaging in prostitution from their youth. In that land their breasts were fondled and their virgin bosoms caressed. The older was named Oholah, and her sister was Oholibah. They were mine and gave birth to sons and daughters. Oholah is Samaria, and Oholibah is Jerusalem.

"Oholah engaged in prostitution while she was still mine; and she lusted after her lovers, the Assyrians—warriors clothed in blue, governors and commanders, all of them handsome young men, and mounted horsemen. She gave herself as a prostitute to all the elite of the Assyrians and defiled herself with all the idols of everyone she lusted after. She did not give up the prostitution she began in Egypt, when during her youth men slept with her, caressed her virgin bosom and poured out their lust on her." (Ezek 23:1–8 NIV)

Israel/Judah and Jerusalem are repeatedly described as a prostitute, a harlot, throughout the Old Testament. The reason they are described as a prostitute and as engaging in prostitution is because they were, from their inception as a nation, God's nation, and then they turned away from him, betrayed him, were faithless towards him, and followed false gods. It's not the following of false gods that defines them as being a prostitute; rather, it is that they were first God's nation, his people, who later turned away from him in faithlessness. It is not the *false religion* that is the prostitute, but the *nation* that betrays its original faithfulness to God.

Throughout the Old Testament, it is only Israel and Judah that are symbolized and represented as a prostitute, for they are the only nation that came into existence as God's nation and then betrayed him. However, there are two other cities in the Old Testament, cities that are not Israel, Judah, or Jerusalem, that are also described as a prostitute—the cities of Tyre and Ninevah.

TYRE

If only Israel/Judah meet the definition of a prostitute in the Old Testament, then how are we to understand the following?:

> At the end of seventy years, the LORD will deal with Tyre. She will return to her lucrative *prostitution* and will ply her trade with *all the kingdoms on the face of the earth*. (Isa 23:17 NIV, italics added)

Isaiah 23:17 specifically tells us that the *city* of Tyre is engaging in prostitution—how are we to understand this if only Israel/Judah are ever described in the Old Testament as being a prostitute? Is this not a contradiction to the definition of a prostitute as being a nation, or city, that came into existence as God's nation and then betrayed him? No, it is not a contradiction, for we can understand this specific example of the city of Tyre, being described as engaging in prostitution, as being an amplification of the same "Babylon the Great" of Revelation 17, as follows.

Isaiah 23 flows into Isaiah 24 as one continuity, as one prophetic narrative, and we see from Isaiah 24 that the time period of the Isaiah 23–24 prophecy is the same time period as the time period of Revelation, the period of time during which the entire Earth will be completely destroyed (Isa 24:3).

> See, the Lord is going to *lay waste the earth*

and *devastate it;*
he will *ruin its face*
and scatter its inhabitants—
it will be the same
for priest as for people,
for the master as for his servant,
for the mistress as for her servant,
for seller as for buyer,
for borrower as for lender,
for debtor as for creditor.
The earth will be completely laid waste
and totally plundered.
The Lord has spoken this word.
The *earth dries up and withers,*
the world languishes and withers,
the heavens languish with *the earth.* (Isa 24:1–4 NIV, italics added)

The *joyful timbrels* are stilled,
the *noise of the revelers* has stopped,
the *joyful harp* is silent.
No longer do they drink wine with a song;
the beer is bitter to its drinkers.
The ruined *city* lies desolate;
the entrance to every house is barred.
In the streets they cry out for wine;
all joy turns to gloom,
all *joyful sounds are banished* from the earth.
The city is left in ruins,
its gate is battered to pieces.
So will it be on *the earth*
and among the nations," (Isa 24:8–13 NIV, italics added)

The term "the foundations of the earth," when used in the Bible, always means the *planet* itself (Ps 102:5; Isa 48:13; Mic 6:2), but the specific term "the earth" always means *only* the *land surface* of the planet (Gen 1:9–10, 9:11 NKJV), while the term "the world" always means *only* the people and life that is upon the surface of the planet (John 3:16 et al.). It is in this context that we understand Isaiah 23–24 when it speaks about the destruction of "the earth"—it is a description of the destruction of the *surface* of the planet, and the destruction as described in Isaiah has not happened since he prophesied it—it is a destruction yet to come, and it is a destruction on a global scale. The only time such a destruction of the Earth on a global scale will happen is during the events of Revelation, described as the Great Tribulation. As a result, we can understand that the time period being prophesied in Isaiah 23–24 is the same time period as is being described in Revelation.

Furthermore, there is a striking parallel in the description of the destruction of a *city* in Isaiah 24 with the description of the destruction of the city Babylon the Great in Revelation 18.

> Then a mighty angel took up a stone like a great millstone and threw it into the sea, saying, "Thus with violence the great city Babylon shall be thrown down, and shall not be found anymore. The *sound of harpists, musicians, flutists, and trumpeters shall not be heard in you anymore*. No craftsman of any craft shall be found in you anymore, and the sound of a millstone shall not be heard in you anymore. The light of a lamp shall not shine in you anymore, and the voice of bridegroom and bride shall not be heard in you anymore. For your merchants were the great men of the earth, for by your sorcery all the nations were deceived. (Rev 18:21–23 NKJV, italics added)

Revelation 18:22 tells us that the sound of music will no longer be heard in the destroyed city of Babylon the Great; Isaiah 24:8–9 tells us that the sound of music will no longer be heard in the destroyed city of Tyre; Revelation 18:17 tells us that all the sea captains and sea merchants will weep over the fall and destruction of Babylon the Great, as will all the merchants of the world (Rev 18:11–19); Isaiah 23:1–14 prophesies moaning and weeping of the ships at sea over the fall and destruction of Tyre; Isaiah 23:17 tells us that God will visit this destruction on Tyre at the end of seventy years; the final judgment of Revelation is described in Daniel as being at the end of seventy weeks (Dan 9:24–27); Isaiah 24:21–23 tells us that, in that day of destruction of Tyre, the "moon will be dismayed, the sun ashamed" (Isa 24:23 NIV), which is an exact parallel of Seal 6 of Revelation, which follows the Great Tribulation and which precedes the destruction of Babylon the Great.

> the sun became black as sackcloth of hair, and the moon became like blood. (Rev 6:12 NKJV)

Furthermore, we are told that, after the fall of Tyre as described in Isaiah 24:23.

> For the LORD Almighty will reign
> on Mount Zion and in Jerusalem,
> and before its elders—with great glory. (Isa 24:23 NIV)

The only time that the Lord Almighty will reign in Jerusalem is after the Second Coming. As a result, we can know that the time period of the Isaiah 23–24 prophecy is the time period that precedes the Second Coming, the same time period as Revelation.

From multiple different angles, we can clearly understand that Isaiah 23–24 is a description of the events that precede the Second Coming, and we see many clear parallels between the city of Tyre, as described in those chapters, and Babylon the Great as described in Revelation 17–18. It is very important to understand that Babylon the Great, as described in Revelation 17–18, is very specifically described as a *city*.

> And the woman whom you saw is that *great city* which reigns over the kings of the earth. (Rev 17:18 NKJV, italics added)

Babylon the Great, the "Mother of Prostitutes," is a *city* (also understood as "nation"), the preeminent city/nation that dominates the world in the days preceding the Second Coming.

The city of Tyre, as prophesied in Isaiah 23, is described as follows:

> At the end of seventy years, the LORD will deal with Tyre. She will return to her lucrative *prostitution* and will *ply her trade with all the kingdoms on the face of the earth*. (Isa 23:17 NIV, italics added)

This is exactly parallel to the description of Babylon the Great.

> with whom *the kings of the earth committed fornication*, and the inhabitants of the earth were made drunk with the wine of her fornication. (Rev 17:2 NKJV, italics added)

The city of Tyre is described as plying her trade, that is, her prostitution, with all the kingdoms on the face of the Earth; Babylon the Great is described as plying her prostitution with all the kings of the Earth.

The historical city of Tyre has never been in such a position of global power that *all* the kingdoms of the Earth participated in Tyre's corruption. As a result, we can understand that the prophecy against the city of Tyre, as related in Isaiah 23–24, is a prophecy that is yet to be fulfilled; that is, it is a prophecy that was not fulfilled by the *historic* city of Tyre, and which now cannot be fulfilled by the *historic* city of Tyre since the historic city of Tyre no longer exists. The city of Tyre in Isaiah 23–24 is a prophetic *symbol* of another city yet to come.

As a result of these many clear parallels, and the fact that the events prophesied in Isaiah 23–24 relate to the time preceding the Second Coming (since the events of Isaiah 23–24 culminate with the Lord ruling on Earth in Jerusalem, Isa 24:23), there is very strong reason to understand that the city of Tyre, as prophesied in Isaiah 23–24, is, in fact, another symbolic representation of the *same* Babylon the Great, the Prostitute, of Revelation 17, a city that, at the time of the prophecy, was a city yet to come.

EZEKIEL 28

There is an additional prophecy against the city of Tyre in Ezekiel 28, and when we examine the details of that prophecy in Ezekiel, we see further affirmation that the city of Tyre is in fact being used as another symbolic representation of Babylon the Great.

The prophecy of Ezekiel 28 is divided into two clear sections—the first section (28:1–10) is a prophecy against the human ruler of Tyre, the "prince" of Tyre, a man who claims to be a god (28:1–10), while the second section of the prophecy (28:11–19) is a lamentation for the "king" of Tyre (28:11–19). This king of Tyre, as described in 28:11–19, is clearly not a human being, for the king of Tyre is described as being created, not born (28:13), and he is specifically described as the greatest angelic being, the "anointed cherub" (28:14). As a result of the many descriptions of the king of Tyre in Ezekiel 28:11–19, we can conclude, with certainty, that the king of Tyre being described here is, in fact, Satan.

How then do we understand the distinction between the human prince of Tyre and the angelic king of Tyre? We can understand it as follows.

In the eyes of the world, the human ruler who rules the city of Tyre would be seen as the *king* of Tyre—that man will be, to the eyes of the world, the ruler, the power, of the city of Tyre. However, in fact, that human ruler is actually only the face of the *real* ruler of Tyre, and the real ruler of the city of Tyre is in fact the king of Tyre, the anointed cherub who sinned, Satan. Ezekiel 28 therefore describes a human ruler of the city of Tyre who claims to be a god (Ezek 28:2), but who is in fact ruling on the authority of a greater power, a power that works through that human ruler, and that greater power is Satan, also called the "great dragon" (Rev 12:9). This scenario is an exact parallel of Revelation 13:2.

In Revelation 13:2, which is a description of the Beast, commonly called the "antichrist," we are told the following:

> Now the beast which I saw was like a leopard, his feet were like the feet *of* a bear, and his mouth like the mouth of a lion. *The dragon gave him his power, his throne, and great authority.* (Rev 13:2 NKJV, italics added)

Revelation 13:2 describes for us a human ruler of the world, a ruler described as the Beast, and this ruler will be seen by the world as the king of the world. This same Beast will also claim to be a god (2 Thess 2:4) and, in fact, will be worshiped as a god (Rev 13:14–15). We are also told that this Beast is in fact ruling on the authority of a greater power, for we are told that the Beast gets his power, his throne and his authority, from the dragon, Satan.

The scenario of the Beast as described in Revelation 13 is the exact same scenario as is described in Ezekiel 28—both prophecies describe a human ruler who claims to be a god, and each human ruler is seen, by the world, as being the king, as being the ruler with authority, and yet both the "prince" of Tyre and the Beast are in fact ruling on the authority of a greater power, and in each case that greater power is Satan, the dragon. The parallels are exact.

As a result, we can conclude that the city of Tyre as prophesied in Isaiah 23–24 is a symbolic representation of the *same* Babylon the Great of Revelation 17–18, and so when Tyre is described in Isaiah 23:17 as returning to her "lucrative prostitution," it is in fact the exact same description as is given of the city Babylon the Great, engaging in its prostitution as the "Mother of Prostitutes."

We see, then, that when Isaiah 23:17 describes the city of Tyre as engaging in prostitution, it is in no way a contradiction of the symbol of a prostitute being used to represent a nation, or city, that from its inception as a nation was a nation unto God, and then turns away from him and betrays him. The city of Tyre in Isaiah 23:17 is just another prophetic representation of Babylon the Great of Revelation 17.

NINEVAH

In the Old Testament, the city of Ninevah is also described as engaging in prostitution.

> Charging cavalry,
> flashing swords
> and glittering spears!
> Many casualties,
> piles of dead,
> bodies without number,
> people stumbling over the corpses—
> all because of the wanton lust of a prostitute,
> alluring, the mistress of sorceries,
> who *enslaved nations* by her *prostitution*
> and peoples by her witchcraft. (Nah 3:3–4 NIV, italics added)

This is a prophecy against the city of Ninevah, and it also describes Ninevah as engaging in prostitution and as enslaving nations by its prostitution.

The historic city of Ninevah, like the historic city of Tyre, was *not* a city or nation that came into existence as a nation unto God and then later betrayed him. Is this not then a contradiction to the meaning of the prostitute symbol? No, it is not, for we can understand this prophecy against Ninevah in exactly the same way as we understand the prophecy against the city of Tyre in Isaiah 23–24—Nineveh here is used as yet another symbolic representation of Babylon the Great.

The historic city of Ninevah was the capital of Assyria. One of the names of the Beast (commonly called the "antichrist") in the Bible is "the Assyrian":

> The Lord Almighty has sworn, "Surely, as I have planned, so it will be, and as I have purposed, so it will happen. I will crush *the Assyrian* in my land; on my mountains I will trample him down. His yoke will be taken from my people, and his burden removed from their shoulders."
>
> This is the plan determined for *the whole world*; this is the hand stretched out *over all nations*. For the LORD Almighty has purposed, and who can thwart him? His hand is stretched out, and who can turn it back? (Isa 14:24–27 NIV)

Isaiah 13, which precedes this passage about the Assyrian, is very clearly a prophecy about "the day of the Lord" (Isa 13:6). The term "the day of the Lord" always and only refers to the time of Revelation, the time of God's wrath and judgment, the time that precedes the Second Coming. As a result, we can know very clearly that Isaiah 13, as a prophecy about the day of the Lord, is a prophecy about the time period of Revelation, a prophecy about the days that will precede the Second Coming. Isaiah 14 continues that prophecy of Isaiah 13, and, as a result, we can understand Isaiah 14:24–27 as also prophesying about the time of Revelation.

Isaiah 14:24–27 prophesies the destruction of the Assyrian, and it relates his destruction to a plan for "the whole world" and for "all nations"—the destruction of the Assyrian is part of a prophecy of events on a global scale. Since the fate of the whole world, and the fate of all nations, is directly tied in with the destruction of the Assyrian, we can understand the Assyrian as being a ruler on a global scale. Also, since we can clearly understand the events of Isaiah 14 as a continuation of the prophecy of Isaiah 13, which is a prophecy about the days that precede the Second Coming, we can therefore know that the destruction of the Assyrian, and the global events tied in with that, will occur in the days preceding the Second Coming, the same time period as described in Revelation.

This same Assyrian is also described in Micah 5:5–8.

> When the Assyrian comes into our land,
> And when he treads in our palaces,
> Then we will raise against him
> Seven shepherds and eight princely men.
> They shall waste with the sword the land of Assyria,
> And the land of Nimrod at its entrances;
> Thus He shall deliver us from the Assyrian,
> When he comes into our land
> And when he treads within our borders.
> Then the remnant of Jacob
> Shall be in the midst of many peoples,
> Like dew from the Lord,
> Like showers on the grass,
> That tarry for no man
> Nor wait for the sons of men.
> And the remnant of Jacob
> Shall be among the Gentiles,
> In the midst of many peoples,
> Like a lion among the beasts of the forest,
> Like a young lion among flocks of sheep,
> Who, if he passes through,
> Both treads down and tears in pieces,
> And none can deliver. (Mic 5:5–8 NKJV)

This description of the Assyrian in Micah 5:5–8 is another description of the Beast, and of his invasion and war against Jerusalem (see also Zech 14:12–16). When

Micah 5:6 tells us that "He [God] shall deliver us from the Assyrian," it is in fact a reference to the Second Coming—Jesus Christ will deliver us from the Assyrian. The Assyrian is the Beast of Revelation.

It is with this understanding that we approach Nahum 3:3–4 and the description of Ninevah as engaging in prostitution.

Since the term "the Assyrian" is one of the symbolic representational names of the Beast, and since Ninevah was, historically, the capital of Assyria, we can understand Ninevah in Nahum 3:3–4 as being itself a symbolic representation of the *kingdom* of the Assyrian, the kingdom of the Beast of Revelation, a kingdom yet to come. As a result, we can understand Ninevah in Nahum 3:3–4 as the capital city of the kingdom of the Assyrian, and as being another symbolic representation of Babylon the Great, for Babylon the Great is the kingdom, or *power base*, of the Beast (the Beast is also symbolically called the "king of Babylon," Isa 14:3–11). Babylon the Great is specifically described as follows:

> the great harlot who sits on many waters, with whom *the kings of the earth* committed *fornication*, and the inhabitants of the earth were made drunk with the wine of her fornication. (Rev 17:1–2 NKJV, italics added)

The prophetic city of Ninevah in Nahum 3:3–4 is described as follows:

> all because of the wanton lust of a *prostitute*,
> alluring, the mistress of sorceries,
> who *enslaved nations* by *her prostitution*
> and peoples by her witchcraft. (Nah 3:4 NIV, italics added)

Likewise, as already discussed, the prophetic city of Tyre is described as follows:

> She will return to her lucrative *prostitution* and will ply her trade with *all the kingdoms* on *the face of the earth*." (Isa 23:17 NIV, italics added)

Babylon the Great, the prophetic Tyre, and the prophetic Ninevah are all described in exactly the same way—as a prostitute engaging in prostitution with all the kings and kingdoms on the face of the Earth. Furthermore, each of these—Babylon the Great, the prophetic Tyre, and the prophetic Ninevah—are described as being ruled by the Beast of Revelation (called the "prince of Tyre" in regard to the prophetic Tyre, and called "the Assyrian" in regard to the prophetic Ninevah). As a result, we can understand that the prophetic Tyre and the prophetic Ninevah are in fact prophetic descriptions of the same Babylon the Great of Revelation 17–18, and since Babylon the Great is described as the Prostitute and as engaging in prostitution and fornication with all the kings and kingdoms of the world, likewise the prophetic Tyre and the prophetic Ninevah, as symbolic representations of Babylon the Great, are described as being prostitutes and as engaging in prostitution.

As a result, the description of the prophetic Tyre and the prophetic Ninevah as prostitutes and as engaging in prostitution is not a contradiction of the meaning of the symbol of the prostitute as being a nation that, from its inception, was a nation born unto God and that then goes on to betray him and turn its back on him. Since the prophetic Tyre and the prophetic Ninevah are a prophecy of the New Testament Babylon the Great, then Israel and Judah remain the only nations in the Old Testament described as being a prostitute, which is in complete accordance with the meaning of the prostitute symbol.

EXODUS 34:11-16

It is in that context that we turn to Exodus 34:11–16.

> Obey what I command you today. I will drive out before you the Amorites, Canaanites, Hittites, Perizzites, Hivites and Jebusites. Be careful not to make a treaty with those who live in the land where you are going, or *they will be a snare among you*. Break down their altars, smash their sacred stones and cut down their Asherah poles. Do not worship any other god, for the LORD, whose name is Jealous, is a jealous God.
>
> Be careful not to make a treaty with those who live in the land; for *when they prostitute themselves* to their gods and sacrifice to them, *they will invite you* and you will eat their sacrifices. And when you choose some of their daughters as wives for your sons and those daughters *prostitute* themselves to their gods, they *will lead your sons* to do the same. (Exod 34:11–16 NIV, italics added)

Exodus 34:11–16 is a warning from God to Israel in regard to the land into which they were about to enter and in regard to the inhabitants of that land—the Amorites, Canaanites, Hittites, Perizzites, Hivites and Jebusites. God says that he will drive out the people of that land, and he warns Israel not to make a treaty with the people who live in that land. God warns *Israel* to not worship the false gods of *those* people. It is in *that* context, in the context of warning *Israel* to not worship the false gods of those people, that God then describes those people as prostituting themselves by worshiping their false gods.

In every other verse in the Old Testament when a people, nation, or city is described as a prostitute, it is always a description of Israel or Judah. The exceptions are in Isaiah 23 and Nahum 3, when both Tyre and Ninevah are described in terms of prostitution, but those two examples are, as discussed, prophecies of the same Babylon the Great of Revelation 17 and 18. In Exodus 34:11–16, God is describing the inhabitants of the land that Israel is about to enter, and those inhabitants were never a people who, from their inception, were a people unto God, nor is Exodus 34:11–16 in any way a prophecy of future events, and certainly not a prophetic description of Babylon the Great, yet to come. And yet, in describing the people of that land and their worship of false gods, God uses the term "prostitute." How are we to understand this? Does this one passage undermine the clear understanding of every other Old Testament passage where the term "prostitute" is used to describe Israel or Judah, or as a prophetic reference to the future Babylon the Great? Or are we to understand this one passage in the light of every other Old Testament passage where the term "prostitute" is used in reference to Israel, Judah, or the future Babylon the Great? We are to understand Exodus 34:11–16 in the light of every other Old Testament passage where the term "prostitute" is used in reference to Israel, Judah, or the future Babylon the Great.

It is important to understand that Exodus 34:11–16 is a *warning* from God to *Israel*. The passage, in its essence, is *not* about the inhabitants of the land that Israel is about to enter; rather, it is a passage specifically about Israel itself. God is very clearly warning *Israel* to not be deceived and worship the false gods of the people who live in the land that Israel is about to enter. Viewed from the perspective of *Israel*, and since it is *Israel* who is being warned to not engage in those practices, then, from *Israel's* viewpoint, those practices are practices of prostitution, for if *Israel* were to participate in the worship of those false gods, then *Israel* would be prostituting itself. So even though, in this one instance, God uses the term "prostitute" in reference to the practices of a foreign people, in fact the use of the term "prostitute" in that instance is to be understood in the context of God warning *Israel* to not engage in those practices. With that understanding of Exodus 34:11–16, the entire passage is in complete accordance with every other Old Testament passage where the term "prostitute" is used in reference to Israel, Judah, or the future Babylon the Great.

We see then, throughout the Old Testament, that the specific description of being a prostitute is only applied to the nation(s) of Israel and Judah, or as a prophetic description of the future Babylon the Great. Israel and Judah are described as a prostitute because Israel came into existence as a nation unto God, a nation that, from its very inception, was born as God's nation, a nation of *God's* people. As a result, when Israel and Judah turn its back and God and turn away from him, in an act of faithlessness, it is that act of turning away from God that leads to Israel and Judah being described as a prostitute. The false religion that Israel embraced during its turning away from God is *not* the prostitute; rather, it is the *nation* of the once faithful *Israel itself* that is the prostitute.

As a result, the symbol of the prostitute, throughout the Bible, always and only represents a nation that, from its beginning/founding/inception, was born as a nation unto God, was born as *his* nation, and then turns its back on him. This is the only meaning of the symbol of the prostitute that is found in the Bible. The prostitute is *not* false religion, *nor* a false religious system.

BABYLON

One of the other key symbols of Revelation is the symbol of Babylon, and the symbol of Babylon is encountered in combination with the symbol of the prostitute.

The name written on her forehead was a mystery:

BABYLON THE GREAT

THE MOTHER OF PROSTITUTES

AND OF THE ABOMINATIONS OF THE EARTH. (REV 17:5 NIV)

The woman of Revelation 17 is the Prostitute, and in fact she is described as the "Mother of Prostitutes." That woman has a name written on her forehead, and her name is "Babylon the Great." That woman, Babylon the Great, the "Mother of Prostitutes," is described as riding the Beast of Revelation 13.

We have already discussed the symbol of the prostitute. How then are we to understand the symbol of Babylon?

BABYLON IS A SYMBOL

A teaching often encountered in studies on Revelation is that the Babylon of Revelation 17–18, and referenced elsewhere in the Revelation, is in fact the literal, historical Middle Eastern city/nation of Babylon. However, as we will see when we look at Babylon the Great closely, that is an impossible argument.

The term "Babylon," as used in Revelation, is *not* a reference to the ancient historical kingdom or nation of the Middle East (in fact, we will see that the Babylon of Revelation is not a nation in the Middle East at all); rather, the term "Babylon" is used as a *symbolic* term, used as a *symbol* to illustrate a deeper meaning.

In fact, the term "Babylon" is used in exactly this same symbolic way elsewhere in the Bible, specifically in 1 Peter.

She who is in Babylon, chosen together with you, sends you her greetings, and so does my son Mark. (1 Pet 5:13 NIV)

It is generally understood that Peter wrote his epistles while he was in Rome, which was also the city if his martyrdom. When Peter says in his letter, "She who is in Babylon . . . ," it is generally understood that the name Babylon, as used by Peter, is a symbolic reference to Rome. There was no real Babylon in existence in Peter's day—the former historical city of Babylon, in Peter's day, was in fact little more than a ruin. Peter here uses the name Babylon in a symbolic way as a representation of Rome.

WHAT IS THE MEANING OF THE SYMBOL BABYLON?

Throughout the Bible, Babylon is portrayed, above all, as a place of immense wealth. As previously discussed, this is most clearly shown in Daniel 2:24–49, where Daniel gives us the vision of the statue that is comprised of four parts, with the head of that statue being the only part of that statue made from pure gold (2:32). Daniel tells us very clearly that the head of that statue, the head of gold, is both King Nebuchadnezzar and his kingdom, Babylon (2:37–38). The kingdom of Babylon is the only part of that statue that is made of gold; every other section is made of an inferior metal. Also, historically, Babylon has always been considered a kingdom of great wealth. As a result, one of the key meanings of the symbol of Babylon is that it is a nation, kingdom, or city of great, exorbitant wealth.

In addition to being a place of immense wealth, Babylon is also historically connected with great immorality and sensual indulgence, and this immorality and sensual indulgence of Babylon is affirmed in the Bible (Isa 47). As a result, the symbol of Babylon also represents a nation of great immorality and sensual indulgence.

Taken together, the symbol of Babylon therefore represents a city or nation of great wealth as well as a place of great immorality. It is in that context that Peter calls Rome "Babylon," for in Peter's day Rome was the greatest, wealthiest, and most powerful city in the world and was also a place of great immorality. Rome was, in that regard, the Babylon of its day.

As a result, when the name Babylon is applied to the Prostitute of Revelation 17–18, we can understand the symbolism of the woman "Babylon the Great, the Mother of Prostitutes" as follows—Babylon the Great is a nation that, from its inception, was born as a nation unto God, coming into existence as God's nation, which then turns away from him, forsakes him, abandons him; it is also a nation of great wealth and great immorality and sensual indulgence. In fact, the clear description of Babylon the Great throughout all of Revelation 17–18 affirms Babylon the Great as being characterized as a city, or nation, of enormous wealth, the world's greatest economic power, whose fall is wept by all the great merchants of the world.

It's important to note that the woman of Revelation 17–18 is not described only as Babylon, but rather is described as "Babylon the *Great*." By being described as Babylon the *Great*, we can understand that, not only is that Babylon a place of enormous wealth and great economic power, but it is the *greatest* such nation that has ever existed, the greatest of all the Babylons that have ever been, whether literal or symbolic.

As a result, we can understand the symbol of Babylon as representing a city or nation of immense wealth, but also a place of great immorality and sensual indulgence.

THE MOTHER OF PROSTITUTES

In Revelation 17, the name of the woman who rides the Beast is "Babylon the Great, the Mother of Prostitutes." How are we to understand the phrase "Mother of Prostitutes"?

Often, in studies on Revelation, the phrase "Mother of Prostitutes" is explained as meaning the *originator* of prostitution, and the prostitution referenced in that definition is itself defined as *false religion*—the term "Mother of Prostitutes," therefore, is understood as meaning the originator of false religion. In this interpretation of the phrase "Mother of Prostitutes," Babylon is usually taken to be the *literal* historical ancient Babylon, rather than a symbolic application of the name.

However, as we have seen clearly outlined in Scripture, the symbol of the prostitute does *not* represent false religion; rather it represents a specific kind of *nation*. As a result, we must understand the meaning of the phrase "Mother of Prostitutes" in that same context, in the context of being a *nation*.

How then do we understand "the mother of . . . "?

In fact, the phrase "the mother of . . . " is a common Middle Eastern phrase that means the *greatest* of . . . This was most recently, and very clearly, seen in the US-led war against Iraq. Prior to the beginning of the US-led attack on Iraq, many televised news reports and news articles showed Iraqi soldiers boasting how they would destroy the US in battle and thereafter turn and destroy Israel. The Iraqis were expecting a US attack, and they described the great battle that would ensue as being "the *mother* of all battles," that is, they were using the phrase "the mother of all battles" to describe their upcoming battle against the US as being the *greatest* of all battles.

This is the exact sense in which we are to understand the phrase "Mother of Prostitutes." The phrase "Mother of Prostitutes" does *not* mean the originator of prostitutes; rather it means the *greatest* of all prostitutes. Since to be a prostitute means to be a nation that, from its inception, was a nation born unto God, but that then turns away from him, we can understand the term "Mother of Prostitutes" as describing a nation that comes into existence as a nation unto God, as a Christian nation, as the greatest and most faithful of Christian nations, but then completely and utterly turns away from him. It is that nation's turning away from God that is the act of prostitution, but it will be such an extreme turning away, a turning away from God that is so calamitous and profound, that it will be the *greatest* act of turning away from God ever, the *greatest* act of prostitution by any nation in history. Such a calamitous and profound turning away from God by that nation, in being the greatest act of prostitution by any nation ever, results in that nation being described as the "Mother of Prostitutes," the *greatest* of all prostitutes.

THE SEA

One other important symbol in Revelation is the symbol of the sea. This is seen primarily in Revelation 13, where the Beast is described as rising from the Sea (Rev 13:1). We are also told in Revelation 21:1 that when this Earth is redeemed, there will no longer be any seas. We are also told in Revelation 20:13 that the "sea gave up the dead."

How are we to understand the symbol of the sea?

One common teaching in regard to the sea, especially as it occurs in Revelation, is that the sea represents many peoples. The reason for that teaching is found in Revelation 17:1 and 17:15.

> Come, I will show you the punishment of the great prostitute, who sits by many waters. (17:1 NIV)

> Then the angel said to me, "The waters you saw, where the prostitute sits, are peoples, multitudes, nations and languages. (17:15 NIV)

Revelation 17:1 describes the Prostitute, Babylon the Great, as sitting on "many waters." In 17:15 the angel explains the symbolism of the term "many waters," telling us that the "many waters" are many "peoples, multitudes, nations and languages." It is for this reason that people often describe the symbol of the sea as representing many peoples.

However, the "many waters" of Revelation 17:1, upon which the Prostitute sits, are *not* the sea; rather, those "many waters" are to be understood as *rivers* and *streams* of humanity. In fact, upon examining the meaning of the sea throughout the Bible, we see that the sea *never* represents peoples or multitudes; rather it always and only represents the *judgment* of God.

THE SEA REPRESENTS JUDGMENT

The clearest example of the sea as the judgment of God is, of course, the flood of Noah's day (Gen 6:11–13, 7). The global flood of Noah's day was God's very clear *judgment* upon the Earth, and that judgment was delivered by way of a flood—a flood not of rivers or streams, but of seas and oceans.

Another clear example of the sea as God's judgment is found in Exodus when the parted Red Sea is released and comes crashing down upon Pharaoh's army, obliterating them.

> Pharaoh's chariots and his army
> He has thrown into the sea;
> And the choicest of his officers
> are drowned in the Red Sea. (Exod 15:4 NASB)

The sea is used as the instrument of God's judgment upon Pharaoh's army, with the sea destroying Pharaoh's entire army.

Also, Job 26:5 describes the sea in connection with anguish.

> The dead are in deep anguish,
> those *beneath* the waters and all that live in them. (Job 26:5 NIV)

Job 26:5 is a description of the Realm of the Dead, in Hebrew called *Sheol*, and in Greek called *Hades*, a place within the Earth where all the dead of humanity went upon their death, but, since the resurrection, where only all non-believers go to await judgment (Heb 9:27; Rev 20:11–15). Job 26:5 specifically identifies the Realm of the Dead as being "beneath" the floors of the waters. These waters are the seas/oceans. The Realm of the Dead is not described as being *in* the waters, but *beneath* the waters. As a result, we can understand the Realm of the Dead, the place where the non-believing dead go to await *judgment*, as being beneath the *floors* of the seas and oceans—this represents the Realm of the Dead as being a place under judgment.

As a further affirmation of that, we turn to Revelation 20:13.

> And the sea gave up the dead who were in it, and Death and Hades gave up the dead who were in them; and they were judged, each one of them according to their deeds." (Rev 20:13 NASB)

This, again, is a description of the Realm of the Dead, *Hades*, giving up its dead for judgment. In this verse, *Hades* giving up its dead is *equated* with *the sea* giving up its dead—in fact, this is the same event. We know from Job 26:5 that the Realm of the Dead (*Hades*) is beneath the floors of the seas/oceans, and so when Revelation 20:13 tells us that *Hades* gave up its dead and then also tells us that the sea gave up its dead, it is, in fact, the same event being described in an amplified form—*Hades* giving up its dead is the same as the sea, which covers *Hades*, giving up its dead. This further connection of the sea and *Hades* is a further affirmation of the sea as a judgment from God.

One other very key place where the sea acts as God's judgment upon Earth is Genesis 1:2.

> And the earth was a *formless* and *desolate emptiness*, and darkness was over the surface of the deep, and the Spirit of God was hovering over the surface of the waters. (Gen 1:2 NASB, italics added)

Contrast this with Isaiah 45:18 and Revelation 12:9; 22:3; 21:1.

> For this is what the Lord says, He who created the heavens (He is the God who formed the earth and made it, He established it and *did not create it as a waste place*, but *formed* it to be *inhabited*): "I am the Lord, and there is no one else." (Isa 45:18 NASB, italics added)

> And the great dragon was thrown down, the serpent of old who is called the devil and Satan, who deceives the whole world; *he was thrown down to the earth*, and his angels were thrown down with him. (Rev 12:9 NASB)

> There will *no longer* be *any curse* . . . (Rev 22:3 NASB)

> Then I saw a new heaven and a new earth; for the first heaven and the first earth passed away, and there is *no longer any sea*. (Rev 21:1 NASB)

Isaiah 45:18 tells us that the Earth, as created in Genesis 1:1, was *not* created empty, nor was it created to be empty; rather it was created perfect and *habitable*, habitable for *man*. Yet, we see by Genesis 1:2 that the Earth is completely *empty*, a desolate emptiness, and is absolutely *uninhabitable* for man, for man cannot live on a global ocean—the global ocean of Genesis 1:2 makes the Earth completely *uninhabitable* for *man*.

Also, we are specifically told in Isaiah 45:18 that when God created the Earth, it was "formed," that is, the Earth had *form*. This is in contrast to Genesis 1:2, where we are very clearly told that the Earth was "formless," that the Earth had *no form*. As a result, since Isaiah 45:18 clearly describes for us the state of the Earth upon its creation as being an Earth that *had form*, and since the description of the Earth in Genesis 1:2 describes the Earth as being *without form*, then Genesis 1:2 is in complete contrast to the description of the Earth as described in Isaiah 45:18. How can we understand this? We can understand it as follows—the Earth as described in Genesis 1:2 is *not* how God created it; rather, the Earth in Genesis 1:2 *became* that way as a result of God's *curse*. The curse upon the Earth in Genesis 1:2 is twofold—it is the curse of a global ocean, making the Earth completely uninhabitable for man, and also the curse of *darkness*.

Why is the Earth in Genesis 1:2 a cursed Earth? The Bible explains for us *why* the Earth in Genesis 1:2 is cursed, for Revelation 12:9 tells us that when Lucifer and the angels rebelled against God, they were cast out of heaven *to Earth*.

In Genesis 1:2, there are two elements of the curse upon the Earth—the global ocean and darkness. The Holy Spirit is there as well, and he is there, hovering over the cursed Earth, as a restrainer of evil, to restrain, or keep down, the fallen angelic horde that was cast down into the Earth, into the place described as the Pit, or the Abyss, which is also located *inside* the Earth, and which is a place of imprisonment, darkness, and chains for fallen angels (Luke 8:31; 1 Pet 3:19; Jude 6–7; Rev 20:1–3).

However, God will redeem this everlasting Earth (Mic 6:2), and in the redemption of the Earth the two curses of seas (oceans) and darkness will be removed. This is specifically described for us in Revelation 21–22:

> And *there shall be no more curse*, but the throne of God and of the Lamb shall be in it, and His servants shall serve Him. (Rev 22:3 NKJV)

> Now I saw a new heaven and a new earth, for the first heaven and the first earth had passed away. Also *there was no more sea*. (Rev 21:1 NKJV)

> *There shall be no night* there: They need no lamp nor light of the sun, for the Lord God gives them light. And they shall reign forever and ever. (Rev 22:5 NKJV, italics added)

We are specifically told that, in its full redemption by God, there will no longer be any *curse* upon the Earth (Rev 22:3). This then is amplified, making clear for us that, at the very least, the curse(s) referred to are the curse of seas, all of which will be removed from the Earth in the Earth's redemption, and the curse of night, or darkness, which will also be removed from the Earth upon the Earth's redemption. As a result, we see that when God redeems this Earth, the two curses present upon Earth in Genesis 1:2—the curse of seas and the curse of darkness—will be fully removed, and there will no longer be any curse upon the Earth (Rev 22:3). All of this, taken together, strongly affirms that, in regard to seas, we can understand seas and oceans as a curse of God's judgment upon the Earth.

The Bible is consistently very clear that the sea, throughout all of Scripture, represents God's judgment. As a result, when the sea is used in a symbolic way in the Bible, it also, always, represents God's *judgment*; it does *not* represent peoples, nations, or multitudes.

We see, then, throughout the entirety of Scripture, that the symbol of the prostitute represents a nation that comes into existence as a nation unto God, coming into existence as God's nation, and then turns away from him; the symbol of Babylon represents a nation of great wealth, great power, and great immorality; the symbol of the sea represents God's judgment. These are the meanings that we apply to those symbols when we encounter them in the book of Revelation.

3

THE RAPTURE

ONE VERY COMMON MODERN teaching concerning the events of Revelation, and the time preceding the Second Coming, is that there will be an event called the "rapture."

The rapture teaching states that, prior to the Second Coming, the church will be supernaturally removed from the Earth, by Jesus Christ, so as to be kept from the judgments that are going to come upon the Earth.

In most versions of the rapture teaching, Jesus Christ will remove the church from the Earth *before* the Beast comes to power (commonly known as the "pre-Tribulation rapture"). In another version of the rapture teaching, Jesus Christ will remove the church from the Earth at the *midpoint* of the Beast's earthly rule (known as the "mid-Tribulation rapture"), while one final version of the rapture teaching states that Jesus Christ will remove his church from the Earth *after* the Tribulation but *before* the Second Coming (known as the "post-Tribulation rapture").

Of the three different views of the rapture, the most commonly held view is the pre-Tribulation rapture, which states that Jesus Christ will remove his church from the Earth *before* the Beast comes to power. As a result, those who hold to this view believe that the church, Christians, will not be on Earth when the events of Revelation occur.

Regardless of which rapture view one may hold to, it is important to understand that the rapture teaching, in any version, is a false and unbiblical teaching, without any biblical support, and it is a teaching that can lead to great harm for believers.

HISTORY OF THE RAPTURE TEACHING

The church is two thousand years old. Apart from one brief comment regarding the idea of a rapture made in the sixteenth century, there is no shred of even the thought of such a teaching in the entirety of church history until the 1830s—for over 90 percent of the church's existence, not even a hint of such a teaching ever existed in the church, was ever taught by the church, nor was it ever believed by the church. The rapture is a very new teaching and it has no biblical support whatsoever.

The idea that God would remove his church from the Earth before the Tribulation events of Revelation was first hinted at in the writings of Francisco Ribera, a Jesuit priest (1537–1591), while he was writing in defense of the pope and Roman Catholicism during the Counter-Reformation. His book *In Sacrum Beati Ioannis Apostoli, & Evangelistiae Apocalypsin Commentarii* was a commentary on the book of Revelation, and in that book he made some comments on the idea that Jesus Christ would remove the church from the Earth before the events of Revelation. This was the very first time, ever, that the idea of a rapture, in any form, had been suggested. However, Ribera's comments and conclusions on the topic of the church being removed from the Earth before the events of Revelation were not accepted. His writings were considered by the Roman Catholic Church as being flawed and unscriptural, and they were filed away, having had no real impact or influence.

Ribera's writings resurfaced over two hundred years later, in England, when they were discovered and then republished by S. R. Maitland (1792–1866) as part of a collection of minor and mostly unknown earlier Christian writings. It was this publication of Maitland's that was read by John Nelson Darby (1800–1882), and it was in Maitland's publication that he read about Ribera's idea of God removing his church from the Earth before the Tribulation events of Revelation. John Darby latched on to the idea of God removing his church from Earth before the Tribulation, and so he took Ribera's writings, embraced them, and invented what is today called the "rapture." It is John Darby, of the nineteenth century, who invented the rapture teaching, and he is in fact considered the father of the rapture teaching.

Of course, in an attempt to try and support his new teaching, Darby invoked a few scriptures that he said supported his view. These were primarily 1 Thessalonians 4:16–17; Matthew 24:31; Matthew 24:40–41 and the parallel Luke 17:34–36; and 1 Corinthians 15:51–53. However, none of these passages teach or support Darby's rapture teaching; in fact, some of them (Matt 24:40–41; 1 Thess 4:16–17 and the parallel Luke 17:34–36) clearly *deny* the very teaching Darby was trying to support.

Even after Darby developed his rapture teaching, the teaching did not go anywhere, and remained confined to Darby and his small band of followers. This began to change in the early twentieth century.

Cyrus Ingerson Scofield (1843–1921) became aware of Darby's rapture teaching and the idea of the church being removed from the Earth prior to the Tribulation events of Revelation, and he embraced Darby's teaching. One of Scofield's major accomplishments is that he is the author of the Scofield Reference Bible. The Scofield Reference Bible is really just the King James Bible with Scofield giving his own commentary opinion on the meaning of the scriptural text. When Scofield would comment on the few verses that Darby invoked to support his rapture idea, then Scofield, in his commentary footnotes on those verses, would describe those verses as teaching the "rapture." The Scofield Reference Bible was published only in 1909, and it was only with the publication of Scofield's commentary that the rapture teaching started to spread. People would buy the Scofield Reference Bible, which was just the King James Bible with Scofield's commentary, then read Scofield's personal commentary opinions in the context of the King James Bible, and then would accept Scofield's personal commentary opinion as being authoritative, since they were reading it in "the Bible." It is for that reason, and that reason alone, that the rapture teaching began to spread, and that only from 1909. The rapture teaching then began to spread more widely throughout the rest of the twentieth century and today is commonly taught as biblical truth, mostly within evangelical circles.

In every respect, the rapture teaching is a completely new, modern teaching without any support throughout church history. In fact, the rapture teaching is completely Darby's invention.

IS THERE SCRIPTURAL SUPPORT FOR THE RAPTURE?

Darby invokes four key verses (one of which has a parallel Gospel verse) to support his rapture teaching. Those verses are as follows:

> For the Lord Himself will descend from heaven with a shout, with the voice of the archangel and with the trumpet of God, and the dead in Christ will rise first. Then we who are alive, who remain, will be caught up together with them in the clouds to meet the Lord in the air, and so we will always be with the Lord. (1 Thess 4:16–17 NASB)

> At that time there will be two men in the field; one will be taken and one will be left. Two women will be grinding at the mill; one will be taken and one will be left. (Matt 24:40–41 NASB)

> I tell you, on that night there will be two in one bed; one will be taken and the other will be left. There will be two women grinding at the same place; one will be taken and the other will be left. Two men will be in the field; one will be taken and the other will be left. (Luke 17:34–36 NASB)

> And He will send forth His angels with a great trumpet blast, and they will gather together his elect from the four winds, from one end of the sky to the other. (Matt 24:31 NASB)

> Behold, I am telling you a mystery; we will not all sleep, but we will all be changed, in a moment, in the twinkling of an eye, at the last trumpet; for the trumpet will sound, and the dead will be raised imperishable, and we will be changed. For this perishable must put on the imperishable, and this mortal must put on immortality. (1 Cor 15:51–53 NASB)

EXAMINING THE VERSES

Two of the key verses invoked as support for the rapture teaching are 1 Thessalonians 4:16–17 and 1 Corinthians 15:51–53.

> For the Lord Himself will descend from heaven with a shout, with the voice of the archangel and with the trumpet of God, and the dead in Christ will rise first. Then we who are alive, who remain, will be caught up together with them in the clouds to meet the Lord in the air, and so we will always be with the Lord. (1 Thess 4:16–17 NASB)

> Behold, I am telling you a mystery; we will not all sleep, but we will all be changed, in a moment, in the twinkling of an eye, at the last trumpet; for the trumpet will sound, and the dead will be raised imperishable, and we will be changed. For this perishable must put on the imperishable, and this mortal must put on immortality. (1 Cor 15:51–53 NASB)

First Thessalonians describes how "the dead in Christ will rise first," and then it describes those "who are alive, who remain, will be caught up . . . to meet the Lord." The description of "we who are alive, who remain, *will be caught up* . . . " is used as support for the rapture teaching. The rapture teaching takes those words and says that they are to be understood in the same way as the "taking away" described by Jesus Christ in Matthew, and the parallel verses in Luke, where, according to Darby, "taking away" is a reference to all living believers being removed from the Earth before the events of Revelation begin, so as to spare the church from going through the tribulations and judgements of Revelation.

First Corinthians 15:51–53 is then further invoked as an amplification of that same rapture event, where the words "we will not all sleep, but we will all be changed" are taken to be a description of the "taking away" of the rapture event.

However, these verses absolutely do *not* support the rapture teaching; rather, these verses are describing a fundamental truth of the Christian faith, which is *resurrection*.

First Thessalonians 4:16–17 is a description of the *resurrection* of believers. This is made absolutely clear in verse 16, which specifically tells us that "the *dead in Christ* will *rise* first"—the *dead* in Christ are *all* believers who have ever lived and died throughout human history. The rising of the dead is the *definition* of "resurrection," so when we are told "the *dead* in Christ will *rise* first," it is absolutely a description of the resurrection of believers.

First Thessalonians 4:16–17, in fact, is a detailed description of what the resurrection of believers will look like, telling us that, in the resurrection, the Christian *dead* will rise *first*, and then, *after* the dead Christians are resurrected, the *living* Christians who are still alive will *then also* be transformed into their *resurrected* selves. This is a description of the resurrection of believers, which occurs just before Jesus Christ descends to Earth at the Second Coming, and from 1 Thessalonians 4:16–17 we can understand the resurrection of believers as having two parts—first, the dead

Christians will be resurrected, and then the other, still-living Christians will be transformed into their resurrected selves.

The resurrection is a fundamental truth of the Christian faith, clearly enunciated in the Creed of the church, and it is described here in 1 Thessalonians 4:16–17. From these verses, as well as from other verses, we know that the resurrection of believers happens at the Second Coming, just before Jesus descends to Earth. As 1 Thessalonians 4:16 tells us, at that moment *all* believers who have died *will be bodily resurrected* and will be raised to meet the Lord Jesus in the air, in the earthly sky, in the clouds, to join with him just before he descends to Earth at the Second Coming. That is Part 1 of the resurrection of believers. Part 2 of the resurrection of believers is described in 4:17, which tells us that, as part of that *same* resurrection event, *after* the dead believers are resurrected, *then* all the believers who are *still alive* and remain on Earth will *then* be transformed into their resurrected selves and will *also* be raised, together with the resurrected dead, to meet the Lord Jesus in the air before he descends to Earth at the Second Coming. All of this is a description of the *resurrection* of believers, and this is all described as happening at the sound of the "trumpet of God."

First Corinthians 15:51–53 is a description of that *same* resurrection event, a description of the *second* part of that resurrection event, describing the resurrection of the *living* believers on Earth at the time of the Second Coming. This is made absolutely clear in 15:52, when we are specifically told that this event will happen when "the trumpet will sound." This trumpet that will sound is exactly the same "trumpet of God" described in 1 Thessalonians 4:16. Furthermore, Paul here also specifically tells us that at the sound of that trumpet, "the *dead* will be raised incorruptible," which is exactly the same as the 1 Thessalonians 4:16 description that "the *dead* in Christ will rise first." Paul then tells us in 1 Corinthians 15:51 that "we shall be changed." The "we" that he is referring to are the same *living* believers of 1 Thessalonians 4:17, who are *not* dead, but who remain alive just prior to the Second Coming. He describes those *living* believers as being "changed." When he says "we shall not all sleep," he means that not all believers shall die, which affirms that this as a description of *living* believers. Paul then tells us that it is those same *living* believers, those believers who "shall not all sleep," who will be "changed." That change is described in verse 53, where he tells us that the "perishable must put on the imperishable, and this mortal must put on immortality." The change that will happen to those living believers is that they will become immortal—the immortality of believers occurs only at the resurrection.

First Corinthians 15:51–53 is describing the exact same event, and moment of time, that 1 Thessalonians 4:16–17 describes, the resurrection of believers, but is just giving us a more detailed description of Part 2 of that resurrection event, the resurrection transformation of the living believers. As a result, we can clearly understand both 1 Thessalonians 4:16–17 and the parallel passage of 1 Corinthians 15:51–53, in describing both dead Christians as rising up and the gathering and rising up of the remaining living Christians, as being a description of the *resurrection* of believers and *not* the rapture.

Another passage used as support for the rapture teaching is Matthew 24:31.

> And He will send forth His angels with a great trumpet blast, and they will gather together His elect from the four winds, from one end of the sky to the other. (Matt 24:31 NASB)

Matthew 24:31 is an excerpt from a larger passage in Matthew 24. The full passage reads as follows:

> But immediately after the tribulation of those days the sun will be darkened, and the moon will not give its light, and the stars will fall from the sky, and the powers of the heavens will be shaken. And then the sign of the Son of Man will appear in the sky, and then all the tribes of the earth will mourn, and they will see the Son of Man coming on the clouds of the sky with power and great glory. And he will send forth his angels with a great trumpet blast, and they will gather together His elect from the four winds, from one end of the sky to the other. (Matt 24:29–31 NASB)

This passage is describing the Second Coming and the *living* believers who remain on Earth just prior to the Second Coming, describing those living believers as being *gathered*. This gathering of living believers is described as happening at the sound of a trumpet, exactly as 1 Thessalonians 4:16–17 and 1 Corinthians 15:51–53 describes it. As a result, we can understand Matthew 24:29–31 as describing the exact same event as are 1 Thessalonians 4:16–17 and 1 Corinthians 15:51–53—the *gathering* and *resurrection/transformation* of the *living* believers just prior to Jesus' descent at the Second Coming, all described as occurring at the sound of a trumpet, and all of which will happen only *after* the dead in Christ rise first. As a result, we can understand Matthew 24:31 in the same way as we understand 1 Thessalonians 4:16–17 and 1 Corinthians 15:51–53, as being a description of the *resurrection* of living believers who are on the Earth just prior to the Second Coming. Matthew 24:31 is therefore *not* a description of the rapture.

One of the other very key passages invoked to support the rapture teaching is Matthew 24:40–41, and the parallel passage, Luke 17:34–36.

> At that time there will be two men in the field; *one will be taken* and *one will be left*. Two women will be grinding at the mill; *one will be taken* and *one will be left*. (Matt 24:40–41 NASB, italics added)

> I tell you, on that night there will be two in one bed; *one will be taken* and *the other will be left*. There will be two women grinding at the same place; *one will be taken* and *the other will be left*. Two men will be in the field; *one will be taken* and *the other will be left*. (Luke 17:34–36 NASB, italics added)

These passages are fundamental to the support of the rapture teaching, and, in fact, it is these very passages that have given the name to the blockbuster *Left Behind* series, the popular work of Christian fiction. From these passages, Darby decided that to be "taken away" means to be *rescued*. Therefore, if two men are in a field, and one is left and the other is *taken*, then the one who is taken is understood as being *rescued*, rescued from the judgments of Revelation, and therefore Darby cited this passage as support for his rapture teaching.

Do these passages teach, or support, the rapture teaching? Does being "taken" mean to be rescued? These passages do not support the rapture teaching; in fact, they actually *deny* it.

How can we understand these passages? It is Jesus himself who explains these passages for us. Matthew 24:40–41 is part of a larger passage that makes the meaning absolutely clear.

> For the coming of the Son of Man will be just like the days of Noah. For as in those days before the flood they were eating and drinking, marrying and giving in marriage, until the day that Noah entered the ark, and they did not understand until *the flood came* and *took them all away*; so will the coming of the Son of Man be. At that time there will be two men in the field; one *will be taken* and one will be left. Two women will be grinding at the mill; *one will be taken* and one will be left. (Matt 24:37–41 NASB)

In this passage, Jesus tells us that the events preceding the Second Coming will be just like the days of Noah. Jesus describes humanity, in the days of Noah, as "eating and drinking, marrying and giving in marriage," and then "the flood came and *took them all away*." What does it mean for the flood to "take them all away"? Did the flood *rescue* humanity? The flood absolutely did *not* rescue humanity; on the contrary, the flood completely *destroyed* and *obliterated* humanity. This destruction and obliteration of humanity by the flood is described by Jesus as being "taken away."

In the exact same breath of his description of the flood as "taking away" humanity, of destroying humanity, Jesus continues to tell us that it will be *exactly the same* with the coming of the Son of Man, the Second Coming. Jesus then describes two men in a field, and describes one as being "taken" and the other as being "left"—what does it mean to be "taken"? Jesus has already specifically defined for us what it means to be taken—to be taken means to be *destroyed*. As a result, we know that the people who are *taken* prior to the Second Coming are people who are being *destroyed*, since Jesus explains for us specifically in verse 39 in regard to the flood of Noah's day that to be "taken away" means to be destroyed. So, when the man who is in the field is described as being "taken," he is being destroyed; when the man who is in the bed is described as being "taken" (Luke 17:34), he is being destroyed, when the woman who is grinding at the mill is described as being "taken," she is being destroyed.

According to the very clear teaching of Jesus Christ, to be "taken away" means to be *destroyed*, but John Darby said that to be "taken away" means to be *rescued*—Darby was wrong, Jesus is right. Matthew 24:40–41 and Luke 17:34–36 do *not* support the rapture teaching; rather, they *deny* it.

OTHER ARGUMENTS USED TO SUPPORT THE RAPTURE TEACHING

In addition to the above verses being used to support the rapture teaching, there are other arguments invoked to support the teaching. One of the other key arguments invoked to support the rapture teaching is as follows: proponents of the rapture teaching say that after chapter 3 of Revelation the church is never mentioned again in the book of Revelation until chapter 20. As a result, since the church is absent in chapters 4–19, this is evidence that supports the fact that the church has been *removed* from the Earth during the events of Revelation 4–19.

Is this true? Is the church in fact not mentioned in the book of Revelation from chapters 4 to 19? It is absolutely *not* true—the church is found *throughout* the *entirety* of the book of Revelation, as the following verses show:

> This calls for patient endurance and faithfulness on the part of *God's people*. (13:10 NIV)

> Here is the patience and the faith of *the saints*. (13:10 NKJV)

> This calls for patient endurance on the part of *the people of God* who keep his commands and remain faithful to Jesus. (14:12 NIV)

> Here is the patience of *the saints*; here are those who keep the commandments of God and the faith of Jesus. (14:12 NKJV)

> It was given power to wage war against *God's holy people* and to conquer them. (13:7 NIV)

> It was granted to him to make war with *the saints* and to overcome them. (13:7 NKJV)

> And I saw the souls of those who had been beheaded because of *their testimony about Jesus* and because of the word of God. They had not worshiped the beast or its image and had not received its mark on their foreheads or their hands. (20:4 NIV)

The church, also referred to as "God's people," as "God's holy people," and as "the saints," is specifically and clearly referred to throughout the events of Revelation 4–19, repeatedly. The church is absolutely present throughout the events of Revelation 4–19.

Further affirmation that the church is present throughout the entire time period of the book of Revelation is also given us by Jesus himself in Mathew 24.

"THEY WILL DELIVER YOU UP AND KILL YOU"

As we shall see, in Matthew 24:3–31 Jesus outlines for us the Seven Seals of Revelation, giving them to us in order and with explanation. Matthew 24:4–8 is a description of Seals 1–4, which, as we will see, cover a period of thirty-three years. Seal 5 is outlined by Jesus in 24:9–28, while Seal 6 is outlined in 24:29, and Seal 7 is outlined in 24:30–31. The entire seven-year period often talked about in studies of Revelation takes place, in its entirety, during Seal 5—Seal 5 is when the Beast comes to power and rules for three and a half years, and is also the time during which the subsequent three-and-a-half-year Great Tribulation takes place. When Jesus begins to describe Seal 6 in 24:29, he begins with the words "Immediately *after* the tribulation of those days"—when Seal 6 is opened, the Great Tribulation is over.

The reason that this is important to understand in any discussion about the rapture teaching is that when Jesus describes for us Seal 5, he begins with these words:

> *Then they will deliver you up to tribulation and kill you*, and *you will be hated* by all nations *for My name's sake*. And then many will be offended, will betray one another, and will hate one another. Then many false prophets will rise up and deceive many. And because lawlessness will abound, the love of many will grow cold. *But he who endures to the end shall be saved*. And this gospel of the kingdom will be preached in all the world as a witness to all the nations, and then the end will come. (Matt 24:9–14 NKJV)

In his description of the events of Seal 5, Jesus specifically tells us that Christians, *the church*, will be *persecuted* and *killed* for his name's sake during that time. This is Seal 5, when the Beast comes to power. This would be impossible if there was such a thing as a rapture, for, if there was a rapture, there would be no church upon the Earth during that time. The fact that Jesus clearly tells us that during the time period of Seal 5 the church will be persecuted and killed for his name's sake, taken together with the numerous passages in Revelation that also affirm the presence of the church on Earth during that same time, we can know, for a certainty, that the church is on the Earth during the events of Revelation.

As a result, the argument that the church is not referred to throughout the events of Revelation 4–19 is a false argument and has no support from Scripture.

"COME UP HERE"

Another argument invoked to support the rapture teaching is Revelation 4:1.

> After these things I looked, and behold, a door standing open in heaven. And the first voice which I heard was like a trumpet speaking with me, saying, "Come up here, and I will show you things which must take place after this." (4:1 NKJV)

Promoters of the rapture teaching describe the words "Come up here" in 4:1 as being spoken to the church, as being a call to the church, on Earth, to come up to heaven, thereby supporting the rapture teaching.

However, to clearly understand to whom those words are addressed, we turn to the following verse, 4:2.

> Immediately *I* was in the Spirit; and behold, a throne set in heaven, and One sat on the throne. And He who sat there was like a jasper and a sardius stone in appearance; and there was a rainbow around the throne, in appearance like an emerald. (4:2 NKJV)

Immediately following the call of 4:1 to "Come up here," the apostle John, to whom the Revelation is being given, tells us that *he* is the one who is taken up into heaven—the call to "Come up here" is given to the apostle John *only*, and to no one else, for immediately after the call to "Come up here" the apostle John describes *himself* as being immediately in the Spirit and in heaven. There is no reason whatsoever to consider those words of 4:1 as applying to the church—there is nothing that even remotely hints at such a thing, and, in fact, 4:2 clearly shows us that those words are *not* spoken to the church; they are spoken *only* to the apostle John.

The "Come up here" of Revelation 4:1 does not support the rapture teaching.

THE SEA OF GLASS

Also invoked to support the rapture teaching is Revelation 4:6.

> Before the throne there was a sea of glass, like crystal. And in the midst of the throne, and around the throne, were four living creatures full of eyes in front and in back. (4:6 NKJV)

Proponents of the rapture teaching claim that the "sea of glass" is the church. Of course, there is nothing in that passage, nor in any other passage in either Revelation or in the entire Bible, that connects a "sea of glass" with the church. So, what then is the "sea of glass," described as being clear as "crystal"? We can understand the "sea of glass" as follows.

The sea of glass, clear as crystal, is described as being before the very throne of God, being mentioned specifically in connection with God's throne. That exact same description of "crystal" before the throne of God is also found in Ezekiel.

> Spread out *above the heads* of the living creatures was what looked something like a *vault*, sparkling *like crystal*, and awesome. (Ezek 1:22 NIV)

> *Above the vault* over their heads was what looked like a *throne* of *lapis lazuli*, and high above on the throne was a figure like that of a man. (Ezek 1:26 NIV)

Ezekiel describes for us four living creatures. These same four living creatures are described in Revelation 4:6 (although in the three instances where the four living creatures are described in the Bible—Ezekiel 1, 10 and Revelation 4—those creatures appear differently in each instance, yet they are always the same four living creatures). Ezekiel tells us that above the heads of the four living creatures there was something that looked like a vault, or platform, of *crystal*, and this crystal is connected with the very throne of God in heaven, the implication being that the throne of God is actually sitting on that crystal platform. The crystal platform is described as sitting on the heads of the four living creatures, and in Ezekiel 10:20 we are told specifically that those four living creatures are, in fact, cherubim. The throne of God is situated on that crystal platform. As a result, since the crystal platform is on the heads of the cherubim (the four living creatures), and since God is sitting enthroned upon that crystal platform, the picture painted here, by Ezekiel, is of God sitting enthroned *between the cherubim*, a picture described repeatedly throughout the Bible.

> The LORD reigns, let the nations tremble; *he sits enthroned between the cherubim*, let the earth shake. (Ps 99:1 NIV)

> And David arose and went with all the people who were with him from Baale Judah to bring up from there the ark of God, whose name is called by the Name, the LORD of Hosts, *who dwells between the cherubim*. (2 Sam 6:2 NKJV)

> Then Hezekiah prayed before the LORD, and said: "O LORD God of Israel, *the One who dwells between the cherubim*, You are God, You alone, of all the kingdoms of the earth. You have made heaven and earth." (2 Kgs 19:15 NKJV)

> And David and all Israel went up to Baalah, to Kirjath Jearim, which belonged to Judah, to bring up from there the ark of God *the LORD, who dwells between the cherubim*, where His name is proclaimed. (1 Chr 13:6 NKJV)

> O LORD of hosts, God of Israel, *the One who dwells between the cherubim*, You are God, You alone, of all the kingdoms of the earth. You have made heaven and earth. (Isa 37:16 NKJV)

The fact that God sits enthroned between the cherubim is affirmed repeatedly throughout Scripture, and that exact description is what we see outlined, in detail, in Ezekiel 1:22, 26. God's throne sits upon a crystal vault, or platform, while the platform itself sits upon the heads of the cherubim, and so God sits enthroned between the cherubim.

Furthermore, in Ezekiel 1:26, God's throne itself is described as looking like *lapis lazuli*, another crystal gemstone. This is strikingly similar to Exodus 24:9–11.

> Moses and Aaron, Nadab and Abihu, and the seventy elders of Israel went up and saw the God of Israel. *Under his feet* was something like *a pavement* made of *lapis lazuli*, as bright blue as the sky. But God did not raise his hand against

these leaders of the Israelites; they saw God, and they ate and drank. (Exod 24:9–11 NIV)

In Exodus 24:9–11, Moses and the leaders of Israel saw God, and they describe God as having something like a "pavement" of lapis lazuli beneath his feet. This lapis lazuli (which is a crystalline gemstone) is the exact same description that Ezekiel gives us of the appearance of God's throne

As a result, we can understand that God's very throne is associated with, and is sitting upon, a crystal platform, a platform which can be understood as being made of precious gemstone, just as God's throne itself is described as having the appearance of a precious gemstone. In fact, precious gemstones are often connected with God throughout the Bible, for the twelve foundations of the New Jerusalem are all made of precious gemstones (Rev 21:19–20).

As a result, we can understand the "sea of glass" in Revelation 4:6 in this same way. The scene described by John in Revelation 4 is a description of God's throne in heaven (Rev 4:2). It is in this context of God's throne that John describes a "sea of glass, like crystal" as being before God's throne. John also tells us, as he describes God's throne and the crystal-like sea of glass before the throne, that around the throne were four living creatures. John's description of God's throne, his description of the crystal-like sea of glass before it, and his description of the throne being surrounded by four living creatures, is virtually the exact same description as Ezekiel gives us of God's throne in Ezekiel 1:22, 26. As a result, we can understand John's description of the "sea of glass, like crystal" as being John's way of describing the same crystal platform upon which sits God's throne, as is described by Ezekiel in his description of God's throne.

As a result, the argument that the "sea of glass, like crystal" mentioned in Revelation 4:6 is the church has no substance or basis in Scripture.

"I GO TO PREPARE A PLACE FOR YOU"

Another Scripture that is invoked to support the rapture teaching is John 14:2–3.

> In My Father's house are many mansions; if it were not so, I would have told you. I go to prepare a place for you. And if I go and prepare a place for you, I will come again and receive you to Myself; that where I am, there you may be also. (14:2–3, NKJV)

In this passage, Jesus tells us that he is going to "prepare a place" for us, the church. It is clear that he is going to *heaven*, to his "Father's house," to prepare this place. He also tells us that he will "come again" to "receive" us to himself—to "come again" is a reference to Jesus' return to Earth at the Second Coming. Jesus tells us that when he returns ("comes again"), he will "receive" the church to himself, so that we will be with him.

Proponents of the rapture teaching cite this Scripture as support for the rapture. But does this passage support the rapture teaching? No, it does not.

It is certainly true that Jesus did go to heaven and, as he tells us himself, while he is in heaven, he absolutely *will* prepare a place for the church, and then, afterwards, he *will* come again and receive the church to himself, so that we will always be with him. If he is not talking about the rapture in this passage, then how are we to understand this passage? What is this place that Jesus said he will prepare for us?

In fact, the Bible makes very clear what that place is—it is the New Jerusalem, and we can know that from the following Scripture:

> Then I, John, saw the holy *city*, New Jerusalem, coming down *out of heaven* from God, *prepared* as a *bride* adorned for her husband. (Rev 21:2 NKJV)

In Revelation 21:1, we are told of a very specific place—that place is named for us—it is the city New Jerusalem.

We are also very specifically told that the city New Jerusalem was "prepared."

We are also very specifically told that the city, the New Jerusalem, is "coming down" from *heaven*, coming to *Earth*.

We are also told that the New Jerusalem is coming down, from heaven, "as a bride."

The term "the Bride" is always and only a reference to *the church*, who is described as "the wife of the Lamb" (Eph 5:31–32; Rev 21:9; 22:17). It is *the church*, the people of God, who are the Bride, so when the New Jerusalem is described "as a bride" adorned for her husband, it is not a reference to the *city* as being the Bride, but rather a reference that the *inhabitants* of that city will be the Bride—that is, the *inhabitants* of the New Jerusalem will be *the church*.

With that in mind, here is what we see—the New Jerusalem is described as a "place," and it is a place that has been "prepared," and it has been prepared in heaven, and it is a place that has been prepared for the church. This is an exact parallel, and fulfillment of, Jesus' words in John 14:2–3—the place that Jesus was referring to in John 14:2–3, the place that he went to heaven to prepare for the church, is the New Jerusalem. The New Jerusalem is *not* inhabited by the church *in heaven*, but is only inhabited by the church *on Earth*, after it descends to Earth *from* heaven.

How then do we understand the rest of Jesus' words, "I will come again and *receive you* to Myself; that where I am, there you may be also" (John 14:3 NKJV)? We can understand it as follows.

When Jesus tells us that he will "come again" and "receive" us to himself, that is a reference to the Second Coming *and* a reference to the *resurrection* of believers.

As we shall see, Scripture clearly teaches that the resurrection of *all* believers happens in Seal 7 of Revelation, just *before* Jesus descends to Earth at the Second Coming. This resurrection of all believers is described as the "marriage" or "wedding feast" of the Bride and the Lamb.

> "Let us be glad and rejoice and give Him glory, for the marriage of the Lamb has come, and His wife has made herself ready." And to her it was granted to be arrayed in fine linen, clean and bright, for the fine linen is the righteous acts of the saints.
>
> Then he said to me, "Write: 'Blessed are those who are called to the marriage supper of the Lamb!' And he said to me, 'These are the true sayings of God.'" (Rev 19:7-9 NKJV)

It is at the resurrection of all believers that all the church is finally fully united with, married to, Jesus Christ, entering into its full redemption by way of resurrection and being fully and permanently indwelt by the Holy Spirit—that is the marriage of the Bride and of the Lamb.

That resurrection of all believers is also outlined for us in 1 Thessalonians 4:15-17.

> For this we say to you by the word of the Lord, that we who are alive and remain until the coming of the Lord will by no means precede those who are asleep. For *the Lord Himself will descend from heaven* with a shout, with the voice of an archangel, and *with the trumpet* of God. And *the dead in Christ will rise first*. Then we who are alive and remain shall be caught up together with them in the clouds to meet the Lord in the air. And thus we shall always be with the Lord. (4:15-17 NKJV)

It is also outlined for us by Jesus himself in Matthew 24 when he describes for us Seal 7.

> Then the sign of *the Son of Man* will *appear in heaven*, and then all the tribes of the earth will mourn, and they will *see the Son of Man coming on the clouds of heaven* with power and great glory. And *He will send His angels* with a great *sound of a trumpet*, and they will *gather together His elect* from the four winds, from one end of heaven to the other. (24:30-31 NKJV)

This exact same event is also described for us in 1 Corinthians.

> Behold, I tell you a mystery: We shall not all sleep, but we shall all be changed—in a moment, in the twinkling of an eye, *at the last trumpet*. For *the trumpet will sound*, and *the dead will be raised* incorruptible, *and we shall be changed*. (15:51-52 NKJV)

All of these verses are a description of the resurrection of believers, and they all agree on the details and the sequence of events—the Trumpet (the *last* Trumpet, which is Trumpet 7 of Revelation) will sound, while Jesus Christ is in the air, in the clouds in the sky of the Earth. At the sound of that last Trumpet, *all* the dead *in Christ* will be raised, *resurrected*, and then *all* the Christians who are still on the Earth, but who have *not* yet died, will be changed into their *resurrected* selves. Then, *all* of these resurrected Christians—the entire church—will be gathered up, into the sky, to meet Jesus, to be received by him. Only *then* does Jesus descend to Earth for the Second

Coming, as all the resurrected church, all the Lord's "holy ones," descends with him, *following* him as he descends to Earth (1 Thess 3:13; Jude 14).

As a result, we can understand Jesus' words in John 14:2–3 as follows. Jesus went to heaven to prepare a place for his church, the place called the New Jerusalem. The New Jerusalem will be inhabited by the church, on Earth. However, before that happens, Jesus will first return to Earth at the Second Coming, and, as he returns to Earth, but before he descends to Earth, the resurrection of all believers first takes place. All believers—living and dead—are resurrected and gathered up into the earthly sky to be with Jesus, who receives his church in the sky. After receiving his church in the sky, Jesus then descends to Earth for the Second Coming. Once the church is gathered to be with Jesus in the air, and before Jesus descends to Earth for the Second Coming, the church will, from that point onwards, always and forever be with Jesus and will never be apart from him. So, when the church is resurrected and gathered up to Jesus just prior to the descent of the Second Coming, this is the fulfillment of Jesus' words "I will come again and receive you to Myself; that where I am, there you may be also." The place that has been prepared for the church, the New Jerusalem, will descend to Earth *later*, and thereafter remain *forever* upon the Earth, where Jesus and the entire church, as well as the Father (Rev 21–22), will dwell. So, the resurrection and gathering up of believers just prior to Jesus' descent at the Second Coming fulfills Jesus' words about him coming again and receiving the church unto himself, while the descent of the New Jerusalem, much later, fulfills Jesus' words about the place that has been prepared for us in heaven, but which will be inhabited by the church on Earth.

As a result, we can see that John 14:2–3 does not support the rapture teaching; rather, it is all and only about resurrection and the New Jerusalem, all of which will be *on Earth*.

JESUS' PRAYER

Another contradiction to the rapture teaching is Jesus' own words in John 17, where Jesus prays specifically for apostles, for believers, for the future church. In that prayer, Jesus prays the following:

> My prayer is *not* that you *take them out of the world* but that you *protect them* from the evil one. (John 17:15 NIV)

In this passage, Jesus is praying for his disciples, but he affirms that his prayer is also for all believers when he says, in John 17:20, that "My prayer is not for them alone" (NIV). In his prayer to the Father, Jesus *specifically* says that Jesus does *not* pray that believers, the church, are *taken from* (or out of) the world; rather he prays for the church's protection.

If there was such a thing as a rapture, a teaching that states that the church is to be *taken out of the* world, then why does Jesus *specifically* say that he is *not* praying for the church to be taken out of the world? It is inarguable that any teaching that states that it is God's will for the church to be taken out of the world, and removed from harmful events, is in direct contradiction with Jesus' own words and prayer for the church—Jesus tells us that he is *not* asking and, by implication, he is not *wanting* the church to be removed from the world during times of trouble or trial. Rather, during times of trouble and trial, Jesus prays for the *protection* of the church during that time of trial. The fact that Jesus prays for the church's protection during the time of trial testifies to the fact that the church *will* go through that time of trial, otherwise there would be no need for the church's protection.

As a result, the rapture teaching is in direct contradiction with Jesus' own words and with his clearly stated will.

THE LETTERS TO THE SEVEN CHURCHES

After the opening introduction to the book of Revelation (chapter 1), Revelation begins with letters from Jesus Christ to the angels of seven churches (chapters 2–3). All of these seven letters take the same tone—Jesus is telling the churches, by way of the angels of each of those churches, to deal with and correct problems and issues within that church because something is going to come upon them. He then describes a variety of issues and problems that those churches are facing that they need to fix in order to be prepared for what is about to come. Jesus then repeatedly tells the churches to persevere and endure through what is to come.

> Do not be afraid of *what you are about to suffer*. I tell you, the devil will put some of you in prison to test you, and *you will suffer persecution* for ten days. Be faithful, *even to the point of death*, and I will give you life as your victor's crown. (2:8 NIV)

> Repent therefore! Otherwise, I will soon come to you and will fight against them with *the sword of my mouth*. (2:16 NIV; also see 19:15 on the "sword of my mouth")

> hold on to what you have until I come. To *the one who is victorious* and does my will to the end, I will give authority over the nations (2:25–26 NIV)

> *I am coming soon*. Hold on to what you have, so that no one will take your crown. (3:11 NIV)

Jesus then tells the churches that if they persevere and endure, they will receive rewards. He then describes the rewards the churches will get—the "victor's crown," "authority over the nations," white robes and their name in the Book of Life (3:5), dwelling in the New Jerusalem (3:12), sitting with Jesus on his throne (3:21). *All* of these rewards are the rewards described as being given by Jesus *after* the Second Coming (Rev 21–22).

The letters to the angels of the seven churches, which begin the book of Revelation, are sent by Jesus to his church as a *warning* of what is to come, an *admonition* to straighten themselves out, to *get ready* for what is about to come, and then giving a promise of rewards to the church if the church *perseveres* and *endures* throughout the trial that is about to come. The church is *not* going to be taken away from the Earth so as to avoid that time of trial; rather, according to Jesus' own words and promises, the church will *go through* that time of trial, and so the church must endure and persevere—this is inarguable and is clearly supported and affirmed by Revelation 2–3.

All of this is the exact *opposite* of the rapture teaching—the rapture teaching is in contradiction to Jesus' own teaching, in contradiction to his own prayers for the church, and in contradiction to the entirety of Scripture.

THE HOUR OF TRIAL

In the letter to the angel of the church in Philadelphia, Jesus tells them the following:

> Since you have kept my command to endure patiently, I will also *keep you from the hour of trial* that is going to come on the whole world to test the inhabitants of the earth. (Rev 3:10 NIV)

In the letter to the church in Philadelphia, Jesus specifically tells them that, since they have kept his command, he will keep them, the church, from the "hour of trial" that is coming upon the world. This "hour of trial" that is coming upon the world is unquestionably the judgment events of Revelation.

Does this not support a rapture teaching? Does 3:10 not teach that the church will be removed from the Earth to be kept from judgment, to be kept from the "hour of trial"? No, it does not. How then are we to understand 3:10? We are to understand it in exactly the same way as we understand the plagues of Egypt and Israel.

During the plagues that God sent upon Egypt, throughout the whole time of those plagues, the nation of Israel was present, there in Egypt, with the Egyptians, while those plagues were raining down upon Egypt. And yet, the Bible is clear that God made a *distinction* between Israel and Egypt—while those plagues were raining down upon Egypt, and while Israel was still in Egypt during the whole time of those plagues, God *protected* Israel from being affected by those plagues—*only* Egyptians were affected by those plagues, *not* Israel. God was keeping Israel "from the hour of trial" that was coming upon Egypt by way of the plagues—Israel was there, present in Egypt, during the whole time of those plagues, but Israel was *protected* from those plagues.

This distinction between Israel and Egypt during the time of those plagues is clearly affirmed by God himself. When God turns the waters of the Nile into blood, he says,

> The fish in the Nile will die, and the river will stink; the *Egyptians* will not be able to drink its water. (Exod 7:18 NIV)

> The fish in the Nile died, and the river smelled so bad that the *Egyptians* could not drink its water. Blood was everywhere in Egypt. (Exod 7:21 NIV)

Even though the plague of blood struck the Nile waters, God tells us, very specifically, that it is the *Egyptians* who will not be able to drink its water, or any other water (7:19). God does not say that *Israel* will be without water, but only the *Egyptians*. Based on what we read of the other, upcoming plagues, and based on the very specific distinction God is making here, we can conclude that Israel *did* have water to drink—Israel was being protected from the plague of blood.

About the plague of frogs, God specifically says that the frogs will come upon *Pharaoh*, and *his* officials, and upon *his* people (8:3–4, 8–10). Once again the plague of frogs is described specifically as coming upon *only* the Egyptians, not upon Israel. Israel was protected from the plague of frogs.

The exact same scenario is seen in the plague of flies (8:21–22)—in fact, in 8:22–23 God specifically tells us that he is making a distinction between the Egyptians and the Israelites in regard to the plague of flies.

> But on that day I will deal differently with the land of Goshen, where my people live; no swarms of flies will be there, so that you will know that I, the LORD, am in this land. *I will make a distinction* between my people and your people. This sign will occur tomorrow. (Exod 8:22–23 NIV)

The plague of livestock is also specifically described as coming *only* upon the *Egyptian* livestock (9:4–6). The plague of boils is also specifically described as coming *only* upon the Egyptians, and *not* upon Israel (9:8–11). The plague of hail is also described as coming *only* upon Egyptians, and *not* upon Israel (9:22–26). Likewise with the plague of darkness—all Egypt was under the plague of darkness, but the Israelites had light (10:21–23). When God sent the plague of the death of the firstborn, he specifically tells us that the plague will come only upon Egyptians, and not upon Israel (11:5–7). Once again, God makes a distinction between Israel, his people, and the Egyptians.

The Bible very clearly shows us that even though Israel was in Egypt during the entire time of all the plagues, God *protected* Israel from those plagues; those plagues did *not* come upon Israel, the plagues came *only* upon the Egyptians—by his protection, God was keeping Israel from the "hour of trial" coming upon Egypt.

It is in exactly that same way that we are to understand Revelation 3:10. There will be an "hour of trial" coming upon the whole world, and the church will be present, on Earth, throughout that entire time of trial, but God, during that time of trial, will make a *distinction* between his church, his people, and those who take the number of the Beast—God will *protect* his church from those trials, even though the church will remain on Earth throughout that entire time. In fact, Revelation 12:14–16 specifically tells us that during that time of Great Tribulation, the church (symbolically represented here as a woman) will be protected, or "taken care of," during that time.

> The woman was given the two wings of a great eagle, so that *she might fly to the place prepared for her in the wilderness*, where *she would be taken care of* for a time, times and half a time, out of the serpent's reach. Then from his mouth the serpent spewed water like a river, to overtake the woman and sweep her away with the torrent. But the earth helped the woman by opening its mouth and swallowing the river that the dragon had spewed out of his mouth. (12:14–16 NIV)

We are told that the woman (the church) will be taken care of for the three and a half years of global Tribulation, and that she will be out of the serpent's reach. When the dragon (Satan) unleashes an onslaught against the woman, she is once again protected from that onslaught, for we are told that the Earth opened its mouth and swallowed that river of onslaught, so as to protect the woman. This is an exact parallel to God's protection of Israel during the plagues of Egypt.

As a result, when Revelation 3:10 tells us that the church will be kept from the "hour of trial" that will be coming upon the whole world, it in no way supports a rapture teaching; rather it affirms that during the time of trial coming upon the whole world, God will *protect* his church from that Tribulation, exactly as he protected Israel during the plagues of Egypt.

THE SECRET COMING

The rapture teaching states that Jesus is coming, quietly and in secret, to take his church out of the world before the events of Revelation unfold. Yet, about the Second Coming of Jesus, we are told the following:

> For the Lord Himself will descend from heaven *with a shout*, with the voice of an archangel, and with *the trumpet* of God. And the dead in Christ will rise first. (1 Thess 4:16 NKJV)

In this passage describing the Second Coming of Jesus, we are told two things. First, when Jesus descends to Earth at his Second Coming, he will descend "with a shout." Second, we are told that his coming will be accompanied by a "trumpet" blast. This is the exact *opposite* of the rapture teaching—there is nothing quiet or secret about the Second Coming of Jesus; rather it will be loud and unmistakable, and Jesus himself will come with a loud shout. This passage completely contradicts the rapture teaching that Jesus will come quietly and in secret.

THREE COMINGS OF CHRIST

One of the very fundamental facts about the rapture teaching is that it teaches there will be *three* comings of Jesus Christ—the first coming, in Bethlehem; a quiet and secret second coming, the rapture; and finally a third coming, Jesus' descent to Earth.

It is the core foundational truth of the church that there are only *two* comings of Jesus Christ—the First Coming, at Bethlehem, and the Second Coming, when Jesus descends to Earth *in glory* and judges the living and the dead. This is in fact stated in the very Creed of the church.

> I believe in one God, the Father Almighty, Maker of heaven and earth, and of all things visible and invisible.
>
> And in one Lord Jesus Christ, the only-begotten Son of God, begotten of the Father before all worlds; God of God, Light of Light, very God of very God; begotten, not made, being of one substance with the Father, by whom all things were made.
>
> Who, for us men for our salvation, *came down from heaven*, and was *incarnate* by the Holy Spirit of *the virgin Mary*, and was made man; and was crucified also for us under Pontius Pilate; He suffered and was buried; and the third day He rose again, according to the Scriptures; and ascended into heaven, and sits on the right hand of the Father; and *He shall come again, with glory, to judge the living and the dead*; whose kingdom shall have no end.
>
> And I believe in the Holy Ghost, the Lord and Giver of Life; who proceeds from the Father [and the Son]; who with the Father and the Son together is worshiped and glorified; who spoke by the prophets.
>
> And I believe in one holy catholic and apostolic Church. I acknowledge one baptism for the remission of sins; and I look for the resurrection of the dead, and the life of the world to come. Amen.[1]

The Creed of the church is clear—at Jesus' *First* Coming, he "came down from heaven" and became "incarnate" in the Virgin Mary—this is the First Coming of Jesus Christ.

The Creed continues and says that Jesus "will come again with glory" and, when he comes that second time, he will come to "judge the living and the dead."

The Creed is very clear—there are only *two* comings of Jesus Christ, and at the *Second* Coming Jesus comes in *glory* and he comes to *judge* both the *living and the dead*. The resurrection of believers, which occurs just prior to Jesus' descent at the Second Coming, is that initial judgment of *both* the living *and* the dead ("the dead in Christ" will rise first, 1 Thess 4:16—the Christian *dead* are judged to *resurrection*, and the *living* Christians are judged and transformed into their resurrected selves). Matthew 25:31–46 describes the judgment of nations by Jesus after his Second

---

1. https://www.ccel.org/creeds/nicene.creed.html.

Coming—again, a judgment of the *living* that follows the Second Coming. That Jesus comes at his *Second* Coming, in *glory*, to *judge the living and the dead* is an unmistakable and foundational truth of the Christian faith, and, as such, it is clearly stated in the very Creed of the church.

However, the rapture teaching teaches something very different. The rapture teaching states that the *Second* Coming of Jesus will be a *secret* coming, one where Jesus does *not* come in glory. Also, at that secret Second Coming, Jesus will *not* judge the living and the dead; rather, he will take his church away from the Earth before, or during, the time of trial that is to come upon the Earth. When Jesus later returns to Earth, some years later, and descends to Earth to judge the living and the dead, that is in fact a *third* coming of Jesus Christ.

Though the rapture teaching may use different wording, the fact is that the rapture teaches that there will be *three* comings of Jesus Christ.

To teach that there will be *three* comings of Jesus Christ, and that one of those comings, the Second Coming, will be a *secret* coming where Jesus does *not* come in glory, where Jesus does *not* come to judge the living and the dead, but instead comes to take the church off of the Earth, is a direct contradiction of the Creed of the church. The Creed of the church is itself a clear summary of the foundational *scriptural* truth of the faith, and so to contradict the Creed of the church is to contradict Scripture. Scripture, the church, and the Creed *all* clearly state that there are only *two* comings of Jesus Christ, *not* three, and at his *Second* Coming the Lord Jesus Christ comes *in glory* and *judges* the living and the dead.

To teach that there are three comings of Jesus Christ, and to teach that the Second Coming is a secret coming to remove the church from the world, rather than a coming of glory to judge the living and the dead, is a contradiction of both Scripture and of the very Creed of the church. Any teaching that contradicts the Creed of the church is heresy. As a result, a very strong argument can be made that the rapture teaching, in its teaching of three comings of Jesus Christ, is a heretical teaching, a modern heresy.

CONCLUSION

The rapture teaching is a new teaching, the invention of John Darby, being invented only in the 1830s, and promoted only since 1909. The small handful of verses that are invoked to support the rapture teaching not only do *not* support the teaching, but they in fact *deny* the teaching (Matt 24:40–41; Luke 17:34–36). Jesus himself tells us specifically that he does *not* ask for the church to be taken out of the world during the time of trial but rather prays for the church's protection as the church *goes through* that time of trial (John 17:15). The church is present throughout the entirety of the events outlined in the book of Revelation (Rev 13:7, 13:10, 14:12, 20:4; Matt 24:9–14), and to teach otherwise is not only a false teaching, but a deadly teaching, for, as we shall see in a close examination of Seal 2, the rapture teaching lays the foundation for believers to potentially worship the Beast to come. The rapture teaching, in its teaching of three comings of Jesus Christ, contradicts the Creed of the church and is therefore a heretical teaching. As a result, the clear conclusion, from Scripture, from history, from the Creed of the church, is that there is no such thing as a rapture of the church.

4

Israel and Judah

ONE OF THE FUNDAMENTAL truths to understand, especially in regard to Bible prophecy, is that there is a distinction between Israel and the Jews.

In the Old Testament, we are given the story of the birth of Israel, a nation born unto God, a nation and a people that he considered his nation and his people. The history of the Israel is as follows.

In approximately 2200 BC, there was a man called Abram, who was called by God to follow him, and who was promised by God that God would make him the father of many nations (Gen 12:1). Abram's name was changed to Abraham (17:5), and Abraham had a son, Isaac, who inherited the promises that God gave to Abraham (17:19).

Isaac had two sons—Esau, the older, and Jacob (Gen 25:19–26). As the older, Esau was to inherit the birthright promises from his father, Isaac, but Jacob manipulated Esau to sell to him, Jacob, the birthright (25:29–34). As a result, Jacob inherited, from his farther Isaac, the promises that God gave to Abraham (Gen 27). Later, Jacob spent an entire night wrestling with a man, a man who was in fact God. As a result of that struggle with God, Jacob's name was changed to Israel, which means "he who struggles with God" (32:22–28; 35:10).

Israel later had twelve sons—Judah, Levi, Benjamin, Gad, Rueben, Asher, Simeon, Dan, Naphtali, Issachar, Zebulun, and Joseph. Israel and his sons, and their families, went to Egypt in Israel's old age to escape the famine that had gripped the land (Gen 46:1–27). Each of Israel's twelve sons had children and, as a result, each son became a father of a tribe of Israel, so the twelve sons of Israel became the fathers of the twelve tribes of Israel. Israel's descendants remained in Egypt for 430 years (Exod 12:40), growing into a nation of millions during that time. Also during that time, the Egyptians made slaves of the people of Israel, until God eventually delivered Israel out of Egypt through Moses (Exod 3:7–10). After God delivered Israel out of Egypt, he brought them to Mount Sinai, where he gave Israel the Ten Commandments (Deut 5:1–22).

After wandering in the wilderness for forty years, God brought Israel to what he described as the promised land (Exod 3:17; 12:25; 13:11; 32:13; 33:1). Once Israel arrived in the promised land, God divided the land among the twelve tribes of Israel (Deut 31:7; Josh 14:5). However, God specifically said that the tribe of Levi, which was the tribe of Moses, Aaron, and, subsequently, the priesthood, was *not* to get a share of the promised land—rather, the people of the tribe of Levi got cities to live in but no share of the land (Josh 14:4; 18:7).

God still wanted there to be twelve divisions of land, though, and so he took the tribe of Joseph and divided it into two *half* tribes—the *half* tribes of Ephraim and Manasseh (Josh 14:4)—so the tribe of Joseph, from that time onward, became *two* tribes, being divided into the two half tribes of Ephraim and Manasseh. As a result, there were now a total of thirteen tribes of Israel—eleven full tribes plus the two half tribes, with twelve divisions of land in the promised land, and with the tribe of Levi, the tribe of the priesthood, having no share in the division of land. This was the makeup of the nation Israel at the time that they entered the promised land.

Some centuries later, in the reign of King Rehoboam, son of King Solomon and grandson of King David, the nation Israel split into *two* nations. Ultimately, ten tribes chose to follow Jeroboam as their king, and those ten tribes came to be known as the northern kingdom. The remaining three tribes—the tribe of Judah (David's tribe, and therefore the tribe of royalty), the tribe of Benjamin, and the tribe of Levi (the tribe of the priesthood) remained loyal to King Rehoboam, and became the southern kingdom (1 Kgs 11:29–32; 2 Kgs 17:21–23; 2 Chr 11:12–17). The northern kingdom kept the name *Israel*, and its capital was Samaria, while the southern kingdom took the name *Judah*, taken from the name of the tribe of David, the tribe of royalty, and had as its capital Jerusalem.

As a result, during the reign of King Rehoboam, at around 945–930 BC, the nation Israel became *two separate kingdom-nations*—the northern kingdom, Israel, comprised of ten tribes, and the southern kingdom, Judah, comprised of three tribes. The people of the southern kingdom, the people of Judah, came to be known as "Jews," with the name Jew coming from the name Judah—so a *Jew* is someone who is from the nation *Judah*, the southern kingdom, being from one of the three tribes of that nation (Judah, Benjamin, Levi).

The people of the northern kingdom, Israel, were *not* Jews; *only* the people of Judah were Jews. Ever since that split of Israel and Judah, God keeps that distinction between Israel and Judah throughout the entirety of Bible prophecy (Isa 8:14; 11:12; Jer 3:8, 11; 11:10; 30:3; 31:31 et al.). Since the division of the one nation Israel into the two nations of Israel and Judah, there is a permanent distinction between Israel and the Jews in prophecy—*only* the people of the southern kingdom, the nation Judah, are Jews, while the people of the northern kingdom, Israel, are not Jews.

At around 750 BC, the kingdom of Israel (the northern kingdom) was conquered by Assyria (2 Kgs 17:5–6; 1 Chr 5:26). The southern kingdom of Judah was *not* conquered by the Assyrians. When the Assyrians conquered the northern kingdom, Israel, they took the people of Israel captive. Ever since that time, the people of Israel, and the ten tribes that made up that kingdom, have been lost to history, while the southern kingdom of Judah, and its three tribes, the Jews, remain to this day.

In the eyes of the Jews, that is, in the eyes of the three tribes that comprised the nation of Judah, the other ten tribes of Israel are not considered Gentiles; rather they are considered brethren to the Jews, but under God's judgment. However, to the eyes of the world, those ten tribes of the nation Israel, since they were not Jews, would be seen as Gentiles—any descendants of those lost ten tribes of Israel would, to this day, be considered, by the world, as Gentile people.

JERUSALEM AND JUDAH

Ever since Israel split into two nations—splitting into the nations of Judah and Israel—God keeps that distinction throughout the Old Testament and throughout all prophecy. When God, in the Old Testament, prophesies about the Jews, he refers to them by their *correct* name, *Judah*, and this remains consistent throughout prophecy.

As an example, in Zechariah 12–14 God prophesies the events that precede the Second Coming, and God specifically talks about Jerusalem in that prophecy.

> Behold, I am going to make *Jerusalem* a cup that causes staggering to all the peoples around; and when the siege is against *Jerusalem*, it will also be against *Judah*. It will come about on that day that I will make Jerusalem a heavy stone for all the peoples; all who lift it will injure themselves severely. And all the nations of the earth will be gathered against it. On that day," declares the Lord, "I will strike every horse with confusion and its rider with insanity. But I will watch over the house of *Judah*, while I strike every horse of the peoples with blindness. Then the clans of *Judah* will say in their hearts, 'The inhabitants of *Jerusalem* are a strong support for us through the Lord of armies, their God.' On that day I will make the clans of *Judah* like a firepot among pieces of wood and a flaming torch among sheaves, so they will consume on the right and on the left all the surrounding peoples, while the inhabitants of *Jerusalem* again live on their own sites in Jerusalem. The Lord also will save the tents of *Judah* first, so that the glory of the house of David and the glory of the inhabitants of *Jerusalem* will not be greater than *Judah*. On that day the Lord will protect the inhabitants of *Jerusalem*, and the one who is feeble among them on that day will be like David, and the house of David will be like God, like the angel of the Lord before them. And on that day I will seek to destroy all the nations that come against *Jerusalem*. (Zech 12:2–9 NASB)

In our own day, the Jews call their nation the modern nation Israel, with Jerusalem as its capital. In this prophecy, detailing events yet to happen in the days that precede the Second Coming, God repeatedly talks about Jerusalem and the nations of the world being gathered against it, and yet, when talking about the *nation* whose capital is Jerusalem, the name Israel is not found anywhere in the prophecy; rather, the name *Judah* is repeatedly named. Why? It is because God is accurate—although the modern nation of the Jews has taken the name Israel for itself, in fact, the modern nation of the Jews is not Israel; the modern nation of the Jews is what it always was—*Judah*. Israel is the nation of the lost ten tribes, the northern kingdom, which had Samaria as its capital, and which was conquered by Assyria ca. 750 BC, while the nation of the Jews, the nation that has Jerusalem as its capital, has always been *Judah*. As a result, in Zechariah 12:2–9, when prophesying about Jerusalem in the days that precede the Second Coming, God specifically names *Judah* as the nation who has Jerusalem as its capital.

As a result, whenever God *prophesies* about the Jews, he calls them "Judah," and when he *prophesies* about "Israel," he is referring to the lost ten tribes of the northern kingdom. The descendants of those lost ten tribes would be today, in the eyes of the world, seen as Gentile peoples.

Also, we should understand that even though the Northern kingdom of Israel, the nation of the lost ten tribes, has been lost to history since ca. 750 BC, those tribes and their descendants are not lost to God—God, alone, knows who those lost tribes are and where their descendants are.

BIBLICAL DISTINCTION BETWEEN ISRAEL AND JUDAH

Throughout the prophecies of the Old Testament, and ever since the split of Israel into the two nations of Israel and Judah, God keeps that distinction between the two nations. In prophecies about the Jews, God refers to them as the nation "Judah," while in prophecies about the other ten tribes, God refers to them as the nation "Israel."

> In the twentieth year of Jeroboam king of *Israel*, Asa became king of *Judah*. (1 Kgs 15:9 NIV; also 1 Kgs 15:25, 33; 16:8 et al.)

> and even *Judah* did not keep the commands of the Lord their God. They followed the practices *Israel* had introduced. (2 Kgs 17:19 NIV)

> Now Jeroboam had sent troops around to the rear, so that while he was in front of Judah the ambush was behind them. Judah turned and saw that they were being attacked at both front and rear. Then they cried out to the Lord. The priests blew their trumpets and the men of Judah raised the battle cry. At the sound of their battle cry, God routed Jeroboam and all Israel before Abijah and Judah. The Israelites fled before Judah, and God delivered them into their hands. Abijah and his troops inflicted heavy losses on them, so that there were

five hundred thousand casualties among Israel's able men. The Israelites were subdued on that occasion, and the people of Judah were victorious because they relied on the Lord, the God of their ancestors. (2 Chr 13:13–18 NIV—Israel and Judah at war with each other)

He will be a holy place; for both *Israel and Judah* he will be a stone that causes people to stumble and a rock that makes them fall. And for the people of Jerusalem he will be a trap and a snare. (Isa 8:14 NIV)

I gave faithless *Israel* her certificate of divorce and sent her away because of all her adulteries. Yet I saw that her unfaithful *sister Judah* had no fear; she also went out and committed adultery. (Jer 3:8 NIV)

The Lord said to me, "Faithless *Israel* is more righteous than unfaithful *Judah*." (Jer 3:11 NIV)

They have returned to the sins of their ancestors, who refused to listen to my words. They have followed other gods to serve them. Both *Israel and Judah* have broken the covenant I made with their ancestors. (Jer 11:10 NIV)

"The days are coming," declares the Lord, "when I will bring my people *Israel and Judah* back from captivity and restore them to the land I gave their ancestors to possess," says the Lord. (Jer 30:3 NIV)

The people of *Israel and Judah* have done nothing but evil in my sight from their youth; indeed, the people of Israel have done nothing but arouse my anger with what their hands have made, declares the Lord. (Jer 32:20 NIV)

"The days are coming," declares the Lord, "when I will fulfill the good promise I made to the people of *Israel and Judah*." (Jer 33:14 NIV)

"In those days, at that time," declares the Lord, "the *people of Israel* and the *people of Judah* together will go in tears to seek the Lord their God." (Jer 50:4 NIV)

He answered me, "The sin of the people of *Israel and Judah* is exceedingly great; the land is full of bloodshed and the city is full of injustice. They say, 'The Lord has forsaken the land; the Lord does not see.'" (Ezek 9:9 NIV)

The word of the Lord came to me: "Son of man, there were two women, daughters of the same mother. They became prostitutes in Egypt, engaging in prostitution from their youth. In that land their breasts were fondled and their virgin bosoms caressed. The older was named Oholah, and her sister was Oholibah. They were mine and gave birth to sons and daughters. Oholah is *Samaria*, and Oholibah is *Jerusalem*. Oholah engaged in prostitution while she was still mine; and she lusted after her lovers, the Assyrians—warriors clothed in blue, governors and commanders, all of them handsome young men, and mounted horsemen. She gave herself as a prostitute to all the elite of the Assyrians and defiled herself with all the idols of everyone she lusted after. She did not give up the prostitution she began in Egypt, when during her youth men slept with her, caressed her virgin bosom and poured out their lust on her. (Ezek 23:1–8 NIV)

Yet the Israelites will be like the sand on the seashore, which cannot be measured or counted. In the place where it was said to them, "You are not my people," they will be called "children of the living God." The *people of Judah* and the *people of Israel* will come together; they will appoint one leader and will come up out of the land, for great will be the day of Jezreel. (Hos 1:10–11 NIV)

All this is because of Jacob's transgression, because of the sins of the people of *Israel*. What is Jacob's transgression? Is it not *Samaria*? What is *Judah's* high place? Is it not *Jerusalem*? (Mic 1:5 NIV)

Just as you, *Judah and Israel*, have been a curse among the nations, so I will save you, and you will be a blessing. Do not be afraid, but let your hands be strong. (Zech 8:13 NIV)

Then I broke my second staff called Union, *breaking the family bond* between *Judah and Israel*. (Zech 11:4 NIV)

Throughout the Old Testament, ever since the split of the one nation Israel into the two nations of Israel and Judah, God keeps that distinction between Israel and Judah, especially throughout prophecy.

BUT WHAT ABOUT EPHRAIM, MANASSEH, AND SIMEON?

There are a few passages in the Old Testament that seem to suggest that, in the land of Judah, the tribes of Ephraim, Manasseh, and Simeon also were part of Judah. Those passages are as follows:

Now the first to resettle on their own property in their own towns were some *Israelites, priests, Levites and temple servants*. Those from Judah, from Benjamin, and from *Ephraim and Manasseh* who *lived in Jerusalem* were: Uthai son of Ammihud, the son of Omri, the son of Imri, the son of Bani, a descendant of Perez son of Judah. Of the Shelanites: Asaiah the firstborn and his sons. Of the Zerahites: Jeuel. The *people from Judah* numbered 690. (1 Chr 9:2–6 NIV)

Then he assembled all *Judah* and *Benjamin* and *the people from Ephraim, Manasseh and Simeon who had settled among them*, for large numbers had come over to him from Israel when they saw that the Lord his God was with him. (2 Chr 15:9 NIV)

In the *towns* of Manasseh, Ephraim and Simeon, as far as Naphtali, and in the ruins around them (2 Chr 34:6 NIV)

How are we to understand these passages? We can understand them as follows:

The passage from 1 Chronicles 9:2–6 is referring to the time of the resettlement of Israel in the promised land, prior to Saul being king, and, as a result, prior to the split of Israel into two nations. We are told that in that period of resettlement there were some people from the tribes of Ephraim and Manasseh who had lived in Jerusalem and had returned at the resettlement of Jerusalem. These were *not* the *tribes* of Ephraim and Manasseh, both of which had their own land divisions; rather, these were only some people, or families, from those tribes that were part of the resettlement. Since this was in the time prior to the split of Israel into two nations, it is *not* telling us that the tribes of Ephraim or Manasseh were a part of the nation Judah.

Ephraim was certainly *not* part of the nation Judah after the split of Israel, for, after the split of Israel into two nations, the northern kingdom of Israel was sometimes referred to by God as "Ephraim" (Jer 31:9; Hos 4:15–17; 5:3), showing that the tribe of Ephraim was an essential part of the northern kingdom of Israel, and was not part of the southern kingdom of Judah.

Second Chronicles 15:9 describes events during the reign of King Asa, which was prior to the Assyrian captivity, and it is affirming the same fact as mentioned in 1 Chronicles 9:2–6—that there were some *people* from the tribes of Ephraim, Manasseh, and Simeon who had settled within the land of Judah. This is after the split of Israel into two nations, but before the Assyrian captivity, and, as such, this is *not* saying that the *tribes* of Ephraim, Manasseh, and Simeon were part of the nation Judah, for we know for a fact that they were not, since ten full tribes comprised the northern kingdom of Israel (1 Kgs 11:29–32). As a result, 2 Chronicles 15:9 is telling us only that some individuals from the tribes of Ephraim, Manasseh, and Simeon had settled within the *land* of Judah.

Second Chronicles 34:6 describes events during the reign of King Josiah, which took place *after* the split of Israel into two nations and *also after* the Assyrian captivity. In the Assyrian captivity, the entire northern kingdom, Israel, and all of its tribes and people was conquered, captured, and taken into captivity by the Assyrians, and this included the *tribes* of Manasseh, Ephraim, and Simeon. How, then, do we understand this passage? We can understand it as follows: the passage is not talking about the *people* of Ephraim, Manasseh, or Simeon; rather it is giving us a description of the *geographic* scope of Josiah's purging of idolatry from Judah, telling us that the purge went even so far north as the *towns* of the (former) territory of Ephraim, Manasseh, and Simeon. The *original* people of those towns, the people of the tribes of Ephraim, Manasseh, and Simeon, were no longer there, but their towns remained, for these were the same settlements of Ephraim, Manasseh, and Simeon referred to in 1 Chronicles 9:2–6 and 2 Chronicles 15:9. So this is *not* saying that the *people* of those tribes were still in Judah; rather, it is only a geographic description of the scope of Josiah's purge.

Also, a further affirmation of settlements within the land of Judah, especially in regard to the tribe of Simeon, is found in Joshua.

> The second lot came out for the tribe of *Simeon* according to its clans. Their inheritance lay within *the territory of Judah*. (Josh 19:1)

This is a description of events prior to the split of Israel into two nations, and in fact it is a description of the original allotment of land among the tribes when they first entered into the promised land. We are told here that when the tribe of Simeon received its land allotment, their land allotment was itself *within* the territory of Judah's land allotment; that is to say, Simeon's share of the land lay entirely within Judah's land.

Why was this the case?

In fact, it is the fulfillment of Jacob's prophecy over his sons Simeon and Levi:

> *Simeon* and *Levi* are brothers—
> their swords are weapons of violence.
> Let me not enter their council,
> let me not join their assembly,
> for they have killed men in their anger
> and hamstrung oxen as they pleased.
> Cursed be their anger, so fierce,
> and their fury, so cruel!
> I will *scatter* them in Jacob
> and *disperse them* in Israel. (Gen 49:5–7 NIV)

In this prophecy over his sons Simeon and Levi, Jacob/Israel says that those two tribes will be "scattered" and "dispersed" among Israel, and, in fact, that is exactly what we see when Israel enters the promised land. In the case of Levi, the tribe of the priesthood, they receive no share in the land; rather they receive numerous cities spread throughout the land of the other tribes, so they are, in every way, scattered and dispersed among Israel. In the case of Simeon, their land allotment falls within the land of Judah, and therefore Simeon is scattered, or dispersed, among the tribe, among the land, of Judah. All of this is the fulfillment of Jacob's/Israel's prophecy over his sons Simeon and Levi.

Also, when Moses pronounces blessings upon the tribes of Israel, Simeon is the only tribe he does not bless (Deut 33). As a result, Simeon, as a tribe, by having its share of land located entirely within the land of Judah, is already losing its identity even before the Assyrian captivity.

The above passages of 1 Chronicles 9:2–6; 2 Chronicles 15:9; and 2 Chronicles 34:6 are consistent with the division of tribes into the two nations of Israel and Judah, with the ten tribes of Reuben, Ephraim, Manasseh, Zebulun, Issachar, Gad, Dan, Naphtali, Asher, and Simeon comprising the northern kingdom of Israel, and with the three tribes of Judah, Benjamin, and Levi comprising the southern kingdom of Judah, the Jews. This distinction between the two nations is a distinction that remains throughout Bible prophecy.

Although God keeps the distinction between Israel and Judah throughout prophecy, how do we understand the many times in the New Testament where it seems like that distinction is *not* kept?

ISRAEL AND JUDAH IN THE NEW TESTAMENT

The nation of Israel, and its ten tribes, have been lost to history since ca. 750 BC. Since that time, only Judah and the Jews remain in the historical record. When Jesus was born in Bethlehem, the town of Bethlehem itself is *not* described as being in the land of Israel; rather it is described as being in the land of *Judah*.

> After Jesus was born in Bethlehem *in Judea*, during the time of King Herod, Magi from the east came to Jerusalem (Matt 2:1 NIV)

"Judea" is just a variant of "Judah," and it is the land of the Jews, and that clear distinction remained in Jesus' own day.

How then do we understand the following?

> "Get up, take the child and his mother and go to the *land of Israel*, for those who were trying to take the child's life are dead." So he got up, took the child and his mother and went to the *land of Israel*. (Matt 2:20–21 NIV)

Jesus was born in Bethlehem, in the land of Judah, and the entire nation, as ruled by Herod, was the kingdom of Judah (Matt 2:22; 3:5; Luke 1:15), and, as a Roman territory, that whole land was called "Judea" (Luke 3:1). Why, then, when the angel told Joseph and Mary to leave Egypt and return to their homeland, are they told to go back to "the land of Israel"?

Also, throughout the gospels, Jesus himself repeatedly refers to the people of Judah as "Israel":

> When Jesus heard this, he was amazed and said to those following him, "Truly I tell you, I have not found anyone *in Israel* with such great faith." (Matt 8:10 NIV)

> When you are persecuted in one place, flee to another. Truly I tell you, you will not finish going through the towns *of Israel* before the Son of Man comes. (Matt 10:23 NIV)

> Then what was spoken by Jeremiah the prophet was fulfilled: "They took the thirty pieces of silver, the price set on him by the *people of Israel*," (Matt 27:9 NIV)

> And the child grew and became strong in spirit; and he lived in the wilderness until he appeared publicly to *Israel*. (Luke 1:80 NIV)

> I assure you that there were many widows *in Israel* in *Elijah's time*, when the sky was shut for three and a half years and there was a severe famine throughout the land. (Luke 4:25 NIV)
>
> I myself did not know him, but the reason I came baptizing with water was that he might be revealed to *Israel*. (John 1:31 NIV)
>
> "You are *Israel's* teacher," said Jesus, "and do you not understand these things?" (John 3:10 NIV)
>
> Therefore let all *Israel* be assured of this: God has made this Jesus, whom you crucified, both Lord and Messiah. (Acts 2:36 NIV)
>
> Now, fellow *Israelites*, I know that you acted in ignorance, as did your leaders. (Acts 3:17 NIV)
>
> At daybreak they entered the temple courts, as they had been told, and began to teach the people. When the high priest and his associates arrived, they called together the Sanhedrin—the full assembly of the *elders of Israel*—and sent to the jail for the apostles. (Acts 5:21 NIV)

Jesus and the apostles were in the land of Judah, Judea, the land of the Jews—why then do they repeatedly refer to that land, and its people, as "Israel"? How can we understand this? Is this not a contradiction to the fact that God makes, and keeps, a distinction between Israel and Judah throughout prophecy? No, it is not a contradiction, and we can understand it as follows.

THE MESSIAH IS THE REDEEMER, THE RESTORER

Jesus Christ, as the Messiah, is Messiah for *all* Israel, which includes *both* Israel *and* Judah.

> But you, Bethlehem, in the *land of Judah*, are by no means least among the rulers of Judah; for out of you will come *a ruler who will shepherd* my people Israel. (Matt 2:6 NIV)
>
> But you, Bethlehem Ephrathah, though you are small among the *clans of Judah*, out of you will come for me one who will be *ruler over Israel*, whose origins are from of old, from ancient times. (Mic 5:2 NIV)

Throughout the New Testament, we do not see that same distinction between Israel and Judah; rather, we see an overall reference to both Israel and Judah as "Israel." The reason for this is that Jesus Christ, as Messiah, *will redeem everything* and *everyone*, beginning with Israel and Judah. As a result, as the Redeemer, the Restorer, the Messiah, Jesus refers to Israel and Judah as they *originally* were, which is as one nation, which is also what they *will become* upon their restoration.

This is affirmed in both Matthew 2:20-21, where the land of Judea is referred to as the "land of Israel." In that day, that land was not known as the "land of Israel"; rather it was known as the "land of Judea", but it was *originally* known as the "land of Israel," *before* the nation split into the two nations of Israel and Judah, and so the reference here to the "land of Israel," and every other reference by Jesus and the apostles to that land and people as "Israel," is a reference to the fact that the divided nation will one day be *restored*, redeemed, and will once again be the one nation as it originally was.

This restoration of the divided nation of Israel is also affirmed by the fact that on the twelve gates of the city New Jerusalem each gate has written on it the name of a tribe of Israel (Rev 21:12), so that *all twelve tribes of Israel* are represented on the twelve gates of the New Jerusalem, the city of the redeemed.

Also, Jesus himself tells us that the redeemed, those who follow him, will judge the twelve tribes of Israel (Matt 19:28; Luke 22:30), once again showing that there is a single collective fate, or destiny, for all twelve tribes, which, when taken together with Revelation 21:12, shows that the ultimate fate, or destiny, of divided Israel and Judah is one of redemption.

We also see in Revelation 7:1-8 that in the days preceding the Second Coming, God chooses twelve thousand people from twelve tribes of Israel and Judah to bring the gospel to the world. Only three of those twelve tribes are Jews—those from the tribes of Judah, Benjamin, and Levi; the rest are from the lost tribes of *Israel*—lost to history, lost to the world, but not lost to God.

All of this shows that there is a redemption, a restoration, a *healing*, of the nations of Judah and Israel, and, as such, in the New Testament, when speaking of the Jews and of Israel, Jesus and the apostles speak with that tone of coming redemption and restoration. In fact, the healing of nations is also addressed in Revelation 22.

> On each side of the river stood the tree of life, bearing twelve crops of fruit, yielding its fruit every month. And the leaves of the tree are for *the healing of the nations*. (22:2 NIV)

As a result, God, throughout prophecy, *does* keep a distinction between Israel and Judah, between the three tribes of Judah, which are the Jews, and the ten tribes of Israel, which are *not* the Jews. However, in the New Testament, that divided nation of Israel is spoken of in tones of the coming redemption and restoration, since the Messiah who will accomplish that redemption, and who himself is King of Israel and King of the Jews, has arrived.

It is also in that context that Jesus, as the Messiah of all Israel, refers to the "other sheep."

THE "OTHER SHEEP"

In John 10:16, Jesus refers to "other sheep."

> I have *other sheep* that are *not of this sheep pen*. I must bring them also. They too will listen to my voice, and there shall be one flock and one shepherd. (John 10:16 NIV)

Who are these "other sheep" to whom Jesus refers? The "other sheep" are also referred to as "not of this sheep pen." The "sheep pen" he is referring to is the *Jews*, the nation of *Judah*, Judea. As a result, when Jesus refers to "other sheep" who are "not of this sheep pen," and since that "sheep pen" is Judah and the Jews, we can know that Jesus is affirming that those "other sheep" who are "not of this sheep pen" are *not* from Judah, that they are *not* Jews. Who are they then? And where are they? In fact, Jesus is referring to the lost ten tribes of Israel. As descendants of Israel, descended from Abraham, Isaac, and Jacob, those ten tribes belong to God, but, since they were scattered in ca. 750 BC, they are now not in Judah, but rather are scattered elsewhere. It is because they are scattered elsewhere, scattered abroad, that they are described as being of a different "sheep pen," yet they remain God's sheep. Jesus affirms the restoration of all twelve tribes of Israel when he says, in that same passage, that *after* he brings those "other sheep," only *then* will there be "one flock," all under "one shepherd." All of this is an affirmation of the restoration of the twelve tribes—the three tribes of Judah, the Jews, and the lost ten tribes of Israel, non-Jews.

JAMES 1:1

James also references the lost tribes in his letter.

> James, a servant of God and of the Lord Jesus Christ, to the *twelve tribes* scattered *among the nations*. (1:1 NIV)

In his letter, James specifically addresses his letter to "the twelve tribes," whom he describes as being "scattered among the nations." How are we to understand this?

Some say that since James addresses his letter to the twelve tribes, that those tribes are not in fact lost but rather that their whereabouts are known. However, the introduction of James' letter does not imply that either he or anyone knows the *whereabouts* of those lost tribes—rather, as he specifically says in his address, he describes those tribes as being "scattered among the nations"—to be "scattered among the nations" means only that those tribes are somewhere, scattered, but not necessarily identifiable.

This address of James' letter to the twelve tribes is also a further affirmation of the restoration and redemption of *all* Israel by the Messiah, who will rule over all Israel and over all Jews, as well as over all humanity.

James' reference to the twelve tribes being "scattered among the nations" is a further affirmation of Jesus' description of those same tribes as being "other sheep" who are "not of this sheep pen." Again, the "sheep pen" Jesus is referring to is the Jews, the people of Judah, so the "other sheep," from a different "sheep pen," are not Jews, are not the people of Judah; rather, they are the people of the other tribes of Israel, "scattered among the nations," lost to history and not identifiable to history since ca. 750 BC. The "nations" among which those lost tribes are scattered is the "sheep pen" of other nations.

SAMARITANS

Another argument that the twelve tribes were not necessarily lost is the reference to the "Samaritan" in Luke 10, the Samaritan woman of John 4, as well as the reference to the towns and villages of the Samaritans in Matthew 10:5 and Acts 8:25.

Samaria was the capital city of the nation Israel, the nation of the ten tribes of Israel (1 Kgs 20:43; 21:1, 18 et al.). A citizen of Samaria was a "Samaritan." However, the Samaritans referred to in Matthew 10:5; Acts 8:25; Luke 10:25–37; and John 4:4–28 are *not* the same Samaritans who inhabited Samaria when it was the capital of the original kingdom of Israel, which was almost a thousand years prior to Jesus' day. That *original* city of Samaria, capital of the northern kingdom of Israel, had been *repopulated* over the centuries, ever since the people of Israel were taken into captivity by Assyria. The new inhabitants of the city of Samaria, and the inhabitants of the towns within the original Samaritan region, came to be also known as "Samaritans," but they were *not* in any way descended from, or connected to, the ten tribes of Israel, who were the original inhabitants of Samaria and its territory. As a result, the Samaritans of Jesus' day were a different people than the people of the ten tribes of Israel.

THE NATION ISRAEL TODAY

Today, the modern state of the Jewish people, founded in 1948, is called "Israel." However, even though the modern nation of the Jewish people calls itself "Israel," in fact, that nation, biblically, is actually Judah, and when the Bible prophesies about the Jewish people, the nation of the Jews is referred to as "Judah," not "Israel," regardless of the modern name of that nation.

This is made clear especially in Zechariah 12–14, which describes the time both preceding and following the Second Coming. Zechariah 12–14 tells us specifically about the city of Jerusalem being besieged by the armies of the world during that time, and the prophecy then continues to outline those events. In that prophecy Zechariah talks specifically about the city of Jerusalem. There has only ever been one city of Jerusalem, and so the Jerusalem talked about in Zechariah is the same Jerusalem of today. Throughout those prophecies of Zechariah, concerning the times before and after the Second Coming, and concerning the city of Jerusalem, the name Israel is never mentioned even once in connection with the city of Jerusalem; rather, the true name of that nation, the nation whose capital city, even today, is Jerusalem, is repeatedly referenced—it is referenced specifically as the nation *Judah*. So even though that nation today goes by the name Israel, it is, in fact, the nation Judah.

This is a profoundly important truth to understand, especially for the purposes of biblical prophecy. The various prophecies concerning the time preceding the Second Coming that reference "Israel" are *not* referring to the Jewish people; rather those prophecies are referring to the ten lost tribes of the northern kingdom of Israel, which have been lost to history (but not to God) since ca. 750 BC. When God talks about the Jewish people in prophecy, he refers to them by their correct name, as the people/nation/kingdom of Judah, from which the term "Jew" derives.

JUDEA

Even in Jesus own day, the nation/kingdom of the Jews, Jesus' homeland, was not called "Israel"; it was in fact called "Judea," which is just a variant of Judah (Matt 2:1, 22, 3:1, 5; 4:25; 19:1; Mark 3:8; 10:1; Luke 1:5 et al.), with Herod being king over all Judea (i.e., the king of the Jews, Luke 1:5).

Judea itself was divided into regions, one of which was Galilee (Matt 19:1), but the area, as a whole, was called "Judea," with Herod as king and with Pontius Pilate as governor (Luke 3:1). Upon King Herod's death, his son, Herod Antipas, was appointed tetrarch of the Judaic region of Galilee, and his brother was appointed tetrarch of some of the other regions (Luke 3:1), but all of these regions were collectively the kingdom of Judea.

Also, in regard to the Roman Empire, there was no such Roman territory known as "Israel"; rather, there was only the territory known as "Judea," the reason being that this was the kingdom/nation of Judah, whose people were Jews. When the Roman emperor Vespasian actually conquered Judea in 70 AD (prior to his conquest Judea was a client kingdom of Rome, with Judea paying tribute to Rome in return for Rome's protection, which is why there was a King Herod at the same time as there was the Roman emperor Augustus), that conquest of Vespasian is commemorated in Roman history and Roman coinage *not* as the conquest and captivity of *Israel*, but rather as the conquest and captivity of *Judea*, with Roman commemorative coinage using the inscription "*Judaea Capta*" to commemorate the conquest. Also, Pontius Pilate, the Roman governor of that land, is specifically called the "governor of Judea" (Luke 3:1).

WHERE ARE THE LOST TRIBES OF ISRAEL TODAY?

The ten tribes of the northern kingdom of Israel have been lost to history since ca. 750 BC, and yet in Revelation 7:3–8, describing events prior to the Second Coming, God lists twelve tribes of Israel, including the lost tribes, telling us that from each of those twelve tribes there will be 12,000 preachers preaching the gospel to the world at that time. (It is important to recognize that one tribe of Israel is *not* on that list—the tribe of Dan is not listed there, and is conspicuous by its absence).

Does this mean that the twelve lost tribes will have been recovered and will be identifiable by that time?

No, it does not. It means only that, even though those tribes remain lost to the world and to history, they are not lost to God—God knows who they are and where they are, even though they have been scattered throughout humanity across the millennia. Except for the 12,000 that are from each of the tribes of Judah, Benjamin, and Levi (Jews), the 12,000 from each of the remaining tribes, as listed in Revelation 7:3–8, will not know, or recognize, that they are from the lost tribes of Israel, unless God supernaturally reveals their identity to them. As a result, since only people from the tribes of Judah, Benjamin, and Levi are Jews, that means that, in the eyes of the world, the people from the remaining tribes listed in Revelation 7:3–8 will be seen as *Gentiles*, and so it will not be 144,000 Jews preaching the gospel upon the Earth during that time, as some declare; rather 36,000 of those 144,000 will be Jews, with 12,000 each from the tribes of Judah, Benjamin, and Levi, and the remaining 108,000 will be Gentiles.

The people of the lost tribes are therefore still upon the Earth, even right now in our own day, but they are not identifiable—to the world, the descendants of those lost tribes would be Gentiles.

Although God knows who and where the lost tribes and their descendants are, is there any way that we might be able to have an idea as to how to identify the people of the lost tribes of Israel?

In fact, there does seem to be a way in which we can at least get a clue as to a possible identity and whereabouts of the descendants of the lost tribes of Israel, and that clue comes from the tribe of Dan.

THE TRIBE OF DAN

When the tribes of Israel settled in the promised land, each tribe settled in its own share of that land. The tribe of Dan seems to have had a particular habit of adding its tribal name to whatever land they settled in.

An example of this can be found in Judges 18:11–12.

> Then six hundred men of the Danites, armed for battle, set out from Zorah and Eshtaol. On their way they set up camp near Kiriath Jearim in Judah. This is why the place west of Kiriath Jearim is called Mahaneh Dan to this day. (18:11–12 NIV)

After the six hundred men from the tribe of Dan set up camp near Kiriath Jearim, that place then came to be called "Mahaneh Dan" (or "Dan's Camp")—the name Dan was added to the name of that land.

Another example is found in Deuteronomy 34:1, where a span of land is described as being "from Gilead to Dan," showing that the land where Dan had settled had taken on the name of that tribe as its place name.

Another example is seen in Joshua 19:47.

> When the territory of the Danites was lost to them, they went up and attacked Leshem, took it, put it to the sword and occupied it. They settled in Leshem and named it Dan after their ancestor. (19:47 NIV)

Once again, we see that when Dan took the land of Leshem and settled there, they changed the name of the land to Dan. The exact same thing is seen again in Judges 18:27–29, where the tribe of Dan conquers the city of Laish, settles there, and then changes the name of the city to Dan as well.

This pattern of Dan adding its tribal name to the land, or to a city that it had conquered, is seen regularly throughout the Old Testament (2 Sam 24:6; 1 Kgs 4:25), and this habit seems particular to the tribe of Dan.

How can this practice of Dan adding its name to any place that the tribe had settled or conquered help us in possibly identifying the lost tribes of Israel? It can help in possible identification as follows.

PRONUNCIATION OF DAN

In Hebrew writing, vowels are not written; rather only consonants are written and vowels are left to be pronounced when spoken. This means that when *Dan* would be written in Hebrew, the vowel would not be written but would be left to be pronounced in the speaking. As a result, when the name Dan was written, it would be the same as if, in English, we were to write it as "D–n," leaving the vowel *a* to be a matter of pronunciation.

This exact same thing is seen in the writing, and pronunciation, of the divine name *YHWH*. When spoken, *YHWH* is sometimes pronounced as "YaHWeH," and other times it is pronounced as "YeHoWaH"—both are correct, as the vowels are left to the pronunciation.

As a result, when *pronouncing* the name Dan, it is equally, and correctly, pronounceable as "Dan," Den," Din," Don," and "Dun."

With these two facts in mind—the fact that Dan had a habit of adding its name to the locations where it settled, and the fact that the vowels of Dan's name were left to the pronunciation—we can use this as a way to glean some possible clues as to the wanderings, or eventual settlements, of the lost tribe of Dan, and, by extension the lost tribes of Israel.

EUROPEAN PLACE NAMES

The northern kingdom of Israel was conquered by the Assyrians ca. 750 BC, and the people of Israel were taken into captivity, into Assyria, at that time. The Assyrian kingdom itself was further north than was the kingdom of Israel, generally in the very northern area of the Middle East, an area that is a close border to Europe.

Since the tribe of Dan had the habit of adding its name to the places where it would settle, and if the lost tribes eventually would migrate, or be freed, from captivity, we could then expect that, as the tribe of Dan would wander and settle after its captivity, it would continue with its practice of adding its name to the land where it would settle.

With that in mind, it is interesting to note the many European place names that contain some variant of the name Dan within their own names—some examples are—Swe*den*, *Den*mark (also called *Dan*mark), Scan*din*avia, Mace*don*ia, the *dan*ube.

This becomes particularly striking when looking at place names across Great Britain—Lon*don*, *Dun*blane, *Don*egal, *Dun*edin, E*din*burgh, *Don*cster, *Den*holme, *Don*agh, *Don*aghadee, *Don*aghcloney, *Don*aghmore, *Don*egore, *Dun*adry, *Dun*-*don*ald, *Dun*drod, *Dun*drum, *Dun*gannon, *Dun*given, *Dun*loy, *Dun*namanagh, *Dun*murry, *Dun*naval, *Dun*severick, and many others.

Some consider the wide prevalence of the "Dan," "Den," "Din," "Don," and "Dun" in place names across Europe as evidence of the subsequent wanderings of the tribe of Dan after the Assyrian captivity. From this, the wanderings of the other lost tribes could also be extrapolated. Since we see the widespread occurrence of "Dan," "Den," "Din," "Don," and "Dun" across the place names of Europe and of the Western world, are the lost tribes of Israel, then, the ancestors of many of the European peoples? Is this why it is the Western, or European, world that is the Christian world, with the descendants of the lost tribes (the "other sheep") having accepted the Messiah?

This is a profound thought and there are many other reasonable arguments that can lead to that conclusion. If this, in fact, is the case, then when God says to Abraham that he will make him the father of many nations (Gen 17:4), this may be true on a much bigger scale than we would normally imagine.

The descendants of the lost tribes of Israel would definitely, in the eyes of the world, be considered Gentiles, therefore, if the lost tribes of Israel are in fact ancestors of many of the European peoples, that means that Abraham is the father of Jews (through Isaac and Jacob), of Arabs (through his son Ishmael), and of many Gentile peoples and their Western nations, by way of the lost tribes of Israel. If the lost tribes of Israel are in fact ancestors of many of the European peoples, then that means Abraham is also father of the nations, and peoples, of the new world. This would then mean that Abraham is father to almost one-third, or more, of the human population of the world today. This would make the fulfillment of God's promise of Genesis 17:4 far greater than we would normally imagine.

However true that may be, it is, however, a fact that the descendants of the lost tribes are alive today, even though they are not identifiable, though God knows who they are and where they are, as is made absolutely clear in Revelation 7:3–8. Those lost tribes of Israel, and all of their descendants, are *not* Jews, but would today be considered *Gentiles*. Even though both Jesus Christ and the apostles, in the New Testament, refer to the tribes of Israel with a view of the coming restoration of the divided nation, God keeps the distinction between Israel and Judah, between the people of Israel and the Jews, throughout Bible *prophecy*, so when God is *prophesying* about "Israel," he is *not* referring to the Jews, but rather he is referring to the Gentiles descended from the ten lost tribes, and when he *does* refer to the Jews in prophecy, he refers to them by their correct name, Judah.

Understanding the symbolism of beasts, horns, the prostitute, Babylon, and the sea; understanding the fact that there is no such thing as a rapture of the church; and understanding the distinction between Israel and Judah, the Jews, throughout Bible prophecy helps us to understand the events described in the book of Revelation. For a yet deeper and clearer understanding of Revelation, we must examine the structure and timelines of the book.

5

Breakdown and Timelines of Revelation

In many studies of the book of Revelation, the events outlined in Revelation are often presented as being chronological and sequential, normally listing the events of the Seven Seals as happening first, followed by the events of the Trumpets, followed by the events of the Bowls. Also, all of this is often presented as occurring during a period of seven years. As we shall see, this is not accurate. It is clear that, from chapters 4 to 18, events are *not* chronological nor sequential. Rather, there are three timelines that are outlined in Revelation and, during the course of those three timelines being described, there is an additional going back and forth in time in the description of events. The three timelines that are outlined in Revelation are as follows.

The Seven Seals

The Seven Seals are the overall, big-picture timeline of Revelation, the Seals are in fact the actual judgments, in their entirety, encompassing a period of forty years; *all* the Trumpet and Bowl events are included in the Seven Seals. We will see that Seals 1–4 encompass a period of thirty-three years, and set the stage for the coming to power of the Beast and the ensuing Great Tribulation; Seal 6 describes the fall of Babylon the Great; Seal 7 is the resurrection of believers and the Second Coming. The key to understanding all of this is Matthew 24:3–31, where Jesus himself outlines for us the Seven Seals, in order, and with explanation.

The Seven Trumpets

The Seven Trumpets are the second timeline and are just a *detailed* description of the three-and-a-half-year period known as the Great Tribulation, with the Great Tribulation being described by Trumpets 1–5, all of which occurs, in its entirety, during Seal 5; Trumpet 6 occurs during Seal 6 and describes the fall of Babylon the Great;

Trumpet 7, the last Trumpet, occurs during Seal 7 and announces the resurrection of believers and the Second Coming.

The Seven Bowls

The Seven Bowls are the third timeline and are an even more detailed description of the Great Tribulation and the fall of Babylon the Great; Bowls 1–5 occur during Trumpet 5 and describe the final five months of the Great Tribulation; Bowls 6 and 7 occur during Trumpet 6 and describe, in more detail, the fall of Babylon the Great.

These are the three timelines of Revelation, and *all* the Trumpet and Bowl timelines and events occur *during* Seals 5, 6, and 7. The events of Revelation 4–18, inclusive, are an outline of the events of these three timelines, and they are presented in those chapters in that order, beginning with the big-picture, overall timeline of the Seven Seals (forty-year period), followed by the more detailed description of the Great Tribulation of Seal 5 (Trumpets 1–5) as well as the fall of Babylon the Great in Trumpet 6 (which occurs during Seal 6), followed by the resurrection of believers and the Second Coming of Seal 7/Trumpet 7. This is then followed by an outline of the Bowl events, which are an even more detailed description of the final *five months* of the three-and-a-half-year Great Tribulation (Bowls 1–5) and the ensuing fall of Babylon the Great (Bowls 6 and 7).

In the description of each timeline, we are brought right up to the point that just precedes the Second Coming, and then the action stops, and Revelation goes back in time to give us added details of those already described events. This then is followed by a description of the next more detailed timeline, which then also is takes us to just before the Second Coming, as follows.

For the first timeline, the overall, total timeline of the Seven Seals, we are given a description of the events of Seals 1–6 (Rev 6), and then Revelation 7 goes back in time to give more details of those earlier events, and then 8:1–5 resumes where Revelation 6 left off, and tells us only that Seal 7 has been opened, and then the action stops (only to resume in 19:11).

Revelation then gives us an outline of the second timeline, the more detailed timeline of the Seven Trumpets, describing the Great Tribulation and beyond, and follows the same pattern as the description of the Seven Seals—Revelation 8:6–13 and Revelation 9 gives us a description of Trumpets 1–6, and then 10:1—11:14 goes back in time to give more details of those earlier events, and then 11:15–19 resumes where Revelation 9 left off, and tells us only that Trumpet 7 has been blown, and then the action stops (only to resume in 19:11).

Revelation then gives us an outline of the third timeline, the even more detailed timeline of the Seven Bowls, describing the final five months of the Great Tribulation and the subsequent fall of Babylon the Great, and follows the same pattern as the description of the Seven Seals and the Seven Trumpets—Revelation 16 gives us a description of Bowls 1–7, and then Revelation 17–18 goes back in time to give more details of the fall of Babylon the Great, and then 19:11 resumes where Revelation 16 left off.

In each case, for each timeline we are brought right up to the point of the Second Coming, and then the action stops, some background information is given, and then all timelines, having been brought to the same point in time, resume as one chronological timeline at 19:11, the Second Coming.

These are the three timelines of Revelation, outlined for us in chapters 4–18, and all following the same descriptive pattern. With that in mind, the overall structural breakdown of Revelation is as follows.

STRUCTURAL BREAKDOWN OF REVELATION

The book of Revelation has a very clear structural layout, and understanding that layout is of great help in understanding the flow of events outlined in Revelation. As described in regard to the timelines of Revelation, from chapters 4 to 18, inclusive, Revelation does *not* present one chronological flow of events; rather, three overlapping timelines are outlined. As those three timelines are being outlined, there is an additional going back and forth in time, the purpose of which is to give us more details of the timelines being described. The overall structural layout of the book of Revelation is as follows:

Chapter 1: Introduction

Chapter 2–3: Letters to the angels of seven churches

Chapter 4–5: In heaven—prelude to the events of Revelation

Chapter 6: The first timeline—description of Seals 1–6, the big, overall timeline

Chapter 7: Break—going back in time, giving background details on events of the Seals, in particular the events of Seal 5

Chapter 8:1–5: Seal 7 opened, but no events outlined

Chapter 8:6–13, 9: The second timeline: a description of Trumpets 1–6

Chapter 10–11:14: Break—going back in time, giving details about the Trumpet 1–6 events

Chapter 11:15–19: Trumpet 7 blown, but no events outlined

Chapter 12–14: Break—going back in time, giving details on the fall of the angels, the birth of Christ and the church, leading to a description of the Beast coming to power

Chapter 15: In Heaven—prelude to events of chapter 16

Chapter 16: The third timeline—a description of Bowls 1–7, the Seven Bowls are completed

Chapter 17–18: Break—Going back in time, giving details on Revelation 16:19, the fall of Babylon

Chapter 19–22: The events of Seal 7 and Trumpet 7 now resume—the Second Coming and beyond

From the above breakdown, we can see that the book of Revelation is regularly going back and forth in time, all while Revelation is outlining three individual timelines—the first timeline is the overall timeline of the Seven Seals; the second timeline is the more detailed Great Tribulation timeline of the Seven Trumpets; the third timeline is the even more detailed timeline of the final five months of the Great Tribulation, and the fall of Babylon, the timeline of the Bowls. For each timeline, we are brought right to the point that precedes the Second Coming, where the action stops, and then the action of all three timelines—the timelines of Seal 7, Trumpet 7, and the action that follows Bowl 7—resumes in Revelation 19:11, the Second Coming. From 19:11 onwards, to the end of the book, the events are all chronological, with no more going back and forth in time.

THE PUNCTUATION OF THE TIMELINES

It is also striking to note that at the point where the description switches from one timeline to the next timeline, the same phrase repeatedly occurs.

> And there were noises, thunderings, lightnings, and an earthquake.
> (Rev 8:5 NKJV)

This phrase occurs after Seal 7 is opened, and where the action of Seal 7 stops. Revelation 8.5 then begins the outline of the Trumpet timeline.

> And there were lightnings, noises, thunderings, an earthquake, and great hail.
> (Rev 11:19 NKJV)

This phrase occurs after Trumpet 7 is sounded, and where the action of Trumpet 7 stops, with the following Revelation 12–14 being a back-in-time description of previous events, and with Revelation 15 being the prelude to chapter 16, and with the next timeline of the Bowls being outlined in Revelation 16.

> And there were noises and thunderings and lightnings; and there was a great earthquake, such a mighty and great earthquake. (Rev 16:16 NKJV)

This phrase occur after Bowl 7 is poured, with the following Revelation 17–18 being a back-in-time description of previous events.

All the action of Seal 7 and Trumpet 7, and the action that follows the end of Bowl 7, resumes at the same point in 19:11, the Second Coming.

Why does the phrase "And there were noises, thunderings, lightnings" repeatedly occur at the point that there is a switch in the timeline narrative? What is significant about that phrase? The significance of that phrase is shown at the place where we first encounter that phrase in the book of Revelation.

The phrase "And there were noises, thunderings, lightnings" is first encountered in Revelation 4.

> And from the throne proceeded lightnings, thunderings, and voices.
> (4:5 NKJV)

John tells us, very specifically, that the "lightnings, thunderings, voices [noises]" are *coming from the throne of God*. As a result, we can understand this as follows:

When Revelation brings a timeline to the point of the Second Coming—which it does with the opening of Seal 7, with the sounding of Trumpet 7 and with the pouring of Bowl 7—it punctuates that same point in the timelines with the "lightnings, thunderings, noises" phrase, so as to indicate that the action of *that* timeline will now stop, and the narrative will now switch. Also, since John initially tells us in 4:5 that the "lightnings, thunderings, voices [noises]" are coming from the throne of God, we can understand that punctuation as coming from the throne of God—it is *God* who is punctuating those points of *his Revelation* for *us*, so that we can understand the flow of the Revelation. So, we can understand the "lightnings, thunderings, voices [noises]" in each of 8:5; 11:19; and 16:16 as coming from the throne of God, and we can therefore understand it as being a *heavenly punctuation* of the Revelation.

If that is the case, then how do we understand the reference to an earthquake in each of 8:5; 11:19; 16:16, as well as the reference to hail in 11:19? Surely there was not an earthquake and hail in heaven? We can understand it as follows.

The phrase "lightnings, thunderings, voices [noises]" is a *heavenly* punctuation that comes from the throne of God, as is made clear in 4:5, but the *added* description of an earthquake and then also hail is a description of the event that occurs *on Earth* at that same point. So, the "lightnings, thunderings, voices [noises]" itself is the *heavenly* punctuation, while the earthquake and hail are the *earthly* counterpart to that same moment in time. As a result, we can understand that when Seal 7 is opened, when Trumpet 7 is sounded, and after Bowl 7 is poured, there is a great earthquake on the Earth accompanied by great hail—this is the *earthly* event at that same point in time.

SILENCE IN HEAVEN

Immediately after Seal 7 is opened, we are told the following:

> When He opened the seventh seal, there was silence in heaven for about half an hour. (8:1 NKJV)

Throughout the entire description of all three timelines—the timeline of the Seals, the timeline of the Trumpets, and the timeline of the Bowls—this is the only time, at the opening of Seal 7, that there is what we can describe as a *dramatic pause*, described as being "silence in heaven." The opening of Seal 7 is completely unique in this regard. *Why* was there silence in heaven for about half an hour upon the opening of Seal 7? How do we understand this? We can understand it as follows.

As we will see when we look closely at the Seal timeline, Seal 7 is the climax and culmination of all things—with the opening of Seal 7, Trumpet 7 sounds and the resurrection of believers occurs at that time, followed by the Second Coming. The dramatic pause at the opening of Seal 7 is an affirmation that what is about to follow will be the greatest of all events—the resurrection and the Second Coming.

Also, John's description of there being "silence in heaven for about half an hour" is a further affirmation of the nature of the heavenly punctuation of the phrase "lightnings, thunderings, noise," as well as an affirmation of the earthly counterpart of the earthquake.

It is clear that Revelation 8:1–5 is a scene in heaven, with John describing for us what he sees in heaven. He affirms this when he describes the opening of Seal 7 being followed by a half-hour of silence *in heaven*. As a result, we can understand all the events of the 8:1–5 description as also being *in heaven*, and this includes 8:5 and the description, "And there were noises, thunderings, lightnings, and an earthquake." The "noises, thunderings, ligthnings" occur *in heaven*, as they did initially in 4:5, and are part of the heavenly scene. As a result, we can understand that 8:1–5 is an affirmation of the phrase "noises, thunderings, ligtnings" as being a heavenly punctuation, coming from the throne of God, which separates the description of the different timelines.

We can then also understand the *added* earthly counterpart of the earthquake and hail as follows.

EARTHQUAKE AND HAIL

After John gives us the heavenly punctuation of "noises, thunderings, lightnings," he then adds the *earthly* counterpart to that moment, which is a description of an earthquake—the earthquake occurs on Earth, not in heaven, and so the earthquake is the additional *earthly* counterpart to the opening of Seal 7. With that moment, we are brought to the point in time that just *precedes* the Second Coming.

Likewise, when Trumpet 7 sounds, whose sounding occurs upon the opening of Seal 7, we are also at the point in time that just precedes the Second Coming, and so when John gives us the heavenly punctuation to denote the end of the Trumpet timeline description, he says,

> And there were lightnings, noises, thunderings, an earthquake, and great hail. (11:19 NKJV)

This is the exact same phrase as the heavenly punctuation of 8:5, but, in addition to the earthly counterpart of an earthquake, John also tells us that, as part of that same earthly counterpart, there was "great hail." As a result, we can know that at the end of Seal 6, and as Seal 7 is being opened and Trumpet 7 is being sounded, the *earthly* conditions of that *same* moment is an earthquake and great hail.

We will see that the opening of Seal 6 results in the sounding of Trumpet 6, which results in the pouring of Bowls 6 and 7. Seal 6 *ends* with the pouring of Bowl 7—after Bowl 7 is poured, we are now at Seal 7/Trumpet 7. Upon the pouring of Bowl 7, which is also the end of Seal 6, we are told the following:

> Then the seventh angel poured out his bowl into the air, and a loud voice came out of the temple of heaven, from the throne, saying, "It is done!" And there were noises and thunderings and lightnings; and there was a great earthquake, such a mighty and great earthquake as had not occurred since men were on the earth. Now the great city was divided into three parts, and the cities of the nations fell. And great Babylon was remembered before God, to give her the cup of the wine of the fierceness of His wrath. Then every island fled away, and the mountains were not found. And great hail from heaven fell upon men, *each hailstone* about the weight of a talent. Men blasphemed God because of the plague of the hail, since that plague was exceedingly great. (16:17–21 NKJV)

Once again, with the pouring of Bowl 7, and *after* we are told that "It is done!," we encounter the heavenly punctuation—"noises and thunderings and lightnings"—which denotes an end to that timeline description. The description then goes on with the same added earthquake description—and we must understand that this is the *same* earthquake of 8:5 and 11:19—this is the *same earthly counterpart* to the heavenly punctuation of "noises, thunderings, and lightnings." However, here in 16:17–21 we are now given greater detail about that earthquake, which is described as being the greatest, most powerful earthquake that has ever been in the history of the world, an earthquake whose power is so strong that it will cause the fall of cities throughout the world.

After the earthquake description, we are then also told about "great hail," which is the exact *same* hail as described in 11:19. Here, in the Bowl 7 description of that great hail, we are given greater detail about that hail, being told that each hailstone had the weight of a "talent" (or approximately one hundred pounds).

As a result, we can conclude the following. Seal 6, and the included Trumpet 6, *ends* with the pouring of Bowl 7—the phrase "It is done!" of 16:17 affirms that with the pouring of Bowl 7 the judgment is done. The conditions *on the Earth* at the pouring of Bowl 7 are a great, cataclysmic global earthquake *and* colossal hail. As the earthquake and hail are occurring upon the Earth, after Bowl 7 has been poured, Seal 7 is opened, and Trumpet 7 sounds, and so, in describing that point in each timeline where the narrative is about to switch to a new timeline, John gives us the heavenly punctuation of "noises and thunderings and lightninings," and then he *adds* a description of the earthly events that are a counterpart to that same point in time—and again, in each case, it is the same description of the earthly events—an earthquake and hail.

All of these events, across all three timelines, line up and affirm that we are now at the same point in time across all three timelines—we are at the point in time that just precedes the Second Coming.

Also, since Bowls 6 and 7 are part of Seal 6, we can know that the earthquake of Seal 6 is the same as the earthquake of Bowl 7.

> I watched as he opened the sixth seal. There was a great earthquake.
> (6:12 NIV)

This earthquake of Seal 6 is the *same* earthquake as in Bowl 7 (since Bowl 7 is included in Seal 6), which, again, is the *same* earthquake referred to in 8:5 and 11:19, the earthly event that occurs together with hail. It is during these earthly events of the great earthquake and great hail that Seal 7 is opened and Trumpet 7 sounds.

Again, all of this affirms the overlapping of the three timelines, as well as the convergence of all three timelines at the same point in time—converging at the point in time that just precedes the Second Coming. We will see that all three timelines resume as one timeline in 19:11, resuming with the Second Coming.

In the three timelines of the Seven Seals, the Seven Trumpets, and the Seven Bowls, there is a fourth time period that is included *within* those three timelines, a clearly defined period of seven years, which is the final seven years of the overall forty-year period. It is during that seven-year period that the Beast comes to power and during which the Great Tribulation occurs. That entire seven-year period occurs in Seal 5.

THE SEVEN-YEAR PERIOD

The seven-year period during which the Beast comes to power and during which the Great Tribulation occurs is outlined for us in Daniel and is affirmed by Jesus Christ in Matthew 24. It is at the start of that seven-year period that the Beast (commonly called the "antichrist") comes to power, with that seven-year period culminating in the Second Coming. It is important to understand that that seven-year period is only the *final part* of the entire forty-year period of the Seven Seals.

Where in Daniel are we told that there will be a seven-year period coming upon the Earth that will be a period of terrible tribulation and destruction?

It is told to us in Daniel 9.

> Seventy "sevens" are decreed for your people and your holy city to finish transgression, to put an end to sin, to atone for wickedness, to bring in everlasting righteousness, to seal up vision and prophecy and to anoint the Most Holy

Place. Know and understand this: From the time the word goes out to restore and rebuild Jerusalem until the Anointed One, the ruler, comes, there will be seven "sevens," and sixty-two "sevens." It will be rebuilt with streets and a trench, but in times of trouble. After the sixty-two "sevens," the Anointed One will be put to death and will have nothing. The people of the ruler who will come will destroy the city and the sanctuary. The end will come like a flood: War will continue until the end, and desolations have been decreed. He will confirm a covenant with many for one "seven." In the middle of the "seven" he will put an end to sacrifice and offering. And at the temple he will set up an abomination that causes desolation, until the end that is decreed is poured out on him. (9:24–27 NIV)

This prophecy of Daniel outlines various judgment periods for Daniel's people, and those judgment periods are described as being periods of "sevens." One "seven" is understood by virtually everyone as being one period of seven years. In total, there are seventy "sevens" described here, and, as a result, since one "seven" is a period of seven years, then seventy "sevens" are therefore a total of 490 years of judgment.

It is important to understand that these 490 years are *not consecutive*; that is, there can be breaks of time between the periods of "sevens." We are told that from the time that the temple in Jerusalem is rebuilt (which happened in the late sixth century BC, ca. 516) to the time that the Anointed One (Jesus Christ) would be put to death, there would be, first, one period of seven "sevens," or a period of forty-nine years, followed by a second period of sixty-two "sevens" (434 years), for a total of sixty-nine "sevens." Therefore we can know that between the rebuilding of the temple in ca. 516 BC to the death of Jesus Christ there is a total of 483 years of *judgment*, even though the total number of actual years between the rebuilding of the temple and the death of Jesus Christ is approximately 549 years (based on Jesus' death being placed at 33 AD, which may not be the exact date, but which has no bearing on the fact that there is a gap between the first forty-nine years of judgment and the following 434 years of judgment)—of those 549 years between the rebuilding of the temple and the death of Jesus Christ, only 483 of those years are years of judgment. We see then that these sixty-nine periods of "sevens" are specifically broken up into two specific parts, which shows that they are not sixty-nine *consecutive* seven-year periods; rather there is a first group of seven seven-year periods, followed later by a second group of sixty-two seven-year periods. By the time of Jesus' death, and resurrection, a total of sixty-nine "sevens" have been accounted for.

After Daniel's description of the sixty-nine "sevens," which end with the death of Jesus Christ, Daniel then telescopes forward in time to a period described as "the end" (Dan 9:26). This time period described by Daniel as "the end" is the time period of Revelation, the time period that precedes the Second Coming. Since there are seventy "sevens," or seventy seven-year periods, in total as described in Daniel's prophecy, and since, by the death of Jesus Christ, only sixty-nine seven-year periods are accounted for, then this final period described here as the time period of "the end" is the *final remaining seven-year period*, the seventieth seven-year period.

Again, since this seventieth seven-year period is described by Daniel as "the end," we know that this final seven-year period is during the period of Revelation, for the events of Revelation are the events of "the end." This final seven-year period includes the Great Tribulation, and this is affirmed by Daniel when he describes that final seven-year period as a time of "desolations" (Dan 9:26). In this final period of "the end" we are told specifically that a "ruler who will come" will confirm a covenant with "many" for a period of "one 'seven'"—this one "seven" is the same final, seventieth seven-year period of Daniel's prophecy. This "ruler who will come" is the Beast of Revelation. As a result, we know that the judgement period of Revelation, the period that will see what is described as the rule of the Beast, and the following Great Tribulation (Matt 24:21 NKJV), is a period of seven years, the final seven-year period of judgment as outlined in Daniel's prophecy.

THE ABOMINATION THAT CAUSES DESOLATION

We are also told here, in Daniel 9, that during the midpoint of that final seven-year period, which would put it at three-and-a-half years into that seven-year period, the "ruler who will come" will put an end to sacrifice (referring to the sacrifices that will be commenced by the Jews in the temple, to be rebuilt), and will set up what Daniel describes as the "abomination that causes desolation" (9:27). This exact same phrase is used by Jesus when he is describing the events that precede the judgment upon the Earth in the days before the Second Coming.

> Therefore when you see the "abomination of desolation," spoken of by Daniel the prophet, standing in the holy place" (whoever reads, let him understand), "then let those who are in Judea flee to the mountains. Let him who is on the housetop not go down to take anything out of his house. And let him who is in the field not go back to get his clothes. But woe to those who are pregnant and to those who are nursing babies in those days! And pray that your flight may not be in winter or on the Sabbath. For then there will be great tribulation, such as has not been since the beginning of the world until this time, no, nor ever shall be. And unless those days were shortened, no flesh would be saved; but for the elect's sake those days will be shortened." (Matt 24:15–22 NKJV)

Jesus here also tells us about the "abomination of desolation," and specifically tells us that this is the same "abomination of desolation" of Daniel's prophecy. Jesus tells us that it is this event, the setting up of the abomination of desolation, that will unleash the great judgment upon the Earth, the Great Tribulation, which Jesus tells us will be the worst time ever in the history of the world, and which will never be equaled again. Jesus also tells us that, during that time, the devastation upon the Earth will be so terrible that if he did not return at his Second Coming ("if those days had not been cut short"), there would be no life left on Earth (Matt 24:22)—the Second Coming of Jesus Christ is what ends that final seven-year period.

As a result, from both Jesus' own words and from Daniel 9, we know that there will be a seven-year period of judgment that precedes the Second Coming, and at the midpoint of that seven-year period, which is three and a half years into that seven-year period, the abomination of desolation will be set up. That abomination of desolation is the event that triggers what Jesus calls the "Great Tribulation," and with that abomination of desolation the final judgment of Revelation will be poured out, which will climax in the return of Jesus Christ at the Second Coming. That judgment period, described as the "Great Tribulation," will last for the second three and a half years of that final seven-year period.

1,290 AND 1,335 DAYS

In addition to the three timelines of the Seven Seals, the Seven Trumpets, and the Seven Bowls, as well as the seven-year period, we are also told about two other time periods—one period of 1,290 days and another period of 1,335 days.

> And from the time that the daily sacrifice is taken away, and the abomination of desolation is set up, there shall be one thousand two hundred and ninety days. Blessed is he who waits, and comes to the one thousand three hundred and thirty-five days. (Dan 12:11–12 NKJV)

We are told that, from the time that the abomination of desolation is set up, there will be 1,290 days. Then separately, we are told that blessed is the one who waits for, and sees, the 1,335th day. It seems very clear that the 1,335 days *includes* the 1,290 days, so the event described as happening at 1,335 days is 45 days *after* the 1,290 days. What does this mean? How do we understand these two time periods? We can understand these two timeframes as follows.

In the Jewish calendar, each month has thirty days, therefore a period of seven years is 84 months, and a period of three and a half years is 42 months. Since there are 30 days in a month, then, in the Jewish calendar, a period of 42 months is 1,260 days (this 42-month/1,260-day period is also specifically outlined in Rev 11:3; 12:6; 13:5).

When Daniel 12:11–12 gives us a time period of 1,290 days, counted from the setting up of the abomination of desolation, that means that this is the same 1,260-day period (three-and-a-half year/42-month period) *plus* one more month of 30 days. We will see that the Great Tribulation itself lasts for the 1,260-day/42-month period, and that the *additional* 30 days after the Great Tribulation describe the subsequent fall of the nation described as "Babylon the Great"—we will see that the nation Babylon the Great falls *after* the Great Tribulation.

As a result, we can understand the 1,290 days as bringing us to the time period following the end of the Great Tribulation, which sees the fall of Babylon the Great.

What then is the 1,335-day period? This is an additional 45 days *after* the fall of Babylon the Great, and a full 75 days *after* the end of the Great Tribulation. In fact, we can understand that this 1,335-day timeframe is telling *exactly* on which day Jesus will return; it is the *specific* day of his Second Coming—Jesus will return 45 days *after* the fall of the nation Babylon the Great, and 75 days *after* the end of the Great Tribulation, returning 1,335 days *after* the setting up of the abomination of desolation. How can we know that this 1,335-day timeframe is referring to the Second Coming?

We can know that it refers to the Second Coming because Daniel tells us very specifically that the one who *waits* for that 1,335th day, the one who is *looking forward* to it, will be *blessed* when they see that day.

The Second Coming is the blessed event that all Christians await, and it is *only* Christians who *wait* for that day, who are *looking forward* to that day, and who, as a result, will be *blessed* by that day upon seeing it, for that day is also the time of the resurrection of believers (Matt 24:30–31; 1 Thess 4:16). We will see that the Great Tribulation is triggered by the setting up of the abomination of desolation, and we will see that the Great Tribulation lasts for 1,260 days—the culmination and climax of events that follows the end of the Great Tribulation is the Second Coming. As a result, since we know that the culmination and climax of events that follows the end of the Great Tribulation is the Second Coming, and since the Second Coming is the only *blessed* event that follows the Great Tribulation, then we know that the Second Coming is the blessed event that all Christians await. So when Daniel tells us that the one who waits for, and sees, the 1,335th day after the setting up of the abomination of desolation is also the one who will be blessed in seeing it, this affirms that the blessed event being waited for, and seen, is in fact the Second Coming of Jesus Christ. As a result, we know that Jesus Christ will descend to Earth at his Second Coming 1,335 days after the abomination of desolation is set up.

In total, we see then that there are three timelines outlined for us in Revelation—the overall big-picture timeline of the Seven Seals, encompassing a total of 40 years; the second timeline of the Seven Trumpets, encompassing the final three and a half years of the 40-year period, and all included within Seals 5, 6, and 7, and the third timeline of the Bowls, encompassing the last five months plus one month of that same 40-year period, and themselves included *within* Trumpets 5 and 6. Included within all of this is the seven-year period outlined in Daniel 9 and referred to and affirmed by Jesus Christ in Matthew 24—the final seven years of the 40-year period of the Seven Seals, during which the Beast comes to power (the first three and a half years of that seven-year period) and during which the entire Great Tribulation occurs (the second three and a half years of that seven-year period). In all of this, the timeline of the Seven Seals is unique, and the Seven Seals themselves are completely distinct from the Trumpets and the Bowls, different in their very character and nature.

THE CONVERGENCE OF THE TIMELINES

In each of the three timelines—the timeline of the Seven Seals, the timeline of the Seven Trumpets, the timeline of the Seven Bowls—Revelation brings us up to the point in time of the Second Coming, and then it stops to give either extra background information or to begin a description of another of the timelines. This means that in the timeline of the Seven Seals we are brought right up to the point of the Second Coming, and then the narrative switches, and in the case of the Seven Seals the narrative switches to a description of the Trumpet outline; in the timeline of the Seven Trumpets, we are brought right up to the point of the Second Coming, and then the narrative switches, and in the case of the Seven Trumpets the narrative switches to the background information of Revelation 12–14; in the timeline of the Seven Bowls, we are brought right up to the point of the Second Coming, and then the narrative switches to the background information of Revelation 17 and 18, the fall of Babylon the Great. The three timelines converge at the point that just precedes the Second Coming, and then they all resume, as one sequential, chronological timeline, at 19:11, the Second Coming. This convergence of the timelines is clearly borne out by the very text of Revelation, where we are given the heavenly punctuation of events.

When Seal 7 is opened, we are given the following description:

> Then the angel took the censer, filled it with fire from the altar, and hurled it on the earth; and there came peals of thunder, rumblings, flashes of lightning and an earthquake. (8:5 NIV)

Once that description is given, the narrative switches to describing the Trumpet timeline (starting at 8:6).

When Trumpet 7 is sounded, we are given the following description:

> Then God's temple in heaven was opened, and within his temple was seen the ark of his covenant. And there came flashes of lightning, rumblings, peals of thunder, an earthquake and a severe hailstorm. (11:19 NIV)

Once that description is given, the narrative switches to the background information of Revelation 12–14, and the heavenly prelude of Revelation 15, and then describes the Bowl timeline (Rev 16).

When Bowl 7 is poured, we are given the following description:

> Then there came flashes of lightning, rumblings, peals of thunder and a severe earthquake. (16:18 NIV)

Once that description is given, the narrative switches to the background information of Revelation 17 and 18, the fall of Babylon the Great.

We see that each timeline takes us to the same point in the narrative—with Seal 7, we are taken to the point described as peals of thunder, rumblings, flashes of lightning and an earthquake; with Trumpet 7, we are taken to the point described as flashes of lightning, rumblings, peals of thunder, an earthquake and a severe hailstorm; with Bowl 7 we are taken to the point described as flashes of lightning, rumblings, peals of thunder and a severe earthquake—this is all the *same* point in time; *all* three timelines *converge* at that same point. Once the three timelines arrive at that point, *then* the action resumes for *all three timelines* as one chronological narrative, which resumes at the Second Coming, 19:11.

Across all three of these timelines, the Seven Seals are unique, for the Seven Seals *alone* are the judgment, and they encompass the entire forty-year period of all the judgments. The Seven Trumpets and the Seven Bowls are all just *details* of Seals 5, 6, and 7. The very nature and character of the Seven Seals differs from the nature and character of the Trumpets and Bowls.

In what way are the Seven Seals different from the Seven Trumpets and the Seven Bowls? How do we know that the Seven Seals are unique? We can understand the utter uniqueness of the Seven Seals as follows.

THE UNIQUENESS OF THE SEVEN SEALS

The Seven Seals of Revelation are unique—they are nothing like the Trumpets or the Bowls. In Revelation, each of the Seven Trumpets can be blown by any angelic being (8:6–13; 9; 11:15–19). Likewise, each of the Seven Bowls can be poured out by any angelic being (Rev 16)—there is nothing special about who blows the Trumpets or who pours the Bowls. This is in complete contrast to the Seven Seals.

We are told, very clearly, in 5:1–4 that no one in the universe can open the Seven Seals except only *one* person, the Lamb, Jesus Christ—*only* Jesus Christ can open the Seven Seals (5:5–10).

> And I saw a mighty angel proclaiming in a loud voice, "Who is worthy to break the seals and open the scroll?" But no one in heaven or on earth or under the earth could open the scroll or even look inside it. I wept and wept because no one was found who was worthy to open the scroll or look inside. Then one of the elders said to me, "Do not weep! See, the Lion of the tribe of Judah, the Root of David, has triumphed. He is able to open the scroll and its seven seals." Then I saw a Lamb, looking as if it had been slain, standing at the center of the throne, encircled by the four living creatures and the elders. The Lamb had seven horns and seven eyes, which are the seven spirits of God sent out into all the earth. He went and took the scroll from the right hand of him who sat on the throne. And when he had taken it, the four living creatures and the twenty-four elders fell down before the Lamb. Each one had a harp and they were holding golden bowls full of incense, which are the prayers of God's people. And they sang a new song, saying: "You are worthy to take the scroll and to open its seals, because you were slain, and with your blood you

purchased for God persons from every tribe and language and people and nation." (5:2–9 NIV)

Only the Lamb, the Son, Jesus Christ, is *worthy* to open the Seven Seals. This is in striking contrast to the Trumpets and the Bowls, which can be blown/poured by any angelic being.

Why is this? *Why* is it that *only* Jesus Christ can open the Seven Seals?

It is because the Seven Seals *are the full judgment* of Revelation; they are the *totality* of the judgment, and *only the Judge* can release the judgments.

So, who is the Judge?

We are told, very clearly, that the Son, alone, is the Judge of all things, and that God the Father judges no one and nothing, but rather has given *all* judgment to the Son, to Jesus Christ.

> Moreover, the Father judges no one, but has entrusted all judgment to the Son. (John 5:2 NIV)

The Bible is very clear—*only* the Son is the Judge; he alone releases judgments. It is because the Seven Seals are the totality of the judgments of Revelation that *only* the Judge can open the Seven Seals, thereby releasing the judgments. This is why only the Lamb, Jesus Christ, the Judge, can open the Seven Seals.

This is a fundamental truth in understanding the events of Revelation—it is *the Son* who sends the judgments of Revelation, *not* the Father.

The Seven Seals are therefore completely unique and different from the Trumpets and the Bowls—any angel can blow a Trumpet, any angel can pour a Bowl, but only the Son can open the Seals. The Seven Seals are the judgments *themselves*, while the Trumpets and the Bowls are only *details* of those Seal judgments. As we shall see, the time period encompassed by the Seven Seals is a period of forty years.

THE TIMELINE OF THE SEVEN TRUMPETS— THREE AND A HALF YEARS

Both the Trumpets and the Bowls are the details of what is called the Great Tribulation, all of which occurs in Seal 5. The name Great Tribulation is the name given to that period by Jesus himself in Matthew 24:21.

> For then there will be great tribulation, such as has not been since the beginning of the world until this time, no, nor ever shall be. (NKJV)

As we shall see, in Matthew 24:3–31 Jesus outlines, in order, the Seven Seals of Revelation, and his description of the Great Tribulation is part of his description of the events of Seal 5. In fact, in Jesus' description and outline of Seal 5 and of the Great Tribulation, he affirms the same "abomination of desolation" spoken of by Daniel as being the event that triggers the Great Tribulation (Dan 9:27; 11:31; 12:11; Matt

24:15). We know from Daniel 9:27 that the abomination of desolation occurs in the middle of a "seven," which is to say that it occurs at the midpoint, or three-and-a-half-year mark, of that final seven-year period. As a result, we know that the Great Tribulation comprises only the second half of that seven-year period.

We will see clearly that the Great Tribulation is released at the sounding of Trumpet 1 and ends with the end of Trumpet 5. Since the Great Tribulation is a duration of three and a half years, then, as a result, we know that Trumpets 1–5 span that same three-and-a-half-year period. We will see that Trumpet 6 announces the thirty days that come *after* the end of the Great Tribulation, during which occurs the fall of Babylon the Great. Trumpet 7, the last Trumpet (1 Cor 15:52; 1 Thess 4:16), sounds forty-five days after the fall of Babylon the Great, announcing the resurrection of believers and the Second Coming. As a result, we know that the Trumpets comprise only the final three and a half years of the forty-year period encompassed by the Seven Seals.

THE TIMELINE OF THE SEVEN BOWLS— THE FINAL SIX MONTHS

As we will see, the Seven Bowls are an even more detailed account of the final *months* of the Great Tribulation; in fact, Bowls 1–5 are the *final five months* of the three-and-a-half-year period of the Great Tribulation, and with all those five Bowls occurring during Trumpet 5.

With the opening of Seal 5, the Beast comes to power. As we will see, the Beast will rule for only three and a half years. He will then set up the abomination of desolation, which is the event that will trigger the Great Tribulation, all of which occurs during Seal 5. The details of the Great Tribulation are described by Trumpets 1–5, with Trumpet 5 releasing, and including, Bowls 1–5. We will see that the time period of Trumpet 5 lasts for five months (Rev 9:5)—these same five months are also the time period of Bowls 1–5 (in fact, we will see that one Bowl is poured during each one of those five months). Once the Great Tribulation is over, Seal 6 is opened, Trumpet 6 is then sounded, and with its sounding Bowls 6 and 7 are poured. Bowl 6 is the fall of Babylon the Great, which happens in the thirty days following the end of the Great Tribulation, while Bowl 7 is a judgment of a great earthquake that levels all the cities of the Earth. With the pouring of Bowl 7, the Bowl timeline is completed and Seal 7 is then opened. Seal 7 includes the blowing of Trumpet 7, which announces the resurrection of believers and the Second Coming.

We will see that the time period covered by the Seven Bowls is in total a six-month period, being the final five months of the three-and-a-half-year Great Tribulation, as well as the following thirty-day period during which occurs the fall of Babylon the Great. This is then followed by the resurrection of believers and Second Coming.

The immense confusion encountered in studies of Revelation is the result of the mistaken idea that the entirety of the events of Revelation all occur during the seven-year period, and that the Seven Seals are no different than the Trumpets or Bowls, and that they are all a description of *subsequent* events. When the false teaching of the rapture is added to this, Revelation becomes almost incomprehensible. It is of vital importance to understand that Revelation outlines three timelines for us—the Seven Seals, the Seven Trumpets, the Seven Bowls. The Seven Seals are the *totality* of all the events that lead to the Second Coming, while the Trumpet and Bowl timelines are *included* in the Seals, being included in Seals 5, 6, and 7. Jesus Christ himself, in Matthew 24, makes clear for us that the seven-year period, and the entirety of the Great Tribulation, *all* happens during Seal 5, for he tells us as he begins his description of Seal 6.

> Immediately after the tribulation of those days *the sun will be darkened*, and the *moon* will *not give its light*; the *stars will fall from heaven*, and the powers of the heavens will be shaken. (Matt 24:29 NKJV)

Jesus' description of Seal 6 in Matthew 24:29 is almost identical to the description of Seal 6 in Revelation.

> I looked when He opened the sixth seal, and behold, there was a great earthquake; and *the sun became black as sackcloth* of hair, and the *moon became like blood*. And *the stars of heaven fell to the earth*. (Rev 6:12–13 NKJV)

When Jesus' begins his description of Seal 6, he begins with the words, "Immediately *after the tribulation* of those days."

As a result, we know that the Great Tribulation occurs in its entirety in Seal 5 and is over at the end of Seal 5.

Understanding these three timelines, and how they are all embedded one into the other, is an essential and fundamental truth in understanding Revelation.

SUMMARY OF TIMELINES

We see, then, that there are three timelines outlined in Revelation—the overall big-picture timeline of the Seven Seals, which covers a period of forty years; the details of the final three-and-a-half-year period of the Great Tribulation, as outlined by the Trumpets; and the final five months of the Great Tribulation, outlined by Bowls 1–5, and the subsequent thirty days, as outlined by the even-more-detailed Bowls 6 and 7. Also, included in Seal 5 is the seven-year period during which the Beast comes to power and during which the entirety of the Great Tribulation occurs

As we examine the Seals, the Trumpets, and the Bowls in detail, we will see that the three timelines, and the seven-year period, lay out as follows:

Seals 1–4

- a thirty-three-year period

- sets the world's stage for the coming of the Beast

Seal 5

- the entire seven-year period
- the Beast comes to power and rules for three and a half years
- the Beast sets up the abomination of desolation three and a half years into his rule, and unleashes the Great Tribulation, which occurs, in its entirety, in the second three and a half years of that seven-year period, and which is described for us by:
    - Trumpet 1
    - Trumpet 2
    - Trumpet 3
    - Trumpet 4
    - Trumpet 5
        - Bowl 1
        - Bowl 2
        - Bowl 3
        - Bowl 4
        - Bowl 5

Seal 6

- includes Trumpet 6, which itself includes Bowls 6 and 7 and which describes the fall of Babylon the Great

Seal 7

- includes Trumpet 7 (the last Trumpet) and announces the resurrection of believers and the Second Coming

This is how the three timelines of Revelation lay out, and we know this for a fact because, as we will see, Jesus himself explains this for us in Matthew 24:3–31, where he outlines for us, in order, the Seven Seals. The Seven Seals are the *entire* forty-year period of Revelation, the entirety of the judgment, while the Trumpets and Bowls are the final three and a half years (the Great Tribulation) of that same forty-year period.

The following is a summary diagram of how these timelines line up:

TIMELINE OF REVELATION

TIMELINE OF EVENTS
(intensity of "birth-pains" increases)

	BEAST comes to POWER HERE * in SEAL 5 — 7 YEARS BEGIN HERE = 42 months	GREAT TRIB begins HERE ** = "abomination of desolation" (Dan. 9.27, Matt. 24.15) 42 months	SECOND COMING HERE *

SEALS (last 40 years)
1 2 3 4 5*   6 7*

TRUMPETS (last 42 months)
1, 2, 3, 4, 5   6 7

BOWLS (last 5 months plus 30 days)
1, 2, 3, 4, 5, 6, 7

Sets the stage **(33 years)**	Peace, prosperity = 42 months	Great Tribulation = 42 months	+30 days

7 YEARS

The Bible clearly affirms that this is the layout of the timelines of Revelation, with the Seven Seals being the totality of all events, and with the Trumpets and Bowls being a more detailed description of the Great Tribulation, the fall of Babylon the Great, and then, with Seal 7/Trumpet 7, the resurrection of believers and the Second Coming. The entirety of those events occurs over a period of forty years, and the seven-year period outlined in Daniel is only the last seven years of that same forty-year period.

6

Introduction—Revelation 1

The first chapter of Revelation is the introduction to the book, telling us who is giving the Revelation, who is receiving the Revelation, and where is it being given. We are also given some details, by way of symbolism and imagery, about what is to unfold.

The very first verse of chapter 1 tells us that the Revelation to follow is given by Jesus Christ, and that it is given to show what must "soon take place," and that it is being given to John. Since the very early church, most have understood, and it has been generally accepted, that this is John the apostle, the disciple whom "Jesus loved" (John 13:23; 19:26; 20:2). Chapter 1 continues to give us a few more details about John.

JOHN

> I, John, your brother and companion in the suffering and kingdom and patient endurance that are ours in Jesus, was on the island of Patmos because of the word of God and the testimony of Jesus. (Rev 1:9 NIV)

John describes himself as a brother in Christ and as our companion in suffering, but also as our companion in God's kingdom as well as a fellow companion in patient endurance. When this Revelation was given, John was on the Greek island of Patmos "because of the word of God and the testimony of Jesus." Most have understood this to mean that John was imprisoned, in exile, on the island of Patmos because of preaching the gospel, though it is also possible that he was on Patmos for the purpose of preaching the gospel. Either way, the Revelation was given to John on the island of Patmos.

It has also traditionally been understood by the church that this Revelation was given to John in his old age, given close to the end of his life. John was the last of the apostles, and he is traditionally believed to have died ca. 98–100 AD. As a result, it has generally been understood that this Revelation was given to John, in Patmos, 94–96 AD or so.

John also tells us that it was on the Lord's Day that he was "in the Spirit," whereupon he received the Revelation (Rev 1:10). The Lord's Day is generally understood as Sunday, and to be "in the Spirit" can be understood as meaning a deep sense of communion with the Lord Jesus Christ.

It is while being "in the Spirit" that the Revelation begins, when John hears a loud voice behind him, as loud as a trumpet blast, and the voice speaks to John and tells him,

> On the Lord's Day I was in the Spirit, and I heard behind me a loud voice like a trumpet, which said: "Write on a scroll what you see and send it to the seven churches: to Ephesus, Smyrna, Pergamum, Thyatira, Sardis, Philadelphia and Laodicea." (1:10–11 NIV)

The voice that John hears tells him to write down what he will see and to send that to seven churches, which churches are then listed—Ephesus, Smyrna, Pergamum, Thyatira, Sardis, Philadelphia, and Laodicea. These are the same seven churches referred to by John in 1:4.

> John, To the seven churches in the province of Asia (1:4 NIV)

It is at that point that John then turns to see who was speaking to him.

> I turned around to see the voice that was speaking to me. And when I turned, I saw seven golden lampstands, and among the lampstands was someone like a son of man, dressed in a robe reaching down to his feet and with a golden sash around his chest. The hair on his head was white like wool, as white as snow, and his eyes were like blazing fire. His feet were like bronze glowing in a furnace, and his voice was like the sound of rushing waters. In his right hand he held seven stars, and coming out of his mouth was a sharp, double-edged sword. His face was like the sun shining in all its brilliance. When I saw him, I fell at his feet as though dead. Then he placed his right hand on me and said: "Do not be afraid. I am the First and the Last. I am the Living One; I was dead, and now look, I am alive for ever and ever! And I hold the keys of death and Hades." (1:12–18 NIV)

There is no question that the one speaking to him is the Lord Jesus Christ, and he is described here in symbolic terms.

THE LORD JESUS CHRIST

We can be certain that this is the Lord Jesus Christ, for he is described as "the Living One," as one who "was dead," but now is "alive for ever and ever." This is a reference to, and affirmation of, the resurrection. Also, this speaker, the one who is speaking to John on Patmos in the first chapter of Revelation, is the same speaker who is speaking to John after the Revelation is given.

INTRODUCTION—REVELATION 1

> I, Jesus, have sent my angel to give you this testimony for the churches. I am the Root and the Offspring of David, and the bright Morning Star. (22:16 NIV)

Here Jesus identifies himself, by name, as the one who is giving the Revelation, also making reference to the same seven churches of 1:4 and 1:11. As a result, there is no question that when John turns to see who is speaking to him on Patmos, the one who is speaking to him is the Lord Jesus Christ.

DESCRIPTION OF THE LORD JESUS

The description of the Lord Jesus given by John in Revelation 1:12–18 is very much a symbolic description. Jesus Christ is described as having hair as white as wool, as white as snow, and as having eyes like blazing fire. His feet are described as looking like bronze glowing in a furnace fire, and as having a voice like rushing, or thundering, waters. He is described as holding seven stars in his right hand, as having a face shining like the sun in all of its brilliance, and as having a sharp double-edged sword coming out of his mouth.

Contrast this description of the Lord Jesus with Daniel's description of "one like a son of man."

> As I looked,
> "thrones were set in place,
> and the Ancient of Days took his seat.
> His clothing was as white as snow;
> the hair of his head was white like wool.
> His throne was flaming with fire,
> and its wheels were all ablaze.
> A river of fire was flowing,
> coming out from before him.
> Thousands upon thousands attended him;
> ten thousand times ten thousand stood before him.
> The court was seated,
> and the books were opened. (Dan 7:9–10 NIV)

There are exact parallels between Jesus as described by John and the person whom Daniel describes. Both have hair white like wool, both are described as "white as snow," both are associated with fire—with John, Jesus is described as having eyes blazing like fire, and in Daniel his throne is described as flaming with fire and with a river of fire flowing out from before him. The description by John of Jesus' feet as looking like bronze glowing in a furnace is also a description of fire. Daniel describes him as "the Ancient of Days."

John also describes Jesus as having a sharp double-edged sword coming out of his mouth. How are we to understand the meaning of this image? We can understand it as follows.

The double-edged sword represents the word of God, the speaking of God.

> For the word of God is alive and active. Sharper than any *double-edged sword*, it penetrates even to dividing soul and spirit, joints and marrow; it judges the thoughts and attitudes of the heart. (Heb 4:12 NIV)

To be "double-edged" means that both edges of the sword are sharp, so that no matter which way the sword swings it can cut equally well. This is a representation of the word of God, the very speaking of God, as being powerful, and, by coming from the mouth of Jesus Christ, it represents that Jesus himself is the one who speaks, or wields, that word. Since the word of God, represented as a double-edged sword, is coming from Jesus' mouth, which is an affirmation of Jesus being the one who speaks that word of power, this is a further, symbolic affirmation of one of the names of Jesus Christ, the "Word of God" (John 1:1–4).

THE SEVEN GOLDEN LAMPSTANDS

John describes Jesus as being in the midst of seven golden lampstands. What are the seven lampstands? Jesus himself explains it for us.

> The mystery of the seven stars that you saw in my right hand and of the seven golden lampstands is this: The seven stars are the angels of the seven churches, and the seven lampstands are the seven churches. (Rev 1:20 NIV)

Jesus tells John that the seven golden lampstands represent the same seven churches to whom John is to send the Revelation, the churches in Ephesus, Smyrna, Pergamum, Thyatira, Sardis, Philadelphia, and Laodicea.

Why are the churches represented as lampstands? It seems certain that the symbolism of the lampstands is meant to represent the fact that just as Jesus is the light of the world (John 9:5), so the churches are to be light to the world.

> You are the light of the world. A town built on a hill cannot be hidden. (Matt 5:14 NIV)

> When Jesus spoke again to the people, he said, "I am the light of the world. Whoever follows me will never walk in darkness, but will have the light of life." (John 8:12 NIV)

> For this is what the Lord has commanded us: "I have made you a light for the Gentiles, that you may bring salvation to the ends of the earth." (Acts 13:47 NIV)

> For you were once darkness, but now you are light in the Lord. Live as children of light. (Eph 5:8 NIV)

> You are all children of the light and children of the day. We do not belong to the night or to the darkness. (1 Thess 5:5 NIV)

All Christians are *light*, and, as a result, each of the seven churches to whom John will be addressing the Revelation are represented as lampstands around the person of Jesus Christ, being represented as a light in the world. The fact that Jesus is described as being in the *midst* of those seven lampstands also denotes that he himself is the *source* of the light of those lampstands, the source of the light of the churches. Also, the lampstands are made of gold, which represents the precious and priceless value of the churches.

THE STARS

Jesus is also described as holding seven stars in his right hand. How are we to understand the meaning of this imagery? Jesus himself explains it for us, telling us that the seven stars in his hand are the seven angels of those same seven churches (Rev 1:20).

Throughout the Bible, angels are often represented as stars. This is seen in Isaiah 14, which describes how Lucifer rebelled in his heart against God, and as part of the description of that rebellion we are told,

> I will raise my throne above *the stars* of God (14:13 NIV)

In desiring to raise his throne above the "stars of God," Lucifer is desiring to raise his throne above the entire angelic host—the "stars" referred to represent angels.

Also, in Revelation 12 we are told the following:

> Then another sign appeared in heaven: an enormous red dragon with seven heads and ten horns and seven crowns on its heads. Its tail swept *a third of the stars* out of the sky and flung them to the earth. (12:3–4 NIV)

This is a description of the angelic rebellion. We are told here that an enormous red dragon (which is the devil, as is made clear in Rev 12:9) swept a third of the stars out of the sky and flung them to the Earth. These stars once again represent the angelic host. As a result, we know that in the angelic rebellion one-third of the angelic host rebelled with Lucifer against God.

Also, the flinging to Earth of the rebellious angels, and Lucifer, is further affirmed in Ezekiel 28:17.

> Your heart became proud
> on account of your beauty,
> and you corrupted your wisdom
> because of your splendor.

So *I threw you to the earth*;
I made a spectacle of you before kings. (NIV)

Ezekiel 28:11–19 is a detailed description of Lucifer before his fall, as well as a description of his rebellion—the rebellion that began only in his own heart and then the subsequent spreading of that rebellion to some of the other angelic host. God makes it very clear in Ezekiel 28:17 that his response to that rebellion was to throw Lucifer, and by extension the entire rebel host, to the Earth, exactly as is described in Revelation 12:3–4. All of this is further affirmation of angels being represented in Scripture as stars.

THE SECOND COMING

At the very outset of the book of Revelation we are told the following:

> "Look, he is coming with the clouds," and "every eye will see him, even those who pierced him"; and all peoples on earth "will mourn because of him." So shall it be! Amen. "I am the Alpha and the Omega," says the Lord God, "who is, and who was, and who is to come, the Almighty." (1:7–8 NIV)

This is a description of the Second Coming of the Lord Jesus Christ, and the references in Revelation 1:7 are referring to Daniel 7:13 and Zechariah 12:10, both of which describe the Second Coming of Jesus Christ.

We also read the following at the *end* of Revelation:

> Look, I am coming soon! My reward is with me (22:12 NIV)

Why does John *begin* Revelation with a reference to the Second Coming, and why does Revelation *end* with Jesus himself telling us that he is "coming soon," also a reference to the Second Coming? The fact that the book of Revelation begins with an affirmation of the Second Coming and then ends with the promise of the Second Coming affirms that the *entire* Revelation is to be understood in the context of the Second Coming. That is to say, Revelation is all about the Second Coming of Jesus Christ, describing what precedes his coming and what follows his coming. As a result, we can know that what is about to follow in Revelation will relate to the Second Coming.

AFFIRMATION OF JESUS' DOMINION

In his greetings to the seven churches (Rev 1:4–5), John describes the resurrected Lord Jesus as the "the ruler of the kings of the earth" (1:5). This is an affirmation of the dominion of Jesus Christ over the Earth. Why does John affirm this dominion here, right at the outset of the book?

INTRODUCTION—REVELATION 1

John's declaration that the Lord Jesus is the ruler of the kings of the Earth is immediately followed by his declaration that Christians have been made a "kingdom," which statement is then followed by the description of the Second Coming (Rev 1:7). All of these are connected. By affirming the Lord Jesus as being the *rightful* ruler of the Earth, and the *rightful* ruler of the *kings* of the Earth, and by then describing his Second Coming, John is affirming the very *purpose* of the Second Coming—the purpose of the Second Coming is Jesus Christ returning to take the dominion of the Earth that he won back at his resurrection, the dominion originally given by God to Adam (Gen 1:28), which Adam then gave up to Satan upon Adam's fall (Luke 4:6), and which Jesus then took back after his resurrection (John 16:8–11; 1 Pet 5:11).

THE SEVEN SPIRITS

In John's greetings to the seven churches, he tells them that he sends greetings of grace and peace.

> Grace and peace to you from him who is, and who was, and who is to come,
> and from the *seven spirits before his throne* (Rev 1:4 NIV)

What are the seven spirits described as being before God's throne? There is some debate over this, without a clear consensus, but what stands out immediately upon reading the verse is that John is addressing seven churches in Asia, and the description of Jesus' holding seven stars in his right hand is explained as each star being an angel who looks out for, and protects, each of the seven churches (1:20). In that context, is it possible that the seven spirits described as being before God's throne are the same seven angels (spirit beings) of the seven churches?

It is a strong possibility that cannot be discounted, especially when, as we shall see, the seven letters that John is to send to the seven churches are in fact specifically *addressed* to the *angel* of each church, and not to the church itself.

As a result, it is possible that the seven angels of the seven churches are the seven spirits before God's throne, since these same seven angels, by way of their position as protectors of each of the seven churches, are, as a result, intimately tied in with this Revelation. Since those seven angelic protectors of the seven churches are so intimately tied in to the Revelation about to be conveyed to those same seven churches, there is very good reason to understand the seven angels of the seven churches as being the seven spirits before God's throne. This also then can explain those same seven spirits as sending peace and grace to those seven churches, which, in that case, would be the seven angels of the churches sending greetings to the very same churches under their protection.

ALPHA AND OMEGA

In Revelation 1:8, the Lord describes himself.

> "I am the Alpha and the Omega," says the Lord God, "who is, and who was, and who is to come, the Almighty." (1:8 NIV)

How are we to understand this? What is the meaning of "the Alpha and the Omega"? We can understand it as follows:

Alpha is the first letter of the Greek alphabet, and Omega is the last letter of the Greek alphabet, and so the phrase "the Alpha and the Omega" is God describing himself as the first and the last (the description "the first and the last" is also specifically used by Jesus to describe himself in Rev 1:17; 2:8; 22:13). The phrase "who is, and who was, and who is to come" is a description of Jesus. "Who is" means that he *is* alive, while "who was" means that he is both eternal and uncreated, but it also means that he walked the Earth as incarnate God, and "who is to come" is a reference to the Second Coming.

WRITE WHAT YOU SEE

In Revelation 1:10–11, John tells us that when he was in the Spirit on the Lord's Day, he heard behind him a loud voice, blaring like a trumpet, and this voice spoke to him and said,

> Write on a scroll what you see and send it to the seven churches: to Ephesus, Smyrna, Pergamum, Thyatira, Sardis, Philadelphia and Laodicea. (1:11 NIV)

It is important to note that John was told specifically to write down what he *sees* and, by implication, what he *hears*. What he *hears* is by implication, since the whole Revelation begins by John *hearing* a voice like a trumpet, so even though he is specifically commanded to write down what he *sees,* we can understand that to also include writing down what he *hears*—in fact, much of what John writes in Revelation is a record of what he hears.

Why is this important? It is important for the following reason. If what is about to follow in the book of Revelation was only a *vision*, then, physically, John would not see anything with his eyes nor hear anything with his ears; it would all be just a vision in his mind. The fact that John is specifically told to write down what he will *see* and, by implication, what he will *hear* affirms that what is about to follow is what John *actually* saw with his own eyes and *actually* heard with his own ears—what is about to follow will not be a vision; rather John will actually see and hear what is about to be shown to him.

Also, the fact that the entire Revelation begins with John being on the island of Patmos, physically hearing a loud voice like a trumpet (1:9–12) and then *turning* to see where the voice was coming from also affirms that John was not experiencing a

INTRODUCTION—REVELATION 1

vision, for, if it was all just a vision, John himself would never need to turn to see who was speaking to him. The very fact that John *turned* to see who was speaking to him affirms that this was something that John was actually experiencing, was actually living through, and was not just a vision.

DEATH AND HADES

When John turns to see who is speaking to him, he sees the Lord Jesus Christ and he sees Jesus appearing in symbolic terms (Rev 1:12–16). When Jesus speaks again to John, one of the things that he says is,

> I am the Living One; I was dead, and now look, I am alive for ever and ever!
> And I hold the keys of death and Hades. (1:17–18 NIV)

What does it mean to hold the "keys of death and Hades"?

Hades is the Greek word used to describe the Realm of the Dead, which in Hebrew is called *Sheol*. The Realm of the Dead is the place where everyone who ever lived and died, from Adam to Jesus' own day, went to when they died, and it is also the place where Jesus went to for the three days that he was dead. Hades/Sheol is the abode of the dead, and it is located inside the Earth (Matt 12:40 et al.).

By describing himself as holding the "keys of death and Hades," Jesus is affirming that he has conquered both—he has conquered and destroyed death, and, as a result, he has conquered the very Realm of the Dead, Hades/Sheol (Rom 6:9; 1 Cor 15:55–56).

Also, to be described as holding the "keys of death" is yet another affirmation of Jesus having reclaimed the dominion of the Earth. When Adam fell, he gave the dominion of the Earth, the dominion that was originally given to him by God (Gen 1:28), to Satan (Luke 4:6; John 12:31; 14:30; Rom 5:12). Once Satan received the dominion to the Earth from Adam, then the whole Earth, and everything on it, came under the dominion of death, coming under bondage to death and decay—people, plants, animals, everything came under the dominion of death (Rom 8:21 et al.). Satan is specifically described as the one who holds to power of death (Heb 2:14), which is to say that Satan holds the dominion of death. As a result, when Jesus describes himself as the one holding the "keys of death and Hades," it means that it is now *Jesus* who has power, or dominion and authority, over death. Since Hebrews 2:14 specifically tells us that it was the devil who had the power of death, and since in Revelation Jesus is described as having power, or dominion, over death, this affirms that the Lord Jesus Christ reclaimed the dominion of the Earth, the same dominion that was originally given by God to Adam, and which was then passed by Adam to Satan upon Adam's fall, and which was then won back by Jesus Christ, the second Adam, upon his resurrection.

THE BLESSING AND THE CURSE

At the very start of the book of Revelation, we are told the following:

> Blessed is the one who reads aloud the words of this prophecy, and blessed are those who hear it and take to heart what is written in it, because the time is near." (1:3 NIV)

Revelation is the only book in the Bible that tells us we are blessed if we read its words aloud, but we are also blessed if we hear its words and take them to heart. Furthermore, in Revelation 22 we are also told the following:

> I warn everyone who hears the words of the prophecy of this scroll: If anyone adds anything to them, God will add to that person the plagues described in this scroll. And if anyone takes words away from this scroll of prophecy, God will take away from that person any share in the tree of life and in the Holy City, which are described in this scroll. (22:18–19 NIV)

Not only are people blessed if they read or hear the words of Revelation, but Jesus himself also says that if anyone tries to *add* or *take away* from what Revelation says, that person will be cursed. No other book of the Bible contains any such blessing or curse upon readers or hearers of the book.

It is interesting to note that the blessing of chapter 1 almost coincides with the chapter 1 declaration of the Second Coming (1:7), while the curse coincides with the promise of Jesus himself that he is coming soon (22:12)—both the blessing and the curse are mentioned in the clear context of the Second Coming.

What are we to make of the blessing and curse of Revelation? We can understand it as follows.

The book of Revelation is a prophecy of the Second Coming, of the events that precede it, of the event itself, and of what ensues after the Second Coming. Both the blessing and the curse are given in the clear context of the declaration of the Second Coming, stated first in 1:7, at the very beginning of the book, and stated again in 22:12, at the very end of the book, with both the blessing and the curse almost bookending Revelation. As a result, we can conclude that the prophecy of Revelation is so important, is to be taken so seriously, that just to hear its words is a blessing, while to take away from its words results in being cursed. The blessing and the curse of Revelation tell us, with absolute clarity, that we are to take the book of Revelation very seriously.

WHAT IS NOW

In Revelation 1:19, Jesus tells John,

> Write, therefore, what you have seen, *what is now* and what will take place later. (1:19 NIV)

Introduction—Revelation 1

Most of Revelation deals with what will take place later. What then does "what is now" refer to? It refers to the seven churches whom John addresses in 1:4, all of which were seven actual churches existing in John's own day, the very same seven churches to whom John was instructed to send the Revelation. In the letters that John is commanded to send to the angels of the seven churches, we will see that Jesus outlines, for each church, the situation of that church, the problems and strengths of that church, and then he admonishes each church to deal with and correct the problems within that church because a trial is about to come. Jesus then tells each church that if they persevere and endure in faithfulness through the coming trial, those churches will receive rewards.

That admonition is given to the actual seven churches to whom John will send the Revelation, but it is also an admonition for the church as a whole, for the seven churches of the seven letters represent the church that will be on the Earth in the days that precede the Second Coming.

7

THE SEVEN LETTERS—REVELATION 2 AND 3

CHAPTERS 2 AND 3 of Revelation are the seven letters to the seven churches that Jesus, in chapter 1 (1:11), had told John to write. The seven churches are located in the following cities: Ephesus, which was a Greek city in modern-day Turkey; Smyrna, also a Greek city in Asia (Minor), which corresponds to modern-day Turkey; Pergamum, another Greek city in modern-day Turkey; Thyatira, again, a Greek city in modern-day Turkey; Sardis, a Persian city in modern-day Turkey; Philadelphia, also a city in modern-day Turkey; and Laodicea, another Greek city in modern-day Turkey. All seven churches are in the Roman province of Asia (1:4), which is *not* the same as the modern continent of Asia, but rather an area that generally corresponds to the modern-day Middle East, with the mentioned seven churches being more specifically in what is modern-day Turkey.

It is important to understand that each and every one of these churches were seven actual churches that existed in John's day, and, upon writing down the Revelation, John would have sent each of these seven actual churches a scroll containing the Revelation, as Jesus had commanded him to do (1:11).

In Jesus' instructions to John in 1:19, he says,

> Write, therefore, what you have seen, what is now and what will take place later. (NIV)

Jesus tells John to write down "what is now" and "what will take place later." The great bulk of Revelation concerns the things that will take place later; the only thing in Revelation that falls in the category of "what is now" are the seven churches—of all the events described in Revelation, only the seven churches existed in John's day. As a result, it is the seven churches that are being described as "what is now."

THE PATTERN OF THE SEVEN LETTERS

In each of the letters to the seven churches, there is a pattern, or form, that is adopted. First, Jesus tells John to address each letter to the "angel" of each church, *not* to the church itself.

Next, Jesus gives a description of himself as being the author of the letter. In each letter, the description that Jesus uses of himself is one of the descriptions of Jesus as witnessed and described by John in chapter 1. In the letter to the angel of the church of Ephesus, Jesus describes himself as "him who holds the seven stars in his right hand and walks among the seven golden lampstands" (2:1), the same description as in 1:12 and 1:16; in the letter to the angel of the church of Smyrna, Jesus describes himself as "the First and the Last" (2:8), the same description as in 1:17; in the letter to the angel of the church of Pergamum, he describes himself as "him who has the sharp, double-edged sword" (2:12), the same description as 1:16; in the letter to the angel of the church of Thyatira, he describes himself as "whose eyes are like blazing fire and whose feet are like burnished bronze" (2:19), the same description as 1:14–15; in the letter to the angel of the church of Sardis, he describes himself as "him who holds the seven spirits of God and the seven stars" (3:1), the same description as 1:4, where the seven spirits are referenced as being before his throne, and the same description as 1:16; in the letter to the angel of the church of Philadelphia, he describes himself as "the words of him who is holy and true, who holds the key of David" (3:7), which is an allusion to the description of 1:18, which references "the keys of death and Hades"; in the letter to the angel of the church of Laodicea, he describes himself as "the Amen, the faithful and true witness, the ruler of God's creation" (3:14), which is an allusion to the description of 1:5.

In the introduction to each letter, the parallel description of Jesus outlined in each letter, together with John's description of him in chapter 1, is affirmation that the one who is giving the Revelation is the same one whom John saw and described in chapter 1.

After the introduction, Jesus then proceeds to tell each church that he "knows" their situation. He first describes what is good in the church, and commends them for it, and then he describes a problem in that church, a problem that they need to address. He tells the church to repent from that problem and then in each case, after his exhortation to repent, he says, "to the one who is victorious . . . ," and then he promises to give them rewards.

At the end of every letter to each church, Jesus ends with the words,

> Whoever has ears, let them hear what the Spirit says to the churches (2:7 NIV)

This is the pattern of each of the seven letters.

THE REWARDS

At the end of each letter, after his exhortation to repent, Jesus says to that church, "to the one who is victorious . . . ," and then follows that with a promise to give rewards. The rewards that Jesus promises are, in fact, all rewards that are described as being given *after* the Second Coming.

For example, to "the one who is victorious" in the church of Ephesus, Jesus promises that they will have the right to eat from the Tree of Life (2:7). This reward is described as being given after the Second Coming in 22:14.

To "the one who is victorious" in the church of Smyrna, he promises that they will not be hurt by the second death (2:11). The second death is described as happening after the Second Coming in 20:14 and 21:8.

To "the one who is victorious" in the church of Pergamum, he promises that they will be given hidden manna and a new name, which is affirmed in 3:12 as happening at the time of the New Jerusalem.

> The one who is victorious I will make a pillar in the temple of my God. Never again will they leave it. I will write on them the name of my God and the name of the city of my God, the new Jerusalem, which is coming down out of heaven from my God; and I will also write on them my new name. (3:12 NIV)

The New Jerusalem descends from heaven to Earth after the Second Coming (21:2). Since the giving of new names is described as happening in the same context as the New Jerusalem, and since the New Jerusalem descends to Earth after the Second Coming, we can understand that the giving of the new names also happens after the Second Coming.

To "the one who is victorious" in the church of Thyatira, he promises that he will give them authority over nations, and that he will also give them the "morning star" (2:26–28). Ruling over the nations of the Earth is described as happening after the Second Coming (21:24), and the "morning star" is further referenced in 22:16, a description of events after the Second Coming.

To "the one who is victorious" in the church of Sardis, he promises that they will be robed in white and that their names will never be blotted out of the Book of Life (3:5). The wearing of white robes is specifically described in 7:9–14, which is a description of the church martyred for Christ during the reign of the Beast (the church is on Earth during the entire reign of the Beast, as well as during the following Great Tribulation, persecuted and killed during the reign of the Beast but protected from the Great Tribulation). This reward of having one's name in the Book of Life is outlined as happening after the Second Coming (21:27).

To "the one who is victorious" in the church of Philadelphia, Jesus promises that they will be a pillar in the temple of God, and that he will write on them the name of God and the name of God's city, the New Jerusalem, and he will also write on them his new name. This reward is similar to the reward outlined for the church of Pergamum, and is likewise tied in with the New Jerusalem, which is described as happening after the Second Coming (21:2).

To "the one who is victorious" in the church of Laodicea, he promises that they will have the right to sit with him on his throne (3:21). This reward is described as happening after the Second Coming (22:1–3, 21:24).

In each of the letters to the seven churches, the church is told to repent and are then told that if they are "victorious," they will be given rewards, and all the rewards that are described are rewards that are given after the Second Coming.

VICTORIOUS, OVERCOMES, CONQUERS

In the letters to the seven churches, the NIV translates the rewards as being given to "the one who is victorious." The NKJV and NASB both translate that same phrase as "he who overcomes," while the RSV translates it as "he who conquers." All of these are correct, and what is important to remember is that, in each case, the terms "victorious," "overcomes" and "conquers" convey the same meaning—to not only repent and align oneself with righteousness, but also to *endure* and to *persevere* through *what is to come*. In fact, the admonition to endure and to persevere is repeated in Revelation.

> This calls for *patient endurance* and faithfulness on the part of God's people. (13:10 NIV)

> This calls for *patient endurance* on the part of the people of God who keep his commands and remain faithful to Jesus. (14:12 NIV)

The call for "endurance" in Revelation 13 and 14 happens during the reign of the Beast, during the persecution of the church. As a result, we can understand the admonition to the seven churches of being "victorious," or of "overcoming" or "conquering," to be this same admonition of chapters 13 and 14, an admonition to *endure* through what is to come and, in enduring, to be victorious, to overcome, to conquer being persecuted. The seven churches are being encouraged to endure the persecution that is to come.

WHY THESE SEVEN CHURCHES?

Why does Jesus tell John to send these letters, and the ensuing Revelation, to these specific seven churches? There were many other churches in the world at the time, so why not send them all a letter with the Revelation; why only these specific seven churches?

As we have seen, these seven churches are the only part of Revelation that falls into the category of things that are "now," that is, they are the only things in Revelation that are actually existing in John's day. However, in Jesus' instructions to John in 1:19, it is important to note that the things that are "now" are inextricably tied to the things that "will take place later"—this means that there is a connection between those seven churches of that day and the events that will happen prior to the Second Coming.

How are we to understand this? We can understand it as follows.

The seven churches were all existing simultaneously in John's day, and they all had different problems and issues to deal with. As a result, we know that those different issues and problems within those churches also existed simultaneously in the world at that time—not only are the churches themselves the "things that are," but their issues and problems are also part of the "things that are." Since the "things that are" have a connection to the "things that will take place later" (1:19), we can understand that these seven churches, and their issues, *represent* the different types of issues and problems *that will exist* within the church that will be on Earth *prior to the Second Coming*. Just as the seven churches, and their problems, all existed simultaneously in John's own day, likewise those same *types* of problems will exist simultaneously within the church that is on Earth in the time prior to the Second Coming.

A PROPHECY OF SUCCESSIVE HISTORY

One proposal for understanding the seven letters is that each church represents successive *ages* of the church; that is, the seven churches represent the different characteristics of the church through future history as history makes its way towards the Second Coming.

So, for example, the first church addressed is the church in Ephesus, described positively as not tolerating wicked people, and as having tested and exposed false apostles. The church in Ephesus is also described as having endured hardships for the sake of Jesus' name. The Ephesian church is also described negatively as having forsaken the love they had at first (2:1–4). The successive-church-history understanding of the seven letters would say that the description of the church in Ephesus in that first letter is in fact a description of the first age of the church, as a whole, over the first few centuries of the church's existence (for example, up to 300 AD or so). This understanding would say that the early church, overall, was predominantly defined by not tolerating wicked people, as having tested and exposed false apostles, as having endured hardships for the sake of Jesus' name, and also as having forsaken the love they had at first.

The second church addressed is the church in Smyrna, described only positively, as enduring persecution and slander. The successive-church-history understanding of the seven letters would say that the description of the church in Smyrna in that second letter is in fact a description of the second age of the church, as a whole, over the *next* few centuries of the church's existence *after* the time period represented by the Ephesus church in the first letter (for example, 300 AD or so to 600 AD or so). This understanding would say that the second age of the church, overall, from 300 AD to 600 AD or so, was predominantly defined as the church being faithful and persecuted.

The third church addressed is the church in Pergamum, described as living where Satan has his throne (2:13), and commended for remaining faithful to Jesus despite living where Satan has his throne. However, they are also described negatively as holding on to, and tolerating, occultic teachings—the teachings of Balaam and the Nicolaitans (2:14–15). The successive-church-history understanding of the seven letters would say that the description of the church in Pergamum in that third letter is in fact a description of the third age of the church, as a whole, over the *next* few centuries of the church's existence after the period represented by *both* the church in Ephesus (to 300 AD or so) and Smyrna (300–600 AD or so), representing, for example, the third age of the church from 600 AD or so to 900 AD or so. This understanding would say that the church, overall, in that third age of the church, from 600–900 AD or so, was located where Satan had his throne, were faithful within that, yet also tolerated occultic teachings and practices.

And so on until we reach the final, or seventh, age of church history, as represented by the church in Laodicea (3:14–22), the only one of the seven churches to whom Jesus has nothing good to say, nothing to commend them for, describing them instead as being neither hot nor cold, as thinking that they are rich and as needing nothing, and yet, in fact, they are poor, needing everything—the Laodicean church is so badly off that Jesus tells this church he is *about* to spit them out of his mouth. In the successive-church-history understanding of the seven letters, the church of Laodicea is a description of the church on Earth in the days preceding the Second Coming, which has often been described as the period from the 1960s onward. As a result, in the successive-church-history understanding of the seven letters, the church on the Earth in the days preceding the Second Coming, the final age of the church, will be like the Laodicean church—neither hot nor cold, full of themselves, thinking they are rich but in fact are poor, and are about to be spit out from Jesus' mouth.

Is there any reason to understand the seven letters as a prophetic description of seven successive ages of future church history?

PROBLEMS WITH THE SUCCESSIVE-CHURCH-HISTORY VIEW

There are many problems with the successive-church-history view of the seven letters. The most immediate one, though it is a more general observational problem, is that there is no reason whatsoever to understand the seven letters in that way.

Yes, it is true that in Daniel 2:31–45, where Daniel describes the statue of Nebuchadnezzar's dream, Daniel does describe the sections of the statue as successive empires that will unfold throughout history after Nebuchadnezzar's Babylon, for Daniel specifically tells us that the head of that statue, the beginning of that sequence of successive empires, is in fact Nebuchadnezzar's Babylon (2:38). Those who hold to a successive-church-history understanding of the seven letters point to the statue of 2:31–45 as precedent and support for that successive view. However, one very striking difference between Daniel 2 and the seven letters of Revelation is that in Daniel we are specifically *told* that the sections of the statue are successive empires that will come after Nebuchadnezzar's Babylon—it is *not* left to be a matter of an interpretation; rather, Daniel specifically makes that meaning clear, so that we are without doubt. No such explanation is given for the letters to the seven churches, and there is nothing in the context of Revelation that would lead us to understand the seven letters as a prophecy of successive church ages.

But another, much more problematic issue with the successive-church-history view is this—when we look back on two thousand years of church history, there is no parallel between two thousand years of church history and the characterizations of the seven churches. For example, in the successive-church-history view, the very early church, or the first age of the church, is represented by the church in Ephesus, which is defined as having not tolerated wicked people, as having tested and exposed false apostles, as having endured hardships for the sake of Jesus' name, but also as having forsaken the love they had at first. This would then mean that, in the successive view, the very early church, the church of that first age of church history, was characterized in this same way, but history says otherwise.

The very early church was persecuted by the Roman emperor Nero in 64 AD, being blamed as the arsonists who started the great fire of Rome. Christian persecution continued under Marcus Aurelius (161–180 AD) and continued, intermittently, but regularly, until 313 AD. Right from the start, the church was persecuted, hunted, their property confiscated, with Christians put to death. To describe this first age of the church as being characterized as having "forsaken its first love" is an impossible argument to make—a church that had forsaken loving Jesus Christ would never welcome being put to death for his name's sake. The very early church cannot be described as a church that had "forsaken its first love."

Also, a major problem arises when trying to find a parallel between the church as described in the letter to Pergamum and a corresponding historical church age.

The church as described in the letter to Pergamum is described as "living where Satan has his throne." In the successive-church-history view, that description must then represent that an entire church age is defined by "living where Satan has his throne," but it is impossible to define any age of the church as fulfilling or meeting that description. If that description is applied to an entire church age, as it must be according to the successive-church-history view, then one has to say, since the church throughout the ages is spread throughout the world, not being confined to any one place or city, that the entire world must be the place "where Satan has his throne"—but this is impossible.

Satan is described as the "ruler of this world" (John 12:31[14:30; 16:11), but he is not God—Satan is a created being, and so, like all created beings, he is a creature subject to time and space, which means that he can only be in one place at any one time. In the letter to Pergamum, he is described as being *specifically* based out of Pergamum, having his "throne" located *there*. It is very likely, almost certain, that Satan, throughout history, has his "throne" somewhere on Earth, but only in one place at any one time, and it is generally always located in the sky above any specific location ("the prince of the power of the air," Eph 2:2). Therefore, as a created being subject to time and space, it is impossible that Satan would be everywhere in the world, across an entire age, all at the same time, yet, if we were to understand the letter of Pergamum as applying to a church age, that is the only conclusion we could reach. As a result, the description of the church in the letter of Pergamum as "living where Satan has his throne" is a powerful witness *against* the successive-church-history view of the seven letters.

Taken together, there is no good biblical reason to understand the seven letters as being an outline of successive ages of future church history.

If this is the case, then how do we understand the seven letters, and *why* are they in Revelation? We can understand the seven letters as being a *prophetic* warning to the church that *will* be on Earth in the days that precede the Second Coming.

A PROPHETIC HISTORICAL PARALLEL

It is important to remember that Revelation is specifically a prophecy about the days and events that precede the Second Coming. This is affirmed right at the outset, in 1:7, at the *beginning* of the book, which specifically invokes the Second Coming, which event is described in chapter 1 even before the Revelation is to be given. Likewise, Jesus himself *ends* the book of Revelation with a declaration that he is coming soon (22:7)—so, the Second Coming is invoked right at the start of the book, *before* the Revelation is given, and again at the *end* of the book, *after* the Revelation is given. Since the entire Revelation is bookended by an invocation and a declaration of the Second Coming, the clear conclusion is that the entire content of the book itself is describing the events and days that lead to the Second Coming. As a result, we can understand the seven letters as being a prophetic description of what the church will be like in *the days that precede the Second Coming*. This is a prophetic historical parallel.

The book of Revelation is clearly a book of symbolism and imagery, and this symbolism and imagery extends to using historical parallels to give understanding of future events. The clearest example of this is the "mark of the Beast."

The mark of the Beast is the numerical equivalent of the name of the Beast, which is 666 (13:16–18). It is also a historical fact that the numerical equivalent of the name of the Roman emperor Nero is also 666. This fact, and the fact of the seven churches of Revelation 2 and 3 existing as actual churches in John's day, has led some people to teach that the events of Revelation have in fact already been fulfilled ("preterism"). The fact that the number of Nero's name is 666 and the fact of the seven actual churches existing in John's day is certainly a historical parallel, but that in no way means that either Nero or the seven churches are the *fulfillment* of the prophecy; rather, both

Nero and the seven churches are used as a prophetic *illustration* of the prophesied *future events*.

For example, since both Nero and the Beast have the same numerical equivalent for their names, this means that Nero is an *illustration* of what the Beast will be like. Nero, as a Roman emperor, was an absolute ruler; therefore, since Nero is being used as a historical parallel to the Beast, which is affirmed by the fact that they have the same numerical equivalent for their name, we can then understand that the Beast, like Nero, will be an absolute ruler. Nero was the very first persecutor of Christians. Therefore, we can understand that the Beast will be a persecutor of Christians. Nero, as a historical parallel to the Beast, is not the *fulfillment* of the prophecies of the Beast; rather, he is a symbolic and prophetic representation of the coming Beast and, as such, gives us understanding of what the Beast will be like.

Likewise, the seven churches of John's day were seven actual churches in the world at that time, but they are *not* the fulfillment of the *prophesied events* being described in Revelation. Rather, like Nero, the seven churches are a historical parallel to the *future* church that *will* be on the Earth in *the days preceding the Second Coming*. As with Nero, by looking at the issues that each of the seven churches were dealing with, and at Jesus' admonition to each of them, we can then understand that the church on the Earth in the days preceding the Second Coming will, in fact, be dealing with those *same* issues as described in the seven letters. As a result, we can understand the seven letters as a prophetic outline of the church on Earth in the days preceding the Second Coming, and just as in John's day all seven churches existed simultaneously with one another, likewise, in the days preceding the Second Coming all the issues described for the seven churches in the seven letters will be existing simultaneously for the church throughout the world at that time. The seven churches of John's day, their issues, and Jesus' admonition to them are a prophetic historical parallel that is fulfilled by the *future church* that will be on Earth in the days preceding the Second Coming.

Also, it is important to remember that the seven churches were all contemporary with one another—they did not exist successively in John's day, but rather they all existed simultaneously with one another. So, at the same time that the Laodicean church was about to be spit out of Jesus' mouth, the Philadelphia church was existing and being commended for its great faithfulness and perseverance. This also applies to the prophetic historical parallel. If, for example, the church in North America in the later twentieth and then twenty-first centuries is like the Laodicean church, then, simultaneous with that, there will be, in communist countries and in even some Islamist countries, churches that are persecuted and that are a beacon and light of faithfulness for Jesus Christ. Again, we can understand the seven churches of Revelation, and their issues and admonitions, as being a prophetic historical parallel that describes the state of the future worldwide church in the days preceding the Second Coming, where some churches will be like the church in Ephesus, some may be like the church in Smyrna, while others may be like the church in Laodicea, and others still like the church in Philadelphia, and all of these churches will be existing on Earth together, at the same time, contemporary with one another.

One other important point to consider is this—why does Jesus *begin* the Revelation with the seven letters to the angels of the seven churches? It is because the judgment of Revelation *begins* with the church.

JUDGMENT BEGINS WITH THE HOUSE OF GOD

As discussed, it is essential to understand that there is no such thing as a rapture—there is no secret coming of Jesus Christ to remove the church from the Earth so as to spare the church from the events described in Revelation, from the rule of the Beast and from the Great Tribulation—such a teaching, in its contradiction to the Creed of the church and the Creed's description of the Second Coming, is a modern heresy. The church *remains* on Earth throughout *all* the events of Revelation (Matt 24:9–10; Rev 13:10; 14:12), is persecuted by the Beast, and is even overcome by the Beast (13:7).

As we will see in discussing the Seven Seals in detail, it is important to understand that the events of Revelation, the *judgments* of Revelation, *begin* with the apostasy, or rebellion, of the church against Jesus Christ.

> Let no one in any way deceive you, for it [the day of the Lord] will not come unless the apostasy comes first, and the man of lawlessness is revealed, the son of destruction. (2 Thess 2:3 NASB)

Paul in 2 Thessalonians specifically affirms the coming apostasy of the church, and he also affirms that the apostasy of the church must happen *before* the Beast comes to power.

Paul here clearly tells us that the "man of lawlessness" (which is the same Beast of Revelation, also commonly called the "antichrist") will *not* come until the church *first* turns away from Jesus Christ. The term "apostasy" means the church abandoning, forsaking, turning away from Jesus Christ. The ESV and the NIV both translate the Greek word for "apostasy" as "rebellion"—describing the church as *rebelling* against Jesus Christ, while the NKJV translates it as "the falling away." In any translation, the meaning is clear—the Beast of Revelation, and all the judgment events of Revelation, will not happen *until after the church* has *first* abandoned Jesus Christ, rebelled against him, and fallen away from him—this is absolutely clear.

The Lord Jesus Christ, in his outline and description of the Seven Seals in Matthew 24:3–31, begins by describing Seal 1 as follows:

> For many will come in my name, claiming, "I am the Messiah," and will deceive many. (24:5 NIV)

As we will see, to come in the name of Jesus Christ means to come as a Christian. When Jesus says that those people that will come in his name will say "I am the

Messiah," he means that those people who come in his name will say that *he*, Jesus Christ, is the Messiah, and then they will teach lies and deceive the church. This is Jesus' description of Seal 1 of Revelation and, like Paul, he affirms that the judgment of Revelation begins with the apostasy of the church. We will see, as we examine the Seven Seals, that Seal 1, as outlined in Matthew 24:5 and Revelation 6:1–2, is *defined* by the apostasy of the church, the same apostasy as affirmed by Paul in 2 Thessalonians 2:3 and by Jesus in Matthew 24:5.

Peter also very clearly affirms that the judgment of God upon the Earth will begin with the judgment of the church, for he tells us,

> For the time has come for *judgment to begin at the house of God*; and if it begins with us first, what will be the end of those who do not obey the gospel of God? (1 Pet 4:17 NASB)

The judgment referred to in 1 Peter is, in fact, the judgment of Revelation—the judgment of God upon the Earth. Peter affirms this when he contrasts the judgment upon the "house of God" (the church) with the judgment of those who do not believe, those who "do not obey the gospel of God"—the judgment of those who do not believe is the judgment of Revelation. Peter tells us that the judgments of Revelation *begin* as a *judgment* upon the church. First Peter 4:17 is in perfect accordance with 2 Thessalonians 2:3 and with Matthew 24:5; *all* of these verses are telling us the same thing—the judgment of Revelation will *begin* as judgment upon the church.

It is for this reason that Jesus precedes the giving of the Revelation with the seven letters, letters that outline for the churches the issues that they need to address in order to remain faithful. Since God's judgment upon the Earth is to *begin* as a judgment upon the *church*, Jesus *begins* Revelation with a warning and admonition to *the church* to repent, to persevere, to overcome, and to be rewarded. Jesus specifically refers to the time of coming global trial in his letter to the angel of the church in Philadelphia when he tells the church to *endure patiently* (compare to Rev 13:10; 14:12), telling them that he will keep them (i.e., *protect* them) from the time of trial coming *upon the whole world* (3:10), and in that context also telling them that he is "coming soon" (3:11). In these seven letters, prior to outlining the unfolding events of Revelation, Jesus, in effect, is telling *all* the church, "Something bad is about to come upon you; get your act together; persevere through it and you will be rewarded."

Second Thessalonians 2:3 is an exact affirmation of 1 Peter 4:17—judgment, the judgment of Revelation, does in fact *begin* with the church. We will also see, when we examine Seal 1 as described in Revelation 6, that Seal 1 is *this same judgment*—Seal 1 is the rebellion, apostasy, falling away of the church described in 1 Peter 4:17 and 2 Thessalonians 2:3, as well as by Jesus himself in Matthew 24:5. It is for this reason— since the judgment of Revelation *begins* with the house of God, the church—that Jesus *begins* Revelation with a *warning* and *admonition* to *the church* to be careful, watchful of sin, to repent, to be *prepared* for what is about to come, and to endure and overcome the coming trial. In so doing, the church will be rewarded.

THE ISSUES OF THE SEVEN CHURCHES

In his warning and admonition to the churches to get prepared for what is about to come upon the whole world (Rev 3:10), Jesus outlines specific issues that each of the churches must deal with, issues over which they need to repent, things they need to overcome, in order to get prepared for the trial that will be coming upon the world. Jesus also tells each of the churches that, in being prepared for that coming trial, they must endure that trial, overcome it, and thereby receive their reward.

Since these seven churches also represent the church on Earth prior to the Second Coming, likewise, the issues with which they were dealing, of which they needed to repent, will also be the same types of issues that the church on Earth before the Second Coming will be dealing with, of which it will need to repent. As a result, by looking at the issues that each of the seven churches were dealing with, we can understand the issues that the church in the world prior to the Second Coming will be dealing with.

THE ISSUES OF THE CHURCH IN EPHESUS

Jesus tells the church in Ephesus,

> you have left your first love. Therefore, remember from where you have fallen, and repent and do the deeds you did at first. (Rev 2:4–5 NASB)

The main issue for the church in Ephesus is that it had "left" its "first love"—that "first love" is Jesus himself; in saying that the church had left its first love, Jesus is telling the church in Ephesus that they have left *him*. This leaving of the church's "first love," in itself, is an affirmation of the same "apostasy" or "falling away" of 2 Thessalonians 2:3.

What does it mean to "have left your first love"? It means that other things had become more important than Jesus Christ to that church. When Jesus tells them to "repent" and to "do the deeds" they "did at first," it gives us an idea as to what that leaving of their first love looked like. At the very least, it tells us that the church was not serving Christ faithfully, that they were either spending their time and effort on all the wrong things or they were just paying lip service to serving Christ—i.e., their *deeds* were empty. As a result, we can know that some of the church on Earth in the time preceding the events of Revelation will likewise be spending their time and effort on all the wrong things, or just paying lip service to serving Christ.

THE ISSUES OF THE CHURCH IN SMYRNA

The church in Smyrna is one of only two churches about whom Jesus has *nothing* bad to say (the other is the church in Philadelphia)—Jesus does not outline *any* issues of which they need to repent. The church in Smyrna is told that they are a faithful church, that they will be tested, will be put in prison, will face "tribulation" (Rev 2:10)—this testing, imprisonment, and tribulation is the same "trial that is coming upon the whole world" of 3:10. Jesus tells the church in Smyrna that they must be faithful unto *death*, and they will receive their reward, the "crown of life" (2:10 NASB). From this we know that some of the church on Earth in the time preceding the events of Revelation will likewise be serving Jesus Christ faithfully, even unto death.

THE ISSUES OF THE CHURCH IN PERGAMUM

To the church in Pergamum, Jesus says,

> But I have a few things against you, because you have some there who hold the teaching of Balaam, who kept teaching Balak to put a stumbling block before the sons of Israel, to eat things sacrificed to idols and to commit sexual immorality. So you too, have some who in the same way hold to the teaching of the Nicolaitans. (Rev 2:14–15 NASB)

The reference to Balaam and Balak is a reference to events in the Old Testament (Num 22), and here Jesus specifically tells us that this church, the church in Pergamum, was similarly holding to teachings that accepted and promoted sexual immorality and occult practices (food sacrificed to idols). Similarly, the Nicolaitans, in essence, taught occult practice, teaching that occult practices were not incompatible with Christian teaching. As a result, we can know that some of the church on Earth in the time preceding the events of Revelation will likewise be accepting of sexual immorality as well as of occult practices.

"WHERE SATAN HAS HIS THRONE"

One other point made by Jesus to the church in Pergamum is that they, the church, live in the city "where Satan has his throne" (Rev 2:13). What does that mean? We can understand it as follows.

Revelation 2:13, in regard to the city of Pergamum being the city where Satan had his throne, can be understood in conjunction with Ezekiel 28:11–19 in regard to the city of Tyre, which describes Satan as the king of that city, as well as in conjunction with Isaiah 14:3–15 in regard to the king of Babylon (that is, Babylon the Great, still to come). In these passages, it is Satan who is described as having his throne in Pergamum (Rev 2:13), Satan who is described as the "king" of Tyre, the real power behind the "prince" of Tyre, a man who claims to be God (Ezek 28:1–2; 2 Thess 2:4;

Rev 13:2), Satan (Isa 14:12–15), who is described as being the real power behind the "king" of Babylon.

From these passages, as well as other verses (Eph 2:2 et al.), we can understand that Satan, as the ruler of this world (Luke 4:5–7; John 12:31; 14:30; 16:11; Eph 2:2), bases his operations within certain major cities upon the Earth, major cities of great influence, and that he moves his base of operations periodically depending on the import, or influence, of the city. For example, in Ezekiel 28:12 Satan is called the "king of Tyre." In its glory days, Tyre was among the most influential and important cities in the world, and Satan, in Ezekiel, is described as its "king." We know that this "king of Tyre" is not a human being, since that "king of Tyre" is described as the "anointed cherub," who was "perfect from the day he was *created*" (Ezek 28:13–14). A Cherub is the highest angelic rank, and to be the "anointed cherub" is to be the *greatest* among the cherubim. Also, human beings are born and not created. As a result, in describing the "king of Tyre" as being "created," we know, for certainty, that this is not a human being, but an angelic being, and since this angelic being is also described as the "anointed cherub," the greatest angelic being among the greatest angelic rank, we know this to be Satan—the "king of Tyre" is Satan. This contrasts with Ezekiel 28:2, which refers to the "prince of Tyre"—this "prince of Tyre" was, in fact, the actual *human* ruler of Tyre; he was a *man* (Ezek 28:2), yet, although God describes that man as a "prince," that human ruler was the one that the world would call "king." However, the *real* power behind that man ("prince of Tyre") is the "king of Tyre," and that "king of Tyre" is Satan. As the king of Tyre, Satan would have had his throne in the city of Tyre.

As a result, we can understand that in the day of Ezekiel Satan had his throne in the city of Tyre, while by the time of Revelation 2:13, in the days of the apostle John and the church in Pergamum, Satan's throne was located in Pergamum. This is why Jesus tells the church in Pergamum that they live "where Satan has his throne" (Rev 2:13 NIV). The fact that the issues that the church in Pergamum had to deal with, and repent of, were issues of sexual immorality and occult practices seems to be almost a natural extension of the fact that they lived in the city where Satan had his throne.

THE ISSUES OF THE CHURCH IN THYATIRA

To the church in Thyatira, Jesus says,

> You tolerate that woman Jezebel, who calls herself a prophet. By her teaching she misleads my servants into sexual immorality and the eating of food sacrificed to idols. (Rev 2:20 NIV)

Jezebel is perhaps the most wicked woman of the Bible. She was the pagan wife of Ahab, king of Judah (1 Kgs 16:31), introduced pagan worship to Judah (the Jews), killed God's prophets (1 Kgs 18:4), and engaged in occult practices (2 Kgs 9:22). For her extreme wickedness, and for her devotion to promote evil, sin, and wickedness across the whole kingdom of Judah, Jezebel suffered a terrible death, being thrown out of a window, trampled by horses and then eaten by dogs (2 Kgs 9:33–37).

Jesus tells the church in Thyatira that they "tolerate the woman Jezebel," and, as a result, are engaging in sexual immorality and occult practices. These are the same issues as the church of Pergamum. Why does Jesus give us *two* churches who are dealing with the *same* issues? It seems it is to emphasize that those two *particular* issues will be very major problems in the church before the events of Revelation. As a result, we can know that the issues of sexual immorality and occult practices will be a major problem for the church on Earth in the time preceding the events of Revelation.

THE ISSUES OF THE CHURCH IN SARDIS

To the church in Sardis, Jesus says,

> I know your deeds; you have a reputation of being alive, but you are dead. Wake up! Strengthen what remains and is about to die, for I have found your deeds unfinished in the sight of my God. (Rev 3:1–2 NIV)

Jesus tells the church in Sardis that they have a good "reputation," but in fact they are a "dead" church. What does it mean to be a dead church? At the very least, it means to hold to a *form* of religion (or faith) but deny its power (2 Tim 3:5). Since Jesus specifically tells them that their "deeds" are unfinished, we can understand that they are not serving him faithfully; rather, we can understand it as just going through the motions, or ritual or ceremony (the form of godliness), but with no power of faith behind that outward appearance. As a result, we can know that some of the church on Earth in the time preceding the events of Revelation will likewise have a good reputation as an organization, but in fact they will be empty and dead in their faith, holding only to a form of religiosity but denying its power.

THE ISSUES OF THE CHURCH IN PHILADELPHIA

As with the church in Smyrna, Jesus has nothing bad to say about the church in Philadelphia; he only has good to say about them. He encourages them to hold on to what they have, and they will receive their reward (Rev 3:7–13).

Just as Jesus gives us two churches who are both dealing with the same issues of sexual immorality and occult practices, so as to emphasize that those two particular issues will be a major problem for the church on Earth in the time preceding the events of Revelation, likewise, the fact that he gives us two churches who are completely faithful and are not engaged in *any* wrong practices tells us that, in the time preceding the events of Revelation, there will be a significant part of the church that will likewise be faithful in every way. It is in this context that we can understand Jesus' words to the church in Philadelphia, where he says,

> I will make those who are of the synagogue of Satan, who claim to be Jews though they are not, but are liars—I will make them come and fall down at your feet and acknowledge that I have loved you. (3:9 NIV)

Jesus here tells the church in Philadelphia that there are people who are calling themselves "Jews," but are actually of the devil ("synagogue of Satan"), and that Jesus will make those people come before the church in Philadelphia, humble themselves before the Philadelphian church, and acknowledge that Jesus has loved them.

The very strong implication is that these people who are calling themselves Jews, but are of the "synagogue of Satan," are in fact other so-called Christians, for, since we are told that Jesus will make those same people come before the church in Philadelphia, humble themselves before the people of that church, and acknowledge that *he* loved the Philadelphian church, we can understand that those same people were telling the Philadelphian church that Jesus did *not* love them. It is hard to imagine that such a condemnation, "Jesus does not love you," would come against Christians except by way of other people who called themselves Christians (i.e., nominal Christians). From this we can understand that in the time preceding the events of Revelation, the true and faithful church of Jesus Christ will be mocked, condemned, and abused by nominal Christians, or by a nominal church.

THE ISSUES OF THE CHURCH IN LAODICEA

The church in Laodicea is the only one of the seven churches to whom Jesus has nothing *good* to say—to them he only has bad things to say.

> I know your deeds, that you are neither cold nor hot. I wish you were either one or the other! So, because you are lukewarm—neither hot nor cold—I am about to spit you out of my mouth. You say, "I am rich; I have acquired wealth and do not need a thing." But you do not realize that you are wretched, pitiful, poor, blind and naked. (Rev 3:15–17 NIV)

Jesus tells the church in Laodicea that they are neither "hot" (full of fiery faith) nor "cold" (full of dead faith), but are only "lukewarm" (a little fiery, a little cold). As a result, Jesus says that he is about to spit them out of his mouth (the Greek term translated as "spit" can also be translated/understood as "vomit"). The Laodicean church says that it is rich and needs nothing, but Jesus tells them that they are, in fact, "wretched, pitiful, poor, blind and naked."

The Laodicean church was a church that was full of itself, a proud church, a church who thought they had everything and needed nothing (this implies that they would have thought that they also did not need God). They would be, in the eyes of the world, a wealthy church, a church engaged in events and gatherings all Christian in name but in fact more like a wealthy social club, justifying its programs by applying the name of Christ to those programs, but programs which, ultimately, were nothing about Christ but rather were more about self-satisfaction and ostentatious accomplishment. The fact that Jesus says, to this church only, that he is about to "spit," or "vomit," them out of his mouth shows just how wretched those particular practices are—even to the churches that engage in, or accept, or tolerate sexual immorality and occult practices, Jesus does not threaten to spit them out of his mouth, but to this church, the Laodicean church, he does threaten to spit them out of his mouth.

As a result, we can know that some of the church on Earth in the time preceding the events of Revelation will likewise be wealthy and will think that they need nothing, but they will be neither hot nor cold; they will be lukewarm, worthy only of being spit out of Jesus' mouth—but they too, like all the other of the seven churches, are called to repent.

LETTERS TO THE ANGELS

It is very important to note that Jesus specifically tells John to address each of the letters to the "angel" of that church:

> To the angel of the church of Ephesus write: (2:1 NIV)
>
> To the angel of the church in Smyrna write: (2:8 NIV)
>
> To the angel of the church in Pergamum write: (2:12 NIV)
>
> To the angel of the church in Thyatira write: (2:18 NIV)
>
> To the angel of the church in Sardis write: (3:1 NIV)
>
> To the angel of the church in Philadelphia write: (3:7 NIV)
>
> To the angel of the church in Laodicea write: (3:14 NIV)

Why does Jesus tell John to address each letter to the angel of that church? What does it mean for a church to have an angel? We can understand it as follows.

Each church has an angel assigned to it so as to *protect* that church. The angel assigned by God to each church congregation throughout the world is God's special, divine protection over his people, over his church, with the angel of that church specifically assigned to protect that church from the attacks of the *enemy*. It is God's additional spiritual protection over each church, his protection over that church from spiritual attack. This would be exactly parallel to Daniel's description of God's angelic protection over Judah and, by extension, Israel.

> At that time Michael, the great prince who protects your people, will arise. (Dan 12:1 NIV)

No one supports me against them except Michael, your prince. (Dan 10:21 NIV)

Michael is one of the mightiest (perhaps the mightiest) of the angelic host, specifically called "*the* archangel" (Jude 9). Twice he contested directly with Satan and twice Michael defeats Satan, all by the power of God (Jude 9; Rev 12:7–9). Michael is described by Daniel as "the great prince who *protects* your people" (Dan 12:1). Daniel was a Jew, of the nation Judah, so his people were the people of Judah, the Jews (but this can also possibly be expanded to include the lost ten tribes of Israel). In Daniel 10 the angel tells Daniel that the reason that Michael came to his (the angel's) aid was because that angel was being opposed, or blocked, from coming to Daniel, blocked by the "prince" of Persia, a fallen angel (Dan 10:13). Since that fallen angel is described as the "prince" of Persia, we see that entire *nations*, and even entire *empires*, have angelic beings assigned to them—those assigned by God are assigned to *protect* the people (as is the case with Michael, assigned to protect Daniel's people), but the enemy also assigns fallen angels to *corrupt* and *harm* people (as is the case with the prince of Persia).

We are also told in Hebrews that angels are sent to serve Christians, the church.

> But to which of the angels has He ever said:
> "Sit at My right hand, till I make Your enemies Your footstool"?
> Are they not all ministering spirits sent forth to minister for those who will inherit salvation? (Heb 1:13–14 NKJV)

As a result, we can understand the "angel of the church" in exactly this same way—just as entire nations have angelic protection assigned to them by God, likewise God's church, and all the individual (local) churches that comprise his one global church, have angelic protection assigned to them to protect them from the attacks of the enemy—God provides supernatural protection for his people, even though his people may not be aware of it.

It is for this reason that Jesus tells John to address the letters to the *angel* of each church, for the angel of each church is the *protector* of that church. In each letter, Jesus is telling each church to repent of the things they need to repent of, but he is *also* telling the *angel* of each church to *especially* look out for that church *in those specific ways*, so that, as the angelic protector of that church, that angel can provide an especially vigilant protection for that church in those areas.

The fact that Jesus addresses each letter to the angel, or protector, of each church further emphasizes, and affirms, that each of those churches need *protection*. As a result, we can know that some of the church on Earth in the time preceding the events of Revelation will likewise need a particularly vigilant angelic protection, protection not only around the issues of sin that will need to be dealt with, but also protection from the attacks of the enemy and from the judgments that are about to come upon the Earth.

8

Prelude to Judgment—Revelation 4 and 5

AFTER THE SEVEN LETTERS are given, the following two chapters of Revelation, chapters 4 and 5, are the prelude to the judgments outlined in the book. After Jesus has finished dictating the seven letters to John, John looks up and sees a door standing open in the sky (4:1), and he hears a voice which sounds the same as the voice previously heard (1:10), and the voice says to John,

> Come up here, and I will show you what must take place after this. (4:1 NIV)

Immediately upon hearing that voice, John is "in the Spirit" (4:2) and is taken to heaven, to the throne room of God, where he sees a throne and someone sitting on the throne. John tells us that the one sitting on the throne "had the appearance of jasper and ruby," and that the throne was surrounded by "a rainbow that shone like an emerald"—this is the throne of God. He also tells us that "Surrounding the great throne were twenty-four other thrones," and upon those thrones were seated twenty-four "elders." The elders "were dressed in white and had crowns of gold on their heads." From God's throne "came flashes of lightning, rumblings and peals of thunder." In front of God's throne were seven blazing lamps, which John tells us are the "seven spirits" of God, or, in some translations, the "sevenfold" Spirit of God. Also, "in front of the throne was what looked like a sea of glass, clear as crystal" (Rev 4:3–6 NIV).

In the center of that scene, around God's throne, were four living creatures, and each creature was covered in eyes. "The first living creature was like a lion, the second was like an ox, the third was like a man, the fourth was like a flying eagle" (4:7 NIV). Each living creature had six wings, and day and night they are constantly giving praise to God, saying,

> Holy, holy, holy is the Lord God Almighty, who was, and is, and is to come. (4:8 NIV)

Every time that the four living creatures speak praise to God, the twenty-four elders also fall down before God, worship him, lay their crowns before God's throne, and say,

> You are worthy, our Lord and God, to receive glory and honor and power, for you created all things, and by your will they were created and have their being. (4:11 NIV)

All of this is described in Revelation 4:1–11. What does this all mean?

JOHN IN HEAVEN

It is important to understand that John was physically taken to heaven, to stand before God's throne, and that he is describing to us what his eyes see and what his ears hear—John is *not* having a vision, but an actual, physical experience; he is taken *bodily* to heaven, to be shown what will take place.

How do we know this is not a vision?

The voice that speaks to John in 4:1 specifically tells him to "Come up here, and I will show you what must take place after this" (NIV). The voice does *not* say, "Stay where you are and behold this vision," or something similar, but rather the voice explicitly tells John to "Come up here," meaning that John is physically to come to the place from which that voice is speaking. John then tells us that, immediately upon being commanded to "come up," he is taken by the Spirit and finds himself in heaven before God's throne. As a result, we know from this description that John is physically taken to heaven, and that he is describing to us what he physically sees and hears, just as he was commanded to, rather than just having a vision while remaining on the island of Patmos.

GOD'S THRONE

The first thing John describes for us, after he is brought to heaven, is God's throne, and someone sitting on that throne. John tells us that the one sitting on that throne had the appearance of precious stones—namely, jasper and ruby. In addition to that, John tells us that a rainbow encircled the throne, and that the rainbow "shone like an emerald" (4:2–3).

Why does John describe God in terms of precious stones, and why does he also describe the rainbow in terms of a precious stone?

THE RAINBOW

Throughout the Bible, God's glory is described as having the appearance of a rainbow.

> Like the appearance of a rainbow in the clouds on a rainy day, so was the radiance around him. This was the appearance of the likeness of the glory of the Lord. (Ezek 1:28 NIV)

> I have set my rainbow in the clouds, and it will be the sign of the covenant between me and the earth. (Gen 9:13 NIV)

In Genesis 9:13, God describes the rainbow as "my rainbow," and Ezekiel 1:28 specifically tells us that the rainbow that surrounded God was, in fact, the appearance of the likeness of God's glory. As a result, we know that God's glory is represented, or displayed, as a rainbow that surrounds his throne, and God himself tells us that the rainbow is his rainbow. When John, in heaven, describes the rainbow surrounding God's throne, he is in fact affirming exactly the same thing that Ezekiel saw when he described God's glory, and also affirms what God himself declares as his own—the rainbow, surrounding God's throne as a display of his glory.

PRECIOUS STONES

Throughout the Bible, precious stones are connected with God, with his presence, and with the physical heaven. The clearest example of this is the city New Jerusalem (Rev 21:15–21), which is described as a physical city that descends from heaven to Earth, to remain forever on Earth, and is described as having a foundation of twelve precious stones, which include jasper, emerald, and ruby, the same three stones that John uses to describe God's person and presence (Rev 4:2–3).

Also, precious stones were part of the high priest's garments, specifically his breastplate (Exod 28:15–21). These twelve stones represented the twelve tribes of Israel and were worn by the high priest when he would go into the tabernacle, and later the temple, to meet with God. The twelve stones upon the high priest's breastplate signified the high priest's representation of the twelve tribes of Israel before God (Exod 28:21).

A similar description is given about Lucifer, prior to his fall, where he is also described as wearing nine precious stones upon his garment (Ezek 28:13). In his case there were only nine stones, not twelve as in the case of the high priest, and that is because there are nine ranks of angels (cherubs, seraphs, thrones, dominions, powers, principalities, rulers, authorities, angels), and, in Lucifer's case, each of the nine stones represented one of the angelic ranks. By wearing those nine stones upon his own garment, this signified that Lucifer, like the high priest in regard to the tribes of Israel, was representing all nine angelic ranks—the entire angelic host—before God. Also, the nine stones on Lucifer's garment are exactly the same as nine of the twelve stones on the high priest's garment, once again affirming the understanding of representation.

Also, in Ezekiel 28:14, the unfallen Lucifer is described as being on the "holy mount of God" (that is, the mount in heaven upon which is situated God's throne), and as walking among the "fiery stones." We are not told the nature of those fiery stones, but they are intimately connected with God's presence, with his throne, and we therefore have very good reason to understand those fiery stones as also being precious stones.

Furthermore, we are told the following:

> Moses and Aaron, Nadab and Abihu, and the seventy elders of Israel went up and saw the God of Israel. Under his feet was something like a pavement made of lapis lazuli, as bright blue as the sky. (Exod 24:9–10 NIV)

Moses, Aaron, and the leaders of Israel saw God, and they described him as having a pavement of precious stone beneath his feet, a pavement of lapis lazuli. Once again, God's presence is connected with precious stones.

When John describes God, and his very presence, as appearing like jasper, ruby, and emerald, it is in complete harmony with the many other passages in the Bible that also connect God's presence with similar precious stones. As a result, we can be certain that precious stones have an intimate connection with God and his very presence.

FLASHES OF LIGHTNING, RUMBLINGS, AND PEALS OF THUNDER

In Revelation 4:5, we are told the following:

> From the throne came flashes of lightning, rumblings and peals of thunder. (NIV)

In John's description of God's throne, he very clearly tells us that *"from the throne came flashes of lightning, rumblings and peals of thunder."* Although it may seem like only a minor detail, it is in fact important, for almost the exact same description occurs a further three times in Revelation.

> and there came peals of thunder, rumblings, flashes of lightning and an earthquake. (8:5 NIV)

> And there came flashes of lightning, rumblings, peals of thunder, an earthquake and a severe hailstorm. (11:19 NIV)

> Then there came flashes of lightning, rumblings, peals of thunder and a severe earthquake. (16:18 NIV)

It is extremely important to understand the occurrence of each of these three additional references to "flashes of lightning, rumblings and peals of thunder." John specifically tells us in 4:5 that the "flashes of lightning, rumblings and peals of thunder" come from the throne of God. This defines the nature of the "flashes of lightning, rumblings and peals of thunder"—they come from God.

The only other three occurrences of that same expression, in the entire book of Revelation, all happen at a very specific time—in 8:5 it occurs only *after* Seal 7 has been opened; in 11:19 it occurs only *after* Trumpet 7 has been sounded; in 16:18 it occurs only *after* Bowl 7 has been poured. Is it a coincidence that the "flashes of lightning, rumblings and peals of thunder" occur *only* after Seal 7, Trumpet 7, and Bowl 7? No, it is not a coincidence, for, as we will see, that very expression— "flashes of lightning, rumblings and peals of thunder"—is used as a sort of punctuation to delineate the three timelines of Revelation. We will see that the three timelines—the timeline of the Seals, the timeline of the Trumpets, the timeline of the Bowls—are not successive; that is, they do *not* come one after the other; rather, the Bowl timeline is contained *within* the Trumpet timeline, and the Trumpet timeline is contained *within* the overall Seal timeline. The descriptions of each of the three timelines are delineated by, are set apart by, the description of "flashes of lightning, rumblings and peals of thunder," which is described as coming from the throne of God, and so is *not* a description of earthly events, but rather is a description of heavenly events.

The three additional occurrences of that expression include the same "flashes of lightning, rumblings and peals of thunder" description—that is the same description as what ensues from the throne of God—but in 11:19 there is the *added* description of "an earthquake and a severe hailstorm," while in 16:18 there is the *added* description of "a severe earthquake." We can understand that as follows—the description of "flashes of lightning, rumblings and peals of thunder" is a description of God's throne, a *heavenly* description, a divine delineation of a timeline, while the *added* elements of an "earthquake" and a "hailstorm" are a description of the corresponding *earthly* event.

We will see that the description of "flashes of lightning, rumblings and peals of thunder" is God's way, in his Revelation, of delineating the three timelines of the Revelation.

THE TWENTY-FOUR THRONES AND ELDERS

In Revelation 4:4, John tells us that, surrounding God's own throne, there were twenty-four other thrones, and upon those thrones were seated elders, with each elder being dressed in white and having a crown of gold upon his head.

Why are there twenty-four thrones? And who are these elders?

HUMAN OR ANGEL?

Discussions of the identity of the twenty-four elders of Revelation usually come down to two possible understandings as to their identity—either they are men or they are angels. It is certain that the twenty-four elders are *not* angels, and here is how we can know that.

First, they are seated on thrones, which means that they are ruling. Holy angels are never depicted, or described, as sitting on any throne, whereas human beings are.

PRELUDE TO JUDGMENT—REVELATION 4 AND 5

> Jesus said to them, "Truly I tell you, at the renewal of all things, when the Son of Man sits on his glorious throne, you who have followed me will also sit on twelve thrones, judging the twelve tribes of Israel. (Matt 19:28 NIV)

Jesus specifically tells his apostles that when he is seated on his glorious throne, the twelve apostles will also sit on twelve thrones.

We are also told,

> To the one who is victorious, I will give the right to sit with me on my throne, just as I was victorious and sat down with my Father on his throne. (Rom 3:21 NIV)

Here, Jesus himself tells us that Christians will sit with him on his throne. Thrones are reserved only for Christians, and never for angels. As a result, since the twenty-four elders are described as sitting on thrones, we can know that they are not angelic beings, but rather they are men.

CROWNS

In addition to being described as seated upon thrones, the twenty-four elders are described as wearing crowns of gold. Once again, throughout the entire Bible, holy angels are *never* described as wearing crowns, but Christians are:

> Blessed is the one who perseveres under trial because, having stood the test, that person will receive the crown of life that the Lord has promised to those who love him. (Jas 1:12 NIV)

> Everyone who competes in the games goes into strict training. They do it to get a crown that will not last, but we do it to get a crown that will last forever. (1 Cor 9:25 NIV)

> Now there is in store for me the crown of righteousness, which the Lord, the righteous Judge, will award to me on that day—and not only to me, but also to all who have longed for his appearing. (2 Tim 4:8 NIV)

> And when the Chief Shepherd appears, you will receive the crown of glory that will never fade away. (1 Pet 5:4 NIV)

> For what is our hope, our joy, or the crown in which we will glory in the presence of our Lord Jesus when he comes? Is it not you? (1 Thess 2:19 NIV)

Christians are repeatedly described as being awarded crowns, and a number of different types of crowns—the "crown of life," the "crown of glory," the "crown of righteousness"—whereas angels are never described as wearing crowns.

As a result, since the twenty-four elders are described as wearing crowns, we can know that they are not angelic beings, but rather they are men.

WHITE ROBES

In addition to being seated upon thrones and wearing crowns, the twenty-four elders are described as being robed in white. This is in exact correspondence to the description of redeemed Christians—Revelation 3:4; 3:18; 6:11; 7:9; and 7:13 all specifically describe Christians as being robed in white.

We see then that the three elements that are ascribed to the twenty-four elders are in fact elements that are specifically ascribed to redeemed humanity—*only* redeemed humanity sits enthroned with Christ, wears crowns, and are robed in white, whereas angels are *never* described in those terms. As a result, there is no question that the twenty-four elders of Revelation 4 are redeemed human beings, and not angels.

ELDERS

Also, those twenty-four crowned and enthroned men are specifically described as "elders." Again, angels are never described in the Bible, in any capacity, as being "elders"; that term is only ever used of human beings.

Throughout the Bible, elders are depicted as people in wise authority over others (Exod 19:7; 24:1; Lev 9:1; Num 11:30; Matt 27:20; Acts 4:8 et al.). As a result, we can understand the elders of Revelation 4 in the same way—they are certainly redeemed men; they are Christians and they are *elders*, which is to say that, as elders, they are in a position of *authority* over the rest of the church. This is further affirmed when these same elders are described as holding the prayers of the saints.

> And when he had taken it, the four living creatures and the twenty-four elders fell down before the Lamb. Each one [elders] had a harp and they were holding golden bowls full of incense, which are the prayers of God's people. (Rev 5:8 NIV)

The elders are described as holding bowls full of incense, which bowls are the prayers of God's people. These are the prayers of the saints (also Rev 8:3–4). To hold the prayers of the saints represents that these elders were in a position of authority over the church, and in fact, just by virtue of being *elders* (i.e., older) the strong implication is that these twenty-four men were *foundational* to the church, which again is further affirmed by the fact that they hold the prayers of the saints.

Once again, their very description as elders affirms that these are not angelic beings, but rather they are men, and they are men in positions of authority within the church, even men who were foundational to the church.

WHO ARE THE TWENTY-FOUR ELDERS?

Why are there twenty-four elders? Why not forty? What is the significance of the number twenty-four? As with everything about the Bible, there is always meaning and significance in the details. We can understand the number twenty-four as follows:

Jesus specifically tells his apostles that they will sit on twelve thrones with him, after he sits upon his glorious throne:

> And Jesus said to them, "Truly I say to you, that you who have followed Me, in the regeneration when the Son of Man will sit on his glorious throne, you also shall sit upon twelve thrones, judging the twelve tribes of Israel." (Matt 19:28 NASB)

Jesus is very clear—his twelve apostles will each sit enthroned with him on twelve individual thrones. Why is that? It is because the twelve apostles are foundational to the birth of the church.

The teachings of the twelve apostles as being the very foundation of the church is specifically attested to in the Creed when it refers to the "apostolic church." The term "apostolic church" means the church as founded upon the teachings of the apostles (which is the writings of the apostles, the New Testament). The teachings of the apostles are foundational to the church.

Furthermore, this foundational role of the apostles within the church is further affirmed by the twelve apostles being specifically and literally described as the very "foundation" of the New Jerusalem.

> And the wall of the city had twelve foundation stones, and on them were the twelve names of the twelve apostles of the Lamb. (Rev 21:14 NASB)

Since Jesus specifically tells his apostles that they will sit with him on twelve thrones, and since the twelve apostles are specifically described as being the very "foundation" of the New Jerusalem, and since the very essence of an elder is a foundational position, and since the elders of Revelation 4 and 5 also hold the prayers of the saints, which in itself represents a position of authority within the church, there is very strong reason to understand that twelve of these twenty-four thrones/elders are, or represent, the twelve apostles.

That being the case, then what about the other twelve thrones/elders? There is good reason to understand the remaining twelve elders to be the twelve sons of Jacob, the fathers of the twelve tribes of Israel. This is affirmed in Revelation 21, again in the description of the New Jerusalem.

> It had a great and high wall, with twelve gates, and at the gates twelve angels; and names were written on the gates, which are the names of the twelve tribes of the sons of Israel. (21:12 NASB)

In addition to the New Jerusalem having twelve foundations, with each foundation bearing the name of one of the twelve apostles, we are told that the New Jerusalem will also have twelve gates that allow entrance to the city, and upon each of the twelve gates is written the names of one of the twelve tribes of Israel, which is to say the names of the *fathers* of the twelve tribes of Israel are each written on one of the twelve gates of the New Jerusalem.

As fathers of the twelve tribes of Israel, Jacob's sons occupy a foundational position in the existence of the nation Israel. Once again, since the position of elder is itself a foundational position, this perfectly ties in with the twelve sons of Jacob having a foundational role, not only in Israel, but also in salvation, since it was through one of the tribes of Israel, the tribe of Judah, that the Messiah himself would be born, accomplishing salvation for all humanity (Heb 7:14; Rev 5:5).

As a result, in light of the foundational role of the twelve sons of Jacob in regard to salvation, we can understand that the remaining twelve elders seated upon the remaining twelve thrones are, or represent, the twelve sons of Jacob, the fathers of the twelve tribes of Israel.

We can therefore understand that twelve of the twenty-four enthroned and crowned elders of Revelation 4 and 5 are the twelve apostles, while the remaining twelve enthroned and crowned elders are the fathers of the twelve tribes of Israel. These twenty-four elders are the crowned and enthroned foundational pillars of the church, just as they are also the twelve foundations of the New Jerusalem and the twelve gates of the New Jerusalem. As such, we can understand these twenty-four elders as being in a special position of authority within the church, and hence their being enthroned on their own individual thrones surrounding the very throne of God.

THE FOUR LIVING CREATURES

John also describes for us what he calls "four living creatures." These are four unusual creatures—these are not animals, but something different. John describes the four living creatures as being in the center, around the throne, and covered everywhere with eyes (Rev 4:6). He also describes them as having six wings and as looking, respectively, like a lion, an ox, a man, and an eagle (4:7–8).

What are these four living creatures? We know that they are cherubim, of the highest angelic rank. How can we know this? These four living creatures also appear in Ezekiel 1 and 10, and Ezekiel explains them for us.

> Also from within it came the likeness of four living creatures. And this was their appearance: they had the likeness of a man. Each one had four faces, and each one had four wings. Their legs were straight, and the soles of their feet were like the soles of calves' feet. They sparkled like the color of burnished bronze. The hands of a man were under their wings on their four sides; and each of the four had faces and wings. Their wings touched one another. The

creatures did not turn when they went, but each one went straight forward. As for the likeness of their faces, each had the face of a man; each of the four had the face of a lion on the right side, each of the four had the face of an ox on the left side, and each of the four had the face of an eagle. Thus were their faces. Their wings stretched upward; two wings of each one touched one another, and two covered their bodies. And each one went straight forward; they went wherever the spirit wanted to go, and they did not turn when they went. (Ezek 1:5–12 NKJV)

Ezekiel describes these four living creatures as *each* having four faces—the face of a man, a lion, an ox, and an eagle—and they are described as having four wings.

Ezekiel also tells us that these four living creatures were each accompanied by a wheel, and he tells us that the rims of these wheels were full of eyes.

As for their rims, they were so high they were awesome; and their rims were full of eyes, all around the four of them. When the living creatures went, the wheels went beside them; and when the living creatures were lifted up from the earth, the wheels were lifted up. Wherever the spirit wanted to go, they went, because there the spirit went; and the wheels were lifted together with them, for the spirit of the living creatures was in the wheels. (Ezek 1:18–20 NKJV)

This is a striking parallel to the four living creatures of Revelation, who are described as having the features of a man, a lion, an ox, and an eagle, multiple wings and covered with, or associated with, many eyes.

We encounter these same living creatures in Ezekiel 10.

And when I looked, there were four wheels by the cherubim, one wheel by one cherub and another wheel by each other cherub; the wheels appeared to have the color of a beryl stone. As for their appearance, all four looked alike—as it were, a wheel in the middle of a wheel. When they went, they went toward any of their four directions; they did not turn aside when they went, but followed in the direction the head was facing. They did not turn aside when they went. And their whole body, with their back, their hands, their wings, and the wheels that the four had, were full of eyes all around. As for the wheels, they were called in my hearing, "Wheel." Each one had four faces: the first face was the face of a cherub, the second face the face of a man, the third the face of a lion, and the fourth the face of an eagle. And the cherubim were lifted up. This was the living creature I saw by the River Chebar. (10:9–15 NKJV)

This is the living creature I saw under the God of Israel by the River Chebar, and I knew they were cherubim. Each one had four faces and each one four wings, and the likeness of the hands of a man was under their wings. And the likeness of their faces was the same as the faces which I had seen by the River

Chebar, their appearance and their persons. They each went straight forward. (10:20–22 NKJV)

In this passage, Ezekiel again describes the four living creatures, and he tells us specifically in 10:15 and 10:20 that these living creatures were *the same* living creatures of Ezekiel 1, which he saw when he was by the River Chebar. He also tells us that these living creatures were cherubim (10:20), members of the highest angelic rank. The four living creatures are again described as having four wings and as having the features of a man, a lion, and an eagle, and each as being accompanied by a wheel, and that *both* the wheels *and the bodies* of the four living creatures were full of eyes.

However, even though Ezekiel tells us specifically in Ezekiel 10 that these four living creatures (who are cherubim) are the same four living creatures of Ezekiel 1 that he saw by the River Chebar, they are slightly differing in their description.

For example, in Ezekiel 1 the living creatures are described as each having four faces—the face of a lion, a man, an *ox*, and an eagle (1:10), and in Ezekiel 10:14 they are also described as each having four faces but the faces are the face of a *cherub*, a man, a lion, and an eagle. In Ezekiel 10, the face of the ox has been replaced by the face of a cherub, yet Ezekiel specifically tells us that these are the same creatures as Ezekiel 1 (10:20).

Furthermore, in Ezekiel 1 the rims of the wheels that accompany the living creatures are described as being full of eyes, whereas in 10:12 the living creatures *themselves*, as well as the wheels that accompany them, are described as being covered everywhere by eyes. How can the description of the same four living creatures differ in Ezekiel 1 and Ezekiel 10?

We know with absolute certainty that the four living creatures of Ezekiel 1 and 10 are the very same creatures (10:20), for Ezekiel specifically tells us that they are the same creatures (10:15, 20), and yet they differ in their appearance (faces) and their covering of eyes. We also know from Ezekiel 10 that these four living creatures are cherubim. Is this a description of *all* cherubim? No, it is not, for cherubim were also depicted on the ark of the covenant (1 Kgs 8:7; Ezek 25:18–22) and depicted as having *two* wings. Cherubim also guard the Tree of Life (Gen 3:24), and Lucifer himself is described as the anointed Cherub (Ezek 28:14, 16). Only in Ezekiel 1 and 10 are these *specific* Cherubim described as the four living creatures, and it seems that their appearance, as depicted in Ezekiel 1 and 10, is a changing appearance because it is a symbolic appearance. In that respect, the appearance of the four living creatures will change depending on the prophecy, or symbolism, being conveyed. It is in that regard that we come to the four living creatures of Revelation 4.

The four living creatures of Revelation 4 are described as being covered completely with eyes (as are the living creatures of Ezekiel 10), but with *one* creature being like a lion, another creature being like an ox, a third creature being like a man, and the fourth being like a flying eagle. These are the exact same descriptions of the four faces that *each* creature had in Ezekiel 1, however, in Ezekiel 1 *each* creature had *all four* of these faces, whereas in Revelation 4 only *one* creature was like a lion, and *another* creature was like an ox, while another was like a man and the fourth was like a flying eagle—each creature in Revelation has only *one* face, but, among the four living creatures of Revelation, they are the same four faces of each of the four living creatures of Ezekiel 1.

Just as the four living creatures of Ezekiel 1 appear again in Ezekiel 10 but look differently than they did in Ezekiel 1, likewise those *same* four living creatures of Ezekiel 1 and 10 appear now in Revelation 4 and are *again* of a slightly differing description. As with the differences in description of the four living creatures between Ezekiel 1 and 10, we can understand the differing description of Revelation 4, of those *same* living creatures, as being the result of the symbolism being conveyed as it relates to the specific prophecy about to unfold—the appearance of the four living creatures in Revelation 4 is representational and is symbolic of what is about to unfold, just as it was in Ezekiel 1 and 10, and the changing appearance is due to the changing message about to be conveyed. However, one thing that we can be certain of is that the four living creatures in Revelation 4 are the very same living creatures of Ezekiel 1 and 10, and they are cherubim.

CHERUBIM AND THE THRONE OF GOD

Throughout the Bible, cherubim are specifically connected to the throne of God.

> The LORD reigns; Let the peoples tremble! He dwells *between* the cherubim; Let the earth be moved! (Ps 99:1 NKJV)

> O LORD of hosts, God of Israel, *the One* who dwells *between* the cherubim, (Isa 37:16 NKJV)

God is repeatedly depicted as being enthroned *between* the cherubim, and, in the scene that John describes in Revelation 4, where he tells us that the four living creatures were *around* the throne, this also places the throne of God *in between* the four living creatures. Since we know from Ezekiel 10 that the four living creatures are cherubim, then the description by John of the four living creatures being *around* the throne of God means that God, in John's description, is in fact enthroned *between* the cherubim, exactly as described in Psalm 99:1 and Isaiah 37:16.

As a result, this is further affirmation that the four living creatures are cherubim between whom sits God enthroned.

THE SCROLL

In Revelation 5, John tells us that, in that heavenly scene, he sees a scroll in the right hand of the one seated upon the throne. He tells us that the scroll had writing on both sides and that it was sealed with *Seven Seals*. An angel then asks, with a loud voice, if there is anyone worthy to open the Seven Seals of the scroll. John tells us that no one, anywhere—not any being in heaven or Earth, not any one in the entire creation—was found "who could open the scroll or even look inside it" (Rev 5:1–3). John then begins to weep because no one was found who could open the Seven Seals of the scroll. Then one of the twenty-four elders speaks to John and tells him not to weep, that there *is* someone who could open the Seven Seals of the scroll—there is only *one* who can open those Seven Seals, and it is the "Lion of the tribe of Judah, the Root of David"; *only he* can open the Seven Seals. John then looks and sees a "Lamb, looking as if it had been slain, standing at the center of the throne," surrounded by the four living creatures and the elders (5:6). The Lamb had seven horns and seven eyes, which John tells us are the "seven spirits" (or the "sevenfold Spirit") of God, and the Lamb approached the throne and took the scroll from the right hand of the one who sat upon the throne. At that, all the elders, the four living creatures and the entire uncountable, vast heavenly host sing worship to the Lamb, declaring the Lamb to be "worthy to take the scroll and to open its seals" (5:9). This Lamb, the only one who was worthy to take the scroll and to open the Seven Seals, is Jesus Christ.

It is extremely important to understand that the Seven Seals are nothing like the Trumpet or Bowl judgments described later in Revelation—the Seven Seals are completely unique. Any one of a number of angels can blow any of the Trumpets (8:2), and any one of a number of angels can pour any of the Bowls (15:7), but *no one*, anywhere, in the entire creation can open the Seven Seals—*only* Jesus Christ can open the Seven Seals. Why is that?

It's because the Seven Seals are the *entirety* of the judgment, and *only* the Judge can release the judgments.

JESUS IS THE JUDGE

The Bible tells us very clearly that it is Jesus Christ, the Son of God, and *only* Jesus Christ, *not* the Father, who is the Judge of all things.

> Moreover, the Father judges no one, but has entrusted all judgment to the Son. (John 5:22 NIV)

God the Father judges *no one* and *nothing*—*all* judgment has been given to the Son, and *only* to the Son; Jesus Christ *alone* is the Judge, the Judge of all things and of all beings. It is because Jesus alone is the Judge of all things that *only* he, the Judge, can open the Seven Seals of judgment. As we shall see, from Jesus' own description and teaching of Matthew 24, the Seven Seals are the *entirety* of the judgment of Revelation, encompassing a period of forty years, and we will see that the Beast (antichrist) comes to power in Seal 5, that the entire Great Tribulation occurs in Seal 5, and that the Second Coming occurs in Seal 7. The Trumpet and Bowl judgments outlined later

Prelude to Judgment—Revelation 4 and 5

in Revelation are just *details* of the Tribulation, details of Seal 5, being details of the final three and a half years of the entire forty-year period, while the Bowls are a more detailed description of the final six months of that same three-and-a-half-year period. We will see this is inarguable, based on a reading of Matthew 24 and Revelation 6.

The description of the Seven Seals judgment encompasses the entirety of Revelation 6–19—the Seven Seals are everything. To understand the book of Revelation, the events that it describes, and the timelines of Revelation and how they all relate, it is essential to understand the Seven Seals.

9

THE SEVEN SEALS

THE SEVEN SEALS ARE the one and only judgment of Revelation—they are the entirety of the judgment, with the Trumpets and Bowls being only details of the Seven Seals, details mostly of Seal 5. The uniqueness of the Seven Seals from the Trumpets and Bowls is made clear right at the outset of Revelation, for any angel can blow any of the Trumpets, any angel can pour any of the Bowls, but *only* Jesus Christ, the one and only Judge (John 5:22), can open the Seven Seals (Rev 5:1–10). The reason that only Jesus Christ can open the Seven Seals is that, as the one and only Judge, only he can release the judgment. As a result, since only the Lord Jesus Christ can open the Seven Seals, we know that the Seven Seals are different, in their very nature, from the Trumpets and the Bowls. In total, the Seven Seals cover a judgment period of forty years.

Here is an overview summary of the judgments of the Seven Seals, a judgment that spans the full forty-year period:

SEAL 1

Seal 1 is defined by the prostitution, or the apostasy, of the church. False Christian teachers will come in the name of Jesus Christ and will declare that Jesus Christ is the Messiah, and then those false Christian teachers will teach lies and falsehoods and will deceive many in the church. As a result of the teaching of those false Christian teachers, the church will abandon Jesus Christ, will fall away from him, rebel against him, turn its back on him (Matt 24:5; 2 Thess 2:3; 1 Pet 4:17; Rev 6:2). Also, at the very opening of Seal 1, the Beast (commonly called the "antichrist") is conceived and then, nine months later, is born as a human baby. Seal 1 covers a period of approximately thirty years.

SEAL 2

Seal 2 is defined by global war—World War III (Matt 24:6–7; Rev 6:4)—and will last approximately two to three years.

SEAL 3

Seal 3 is global famine (Matt 24:6–7; Rev 6:6); it is opened after Seal 2 is opened, but its impact is simultaneous with Seal 2.

SEAL 4

Seal 4 is global disease and death (Matt 24:7–8; Rev 6:8); as with Seal 3, Seal 4 is opened after Seal 2 and also after Seal 3, but its impact is simultaneous with Seal 2 and with Seal 3.

SEAL 5

The Beast appears on the world's stage in Seal 5, bringing world peace by bringing the global war of Seal 2 to an end, which he does by making a global peace covenant with many (Dan 9:27). As a result of this global peace, the Beast will also bring an end to the global famine and the devastating death that resulted from Seals 2–4. It is almost certain that the Beast will be around thirty-three years of age when he comes to power. Soon after rising on the world's stage and bringing global peace, the Beast will be fake-assassinated (that is, the world will see him assassinated, but he will not actually have died, though the world will believe him to have been killed); his wounds will be to his right eye and to his arm, and by implication the wound will be to his *right* arm (Zech 11:17). After the fake death of the Beast, the Beast will be fake resurrected (that is, he will appear alive again, after his fake death, and so the world, who had believed him to have been killed, will hail him as being resurrected). The world will be astonished at his "resurrection" (Rev 13:3–4). At that same time, and upon the supposed resurrection of the Beast, a great Christian leader, described as the "false prophet," will proclaim the Beast to be the Second Coming of Christ, and this False Prophet will then perform great miracles in full view of the world to prove that he speaks the truth. As a result of the Beast's witnessed death and resurrection, and as a result of the False Prophet's proclamation that the Beast is the Second Coming of Christ, together with the miraculous signs performed by the False Prophet, the world will worship the Beast as Christ returned. The Beast will then persecute and overcome the true church (Dan 7:21, 7:25; Matt 24:9–10; Rev 6:9–11; 13:7), killing most of the church. He will also, as part of his global peace, cause the Jews to begin, and finish, the rebuilding of the (third) temple, and as a result the Jews will hail him as Messiah. The rebuilding of the temple will take three and a half years. When that rebuilt temple is complete, and when the Jews have just started to offer the daily sacrifice in the rebuilt temple, the Beast will almost immediately put a stop to the daily sacrifice and will go into the holy of holies of the rebuilt temple and enthrone himself there. The enthroning of himself in the holy of holies in the rebuilt temple is described by Daniel and by Jesus Christ as the "abomination of desolation" (Dan 9:27; 11:31; 12:11; Matt 24:15). By enthroning himself in the holy of holies in the rebuilt temple, the Beast will be proclaiming himself as God Almighty (2 Thess 2:4). From the time that the Beast comes to power to the time that he sets up his throne in the holy of holies will be a period of three and a half years (Dan 9:27). When the Beast sets up his throne in the holy of holies, in the rebuilt temple, that abomination of desolation is the specific event that unleashes the Great Tribulation. The Great Tribulation begins three and a half years after the Beast comes to world power and will itself last for an additional three and a half years. The details of the Great Tribulation are described by the Trumpets (Trumpets 1–5) and by the Bowls (Bowls 1–5)—*all* of this happens in Seal 5 (Matt 24:9–28).

SEAL 6

After the Great Tribulation has ended (Matt 24:29; Rev 6:12–14), Seal 6 is opened. Seal 6 is defined by the judgment and destruction of the nation called "Babylon the Great, the Mother of Prostitutes." Babylon the Great will be destroyed in Seal 6, and Seal 6 will last a total of thirty days (Dan 12:11; Rev 11:3; 12:6, 17–18). Seal 6 includes Trumpet 6, which itself includes Bowls 6 and 7.

SEAL 7

Seal 7 is opened forty-five days *after* the end of Seal 6, which is seventy-five days *after* the end of the Great Tribulation. Seal 7 includes the sounding of Trumpet 7, the last Trumpet, and the sounding of that last Trumpet results in the resurrection of *all* believers (Matt 24:31)—first, *all* the dead believers are resurrected (1 Thess 4:16), and then all the *living* believers will be *transformed* into their resurrected selves (1 Cor 15:52; 1 Thess 4:17)—all of this happens at the last Trumpet, Trumpet 7. All the resurrected believers will then rise into the sky to meet Jesus Christ in the air, for he has arrived at Earth and awaits his resurrected church to join him in the sky before he descends to the Earth for the Second Coming. This meeting of the entire resurrected church with Jesus Christ in the earthly sky is described as the "wedding" and "wedding supper" of the Lamb and his Bride (Rev 19:6–9). Once the entire resurrected church joins Jesus Christ in the earthly sky, then Jesus Christ descends to Earth, together with the entire resurrected church—these are the "holy ones" who come with him (Zech 14:5; 1 Thess 3:13; Jude 14), who descend with him, at the Second Coming. The church, which descends to Earth with Jesus Christ at the Second Coming, will witness his judgment and the establishing of his dominion on Earth (Dan 7:18, 22; Matt 6:10). These are the events of Seal 7.

From this general summary, we see that Seals 1–4 encompass a period of thirty-three years, while Seals 5–7 encompass seven years. As a result, the totality of the judgments of the Seven Seals encompasses a period of forty years.

Seals 1–4 set the world's stage, prepare the world, for the coming of the Beast, with the Beast coming to power with the opening of Seal 5. He will rule for a total of three and a half years, at which time he will enthrone himself in the holy of holies of the rebuilt temple, at which point the Great Tribulation is unleashed, which will last an additional three and a half years—all of this, from the Beast coming to power to the end of the Great Tribulation, occurs, in its entirety, in Seal 5. This gives Seal 5 a total duration of seven years.

After the end of the Great Tribulation of Seal 5, Seal 6 is opened, which results in the destruction of the nation symbolically described as Babylon the Great—Seal 6 lasts for a period of thirty days.

Forty-five days after Babylon the Great is destroyed, which is forty-five days after the end of Seal 6, Seal 7 is opened, which results in the resurrection of all believers, living and dead, and the meeting of the resurrected church with Jesus Christ in the sky. Jesus Christ then descends to Earth, in glory, with his entire resurrected church, 1,335 days after the Beast set up his throne on the holy of holies. At his Second Coming, Jesus Christ judges the living and the dead, and then, with his resurrected church, establishes his everlasting kingdom on Earth.

This is the entirety of the book of Revelation from chapters 6 to 19.

So how can we be sure of these details?

The foundational key to understanding the events and the timelines of Revelation, and of the Seven Seals, is Matthew 24:4–33. Read side by side with Revelation 6; 8:1–5; 19:11–21, Matthew 24:4–33 is an outline, by Jesus Christ himself, of the Seven Seals, in order, with explanation—that's how we can know the details of the Seven Seals.

SEAL 1—THE PROSTITUTION AND REBELLION OF THE CHURCH

> I watched as the Lamb opened the first of the seven seals. Then I heard one of the four living creatures say in a voice like thunder, "Come!" I looked, and there before me was *a white horse!* Its *rider held a bow,* and *he was given a crown*, and *he rode out as a conqueror* bent on conquest. (Rev 6:1–2 NIV)

> Jesus answered: "Watch out that no one deceives you. For many will *come in my name*, claiming, *'I am the Messiah,'* and *will deceive many*." (Matt 24:4–5 NIV)

> For it is time for *judgment to begin with God's household*; and if it begins with us, what will the outcome be for those who do not obey the gospel of God? (1 Pet 4:17 NIV)

> Concerning *the coming of our Lord Jesus Christ* and our being gathered to him, we ask you, brothers and sisters, not to become easily unsettled or alarmed by the teaching allegedly from us—whether by a prophecy or by word of mouth or by letter—asserting that the day of the Lord has already come. *Don't let anyone deceive you* in any way, for *that day will not come until the rebellion occurs* and the man of lawlessness is revealed, the man doomed to destruction. (2 Thess 2:1–3 NIV)

How are we to understand Seal 1, as outlined in Revelation 6:1–2? Seals 2–4 are straightforward as to their meaning and description—war, famine, and death, respectively—but Seal 1 is less straightforward. What do we make of the white horse and the rider upon it, a rider who wears a crown, who has a bow and is bent on conquest? As with all the Seven Seals, the only way we can understand Seal 1 is from Jesus himself, who gives us the Seven Seals of Revelation, in order, and with explanation, in Matthew 24:3–33. Here is that passage in its entirety:

> Now as He sat on the Mount of Olives, the disciples came to Him privately, saying, "Tell us, when will these things be? And what will be the sign of Your coming, and of the end of the age?" And Jesus answered and said to them: "Take heed that no one deceives you. For many will come in My name, saying, 'I am the Christ,' and will deceive many. And you will hear of wars and rumors of wars. See that you are not troubled; for all these things must come to pass, but the end is not yet. For nation will rise against nation, and kingdom against kingdom. And there will be famines, pestilences, and earthquakes in various places. All these are the beginning of sorrows. "Then they will deliver you up to tribulation and kill you, and you will be hated by all nations for My name's sake. And then many will be offended, will betray one another, and will hate one another. Then many false prophets will rise up and deceive many. And because lawlessness will abound, the love of many will grow cold. But he who endures to the end shall be saved. And this gospel of the kingdom will be preached in all the world as a witness to all the nations, and then the end will come. "Therefore when you see the 'abomination of desolation,' spoken of by Daniel the prophet, standing in the holy place" (whoever reads, let him understand), "then let those who are in Judea flee to the mountains. Let him who is on the housetop not go down to take anything out of his house. And let him who is in the field not go back to get his clothes. But woe to those who are pregnant and to those who are nursing babies in those days! And pray that your flight may not be in winter or on the Sabbath. For then there will be great tribulation, such as has not been since the beginning of the world until this time, no, nor ever shall be. And unless those days were shortened, no flesh

would be saved; but for the elect's sake those days will be shortened. "Then if anyone says to you, 'Look, here is the Christ!' or 'There!' do not believe it. For false christs and false prophets will rise and show great signs and wonders to deceive, if possible, even the elect. See, I have told you beforehand. "Therefore if they say to you, 'Look, He is in the desert!' do not go out; or 'Look, He is in the inner rooms!' do not believe it. For as the lightning comes from the east and flashes to the west, so also will the coming of the Son of Man be. For wherever the carcass is, there the eagles will be gathered together. "Immediately after the tribulation of those days the sun will be darkened, and the moon will not give its light; the stars will fall from heaven, and the powers of the heavens will be shaken. Then the sign of the Son of Man will appear in heaven, and then all the tribes of the Earth will mourn, and they will see the Son of Man coming on the clouds of heaven with power and great glory. And He will send His angels with a great sound of a trumpet, and they will gather together His elect from the four winds, from one end of heaven to the other. "Now learn this parable from the fig tree: When its branch has already become tender and puts forth leaves, you know that summer is near. So you also, when you see all these things, know that it is near—at the doors! (NKJV)

Matthew 24:3–33 is the parallel passage to Revelation 6; 8:1–5; 19:11–21, the Seven Seals, and this is clearly apparent when we set these passages side by side, as follows:

Matthew 24	Revelation 6 (NKJV)
Seal 1	
Take heed that no one deceives you. For many will come in My name, saying, 'I am the Christ,' and will deceive many. (vv. 4–5)	And I looked, and behold, a white horse. He who sat on it had a bow; and a crown Was given to him, and he went out conquering and to conquer. (v. 2)
Seal 2	
And you will hear of wars and rumors of wars. See that you are not troubled; for all these things must come to pass, but the end is not yet. For nation will rise against nation, and kingdom against kingdom. (vv. 6–7a)	Another horse, fiery red, went out. And it was granted to the one who sat on it to take peace from the earth, and that people should kill one another; and there was given to him a great sword. (vv. 3–4)

Seal 3	
And there will be famines, (v. 7b)	When He opened the third seal, I heard the third living creature say, "Come and see." So I looked, and behold, a black horse, and he who sat on it had a pair of scales in his hand. And I heard a voice in the midst of the four living creatures saying, "A quart of wheat for a denarius, and three quarts of barley for a denarius; and do not harm the oil and the wine." (vv. 5–6)
Seal 4	
pestilences, and earthquakes in various places (v. 7b)	When He opened the fourth seal, I heard I heard the voice of the fourth living creature saying, "Come and see." So I looked, and behold, a pale horse. And the name of him who sat on it was Death, and Hades followed with him. And power was given to them over a fourth of the earth, to kill with sword, with hunger, with death, and by the beasts of the earth. (vv. 7–8)

Seal 5	
Then they will deliver you up to tribulation and kill you, and you will be hated by all nations for My name's sake. And then many will be offended, will betray one another, and will hate one another. Then many false prophets will rise up and deceive many. And because lawlessness will abound, the love of many will grow cold. But he who endures to the end shall be saved. And this gospel of the kingdom will be preached in all the world as a witness to all the nations, and then the end will come. "Therefore when you see the 'abomination of desolation,' spoken of by Daniel the prophet, standing in the holy place" (whoever reads, let him understand), "then let those who are in Judea flee to the mountains. Let him who is on the housetop not go down to take anything out of his house. And let him who is in the field not go back to get his clothes. But woe to those who are pregnant and to those who are nursing babies in those days! And pray that your flight may not be in winter or on the Sabbath. For then there will be great tribulation, such as has not been since the beginning of the world until this time, no, nor ever shall be. And unless those days were shortened, no flesh would be saved; but for the elect's sake those days will be shortened. "Then if anyone says to you, 'Look, here is the Christ!' or 'There!' do not believe it. For false christs and false prophets will rise and show great signs and wonders to deceive, if possible, even the elect. See, I have told you beforehand. "Therefore if they say to you, 'Look, He is in the desert!' do not go out; or 'Look, He is in the inner rooms!' do not believe it. For as the lightning comes from the east and flashes to the west, so also will the coming of the Son of Man be. For wherever the carcass is, there the eagles will be gathered together. (vv. 9–28)	When He opened the fifth seal, I saw under the altar the souls of those who had been slain for the word of God and for the testimony which they held. And they cried with a loud voice, saying, "How long, O Lord, holy and true, until You judge and avenge our blood on those who dwell on the earth?" Then a white robe was given to each of them; and it was said to them that they should rest a little while longer, until both the number of their fellow servants and their brethren, who would be killed as they were, was completed. (vv. 9–11)

Seal 6	
Immediately after the tribulation of those days the sun will be darkened, and the moon will not give its light; the stars will fall from heaven, and the powers of the heavens will be shaken. (v. 29)	I looked when He opened the sixth seal, and behold, there was a great earthquake; and the sun became black as sackcloth of hair, and the moon became like blood. And the stars of heaven fell to the earth, as a fig tree drops its late figs when it is shaken by a mighty wind. Then the sky receded as a scroll when it is rolled up, and every mountain and island was moved out of its place. And the kings of the earth, the great men, the rich men, the commanders, the mighty men, every slave and every free man, hid themselves in the caves and in the rocks of the mountains, and said to the mountains and rocks, "Fall on us and hide us from the face of Him who sits on the throne and from the wrath of the Lamb! For the great day of His wrath has come, and who is able to stand?" (vv. 12–17)
Seal 7	
Then the sign of the Son of Man will appear in heaven, and then all the tribes of the earth mourn, and they will see the Son of Man coming on the clouds of heaven with power and great glory. And He will send His angels with a great sound of a trumpet, and they will gather together His elect from the four winds, from one end of heaven to the other. (vv. 30–31)	When He opened the seventh seal, there was silence in heaven for about half an hour. (8:1) Let us be glad and rejoice and give him glory, for the marriage of the Lamb has come, and His wife has made herself ready." (19:7) Now I saw heaven opened, and behold, a white horse. And He who sat on him was called Faithful and True, and in righteousness He judges and makes war. His eyes were like a flame of fire, and on His head were many crowns. He had a name written that no one knew except Himself. He was clothed with a robe dipped in blood, and His name is called The Word of God. And the armies in heaven, clothed in fine linen, white and clean, followed Him on white horses. (19:11–14)

These are the Seven Seals of Revelation, in parallel with Jesus' own words from Matthew 24:4–33. In Matthew 24:6–31, Jesus gives us, in order, war (Seal 2); famine (Seal 3); death, disease, and pestilence (Seal 4); persecution of the church (Seal 5); the sun darkened, the moon doesn't give its light/is like blood, and stars fall from heaven

(Seal 6); the resurrection of believers and the Second Coming (Seal 7)—these are an exact parallel.

Since we can see that Seals 2–7 of Revelation are an exact parallel with Matthew 24:6–31, we can then also clearly understand, from that same context, that Jesus' words in Matthew 24:4–5 are his description of Seal 1.

With that in mind, how does Jesus describe Seal 1?

JESUS' DESCRIPTION OF SEAL 1 IN MATTHEW 24:4–5

> Take heed that no one deceives you. For many will come in My name, saying, "I am the Christ," and will deceive many (Matt 24:4–5 NKJV)

How is Seal 1 described in Revelation?

> And I looked, and behold, a white horse. He who sat on it had a bow; and a crown was given to him, and he went out conquering and to conquer." (Rev 6:2 NKJV)

At first, these seem like two differing descriptions, however, since we know that Matthew 24:6–31 is a description of Seals 2–7 in Revelation, we can then also understand that Jesus' description of Matthew 24:4–5 is his description of Seal 1. Putting these two descriptions together gives us an understanding of Seal 1.

"IN MY NAME"

Jesus begins describing Seal 1 with a warning to the church to not be deceived. He tells us, in his description of Seal 1, that many people will come in *his* name, in the name of Jesus Christ, and they will say that "Jesus is the Christ" ("I am the Messiah") and they will deceive many. Seal 1 is *defined* by the *deception* of the church.

What does this mean?

The very heart of Jesus' description is that there will be people who will be "deceiving many," and those deceivers are people who will come in *his* name—that is, they will be deceiving teachers who will come in the name of Jesus Christ. Those people will *not* be false Christs, rather, they will be *Christian teachers* who will acknowledge that Jesus is the Christ.

How do we know that those false teachers are not false Christs?

Jesus explains for us in John 5:43 what defines a "false Christ."

> I have come in My Father's name, and you do not receive Me; if another comes *in his own name*, him you will receive." (5:43 NKJV)

Jesus tells us that he comes in his "Father's name," and that the Jews will not receive him, but one day *another* will come "in his own name," and *him* they will receive. The one who will come "in his own name" is the Beast, commonly called the "antichrist," and the Jews will receive him as their Messiah. But what is important to note is that Jesus describes the false Christ as coming in his *own* name—false Christs come *in their own name*. Therefore, when Jesus describes the false teachers of Seal 1 as coming "in *my* name," they are *not* false Christs, because false Christs come in their *own* name, but the false teachers of Seal 1 come as *teachers* in *his* name, coming in the name of Jesus Christ. By coming in the name of Jesus Christ, rather than coming in their own name, we know that those deceivers are not false Christs; rather they are teachers who come in the name of Jesus Christ and who will then teach false teachings.

This is further affirmed when Jesus tells us that those same false teachers will say "I am the Christ." When those false teachers say "I am the Christ," they are *not* saying that *they themselves* are Christ, since then they would be false Christs and, as we have seen, false Christs come in their own name, while these false teachers come in the name of Jesus Christ. Rather, when those false teachers say "I am the Christ," they will be saying that *Jesus* is the Christ. Remember that in this passage it is *Jesus* who is talking, and so, when he describes the people as saying "I am the Christ" he is in fact referring to *himself*—those false teachers will say that Jesus is, in fact, the Christ.

Once again, these people will not be false Christs, but rather they will be false Christian *teachers*, who will *affirm* that Jesus is the Christ, and then they will teach lies, and by their false teachings they will deceive the church, and the church will embrace those false teachings. In embracing those false teachings, the church will be prostituting itself, turning away from the truth, turning away from Jesus Christ, abandoning him. This is how the judgment of Revelation begins—it begins with the house of God; it begins with the church.

This is also exactly what Peter tells us.

> For the time has come for judgment to begin at the house of God; (1 Pet 4:17 NKJV)

Peter tells us that the judgment—which is in fact referring to the coming judgment of Revelation—will *begin* with the church; this is in exact accordance with, and a complete affirmation of, Jesus' words of Matthew 24:4-5—the judgment of Revelation begins with Seal 1, and Seal 1 is the church's embrace of false teachings, leading to the apostasy of the church.

Paul affirms exactly this same truth:

> Now we ask you, brothers and sisters, regarding the coming of our Lord Jesus Christ and our gathering together to Him, that you not be quickly shaken from your composure or be disturbed either by a spirit, or a message, or a letter as if from us, to the effect *that the day of the Lord* has come. *No one is to deceive you* in any way! For it will not come unless *the apostasy comes first*, and the man of lawlessness is revealed, the son of destruction, who opposes and exalts himself above every so-called god or object of worship, so that he

takes his seat in the temple of God, displaying himself as being God. (2 Thess 2:1–4 NASB)

Paul here warns the church to *not be deceived*—this is an exact harkening back to Jesus' own words of Matthew 24:4–5, where he describes the deception of the church. Paul then tells us that the day of the Lord, the day of judgment that precedes the Second Coming, will not happen until the *apostasy* of the *church* happens *first*. Paul makes it very clear that it is only *after* the apostasy of the church that the "man of lawlessness," the Beast, commonly called the "antichrist," will be revealed. This word translated as "apostasy" (NASB, AMP) is also translated as "falling away" (NKJV, YLT), "rebellion" (ESV, NIV, RSV, NLT), and "revolt" (DRA)—across any and every translation, it is clear that the word is referring to the *church*—it is the *church* that will "fall away," the *church* that will "rebel," the *church* that will commit "apostasy." Rebel against what? Fall away from whom? The church will rebel against Jesus Christ, will turn away from him—this is the apostasy. The church will commit this great apostasy by its embrace of the deceptive teachings of false Christian teachers.

THE APOSTASY OF THE CHURCH—THE SEVEN LETTERS

Also, it is because the judgment of Revelation will begin with the church that Jesus himself begins Revelation with the letters to the *angels* (i.e., the protectors) of the Seven churches, telling the *churches* to get their act together, to strengthen what remains and to "endure" and "persevere" through what is about to come, and, if they endure and persevere, they will be rewarded. Jesus then tells us what those rewards are, and those rewards are all outlined in Revelation 21–22, rewards that come *after* the Second Coming.

Why does Jesus *begin* Revelation with the warning to the churches, which is, in fact, his warning to the church as a whole? It is because the judgment of Revelation, the judgment of Seal 1, *begins* with the church, with great forces arrayed against the church so as to deceive the church and to corrupt the church, and to thereby cause the rebellion and the apostasy of the church.

This is Seal 1—the corruption, prostitution, rebellion, and apostasy of the church—that is the clear meaning of Jesus' own words as he describes Seal 1 in Matthew 24:4–5. The church will be deceived by false Christian teachers and, as a result of that deception, the church will turn away from, or rebel against, Jesus Christ. Jesus' words in Matthew 24:4–5 are a parallel description to Seal 1 as described in Revelation 6:2, and so Matthew 24:4–5 can help us understand the imagery of Seal 1 as outlined in Revelation 6:2. Seal 1, the beginning of the judgment of Revelation, is defined by the apostasy of the church.

JESUS' WORDS VS. DARBY'S RAPTURE

From Jesus' description of the church in Matthew 24:4–5, as well as from the parallel passages of 1 Peter 4:17 and 2 Thessalonians 2:1–4, we can see the striking contradiction between the rapture teaching and Scripture. The rapture teaching states that the church will be removed from the Earth *before the judgment* of Revelation *begins*, but Scripture, and the very words of Jesus Christ himself, tells us that the church not only will *not* be removed from the Earth prior to the judgment of Revelation, but rather the judgement of Revelation will itself *begin* with the church—the church will not be removed from the Earth to be kept from judgment, but rather the church will be deceived, will prostitute itself, will corrupt itself, will commit rebellion and apostasy, all as clearly affirmed by Matthew 24:4–5; 1 Peter 4:17; and 2 Thessalonians 2:3—the rapture teaching is in contradiction to all of these scriptures.

From any and every angle, the rapture teaching is in complete contradiction to Scripture, even to Jesus' own words. There is no rapture of the church, in fact, the judgment of Revelation *begins* with the church.

THE RIDER ON THE HORSE

If Seal 1, in accordance with the parallel passages of Matthew 24:4–5; 1 Peter 4:17; and 2 Thessalonians 2:3, is in fact defined by the apostasy of the church, how then do we understand the very clear image of the rider on a white horse of Revelation 6:2, a rider who has a crown and a bow, and who goes out to conquer?

It is very clear, from the entire context of Matthew 24:3–31, that the words of Jesus Christ in Matthew 24:4–5 is certainly a description of Seal 1. As a result, we must understand Revelation 6:2 in the light of Matthew 24:4–5, as well as in the light of 1 Peter 4:17; 2 Thessalonians 2:3; and also Revelation 19:11–21. Revelation 6:2 gives us added information and additional details of Seal 1—the details of Seal 1 as presented and outlined in Revelation 6:2 are just an amplification of the details of Seal 1 as outlined by Jesus Christ in Matthew 24:4–5.

How do we begin to understand the image of the rider on a white horse as described in Revelation 6:2? We can understand it in light of Revelation 19:11–21.

THE RIDER ON A WHITE HORSE—REVELATION 19:11–21

Revelation 19:11–21 gives us the exact picture of the real Second Coming of Jesus Christ. In that passage, the Lord Jesus Christ is described as riding a white horse, as having eyes of fire, and as wearing many crowns, and also as wearing a robe dipped in blood and as having a sword coming out of his mouth.

This is a striking parallel to the image of Revelation 6:2—both Revelation 6:2 and Revelation 19:11–21 describe a rider on a white horse; both passages describe the rider as wearing a crown or crowns; both passages describe the rider as being armed.

However, despite these clear parallels, there are many differences between the two images.

One of the very clear differences between the Revelation 6:2 and 19:11–21 passages is that is that the rider of Revelation 6:2 has a bow, and not a sword. What does this mean? We can understand it in the context of Ephesians 6:16.

> In addition to all this, take up the shield of faith, with which you can extinguish all *the flaming arrows* of the evil one. (NIV)

Ephesians 6:16 describes Satan's tactics, his attacks, as "flaming arrows." In being described as "flaming *arrows*," there is an immediate connection made between arrows and a bow. This of course brings to mind the rider on the horse on Revelation 6:2, having a bow. It is striking to note that, in the Revelation 6:2 description of the rider on the horse, that rider is described as having a bow but there is *no mention* of having arrows—why is that? Is it because the arrows that will be fired from the bow of Revelation 6:2 are in fact the same "flaming arrows" of Satan as described in Ephesians 6:16? If so, then the rider of Revelation 6:2 is firing Satan's flaming arrows—it is *Satan* who is arming that bow.

Ephesians 6:16 also tells us, in the context of Satan's flaming arrows, that the *defense* against those flaming arrows is the "shield of faith." Since Satan's flaming arrows can be extinguished, or made worthless, by the shield of faith, we can then understand that Satan's flaming arrows are in fact an attack against the *faith* of believers. As a result, when the rider of Revelation 6:2 is firing Satan's "flaming arrows" (since the rider himself has no arrows of his own), we can then understand that the rider of Revelation 6:2 is launching an attack against the *faith* of Christians, against the *faith* of the church. Since Satan is the source of those flaming arrows, and since we know that Satan is very clearly a liar and the father of lies (John 8:44), then we can understand those flaming arrows as fired by the rider of Seal 1 as being an attack *by way of lies and deception* upon the faith of the church—it is a great attempt by the enemy to *deceive* the church.

This then is in exact accordance with Jesus' own words of Matthew 24:4–5, where he specifically describes Seal 1 as being a deception of the church.

Also, the fact that the rider of Revelation 6:2 is on a white horse clearly connects that rider to Jesus Christ himself, who is also described as being on a white horse (Rev 19:11–21). But the rider in Revelation 6:2 is *not* the real Christ, is *not* a *true* Christianity, but is a counterfeit Christ, a counterfeit Christianity. As a result, we can understand that the rider on the white horse, who is firing Satan's flaming arrows as an attack on the faith of the church, is a *false Christianity*, which rides out to conquer the world.

THE RIDER—A MAN OR A FORCE

Of course, due to the similarity of the description of the rider in Revelation 6:2 with the description of Jesus Christ in 19:11–21, many teach that the rider of 6:2 is in fact the *person* of the Beast, the *person* of the antichrist. Is this true? Is the rider of Seal 1 an individual *person* who comes upon the world's stage, or is the rider a *force* unleashed upon the world? There is very strong basis for understanding the rider of Seal 1 as representing primarily a *force* unleashed upon the world, rather than a specific *person*, for the following reasons.

We know, with certainty, from 1 Peter 4:17; 2 Thessalonians 2:3; and Matthew 24:4–5, that the beginning of the judgment of Revelation is upon the *church*, and that the Beast will *not* be revealed until *after* the apostasy of the church. So, once again, the apostasy of the church happens *before* the Beast comes to power.

Also, when looking at the other six Seals, *none* of them describe or identify with a *person*; they *all* describe global *forces* and global *events*.

As a result, putting all this together, there is very strong, and consistent, reason to understand that the rider on the white horse of Seal 1 in Revelation 6:2 represents primarily a *force* or *events* rather than a specific person—in this case, representing the force of a prostituted Christianity, the great rebellion and apostasy of the church. This is in perfect accordance with Jesus' own words of Matthew 24:4–5, as well as with 1 Peter 4:17; 2 Thessalonians 2:3; and also Revelation 2–3, the seven letters containing Jesus' warning to the church to not be deceived and to not abandon its first love.

THE BEAST

However, that being the case, why does the imagery of Seal 1 bear such a striking, yet superficial and shallow, resemblance to Jesus Christ as he is described in Revelation 19:11–21? The rider of Seal 1, as described in Revelation 6:2, is a very poor reflection of the rider of 19:11–21, the Lord Jesus Christ. The rider of Seal 1 certainly represents a false Christianity, a Christianity that has been deceived by lies and corruption, the apostasy of the church, but does the rider of Seal 1 represent *only* that? Is it possible that the rider of Seal 1 *also* represents an additional *parallel* meaning, representing *two* simultaneous things, rather than just one?

In fact, there is good reason to understand that the rider on the white horse of Seal 1, as described in 6:2, in addition to representing the *force* of a false Christianity, *also* represents the coming *false Christ*, who himself will be the *culmination* of that force of false Christianity. Why would the rider of Seal 1 represent *both* the false, corrupted, apostate church *and* the coming false Christ, the Beast? How do we understand that parallel representation? We can understand it as follows.

As we shall see, the Beast comes to prominence in Seal 5, and he will almost certainly be thirty-three years of age when he comes to power. Seals 1–4 prepare the world for his coming, creating the conditions in the world out of which he will arise.

Prior to coming to power, the Beast must, of course, first be born. When will he be born?

The Beast will be at the very heart of the coming events and judgments of Revelation; therefore it is inconceivable that the Beast can be born at any time *before* the beginning of judgment; that is, it is impossible to imagine that the Beast will be born at any time prior to the opening of Seal 1, which is the beginning of judgement. As a result, the Beast must be born sometime during Seals 1–4. When we examine Seals 1–4, the only Seal that contains anything even remotely resembling the coming false Christ is Seal 1—Seal 2 is global war; Seal 3 is global famine; Seal 4 is global death from the war, the famine, and from disease—only Seal 1 contains a clear representation of a false Christianity *and* a simultaneous false Christ. As a result, we can conclude that the rider on the white horse of Seal 1 in 6:2 is simultaneously representing both the force of a false Christianity *and* the coming Beast—but it does *not* represent the Beast coming to *power*; rather it represents the fact that the Beast will be *born*, on Earth, as a human baby, in Seal 1.

The birth of the Beast in Seal 1 is also powerfully appropriate. Seal 1 is *defined* by the apostasy of the church; as a result, it is fitting that the Beast is born during the time of the apostasy of the church. In fact, this idea is also implicitly affirmed in 2 Thessalonians 2:3.

> Let no one deceive you by any means; for that Day will not come unless the falling away comes first, and the man of sin is revealed, the son of perdition
> (2:3 NKJV)

In 2 Thessalonians 2:3, the Beast (the "son of perdition") is described as being "revealed." That revealing of the "man of sin" (the Beast) is specifically connected with the apostasy of the church, with the apostasy of the church happening *first*. Since Seal 1 is defined by the apostasy of the church, and since the Beast is revealed only *after* the start of the apostasy of the church, we can understand the revealing of the Beast to occur together with that apostasy, and so we can understand the revealing of the Beast as also occurring in Seal 1, happening *after* the start of the apostasy of the church.

We will see, very clearly, that this revealing of the Beast is *not* the Beast coming to *power*, for the Beast's coming to power clearly occurs in Seal 5. What then does it mean for the Beast to be "revealed"? There is strong reason to understand the description of the "man of sin" as being "revealed" as describing his *birth* upon this Earth—the Beast is "revealed" upon the Earth by being *born*. As a result, we can understand that the Beast is born soon after the opening of Seal 1, being born while the church is prostituting itself, corrupting itself and embracing faithlessness and apostasy.

Also, in this parallel and simultaneous representation of the "rider on a white horse" as representing the birth of the Beast, the fact that the rider has no arrows gains an added meaning. In the case of the rider representing the *force* of a false Christianity, the lack of arrows can be understood in conjunction with Ephesians 6:16, where it will be Satan's "flaming arrows" of deception fired against the faith of the church. In the case of the rider also representing the birth of the Beast, the lack of arrows can be understood as signifying that the Beast, at that time, will have no power—he is only born, but he is powerless, and will come to power thirty-three years later.

THE CONCEPTION OF THE BEAST

Just as it is almost impossible to imagine that the Beast is born at any time prior to the opening of Seal 1, it is likewise impossible to imagine that the Beast is *conceived* at any time prior to the opening of Seal 1. As a result, we can understand that the Beast is not only *born*, or "revealed," in Seal 1, but he is in fact *conceived* with the very opening of Seal 1, being born nine months after Seal 1 has been opened. As a result, we can understand Seal 1 as including *both* the conception of the Beast and his birth.

These are the events of Seal 1, which is defined primarily by the rebellion and apostasy of the church, represented by the "rider on a white horse" as the *force* of a false Christianity. We can also understand that image of the rider on a white horse as representing the Beast being conceived and then born as a human baby during Seal 1, during the apostasy of the church. The rider on the white horse as described in Seal 1 of Revelation 6:2 therefore represents *both* the *force* of a corrupted and false Christianity *and* the conception and birth of the person of the Beast.

SEAL 2—GLOBAL WAR

> When the Lamb opened the second seal, I heard the second living creature say, "Come!" Then another horse came out, a fiery red one. Its rider was given power to take peace from the earth and to make people kill each other. To him was given a large sword. (Rev 6:3–4 NIV)

> You will hear of wars and rumors of wars, but see to it that you are not alarmed. Such things must happen, but the end is still to come. Nation will rise against nation, and kingdom against kingdom. (Matt 24:6–7 NIV)

The Second Seal is very clear—it is global war. How do we know that this war is a global war and not a regional war? We can know that this is a global war for Revelation 6:4 specifically tells us that the Seal 2 judgment will "take peace *from the earth*"—this is *not* a localized or regional event; rather, it is a *global* event, for peace is not taken from a region, but peace is taken from the whole Earth.

In Jesus' description of Seal 2 in Matthew 24:6–7, he describes it as "nation rising against nation," and "kingdom against kingdom." In describing these wars as involving "nations" and "kingdoms," this, again, is not describing a localized or regional event; rather, as with Revelation 6:3–4, it is a description of a global event, an event of nations.

Jesus also begins his description of Seal 2 by saying that we will hear of "wars and rumors of wars"—not that we will hear of a war and rumors of a war, but of "*wars and rumors of wars*"—these are multiple wars, wars of kingdoms and nations, wars throughout the Earth. This description of "wars and rumors of wars" again affirms that this is a description of a global conflict, exactly as is described in the Revelation 6:3–4 description of Seal 2. In fact, that global war of Seal 2 will be what we would call World War III, a devastating global event. We must remember that all of this *precedes* the coming of the Beast.

JESUS' SIDE COMMENT

It is very important to note that throughout the Matthew 24:3–33 passage, when Jesus is giving us the Seven Seals in order and explaining them for us, on only two occasions in that description does he add a side comment.

The first side comment is in his description of Seal 2, when, after telling us of the "wars and rumors of wars," he adds "but the end is still to come" (Matt 24:6). The second side comment is in Seal 4, when he says, as a summary of Seals 1–4, "All these are the beginning of birth pains" (24:8).

Why does Jesus stop on those two occasions to add those side comments? In fact, those two comments are profound and instructional. The first of those two side comments is in reference to Seal 2.

"BUT THE END IS STILL TO COME"

In Matthew 24:6, in his description of the "wars and rumors of wars," and of "nation rising against nation" and "kingdom against kingdom," Jesus adds, "but the end is still to come." Matthew 24:6 is also translated as "but that is not yet the end" (NASB) and "but the end is not yet" (NKJV, RSV). Why does Jesus add this comment, and why does he add it in his description of Seal 2? We can understand it as follows.

When the global war of Seal 2 occurs, people throughout the world will think that the war, which will be considered to be World War III, will be the end—in fact, people will think that that war is Armageddon. It is for that reason that Jesus stops to tell us that the global war of Seal 2 is *not* the end, that it is *not* Armageddon; rather it is only part of the *preparation* for the rise of the Beast. As we shall see, it is the Beast himself who will bring that global war of Seal 2 to conclusion, bringing global peace (Dan 9:27), resulting in him being hailed as the savior of the world. Jesus knows that many people will consider the Seal 2 global war as being Armageddon, as being the end, and so he makes a point of telling us that that war is *not* Armageddon, is *not* the end.

Why is this point so important that it necessitates Jesus clarifying it for us? It is important for the following reason.

THE RAPTURE—THE TICKING TIME BOMB

It is in the context of the global war of Seal 2 that the great danger of the rapture teaching will be revealed. Until Seal 2 is opened, the destructiveness of the rapture teaching will not yet be present, for the false rapture teaching is a ticking time bomb that will only truly go off during Seal 2, during the time of the global war, the war that the world will *think* is Armageddon. In fact, it will be in the context of the Seal 2 global war that the rapture teaching will act as the foundation upon which Christians can be deceived to worship the Beast—the false rapture teaching will be one of the primary means whereby Jesus' words, and warning, can be fulfilled, for Jesus tells us,

> For false messiahs and false prophets will appear and perform great signs and wonders to deceive, if possible, even the elect. See, I have told you ahead of time. (Matt 24:24–25 NIV)

Jesus tells us that the deception of those days will be so great that, if it were possible, even Christians would be deceived to worship the Beast. How can this be? How could Christians possibly be deceived to worship the Beast? The false rapture teaching makes it possible, and here's how.

Jesus himself tells us, in his Matthew 24:6–7 description of Seal 2 and the global war that it unleashes, that that war is *not* the end. The reason he stops and adds that special side comment is because the world will believe that the global war of Seal 2 *is*, in fact, *the end*; they will believe that that war is Armageddon, the great global war that will *precede* the Second Coming, the great war that will be stopped by Jesus himself at his Second Coming (Rev 19:19–21).

For those Christians who would have believed the rapture teaching, and who then find themselves in the midst of the Seal 2 global war, they too will believe that they are in the midst of Armageddon, and they will be dismayed. In having believed Darby's rapture teaching, those Christians would have been expecting to be removed from the Earth before any of the Revelation events happen, and, as a result, they would expect that they would not be present on Earth during the Seal 2 global war. However, when those same Christians find themselves on Earth during the global war of Seal 2, they will then realize, in the midst of the Seal 2 global war, that, in regard to the rapture teaching, they were taught *falsely*, for they will see, firsthand, that there is no rapture. For many rapture-believing Christians this will rock their world and, in many instances, be a shock to their faith. As a result, in their shock and dismay, those same Christians will then question other Christian teachings, and ask, in light of having been taught the false rapture teaching, "What else was I taught that was false?" *That* question will then lead to, "Was I also taught falsely as to what the Second Coming will look like?," and that is the question that can be the foundation for destruction.

Those rapture-believing Christians will know that at the height of Armageddon Jesus Christ is to return at the Second Coming, bringing a stop to that war, ushering in world peace and establishing his kingdom. Since those Christians will find themselves in the midst of a war that they will *think* is Armageddon, and since, upon realizing the falsehood of the rapture teaching, they will question what else they have believed that might be a false teaching, including questioning what the Second Coming might *actually* look like, then when a man arises on the world's stage and brings an end to that global war that is supposedly Armageddon, and when that man is then proclaimed as Christ returned, those very same Christians will look at that man and say, "Maybe *that's* what the Second Coming *actually* looks like!"—and they will be referring to the Beast. This is how the ticking time bomb of the rapture teaching explodes, and this is why Jesus makes a point to tell us that the global war of Seal 2 is *not* the end.

As a result, the rapture teaching lays the foundation, during Seal 2, upon which Christians could worship the Beast as Christ returned, and, in so doing, the words of Jesus Christ would be fulfilled, that many will be deceived, if possible, *even the elect*. It is for this reason, above all reasons, that the false rapture teaching must be confronted and exposed whenever it is encountered, for it is a teaching that can lead to Christians worshiping the Beast.

SEAL 3—GLOBAL FAMINE

> When the Lamb opened the third seal, I heard the third living creature say, "Come!" I looked, and there before me was a black horse! Its rider was holding a pair of scales in his hand. Then I heard what sounded like a voice among the four living creatures, saying, "Two pounds of wheat for a day's wages, and six pounds of barley for a day's wages, and do not damage the oil and the wine!" (Rev 6:5-6 NIV)

> There will be famines . . . (Matt 24:7)

Seal 3 is very clear—preceding the rise of the Beast, there will be global famine, as Jesus himself specifically affirms in his description of Seal 3 in Matthew 24:7.

SEAL 4—GLOBAL PESTILENCE AND DEATH

> When the Lamb opened the fourth seal, I heard the voice of the fourth living creature say, "Come!" I looked, and there before me was a pale horse! Its rider was named Death, and Hades was following close behind him. They were given power over a fourth of the earth to kill by sword, famine and plague, and by the wild beasts of the earth. (Rev 6:7-8 NIV)

> . . . pestilences, and earthquakes in various places. (Matt 24:7 NKJV)

Seal 4 is the release of death upon the world, and we are told, very specifically, that this death is the result of the war of Seal 2 ("kill by the sword"), of the global famine, and also by way of global plague and disease.

What does it mean when it says that death also comes "by the wild beasts of the earth"? Does that mean that lions will be roaming the streets and tearing people apart? No, it does not. In fact, to say that death will come "by way of the wild beasts of the Earth" is in fact just an expansion of the very previous word—"plague"—the "plagues," or "pestilences," that will come upon humanity are diseases that will be carried, and spread, by wild animals, much like the bubonic plague of the Middle Ages was spread by rats.

We are also told that, from the global war, the global famine, and the plagues to come, a quarter of the human population will die—so if the human population at that time is eight billion people, then two billion people will die.

From the description of Seal 4 in Revelation 6:7–8, there is the strong implication that the famine of Seal 3 and the plagues of Seal 4 are happening simultaneously with the global war of Seal 2—in fact, we can easily see how a global war can result in global famine and global disease. The global famine and global disease will begin sometime after the global war is underway, but they will occur simultaneous with the global war. This means that by the time Seal 5 is opened, the entire world, the whole of humanity, will be suffering from a devastating global war, a global famine, and global pestilence. This is important because it is in Seal 5 that the Beast rises to prominence and puts an end to the war and brings global peace, also bringing an end to the global famine and global pestilences.

Once again, Jesus himself affirms the details of Seal 4 when he tells us,

> . . . pestilences, and earthquakes in various places. (Matt 24:7 NKJV)

Jesus specifically tells us that Seal 4 is defined by "pestilences," that is, plagues and diseases, which is exactly what we are told in Revelation 6:7–8. Jesus though adds that during Seal 4 there will also be multiple earthquakes throughout the world. As a result, we know that Seal 4 is defined by global death from the plagues, pestilences, global war, and global famine, and that there will also be many earthquakes throughout the world during that same time.

THE BEGINNING OF BIRTH PAINS

It is at the end of Seal 4 that Jesus makes his second side comment when he tells us,

> All these are the beginning of birth pains. (Matt 24:8 NIV)

Why does Jesus stop to make this point, and why does he do it now, after his description of Seal 4?

The reason Jesus stops to make this point here, immediately after his description of Seal 4, is to clearly show that the entirety of Seals 1–4 is only *preliminary* to what is coming next, that the *real* judgment has not yet started, but will begin only *after* Seal 4. Seals 1–4 only set the stage for the Beast to come to power; they only prepare the world for his rise. His rise, as well as his entire rule and the entire Great Tribulation, all happen in Seal 5.

Also, it is very important to note the term that Jesus uses in describing the Seven Seals—he describes them as "birth pains." How are we to understand this? We are to understand it as follows.

The judgments of the Seven Seals are like birth pains that will culminate in a birth—that birth is the Second Coming of the Lord Jesus Christ and the establishing of his everlasting kingdom upon Earth. Just like birth pains, once Seal 1 is opened and those events have started to unfold, the closer we get to that moment of the birth, the moment of the Second Coming, the judgments that precede that birth will increase in both frequency and intensity, exactly as do labor pains during human birth. In fact, that is exactly what we see in Revelation with the Trumpet and Bowl events. Of the entire forty-year period of the Seven Seals, the Trumpet and Bowl events occur in the immediate three and a half years that precede the Second Coming, bringing an increasing frequency and intensity of judgment as we approach the moment of the Second Coming. Jesus' description of the judgment of the Seven Seals as "birth pains" is perfect and exact.

AN IMPORTANT OBSERVATION

Before looking at Seal 5, it is fundamentally important that we first look at how Jesus describes Seal 6 in Matthew 24:29—here is what he says:

> Immediately after the tribulation of those days **the sun will be darkened**, and **the moon will not give its light**; **the stars will fall from heaven**, and the **powers of the heavens will be shaken**. (Matt 24:29 NKJV)

Compare this to the description of Seal 6 in Revelation 6:12–13.

> I looked when He opened the sixth seal, and behold, there was a great earthquake; and *the sun became black* as sackcloth of hair, and *the moon became like blood*. And *the stars of heaven fell to the earth*, as a fig tree drops its late figs when it is shaken by a mighty wind. (NKJV)

In Matthew 24:29, Jesus tells us that the sun will be darkened, the moon will not give its light, and the stars will fall from heaven. He also tells us that the powers of the heavens will be shaken.

This is almost exactly the same language that is used to describe Seal 6 in Revelation 6:12–13, where we are told that the sun became black, the moon became like blood, and the stars fell from heaven to Earth. There is absolutely no question that in Matthew 24:29 Jesus is describing Seal 6—the parallel with Revelation 6:12–13 is exact.

What is exceedingly important to note is how Jesus *begins* his description of Seal 6 in Matthew 24:29—He begins with these words:

> Immediately *after* the tribulation of those days . . . (NKJV)

Jesus is very clear—*the entire Great Tribulation is over by the end of Seal 5*. This is a foundational truth, for it is with these words that we know the full nature of the Seven Seals, that the Seven Seals are the *entirety* of the judgment of Revelation, for the *entire* Great Tribulation occurs, completely, during Seal 5. This is unquestionable and inarguable, for Jesus himself makes it unequivocally clear in Matthew 24:29—when Seal 6 begins, the Great Tribulation is over.

SEAL 5—THE BEAST, THE FALSE PROPHET, THE GREAT TRIBULATION

When Jesus describes for us Seals 1–4 in Matthew 24:4–8, he spends about one verse, or less, on each Seal. When he describes for us Seal 6 (24:29) and Seal 7 (24:30–31), he spends one verse on Seal 6 and two verses on Seal 7. But in his description of Seal 5, Jesus spends *twenty* verses describing Seal 5 (24:9–28). This is a striking difference. Why does Jesus spend twenty verses describing Seal 5? It is because it is in Seal 5 that the fullness of judgment happens, for it is in Seal 5 that the Beast first rises to power, then rules the world for three and a half years, with the False Prophet as his accomplice, during which time he persecutes, and overcomes, the church on Earth. That three-and-a-half-year rule of the Beast is then followed by the three and a half years of the Great Tribulation, which also occurs, in its entirety, in Seal 5. Seal 5 is where everything happens—Seals 1–4 are, as Jesus said, only the *beginning* of the "birth pains," only setting the stage for Seal 5.

Here is Jesus' description of Seal 5:

> "Then they will deliver you up to tribulation and kill you, and you will be hated by all nations for My name's sake. And then many will be offended, will betray one another, and will hate one another. Then many false prophets will rise up and deceive many. And because lawlessness will abound, the love of many will grow cold. But he who endures to the end shall be saved. And this gospel of the kingdom will be preached in all the world as a witness to all the nations, and then the end will come.
>
> "Therefore when you see the 'abomination of desolation,' spoken of by Daniel the prophet, standing in the holy place" (whoever reads, let him understand), "then let those who are in Judea flee to the mountains. Let him who is on the housetop not go down to take anything out of his house. And let him who is in the field not go back to get his clothes. But woe to those who are pregnant and to those who are nursing babies in those days! And pray that your flight may not be in winter or on the Sabbath. For then there will be great

tribulation, such as has not been since the beginning of the world until this time, no, nor ever shall be. And unless those days were shortened, no flesh would be saved; but for the elect's sake those days will be shortened.

"Then if anyone says to you, 'Look, here is the Christ!' or 'There!' do not believe it. For false christs and false prophets will rise and show great signs and wonders to deceive, if possible, even the elect. See, I have told you beforehand.

"Therefore if they say to you, 'Look, He is in the desert!' do not go out; or 'Look, He is in the inner rooms!' do not believe it. For as the lightning comes from the east and flashes to the west, so also will the coming of the Son of Man be. For wherever the carcass is, there the eagles will be gathered together." (Matt 24:9–28 NKJV)

There is a great wealth of information here, information that is foundational to our understanding of Revelation and the events and timelines outlined therein.

THE PERSECUTION OF THE CHURCH

Jesus begins Seal 5 by describing the persecution of the church, telling us that Christians will be hated by all nations for his name's sake. This is exactly the same as the description of Seal 5 in Revelation 6:9–11.

> When He opened the fifth seal, I saw under the altar the souls of those who had been slain for the word of God and for the testimony which they held. And they cried with a loud voice, saying, "How long, O Lord, holy and true, until You judge and avenge our blood on those who dwell on the earth?" Then a white robe was given to each of them; and it was said to them that they should rest a little while longer, until both the number of their fellow servants and their brethren, who would be killed as they were, was completed. (NKJV)

Revelation 6:9–11 describes the persecution, unto death, of the church, exactly the same as Jesus' description of Seal 5 in Matthew 24:9—it is in Seal 5, as Jesus makes absolutely clear, that the church will be persecuted, unto death.

Once again, Jesus' own words show the falsehood of the rapture teaching. According to Jesus' own words in his description of Seal 5, not only is the church present on Earth throughout that entire time of judgment, but the church will also face great, worldwide persecution—where John Darby teaches that the church will not be on Earth, Jesus teaches that the church *will* be on Earth; where John Darby teaches that the church will be *rescued* and *kept* from harm and judgment, Jesus teaches that the church will be persecuted and put to death. Once again, the contradiction of Darby's rapture teaching with scriptural truth is striking—Darby teaches the church will be rescued and kept from harm during the events of Revelation, whereas Jesus teaches that the church will be persecuted and put to death during that same time; this is made unquestionably clear in Jesus' description of the persecution of the church in Matthew 24:9, all happening during Seal 5.

Jesus continues in his description of Seal 5, telling us in verse 11 that "many false prophets will arise and deceive many." Not only is this a description of "many false prophets" arising but, when taken together with Revelation 13, it is also a clear affirmation of one prominent False Prophet—the rise of that preeminent False Prophet is placed by Jesus here in Seal 5.

Jesus also describes this same time as being a time of "lawlessness" (v. 12). This use of the word "lawlessness" is a striking echo of 2 Thessalonians 2:3.

> that day will not come until the rebellion occurs and the man of *lawlessness* is revealed (NKJV)

The "man of lawlessness" described in 2 Thessalonians 2:3 is the Beast, and so when Jesus describes the period of Seal 5 as being one of "lawlessness," it is an affirmation of the same "lawlessness" of 2 Thessalonians 2:3, the "lawlessness" of the "man of lawlessness," which is described by Jesus as happening in Seal 5. This then puts that "lawlessness," as well as the "man of lawlessness," in the same context as the false prophets and the preeminent False Prophet, all of which are described by Jesus as being in Seal 5.

Jesus also then tells us that "he who endures to the end will be saved" (Matt 24:13). This is a striking echo of Jesus' own words in the Seven Letters, where he also tells the church to "endure" (Rev 2:3 NASB), to "persevere" (Rev 3:10 NKJV), and to "overcome" (Rev 2:7, 11, 17, 26; 3:5, 12, 21; 21:7). In each of these contexts—in the Matthew 24:13 context and in the various Revelation contexts listed above—the admonition to "endure" and to "persevere" is an admonition in regard to the persecution of the church, unto death, all occurring in Seal 5.

Jesus also says that "the gospel of the kingdom will be preached in all the world" (Matt 24:14). As we will see, this is in fact a reference to, and an affirmation of, the 144,000 of Revelation 7, who will be present, and released upon the Earth, in Seal 5, during the three-and-a-half-year rule of the Beast.

As Jesus continues with his description of Seal 5, he tells us of the "abomination of desolation" (v. 15) and affirms that it is the exact same abomination of desolation spoken of by Daniel in Daniel 11:31 and 12:11. Jesus tells us that when we see that event, the abomination of desolation, it will mark the beginning of the Great Tribulation. We know from Daniel 9:27 that the abomination of desolation begins midway through the seven-year period of the Beast's reign on Earth, and so we can understand clearly that the abomination of desolation occurs three and a half years into the rule of the Beast.

Jesus describes this Great Tribulation as being the worst time that the Earth will have ever witnessed or experienced, worse than any other time ever in Earth's history, a destruction and devastation so great that it will never again to be equalled (v. 21). Jesus tells us that it will be a destruction so great that unless he comes to put an end to that Tribulation, no life would remain on Earth (v. 22).

It is then that Jesus specifically warns us to beware of a false Christ—he is *not* referring to *multiple* false Christs but to *one* false Christ in particular (vv. 23, 26)—this is the Beast, the antichrist.

> Then if anyone says to you, "Look, here is *the* Christ!" or "There!" do not believe it. For false christs and false prophets will rise and show great signs and wonders to deceive, if possible, even the elect. See, I have told you beforehand. Therefore if they say to you, "Look, *He* is in the desert!" do not go out; or "Look, *He* is in the inner rooms!" do not believe it. For as the lightning comes from the east and flashes to the west, so also will the coming of the Son of Man be." (Matt 24:23-27 NKJV)

In Matthew 24:24 Jesus refers to "false christs," but this is in contrast to Matthew 24:23, where he refers specifically to "*the* Christ." The "false christs" of verse 24 are very different from "*the* Christ" of verse 23—"*the* Christ" of verse 23 is a *specific individual*, and this is affirmed in verse 26 when Jesus, referring to this same individual, says,

> Therefore if they say to you, "Look, *He* is in the desert!" do not go out; *or* "Look, *He* is in the inner rooms!" do not believe it. (Matt 24: 26 NKJV)

In Matthew 24:26, Jesus is referring to a *specific individual* when he describes that false Christ as "he"—this is *not* one of the "false christs" referred to in verse 24, but rather this is the same false Christ who is described as "*the* Christ" in verse 23—this false Christ, this specific individual, is the Beast of Revelation, commonly called the "antichrist"—and Jesus speaks of him in his description of Seal 5.

Jesus again reaffirms, in connection with this specific false Christ of Seal 5, that false prophets, and, as we know from Revelation 13, the one preeminent False Prophet will be present on Earth during that same time—the False Prophet will be present on Earth in conjunction with the false Christ. Those false prophets, and above all the one False Prophet, will deceive many by way of great signs and wonders that will be performed for all the world to see, wonders that will deceive people to worship the false Christ, the Beast, to worship him as Christ returned. These are the same signs, wonders, and miracles ascribed to the False Prophet in Revelation 13:13-14—again, Jesus places this all in Seal 5.

We see then that it is in Seal 5 that the Beast will come to power, that the False Prophet will be present, that the church will be persecuted unto death, and during which the entire Great Tribulation will occur—*all* of these events happen in Seal 5, and this is inarguable based on Jesus' own words in Matthew 24:9-28, in conjunction with both Daniel and Revelation. Seal 5 is where the huge events happen, and it is for that reason that Jesus spends twenty verses describing Seal 5, whereas for all the other Seals he describes them all in one verse or less.

SEAL 6—AFTER THE GREAT TRIBULATION

> I looked when He opened the sixth seal, and behold, there was a great earthquake; and the sun became black as sackcloth of hair, and the moon became like blood. And the stars of heaven fell to the earth, as a fig tree drops its late figs when it is shaken by a mighty wind. Then the sky receded as a scroll when it is rolled up, and every mountain and island was moved out of its place. And the kings of the earth, the great men, the rich men, the commanders, the mighty men, every slave and every free man, hid themselves in the caves and in the rocks of the mountains, and said to the mountains and rocks, "Fall on us and hide us from the face of Him who sits on the throne and from the wrath of the Lamb! For the great day of His wrath has come, and who is able to stand?" (Rev 6:12–17 NKJV)

> Immediately after the tribulation of those days the sun will be darkened, and the moon will not give its light; the stars will fall from heaven, and the powers of the heavens will be shaken. (Matt 24:29 NKJV)

Seal 6 occurs *after* the Great Tribulation, and both Jesus in Matthew 24:29 and also Revelation 6:12–13 describe the events with virtually the exact same language, referring to the sun being dark, the moon looking like blood and not giving off its light, and the stars falling to Earth. Revelation 6:14 also tells us that during that time, every mountain and island will be moved out of its place and that all humanity will hide in caves and mountains, hiding from God's judgment.

Remember, this is taking place *after* the Great Tribulation, so the humanity that is terrified and hiding has just witnessed, and lived through, the Great Tribulation. Those same people of Revelation 6:16, the ones who have lived through the Great Tribulation, are the ones who are running from God, calling on the mountains and rocks to fall on them and hide them from the "wrath of the Lamb."

This is profound—Revelation 6:16 makes it very clear that these people, people who have survived the Great Tribulation and who are now in hiding, clearly *know* that what they have just witnessed and lived through was from the hand of God, and we are told that they *know* that it is *specifically* the wrath of Jesus Christ, the Lamb. Even though they *know* that this is the judgment of Jesus Christ, the one and only Judge, they are running from him and hiding from him, rather than turning to him—such is their corruption. We will see that these people who are running from God during that time are the ones who have taken the "mark of the Beast," and this running away from Christ is the fruit of their choice, for in having taken the mark of the Beast they have confirmed themselves in opposition to Jesus Christ, and so, even though they will know that the colossal events through which they have just lived are from the very hand of God, from the Lord Jesus Christ, they will not turn to him, but will instead run from him.

THE SEVEN SEALS

We shall see, when we look at the details of the Trumpets and Bowls, that Seal 6 is in fact the fall of the nation Babylon the Great, the nation referred to as the "Mother of Prostitutes," the nation that at one time was the greatest Christian nation and that later utterly and completely turned its back on Jesus Christ—that is the prostitution. The destruction of the nation Babylon the Great happens *after* the end of the Great Tribulation, taking place, in its entirety, in Seal 6.

HOW LONG DOES SEAL 6 LAST?

We know that the entire Great Tribulation happens in Seal 5. We know, from Revelation 11:2–3; 12:6 and from Daniel 7:25; 9:27; 12:7, that the entire Great Tribulation will last 1,260 days, or 42 months ("a time, times, and half a time"). We know that the Great Tribulation begins with the abomination of desolation (Dan 11:31; 12:11; 9:27; Matt 24:15). As a result, we know that 1,260 days *after* the abomination of desolation is set up, the Great Tribulation is over.

How the do we understand the following?

> From the time that the daily sacrifice is abolished and the abomination that causes desolation is set up, there will be 1,290 days. Blessed is the one who waits for and reaches the end of the 1,335 days. (Dan 12:11–12 NIV)

Why does Daniel tell us of 1,290 days, and then of 1,335 days? We can understand it as follows.

From the time of the abomination of desolation to the *end* of the Great Tribulation is 1,260 days, or 42 months (Dan 7:25; 9:27; Rev 11:2–3; 12:6, with months counted as 30 days per month, as per the Jewish calendar). We know that the Great Tribulation begins *and ends* in Seal 5 and, based on Jesus' own words of Matthew 24:29, we know that Seal 5 itself *ends* with the end of the Great Tribulation. So, as a result, we know that from the setting up of the abomination of desolation to the *end* of Seal 5 is 1,260 days.

As a result, we know that Seal 6 *begins* 1,261 days *after* the setting up of the abomination of desolation. So, when Daniel tells us of the 1,290 days, he is in fact taking us to the *end* of Seal 6—Seal 6 *begins* 1,261 days *after* the setting up of the abomination of desolation and *ends* 1,290 days after the setting up of the abomination of desolation—as a result, we know that Seal 6 will last thirty days.

Why does Daniel take us to 1,290 days *after* the setting up of the abomination of desolation, 30 days *after* the *end* of the Great Tribulation?

It is because, even though the great judgment of the Tribulation is over, there is still one judgment left—that judgment is *not* a Great Tribulation judgment; rather, it is the judgment on the nation Babylon the Great, the nation that was the foundation of the Beast and his rise to power, the nation that is the bringer of the greatest of human evils upon the Earth. For this reason, Daniel takes us to the *end* of that *complete* judgment, taking us to 30 days *after the* Great Tribulation.

What then do we make of the 1,335 days of Daniel 12:12, where we are told that whoever waits for that 1,335th day, and sees it, is blessed?

This 1,335th day is 1,335 days after the setting up of the abomination of desolation. We know that Seal 6 *ends* with day 1,290, and so we now have 45 days between the end of Seal 6 and this next event. What is this next event? After Seal 6, there is only one remaining event—the events of Seal 7, the resurrection of all believers and the Second Coming itself. *Only* Christians will be *waiting* for that event, and so Daniel tells us that whoever has been *waiting* for that event, and *sees* it, that person is *blessed*. Since it is only Christians who will be waiting for that event, then, when that event comes, and when Christians upon the Earth *see* that event, they are blessed.

As a result, from Daniel 12:11–12, we know that Seal 6 lasts for 30 days, and then 45 days after the end of Seal 6, or 1,335 days *after* the setting up of the abomination of desolation, Jesus Christ returns to Earth at the Second Coming—the Second Coming happens on the 1,335th day after the setting up of the abomination of desolation, and it occurs in Seal 7.

SEAL 7—THE RESURRECTION OF BELIEVERS AND THE SECOND COMING

> Then the sign of the Son of Man will appear in heaven, and then all the tribes of the earth will mourn, and they will see the Son of Man coming on the clouds of heaven with power and great glory. And He will send His angels with a great sound of a trumpet, and they will gather together His elect from the four winds, from one end of heaven to the other. (Matt 24:30–31 NKJV)

> When He opened the seventh seal, there was silence in heaven for about half an hour. (Rev 8:1 NKJV)

Jesus himself, in Matthew 24:30–31, describes Seal 7 as being his Second Coming, and as the gathering of "his elect," the gathering of all Christians, which, we will see, includes *first* all the believers who have ever lived and *died*, and *then* those believers who had *not* yet died, but who are still *alive* upon the Earth, and who are waiting for the Coming of Jesus Christ, the same ones referred to in Daniel 12:12 as waiting for the Second Coming and as being blessed when they see it.

This resurrection of all believers is described clearly in 1 Thessalonians 4:16–17 and is described as happening at "the trumpet" (which is Trumpet 7 of Revelation, the "last trumpet"). Jesus also affirms that the resurrection of believers occurs at the sound of the Trumpet (Matt 24:31), and 1 Corinthians 15:52 tells us more specifically that this happens at the "*last* trumpet."

at the *last trumpet*. For the *trumpet will sound*, and *the dead will be raised* incorruptible, *and <u>we</u> shall be changed.* (1 Cor 15:52 NKJV)

The "last trumpet" of 1 Corinthians 15:52 is the same Trumpet of 1 Thessalonians 4:16–17, which is the same Trumpet as Matthew 24:31—this is all in Seal 7, and, in fact, this "last trumpet" is the same Trumpet 7 of Revelation (Rev 11:5)—the Seventh Trumpet. The "last trumpet," Trumpet 7, announces the Second Coming, which is preceded by the resurrection of all believers, living and dead. All of this is made clear by Jesus' own words in Matthew 24:30–31 in his description of Seal 7.

Why then does Revelation 8:1 tell us that Seal 7 is opened, and that there is then "silence in heaven for about half an hour"? How is this parallel to Jesus' description of Seal 7 in Matt.24.30-31? We can understand it as follows.

It is important to remember that in Revelation 6—19:11 there are three timelines being described: the overall, big-picture timeline of the Seven Seals, which is the entirety of the judgment, encompassing a total of forty years; the timeline of the Seven Trumpets, which is the three-and-a-half year Great Tribulation, all of which happens in Seal 5, and the following Seal 6/Trumpet 6 fall of the nation Babylon the Great, and the following Seal 7/Trumpet 7 resurrection of believers and the Second Coming, all of which happens in the final three and a half years of that same forty-year period; and the timeline of the Seven Bowls, which are just more specific details of the final six months of that same forty-year period. In between the descriptions of each of those timelines, Revelation goes back and forth in time to give us more details about the timeline just described, in most instances details specifically about the events of Seal 5, before moving on to the next timeline.

When Seal 7 is opened, and we are told that there was "silence in heaven", this brings us right up to the point of the Seal 7 resurrection of believers and the following Second Coming about to happen, but the action of Seal 7 stops there, and the narrative now switches to the description of a new timeline, the Trumpet timeline (starting at Rev. 8.6). Just after Seal 7 is opened, and before the Trumpet timeline begins to be described, we encounter the heavenly punctuation of "thunder, rumblings, flashes of lightning and an earthquake." (8.5). With this heavenly punctuation, we know that we are now switching to the description of a new timeline. As a result, the action of Seal 7 resumes later, resuming in 19.6, describing the marriage of the bride and the Lamb (the resurrection of believers) and the Second Coming at 19.11. As a result, when we take into account the fact that the events of Seal 7 are outlined in Revelation 19.6-9, and 19.11-21, we see that the events of Seal 7 as described in Revelation are in fact an exact parallel to Jesus' description of Seal 7 in Matt. 24.30-31.

THIS GENERATION – FORTY YEARS

In Matthew 24:34, after outlining for us the Seven Seals, Jesus tells us the following:

Truly I tell you, this generation will certainly not pass away until all these things have happened. (NIV)

Some have taken these words of Jesus and presented them as an example of how Jesus was mistaken, thereby using his supposed mistake as a foundation upon which to deny his divinity.

It is certainly true that after Jesus finishes describing to his apostles the Seven Seals, he specifically tells them that "this generation" will not pass till all the events he just described have happened. However, the generation of the apostles *did* pass and those events as described by Jesus did *not* happen—so, was Jesus wrong? How can we understand this?

No, Jesus was not wrong, and we can understand it as follows.

It is important to remember that Jesus makes the "this generation" comment specifically *after* he has just finished describing the entirety of the Seven Seals. It is also important to remember that the Seven Seals encompass a period of forty years. With that in mind, it is important to understand that a biblical generation is considered as forty years.

For example, after Israel rebelled at Mount Sinai, after Moses received the Ten Commandments, God made Israel wander in the wilderness for *forty years*, and we are told specifically that the purpose of that forty-year wandering was so that the *generation* that rebelled at Mount Sinai would die off.

> The Lord's anger burned against Israel and he made them wander in the wilderness *forty years*, until *the whole generation* of those who had done evil in his sight was gone. (Num 32:13 NIV)

Biblically, a generation is considered as forty years.

It is in that context that we are to understand the words of Jesus in Matthew 24:34. Simply put, it is this—the *generation* of which Jesus was speaking was *not* the generation of *his* day, the generation of the apostles; rather it was *the generation that will see the events that he has just finished describing*—it is the *future* generation on Earth in the days that precede the Second Coming, the generation that will see the events of Seals 1–7 as just described by Jesus in Matthew 24:3–31.

This is further affirmed when we remember that one generation in the Bible is considered as *forty years*, and that the events of the Seven Seals encompass a period of *forty years*—as a result, we can know that the events of the Seven Seals unfold over *one generation*. Seeing as Jesus just finished describing the events of the Seven Seals, events that will unfold over a forty-year period, over the period of one generation, then when Jesus makes the comment in Matthew 24:34 about "this generation," he is referring to that same future generation that will see the unfolding of the events of the Seven Seals which he just finished describing—*that* is the generation that, once the Seven Seal events begin, will not pass until *all* those things (the Seven Seals events) have happened, all occurring over the course of that one generation, a period of forty years.

CONCLUSION

From Jesus' own words, and his clear description of the Seven Seals in Matthew 24:3–33, and from the description of the Seven Seals in Revelation 6 and 8:1, we can know, with certainty, that the Seven Seals are the *entirety* of the judgment of Revelation, and that the later Trumpets and Bowls are all just *details* of Seal 5 and 6, and with Trumpet 7, the last Trumpet, being sounded in Seal 7 to announce the Second Coming,

When we look at the details of the Beast, we will see that, almost certainly, he will come to power at age thirty-three. It is almost certain that he will be conceived with the opening of Seal 1 and will be born nine months later, and it is certain that Seals 1–4 prepare the world for his coming. As a result, since the Beast will be born at the start of Seal 1, and since Seals 1–4 prepare the world for his coming, and since the Beast will almost certainly be thirty-three years of age when he comes to power at Seal 5, we can know that Seals 1–4 span a period of thirty-three years.

We also know that Seal 5 is the entirety of the Beast's three-and-a-half-year rule, as well as the entirety of the following three-and-a-half-year Great Tribulation, giving a total duration of seven years for Seal 5.

We also know that the duration of Seal 6 is thirty additional days *after* the end of Seal 5.

We also know that Seal 7 is the resurrection of all believers (both dead and living) and the Second Coming, with the Second Coming occurring forty-five days after the end of Seal 6.

As a result, we can know that the Seven Seals cover a period of thirty-three years (Seals 1–4) + seven years (Seal 5) + seventy-five days (Seal 6 and Seal 7) = forty years.

The Seven Seals cover a period of forty years, and they are the *entirety*, the *totality*, of the judgment of Revelation. This is why no one except the Judge himself, Jesus Christ, can open the Seven Seals—the opening of the Seven Seals is the Judge releasing the judgments. Jesus' own words in Matthew 24:3–31 are foundational to understanding this truth.

10

THE GREAT TRIBULATION—
THE TRUMPETS AND THE BOWLS

IN ADDITION TO THE Seven Seals outlined in Revelation, there are also two other timelines outlined in Revelation—the timeline of the Seven Trumpets and the timeline of the Seven Bowls. As we have already seen, the Seven Seals are the entirety of the judgment, spanning a period of forty years. What then are the Trumpets and the Bowls? The Trumpets and Bowls are in fact *details* of the Great Tribulation, which occurs *in its entirety* during Seal 5. In fact, the Trumpet and Bowl details break down as follows:

Seal 5 (Midway through)—the Great Tribulation

- Trumpet 1
- Trumpet 2
- Trumpet 3
- Trumpet 4
- Trumpet 5
    - Bowl 1
    - Bowl 2
    - Bowl 3
    - Bowl 4
    - Bowl 5

Seal 6—the Fall of Babylon the Great

- Trumpet 6
    - Bowl 6
    - Bowl 7

Seal 7—the Resurrection of Believers and the Second Coming

- Trumpet 7

This is how the details of the Trumpets and Bowls line up with the overall forty-year period of the Seven Seals. There are no Trumpets or Bowls during Seals 1–4—the Trumpets commence midway through Seal 5, and the sounding of Trumpet 1 is what begins the Great Tribulation, and Trumpets 1–5, in total, outline the overall details of the *entire* three-and-a-half-year Tribulation.

With the sounding of Trumpet 5, which lasts for a period of five months (Rev 9:10), and included as part of Trumpet 5, are Bowls 1–5, with those Bowls being the more specific details of the last five months of the Great Tribulation. Trumpet 5 is the last Trumpet of the Tribulation, which is brought to conclusion by the pouring of Bowls 1–5.

Seal 6 is opened *after* the end of the Great Tribulation (Matt 24:29) and is the fall of the nation Babylon the Great. When Seal 6 is opened, Trumpet 6 is sounded, and Trumpet 6 outlines the *details* of the Seal 6 fall of Babylon the Great. When Trumpet 6 sounds, it also unleashes Bowls 6 and 7, which are an even more detailed account of the fall of Babylon the Great. All of this is part of Seal 6. The pouring of the Bowls is complete with the end of Seal 6/Trumpet 6

Seal 7 is opened after the end of Seal 6, after the fall of Babylon the Great. With the opening of Seal 7, Trumpet 7, the "last trumpet," is sounded, and the sounding of Trumpet 7 brings forth the resurrection of believers and the Second Coming. The details of the resurrection of believers and the Second Coming are all part of Trumpet 7, the "last trumpet" (1 Cor 15:52; 1 Thess 4:16; Rev 11:15), which is itself part of Seal 7.

THE DEVASTATION OF THE TRUMPETS AND THE BOWLS—THE GREAT TRIBULATION

The sounding of the Trumpets and the pouring of the Bowls outlines, progressively, the details of the Great Tribulation, describing total, global devastation, as follows:

Trumpet 1

> The first angel sounded: And hail and fire followed, mingled with blood, and they were thrown to the earth. And a third of the trees were burned up, and all green grass was burned up. (Rev 8:7 NKJV)

With Trumpet 1, a third of all the trees on Earth are burned up, as well as *all* the grass.

Trumpet 2

> Then the second angel sounded: And something like a great mountain burning with fire was thrown into the sea, and a third of the sea became blood. And a third of the living creatures in the sea died, and a third of the ships were destroyed. (8:8–9 NKJV)

With Trumpet 2, a third of the sea is described as becoming like blood, and a third of all sea creatures die, and a third of all ships are destroyed.

Trumpet 3

> Then the third angel sounded: And a great star fell from heaven, burning like a torch, and it fell on a third of the rivers and on the springs of water. The name of the star is Wormwood. A third of the waters became wormwood, and many men died from the water, because it was made bitter. (8:10–11 NKJV)

With Trumpet 3, a third of all the fresh water becomes poisoned.

Trumpet 4

> Then the fourth angel sounded: And a third of the sun was struck, a third of the moon, and a third of the stars, so that a third of them were darkened. A third of the day did not shine, and likewise the night. (8:12 NKJV)

With Trumpet 4, a third of the sun and moon and the stars are darkened, and do not give light.

The events of Trumpets 1–4 are enormous global devastation, the likes of which has never before been seen on Earth. This devastation is the explicit fulfillment of Jesus' own words from Matthew 24.

> For then there will be great tribulation, such as has not been since the beginning of the world until this time, no, nor ever shall be. And unless those days

were shortened, no flesh would be saved; but for *the elect's sake* those days will be shortened. (Matt 24:21–22 NKJV)

This is the Great Tribulation, a devastation so great that, according to Jesus Christ himself, unless Jesus returns at the Second Coming to put an end to that Tribulation, no life would remain on Earth.

In fact, in the Matthew 24:21–22 passage Jesus again affirms the full presence of the church upon the Earth during that time of the Great Tribulation, for he explicitly tells us that he is returning for the sake of the elect. Once again, as specifically affirmed by Jesus himself, the church remains on Earth during the entire Tribulation, right to the end, for whose sake he returns.

TRUMPET 5

There is a specific break between the account of Trumpets 4 and 5, and that break is found in 8:13.

> And I looked, and I heard an angel flying through the midst of heaven, saying with a loud voice, "Woe, woe, woe to the inhabitants of the earth, because of the remaining blasts of the trumpet of the three angels who are about to sound!" (NKJV)

After the events of Trumpet 4, and before the sounding of Trumpet 5, the action stops and an angel makes a declaration to the world that what is now about to follow will be especially terrible. Why does this declaration happen here, after Trumpet 4 but before Trumpet 5? It is because, with the sounding of Trumpet 5, the Bowls begin to be poured. The blast of Trumpet 5, in addition to releasing its own Trumpet judgment, also unleashes the pouring of Bowls 1–5—Bowls 1–5 are part of the Trumpet 5 judgment.

Trumpet 5 is described as follows:

> Then the fifth angel sounded: And I saw a star fallen from heaven to the earth. To him was given the key to the bottomless pit. And he opened the bottomless pit, and smoke arose out of the pit like the smoke of a great furnace. So the sun and the air were darkened because of the smoke of the pit. Then out of the smoke locusts came upon the earth. And to them was given power, as the scorpions of the earth have power. They were commanded not to harm the grass of the earth, or any green thing, or any tree, but only those men who do not have the seal of God on their foreheads. And they were not given authority to kill them, but to torment them for five months. Their torment was like the torment of a scorpion when it strikes a man. In those days men will seek death and will not find it; they will desire to die, and death will flee from them. The shape of the locusts was like horses prepared for battle. On their heads were crowns of something like gold, and their faces were like the faces of men. They

had hair like women's hair, and their teeth were like lions' teeth. And they had breastplates like breastplates of iron, and the sound of their wings was like the sound of chariots with many horses running into battle. They had tails like scorpions, and there were stings in their tails. Their power was to hurt men five months. And they had as king over them the angel of the bottomless pit, whose name in Hebrew is Abaddon, but in Greek he has the name Apollyon. (9:1–11 NKJV)

With the blast of Trumpet 5, we are told of a fallen angel (the "star fallen from heaven," see also Isa 14:13; Rev 12:4), and we are told that that fallen angel was "given the key to the bottomless pit," and that the fallen angel opened the bottomless Pit, which is located inside the Earth (Rev 9:1). Upon the opening of the Pit, smoke arises from the Pit to darken the sun and the earthly sky. We are told that strange creatures, described as looking like locusts, come out of the Pit, coming upon the Earth, and having authority to harm *only* those people who worshiped the Beast, with those locust-like spirits being specifically described as *not* being *allowed* to harm the church, the people belonging to God. The church itself is then described as having the "seal of God on their foreheads." As a result, the church on the Earth continues to be protected from the judgments of the Great Tribulation, a fulfillment of Revelation 3:10, where Jesus promises the church that, though fully on the Earth during this entire Tribulation time, it will be protected from, or will be kept from, the trial that has come upon the Earth (just as Israel was present in Egypt during the plagues but was protected from being harmed by those same plagues).

The locust-like spirits coming out from the Pit are described as having crowns on their heads, as having human faces, and also as having hair like women, teeth like lion's teeth, and breastplates of iron. They are described as having wings that thunder like the running of chariots, and also as having tails like scorpions. We are told that those locust-like spirits have power to torment, but not kill, *only* the people who had the mark of the Beast, and that their torment would last for a period of five months. We are told that the people who have the mark of the Beast, the people who are suffering that torment, will seek death, but will be unable to die. We are also told that a fallen angel from the Pit named Abaddon, or Apollyon, is king over the locust-like spirits.

This is the description of the events of Trumpet 5.

Where Trumpets 1–4 describe enormous earthly devastation, Trumpet 5 describes human torment, but only for those people who do not belong to God, who have taken the mark of the Beast—the church is kept safe during this time, protected from harm, for only those who have the mark of the Beast will suffer torment.

The events described during Trumpet 5, events of human torment that will come upon only those who have the mark of the Beast, are not even remotely in the same league of devastation as was described by Trumpets 1–4, and yet Trumpet 5 is preceded by the declaration of an ominous warning to the inhabitants of the Earth, a warning that basically says that what is now about to come upon the Earth with the sounding of Trumpet 5 will be far worse than what was experienced with Trumpets 1–4. When we compare the event of human torment ascribed to Trumpet 5 to the colossal global devastation events of Trumpets 1–4, Trumpet 5 does not in any way seem to be as bad as Trumpets 1–4, so how then can we understand the angel's declaration of a coming devastation, to come with the sounding of Trumpet 5, that, implicitly, is to be much worse than Trumpets 1–4? We can understand it as follows.

The declaration that precedes the sounding of Trumpet 5, where the angel declares "woe" to the inhabitants of the Earth for what is about to come (8:13), is in fact an announcement that the *Bowls* are about to be poured out, poured out as *part* of the Trumpet 5 *details*. When Trumpet 5 sounds, it unleashes the pouring of Bowls 1–5—Bowls 1–5 are all part of Trumpet 5. The declaration by the angel of "woe, woe, woe to the inhabitants of the earth" is a reference to the pouring of Bowls 1–5.

BOWLS 1 TO 5

Here are the details of the Bowls being poured out:

Bowl 1

> So the first went and poured out his bowl upon the earth, and a foul and loathsome sore came upon the men who had the mark of the beast and those who worshiped his image. (16:2 NKJV)

With the pouring of Bowl 1, all people who had the mark of the Beast are afflicted with foul and loathsome sores. This is almost an exact representation of Trumpet 5, where we are told that the locusts had power to hurt people who took the mark of the Beast, to hurt them only, not kill them, for a period of five months. When Trumpet 5 is blown, Bowl 1 is poured, and *only* the people who have the mark of the Beast are afflicted with foul and loathsome sores, and those people will seek death but will not find it (Trumpet 5, 8:4–5). The foul and loathsome sores of Bowl 1 are in fact the exact *same* torment as described by Trumpet 5, inflicted only upon people who have the mark of the Beast, inflicted upon them by the locusts—that affliction is *generally* described in 9:1–11, the description of Trumpet 5, but *in more detail* in 16:2, the description of Bowl 1. Both of these descriptions, the description of Trumpet 5 and the description of Bowl 1, are a description of the *same* event.

Bowl 2

> Then the second angel poured out his bowl on the sea, and it became blood as of a dead man; and every living creature in the sea died. (16:3 NKJV)

The details of Trumpet 5 continue with Bowl 2, which is poured upon the sea, this time resulting in the death of *every* living thing in the sea.

Bowl 3

> Then the third angel poured out his bowl on the rivers and springs of water, and they became blood. (16:4 NKJV)

Trumpet 5 continues with the pouring of Bowl 3, where *all* the remaining freshwater becomes like blood, that is to say, undrinkable.

Bowl 4

> Then the fourth angel poured out his bowl on the sun, and power was given to him to scorch men with fire. And men were scorched with great heat, and they blasphemed the name of God who has power over these plagues; and they did not repent and give Him glory. (16:8–9 NKJV)

With the pouring of Bowl 4, also part of Trumpet 5, the sun becomes intensely hot and burns *only* those people who have the mark of the Beast. We know this is true because we are specifically told that those people who are suffering this extreme scorching heat blaspheme God and refuse to repent—the *only* people who will blaspheme God and refuse to repent are the people who have the mark of the Beast, while everyone else on Earth who does *not* have the mark of the Beast will *not* be tormented by the extreme scorching heat.

Bowl 5

> Then the fifth angel poured out his bowl on the throne of the beast, and his kingdom became full of darkness; and they gnawed their tongues because of the pain. (16:10 NKJV)

With the pouring of Bowl 5, also part of Trumpet 5, the very throne of the Beast, and his entire kingdom, is cursed with a *painful* darkness, described as being so painful that it results in people "gnawing their tongues." Again, this darkness and pain is *only* upon those who are of the Beast's kingdom, and is *not* upon those who are not of his kingdom.

In fact, this darkness that is poured out upon the throne of the Beast, and upon his kingdom, is an exact parallel to the curse of darkness upon Egypt, where that darkness fell *only* upon the Egyptians but *not* upon the Israelites, even though the Israelites dwelt in that same land of Egypt.

Then the LORD said to Moses, "Stretch out your hand toward heaven, that there may be darkness over the land of Egypt, darkness which may even be felt." So Moses stretched out his hand toward heaven, and there was thick darkness in all the land of Egypt three days. They did not see one another; nor did anyone rise from his place for three days. But all the children of Israel had light in their dwellings. (Exod 10:21–23 NKJV)

In exactly this same way, when Bowl 5 is poured upon the throne and kingdom of the Beast, *only* the Beast and those who have his mark, only those who belong to his kingdom, will be afflicted with that painful darkness, but the church, though fully present upon Earth during that entire time, will *not* be afflicted by that painful darkness, for the church is kept from, is protected from, the trial, or Tribulation, that will come upon the Earth (Rev 3:10).

Bowls 1–5 are an enormous devastation, a degree of total, global devastation that *exceeds* the devastation of Trumpets 1–4. Bowls 1–5 occur *during* Trumpet 5, which is why Bowl 1 describes the exact same affliction poured out upon the people who have the mark of the Beast as is inflicted by the locusts of Trumpet 5, also inflicted only upon those people who have the mark of the Beast—the Trumpet 5 affliction and the Bowl 1 affliction are a description the same event.

The blast of Trumpet 5 unleashes the pouring of the Bowls, and the devastation brought by the pouring of Bowls 1–5 greatly exceeds the devastation brought by Trumpets 1–4. It is for this reason that the angel declares a warning to the inhabitants of the Earth, declaring "woe, woe, woe to the inhabitants of the earth" just before Trumpet 5 is sounded—with the sounding of Trumpet 5, the pouring of the Bowls begins.

Once Bowl 5 is poured, the events of Trumpet 5 are over, the Great Tribulation is finished, for we will see that Bowls 6 and 7 are part of the Trumpet 6 events, which itself is sounded during Seal 6, with Seal 6 being opened *after* the end of the Great Tribulation (Matt 24:29; Rev 6:12–13).

HOW LONG IS THE PERIOD OF TRUMPET 5/BOWLS 1–5?

The Great Tribulation begins at the midpoint of the seven-year period described by Daniel in Daniel 9:27, beginning after the Beast rules for three and a half years and after he seats himself upon a throne on the holy of holies of the rebuilt temple—the abomination of desolation. The Great Tribulation is unleashed by the sounding of Trumpet 1. That same Great Tribulation *ends* with the conclusion of Trumpet 5—that entire Tribulation period, the period of Trumpets 1–5, lasts 1,260 days, 42 months, or three and a half years.

As we have seen, Bowls 1–5 are all part of the Trumpet 5 judgment, being just the *details* of Trumpet 5—with the pouring of the final Bowl, Bowl 5, the Great Tribulation is over. That being the case, then how long do those Five Bowls last? Bowls 1–5 cover a period of five months, the final five months of the three-and-a-half-year Great Tribulation.

How can we know that? We can know it as follows:

We are specifically told in the Revelation 9:1–5 description of Trumpet 5 that the locust torment released upon those who have the mark of the Beast will last for five months. It is implicit in this that Trumpet 5 *itself* lasts a total of five months. As a result, since we know that Bowls 1–5 occur during Trumpet 5, and since Trumpet 5 lasts for five months, we can conclude that Bowls 1–5 last a total of five months. Also, the fact that there are *five* Bowls included in the Trumpet 5 judgment, and that the entire Trumpet 5 judgment lasts for *five* months, indicates that one Bowl will be poured out every 30 days during the five-month period of Trumpet 5. As a result, we can understand that *each* of Bowls 1–5 will last a period of 30 days, with all five Bowls collectively lasting 150 days, five months, constituting the *final* five months of the Great Tribulation period.

Once Bowl 5 has been poured, the Trumpet 5 judgment is completed, and the Great Tribulation is over.

TRUMPET 6

After the end of the Trumpet 5 judgment, after the end of the Great Tribulation, Seal 6 will be opened. With the opening of Seal 6, Trumpet 6 will sound, and we are told the following about Trumpet 6:

> Then the sixth angel sounded: And I heard a voice from the four horns of the golden altar which is before God, saying to the sixth angel who had the trumpet, "Release the four angels who are bound at **the great river Euphrates**." So the four angels, who had been prepared for the hour and day and month and year, were released to kill a third of mankind. Now the number of the army of the horsemen was two hundred million; I heard the number of them. And thus I saw the horses in the vision: those who sat on them had breastplates of fiery red, hyacinth blue, and sulfur yellow; and the heads of the horses were like the heads of lions; and out of their mouths came fire, smoke, and brimstone. By these three plagues a third of mankind was killed—by the fire and the smoke and the brimstone which came out of their mouths. For their power is in their mouth and in their tails; for their tails are like serpents, having heads; and with them they do harm. (9:13–19 NKJV)

We are also told the following about Bowls 6 and 7:

Bowl 6

> Then the sixth angel poured out his bowl on the great river Euphrates, and its water was dried up, so that the way of the kings from the east might be

prepared. And I saw three unclean spirits like frogs coming out of the mouth of the dragon, out of the mouth of the beast, and out of the mouth of the false prophet. For they are spirits of demons, performing signs, which go out to the kings of the earth and of the whole world, to gather them to the battle of that great day of God Almighty. "Behold, I am coming as a thief. Blessed is he who watches, and keeps his garments, lest he walk naked and they see his shame." And they gathered them together to the place called in Hebrew, Armageddon. (16:12–15 NKJV)

Bowl 7

Then the seventh angel poured out his bowl into the air, and a loud voice came out of the temple of heaven, from the throne, saying, "It is done!" And there were noises and thunderings and lightnings; and there was a great earthquake, such a mighty and great earthquake as had not occurred since men were on the earth. Now the great city was divided into three parts, and the cities of the nations fell. And great Babylon was remembered before God, to give her the cup of the wine of the fierceness of His wrath. Then every island fled away, and the mountains were not found. And great hail from heaven fell upon men, each hailstone about the weight of a talent. Men blasphemed God because of the plague of the hail, since that plague was exceedingly great. (16:17–21 NKJV)

It is important to notice that both Bowls 6 and 7 are different in their nature and character from Bowls 1–5. Where Bowls 1–5 describe enormous global judgments upon the inhabitants of the Earth (a specific fulfillment of the angel's Trumpet 5 warning declaration of "woe" in 8:13), Bowls 6 and 7 do *not* describe a similar global devastation. Rather, with Bowl 6, the Euphrates dries up, spirits come out of the mouth of the dragon, out of the mouth of the Beast, and out of the mouth of the False Prophet, and those three spirits then gather the armies of the world to Armageddon for battle, while Bowl 7 describes the fall of Babylon the Great. The nature of the judgments of Bowls 6 and 7 is strikingly different than the nature of the Bowl 1–5 judgments—why? It is because Bowls 1–5 are describing the final months of the Great Tribulation, while Bowls 6 and 7 describe events *after* the Great Tribulation.

BOWL 6

Compare Trumpet 6, as described in 9:14, with Bowl 6, as described in 16:12.

> . . . saying to the sixth angel who had the trumpet, "Release the four angels who are bound at *the great river Euphrates.*" (9:14 NKJV, Trumpet 6)

> Then the sixth angel poured out his bowl on *the great river Euphrates*, and its water was dried up, so that the way of *the kings from the east* might be prepared. (16:12 NKJV, Bowl 6)

Both 9:14 (Trumpet 6) and 16:12 (Bowl 6) describe events at the river Euphrates. We see from 9:16 that the Trumpet 6 events are in fact *military* events that are unfolding at the river Euphrates. Likewise, in 16:12, Bowl 6 also describes *military* events unfolding at the river Euphrates.

So, are these military events at the river Euphrates happening twice? No—they only happen once, for the Trumpet 6 description and the Bowl 6 description are describing the same event—the drying up of the Euphrates river and the army of two hundred million coming from the east, which will cross over the dried-up Euphrates river. The blast of Trumpet 6 results in Bowl 6 being poured out, and so both the Trumpet 6 and Bowl 6 descriptions are describing the same event.

Furthermore, both Trumpet 6 and Bowl 6 give a corroborating detail about the specific military events at the river Euphrates, which further affirms that Trumpet 6 and Bowl 6 are describing the same event.

In the Bowl 6 description of that event, we are told that the drying up of the Euphrates river makes way for the "kings of the east" to come (Rev 16:12). Likewise, in the Trumpet 6 description of that event, we are told that an army of two hundred million has been mustered and is on the move (9:16). There is only one nation on Earth that could muster an army of two hundred million, and that is the most populous nation on Earth—China. It so happens that China is also in the "east." As a result, we can understand the Bowl 6 description of the "kings of the east" and the Trumpet 6 description of an army of two hundred million as being a description of the same event.

BOWL 7

Also included in the Trumpet 6 events is Bowl 7. Bowl 7 is poured out after Bowl 6 is poured out and describes the fall of Babylon the Great, the great city/nation that is the dominant nation on Earth, and which, as we shall see, will be the initial power base of the Beast. Bowl 7 *also* occurs during Trumpet 6, and we can know that by looking at Trumpet 7.

TRUMPET 7

When Seal 7 is opened, Trumpet 7, the last Trumpet, will sound. Trumpet 7 is described as follows:

> The seventh angel sounded his trumpet, and there were loud voices in heaven, which said: "The kingdom of the world has become the kingdom of our Lord and of his Messiah, and he will reign for ever and ever." (Rev 11:15 NIV)

The Great Tribulation—The Trumpets and the Bowls

Trumpet 7, the last, or final, Trumpet, announces the Second Coming. This is in exact accordance with Jesus' own words.

> Then will appear the sign of the Son of Man in heaven. And then all the peoples of the earth will mourn when they see the Son of Man coming on the clouds of heaven, with power and great glory. And he will send his angels with *a loud trumpet call*, and they will gather his elect from the four winds, from one end of the heavens to the other. (Matt 24:30–31 NIV)

Here, Jesus describes his coming, and the gathering, or resurrection, of the church, happening at the sound of a Trumpet. This exact same Trumpet scenario and description is given by other scriptures.

> In a flash, in the twinkling of an eye, at the *last trumpet*. For the *trumpet* will sound, *the dead will be raised imperishable*, and we will be changed. (1 Cor 15:52 NIV)

This is specifically a description of the resurrection of believers, and it is described as happening at the "last trumpet," which is Trumpet 7 of Revelation, and which is the same Trumpet referred to by Jesus in Matthew 24:30–31.

> For *the Lord himself will come down from heaven*, with a loud command, with the voice of the archangel and with the *trumpet* call of God, and *the dead in Christ will rise first*. (1 Thess 4:16 NIV)

In 1 Thessalonians 4:16, we are once again specifically told about the Second Coming, and, once again, we are told that at the blast of the Trumpet the "dead in Christ" (all Christians who have ever died) will now be resurrected. This Trumpet of 1 Thessalonians 4:16 is the same "last trumpet" of 1 Corinthians 15:52, which is also the same Trumpet referred to by Jesus in Matthew 24:30–31 when he describes the "gathering of the elect" (i.e., the resurrection of Christians) and his Second Coming. All of these Trumpet references are referring to the same Trumpet and the same events, and the Trumpet referred to in all of these scriptures is in fact the "last trumpet" of Revelation, Trumpet 7.

As a result, from these various scriptures, we know, with certainty, that Trumpet 7 announces the resurrection of believers as well as the Second Coming.

Since we know that Bowl 7 is the fall of the city/nation Babylon the Great, and since we know that Trumpet 7 specifically announces the resurrection of believers as well as the Second Coming, and since we know, for a fact, that the fall of Babylon the Great happens before the Second Coming (Rev 19:1–11), then we can know, with certainty, that Bowl 7 does *not* occur during Trumpet 7. As a result, we can know that Bowl 7, together with Bowl 6, *also* occurs during Trumpet 6.

SUMMARY OF THE TRUMPETS AND BOWLS

Here then is a summary of the Trumpets and Bowls, of how they line up together as is clearly laid out for us in Revelation:

Seal 5

- Trumpet 5
    - Bowl 1
    - Bowl 2
    - Bowl 3
    - Bowl 4
    - Bowl 5

Seal 6

- Trumpet 6
    - Bowl 6
    - Bowl 7

Seal 7

- Trumpet 7

HOW LONG DOES TRUMPET 6 AND TRUMPET 7 LAST?

As we have seen, the entire Great Tribulation is described by Trumpets 1–5, with Bowls 1–5 being included in Trumpet 5. That entire Great Tribulation time period spans three and a half years. All of this, as well as the preceding three-and-a-half-year rule of the Beast, is part of Seal 5.

We also know that Seal 6 is opened *after* the Great Tribulation (Matt 24:29), and, since Trumpet 6 is sounded with the opening of Seal 6, we know that Trumpet 6 is sounded *after* the Great Tribulation. As we have seen, both Bowl 6 and Bowl 7 are themselves included in the Trumpet 6 events, therefore we can know that Bowls 6 and 7 are poured during Trumpet 6, *after* the Great Tribulation.

How do we know that the Great Tribulation lasts for three and a half years? And how long does Trumpet 6/Bowls 6 and 7 last?

We will see that the Great Tribulation/Trumpets 1–5 lasts 1,260 days, or 42 months/three and a half years (also described as "a time, times and half a time"—Dan 7:25; 12:7), and that Bowls 1–5 are the final five *months* of that *same* period.

We will see that Trumpet 6 lasts for 30 days, being the 30 days *following* the Great Tribulation.

We will also see that the events announced by Trumpet 7—the resurrection of all Christians, dead and living, and the Second Coming—occur 45 days *after* the end of Trumpet 6.

How do we know that? We can know this by understanding the event that triggers the Great Tribulation.

THE EVENT THAT TRIGGERS THE GREAT TRIBULATION

Jesus specifically tells us, in his description of Seal 5 in Matthew 24:15–21, that the event that triggers the Great Tribulation is the abomination of desolation. He also tells us that this abomination of desolation is the same event as described by the prophet Daniel. As a result, by referring to Daniel, we can know specifically when the Great Tribulation begins.

We are told the following in Daniel:

> He will confirm a covenant with many for *one "seven."* In *the middle of the "seven"* he will put an end to sacrifice and offering. And at the temple *he will set up an abomination that causes desolation*, until the end that is decreed is poured out on him. (Dan 9:27 NKJV)

As we have discussed, the periods of "sevens" referred to in Daniel 9 are periods of seven years, and each period of seven years is described in Daniel as being one "seven" or one "week." As a result, when Daniel tells us that a person will confirm a covenant with many for "one week," he is telling us that this covenant will be for a seven-year period, which itself will be the *final* seven-year period of Daniel's seventy seven-year periods as described in Daniel 9:24–27, with that final seven-year period culminating in God's kingdom being established forever on Earth (Dan 7:23–27). This final seven-year period is the period during which the Beast comes to power and during which the Great Tribulation occurs.

Daniel tells us that the Beast will dominate the world for a period of seven years (Dan 7:23–27; 9:24–27), and that he will come to power by establishing a global covenant with the nations of the world, described as the "covenant with many"—this covenant will be a covenant of peace, for that man, the Beast of Revelation, is described as coming in peace (Dan 11:21; 11:24). This "covenant with many," the covenant of peace that will be brought about by the Beast, is the peace treaty that brings to an end the global war of Seal 2. The establishing of that covenant is what will *begin* that final seven-year period. Daniel then tells us, very specifically, that in the *middle* of that "seven," or in the *middle* of that seven-year period, that same one who makes the covenant of peace will "put an end to sacrifice and offering" and set up the abomination of desolation. As a result, we know, for a fact, that the abomination of desolation occurs in the middle of that final seven-year period, or three and a half years into that seven-year period.

THREE AND A HALF YEARS, 42 MONTHS, 1,260 DAYS

As previously discussed, the periods of months described in Revelation are based on the Jewish calendar month of 30 days. So, a three-and-a-half-year period is a period of 42 months; 42 months, calculated as based on 30 days in a month, is a total of 1,260 days. As a result, Daniel's period of three and a half years is also equal to a period of 42 months or 1,260 days.

Why is this significant? It is significant because the period of 42 months, and 1,260 days, is specifically and constantly reaffirmed in Revelation.

> And he was given a mouth speaking great things and blasphemies, and he was given authority to continue for *forty-two months*. (13:5 NKJV)

> And they will tread the holy city underfoot for *forty-two months*. (11:2 NKJV)

> And I will give *power* to my *two* witnesses, and they will prophesy *one thousand two hundred and sixty days*, clothed in sackcloth. (11:3 NKJV)

> Then the woman fled into the wilderness, where she has a place prepared by God, that they should feed her there *one thousand two hundred and sixty days*. 12:6 NKJV)

The 42 months, and the 1,260 days, repeatedly mentioned in Revelation are in fact the exact same three-and-a half-year period as mentioned in Daniel. We also must remember that there are in fact *two* periods of three and a half years in Daniel— the first three-and-a-half-year period *precedes* the abomination of desolation, while the second three-and-a half-year period *follows* the abomination of desolation. Together, these *two* three-and-a-half-year periods make up the entire seven-year period of Daniel 9.

When looking at Revelation, and its description of the 1,260 days in 11:3, and the 42 months in 13:5, we will see, based on the presence of the Two Witnesses, that this is a description of the *first* 1,260-day, or three-and-a-half-year, period, the period during which the Beast will rule as the global ruler of the world (referred to by 13:5 as the period of the Beast's "authority"), and during which time the Beast will persecute the church. The 1,260 days of Revelation 12:6 is the *second* three and a half years of that seven-year period, and this is the time of the Great Tribulation spoken of by Jesus in Matthew 24:15–28, during which time the church will be protected.

This protection of the church during the time of the Great Tribulation is specifically affirmed in Revelation 12:6. In 12:6, the woman (here representing the church on Earth) flees to a place of safety during that second 1,260 days, the time of the Great Tribulation. The protection described in Revelation 12:6 is, in fact, yet another affirmation of Jesus' words of Revelation 3:10, where he tells us that the church will be kept from, or *protected* from, the trial that is to come upon the world. The church *is* protected from that trial, *not* by being removed from Earth (as affirmed by Jesus himself in John 17:15, when he tells the Father that he is not asking for the apostles or the church to be taken out of the world during the time of trial, but to be *protected* from that trial), but rather by having a place of safety and refuge upon the Earth during that time. That place of safety and refuge for the church is what is being described in Revelation 12:6, where the church is described as fleeing into the wilderness to a place prepared for her by God where she will be fed (i.e., kept safe) for the 1,260 days of the Great Tribulation.

Once again, this is yet another scriptural affirmation that the church is present fully on Earth during the entire time of the Great Tribulation, in complete contradiction to the rapture teaching.

We see then that both Revelation and Daniel consistently affirm the seven-year period, and the two halves of that period—the first half being the Beast's three-and-a-half-year rule of the world, and the second half being the three-and-a-half-year Great Tribulation.

But what triggers the Great Tribulation? *Why* does it start three and a half years into the rule of the Beast?

We know, from both Jesus own words in Matthew 24:15–21 as well as from Daniel 9:27, that the event that triggers the Great Tribulation is the abomination of desolation and that it occurs at the midpoint of the seven-year period, which is 1,260 days, or 42 months (three and a half years) *after* the Beast makes the "covenant with many" (Dan 9:27).

What is the abomination of desolation?

THE ABOMINATION OF DESOLATION

Jesus himself tells us that the abomination of desolation is what triggers the Great Tribulation (Matt 24:15–21), and he also tells us that this is the same abomination of desolation spoken of by the prophet Daniel. The abomination of desolation is spoken of by Daniel in Daniel 9:27, and Daniel tells us that the abomination of desolation occurs in the *middle* of the "week," which is to say it occurs in the middle of that final seven-year period, or three and a half years into the rule of the Beast. Daniel also specifically connects the abomination of desolation with bringing an "end to sacrifice and offering." To what "sacrifice and offering" is Daniel referring?

The sacrifices and offerings to which Daniel is referring are the sacrifices and offerings performed by the Jews at the temple. Jewish sacrifices and offerings could *only* take place in the temple, but the temple was destroyed in 70 AD, and has not existed since that time. Since Daniel is telling specifically that the abomination of desolation will occur at the same time that the sacrifices and offerings are stopped, and since those same sacrifices and offerings can *only* be performed in the temple, then that means, in order for there to be sacrifices and offerings in the first place during that time, the destroyed temple must be rebuilt, otherwise sacrifices and offerings cannot happen.

This is also further affirmed in Daniel 11:31.

> And forces shall be mustered by him, and *they shall defile the sanctuary fortress*; then *they shall take away the daily sacrifices*, and *place there the abomination of desolation*. (Dan 11:31 NKJV)

Once again, Daniel here affirms for us that the daily sacrifices will be stopped, and *in that same place where the sacrifices would occur* is where the abomination of desolation will be placed, and Daniel describes this as a defilement of the "sanctuary."

As a result, we can know that the abomination of desolation will be set up in the temple, and it is for this reason that we can know that the temple in Jerusalem must be rebuilt in order for that to happen, since the temple has not existed since 70 AD and does not currently exist.

Since the founding of the modern state of Israel in 1948, there have been continuous calls by the Jews to rebuild the temple, but the sacred spot upon which the temple must be rebuilt is on the Muslim territory of Jerusalem, currently occupied by the Muslim Dome of the Rock. How then will the temple be rebuilt? We shall see almost certainly that it will be the Beast himself who will instigate, and make possible, the rebuilding of that temple as part of the global "peace/covenant with many" that he will make with the nations of the world. As a result of the Beast making possible the rebuilding of the temple, the Beast will be hailed by the Jews as Messiah.

ANTIOCHUS EPIPHANES

The prophecies of Daniel 9 and of Matthew 24 refer specifically to the events that will precede the Second Coming and describe the events of the time of the Beast. However, there is also a parallel historical example of an event that illustrates an abomination of desolation, a historical event that shows how the temple could be defiled, and that event is the sacrilege of the temple by Antiochus Epiphanes in 167 BC.

Antiochus Epiphanes, or Antiochus IV, was a Seleucid ruler who captured Jerusalem, stopped the Jewish sacrifices of the temple, and then, going into the holy of holies, the very sacred heart of the temple accessible only by the high priest once a year in order to make sacrifice for the people of Judah, Antiochus erected an altar to the pagan Greek god Zeus and sacrificed a pig to Zeus. That altar to Zeus, and that pig sacrifice to Zeus, in the holy of holies, was a desecration of the temple that came to be known in Jewish history as the abomination of desolation. That abomination of desolation by Antiochus Epiphanes was the complete sacrilege of the holy of holies, the very heart of the temple, and involved the worship of, and sacrifice to, a false god in the holy of holies.

With this historical event in mind, we can understand the coming abomination of desolation that will be instituted by the Beast in a similar way. The temple will be rebuilt, and daily sacrifices will only *begin* to happen but will almost immediately be stopped by the Beast himself. Upon stopping the sacrifice in the rebuilt temple, the Beast will then himself go into the holy of holies, exactly as did Antiochus Epiphanes, and set up his *own* throne *in the holy of holies*, and he will sit upon that throne and, in so doing, he will proclaim *himself* as God Almighty. This is specifically affirmed in 2 Thessalonians.

> who opposes and exalts himself above all that is called God or that is worshiped, so that *he sits as God in the temple of God*, showing himself *that he is God*. (2:4 NKJV)

Based on 2 Thessalonians 2:4, and in conjunction with Matthew 24 and Daniel 9's reference to the abomination of desolation, we can understand the following. The Beast will cause the temple to be rebuilt as part of the global "peace/covenant with many" that he will institute, and, as a result, he will be hailed by the Jews as the Messiah (Isa 28:15–18; John 5:43). We will see that it will almost certainly take three and a half years to rebuild the temple, and once it is rebuilt the Jews will begin to offer the daily sacrifice and offerings. At that point, the Beast, who (as we shall see) will be in Jerusalem at exactly that three-and-a-half-year point (Rev 11:1–10), will go to the rebuilt temple and put a stop to the daily sacrifice and offerings that the Jews were just beginning to make. Once he puts a stop to that daily sacrifice, the Beast will then go into the holy of holies of the rebuilt temple, set up a throne in the holy of holies, and then seat himself upon that throne, in the holy of holies, thereby proclaiming *himself* to be God Almighty. *That* will be the abomination of desolation and that is the event that triggers the Great Tribulation.

Why is that the event that triggers the Great Tribulation?

The reason the abomination of desolation triggers the Great Tribulation is that in seating himself in the holy of holies, upon a throne, the Beast is, in fact, claiming the very throne of Jesus Christ as his own, for when Jesus Christ returns to Earth at the Second Coming, and rules the Earth as King of God's everlasting kingdom on Earth, his throne will be in the holy of holies of that same rebuilt temple. In seating himself upon a throne in the holy of holies of the rebuilt temple, the Beast is claiming the throne of Jesus Christ for himself.

That event, the abomination of desolation, the setting up of a throne in the holy of holies of the rebuilt temple, and the Beast seating himself upon that throne, occurs 1,260 days, 42 months, or three and a half years *after* the Beast comes to power by bringing global peace to the world, which is the "covenant with many" (Dan 9:27), and *after* ruling the world for those three and a half years. Once the Great Tribulation is triggered, it will last an additional three and a half years, or 1,260 days/42 months, and will be described, in totality, by Trumpets 1–5, and by Bowls 1–5, which are themselves part of the Trumpet 5 events. Again, *all* of this—the Beast's global peace, his initial three-and-a half-year rule, the subsequent setting up of the abomination of desolation, and the ensuing three-and-a-half-year Great Tribulation—that entire seven-year period, occurs in Seal 5.

BIRTH PAINS

We see then, with the inclusion of the Trumpets in Seals 5–7, and with the inclusion of the Bowls in Trumpets 5 and 6, that the closer we get to the Second Coming, the more intense are the judgments of Seal 5 *and* the more *frequently* do they occur. This increase in intensity and frequency of the judgments as we get closer to the Second Coming is an exact fulfillment of Jesus' own words of Matthew 24:8, where he summarizes Seals 1–4:

> All these are the beginning of birth pains. (NIV)

Jesus here describes the events of Seals 1–4 as the "beginning of birth pains." Since Seals 1–4 are the *beginning* of birth pains, then what is to come in Seals 5–7 will be the *culmination* of those same birth pains, resulting in the actual *birth* itself, which is the Second Coming of Jesus Christ and the birth of his established kingdom on Earth.

What happens during birth pains?

During any pregnancy, when the birth pains begin, they are relatively infrequent and not so intense, but as the time of birth approaches, those same birth pains greatly increase in *both* frequency *and* intensity, culminating in the actual birth.

This is *exactly* what we see with the Seven Seals, and the attendant Trumpets and Bowls. Seals 1–4 *prepare* the world for the coming of the Beast—they are the "*beginning* of birth pains." Seal 5 is when the Beast comes to power, ruling for three and half years, during which time he persecutes, and overcomes, the church. Once he seats himself upon the throne in the holy of holies in the rebuilt temple, the Great Tribulation begins—this is still all in Seal 5, with the entire Great Tribulation being described by Trumpets 1–5. As the Great Tribulation unfolds, starting with Trumpets 1–4, the "birth pains," or the "devastations," increase, growing in both intensity and in frequency the closer we get to the birth, the Second Coming. The last five months of that Great Tribulation are described by Trumpet 5, whose sounding unleashes Bowls

1–5—Bowls 1–5 are enormous in the *intensity* of their devastation, and are also occurring at a greatly increased *frequency*, with all Five Bowls being poured out over a period of only five months—one Bowl every thirty days—which constitutes the *last* five months, or *end*, of the Great Tribulation.

We see then that as we get closer to the Second Coming, the frequency and intensity of the judgment increases, for the birth is nearing, which is exactly in keeping with Jesus' perfect description of those events as "birth pains." *All* of this is in Seal 5.

HOW LONG DOES SEAL 6/TRUMPET 6/BOWLS 6 AND 7 LAST?

The *entire* Great Tribulation is *over* at the end of Seal 5 (Matt 24:29), lasting 1,260 days (three and a half years/42 months). That 1,260-day period of the Great Tribulation is calculated from the time that the abomination of desolation is set up, so the Great Tribulation is over 1,260 days *after* the abomination of desolation is set up. Since Trumpets 1–5 and Bowls 1–5 are the events and judgments of the Great Tribulation, all occurring as part of Seal 5, then we know, with certainty, that Trumpets 1–5 and Bowls 1–5 are themselves *over* when Seal 6 is opened, for we know, without question, that Seal 6 is opened *immediately after* the end of the Great Tribulation (Matt 24:29). The opening of Seal 6, as we have seen, results in the blast of Trumpet 6, which itself results in the pouring of Bowls 6 and 7, resulting in the fall of the nation Babylon the Great and the gathering of armies to Armageddon for war.

How long does Seal 6 last?

1,290 DAYS

We are told the following in Daniel:

> And from the time that the daily sacrifice is taken away, and the abomination of desolation is set up, there shall be one thousand two hundred and ninety days. Blessed is he who waits, and comes to the one thousand three hundred and thirty-five days. (12:11–12 NKJV)

As previously discussed, since we know that the Great Tribulation lasts specifically for 1,260 days, or 42 months ("a time, times and half a time"), and since we know that the Great Tribulation is over at the end of Seal 5 (Matt 24:29), therefore we know that once we get to Seal 6, Seal 5 is over and it has been 1,260 days, or 42 months, since the abomination of desolation has been set up. As a result, once we are at day 1,261 after the abomination of desolation, we know we are in Seal 6.

When we put all of these pieces together, we can conclude the following.

Seal 6 begins after the 1,260-day Great Tribulation is over (Matt 24:29), beginning on day 1,261 after the abomination of desolation is set up. Seal 6 ends at day 1,290 after the setting up of the abomination of desolation. This is why Daniel 12:11

specifically tells us that the events that began with the abomination of desolation will culminate 1,290 after that event. Since we know that Trumpet 6/Bowls 6 and 7 are part of Seal 6, and since Seal 6 begins 1,261 days after the setting up of the abomination of desolation, and ends at day 1,290 after the setting up of the abomination of desolation, we can understand that Seal 6/Trumpet 6/Bowls 6 and 7 will last a total of 30 days after the Great Tribulation is over.

It is during those 30 days of Seal 6/Trumpet 6/Bowls 6 and 7 that the nation Babylon the Great will fall and be utterly destroyed, being destroyed by the armies of the Beast and of the world (Rev 17:16–17). Those same armies, the armies of the Beast, the armies that destroy Babylon the Great, will then be gathered to Armageddon for the Second Coming (Rev 16:16).

1,335 DAYS

But after telling us of the 1,290 days, Daniel tells us the following:

> Blessed is the one who waits for and reaches the end of the 1,335 days. (12:12 NIV)

What is the meaning of the 1,335 days? As with the 1,260- and 1,290-day periods, this 1,335-day period is *also* counted from the day that the Beast sets up the abomination of desolation, enthroning himself in the holy of holies in the rebuilt temple in Jerusalem.

What is the significance of the 1,335 days? As discussed, we can understand day 1,335 after the abomination of desolation is set up as being the specific day of the Second Coming, the specific day that Jesus Christ descends to Earth, for that event will be the only blessed event that follows the Seal 6 fall of Babylon the Great, and which will be awaited by Christians, who will be blessed when they see it. The Second Coming happens in Seal 7 with the sounding of Trumpet 7, the last Trumpet (Matt 24:30–31; 1 Cor 15:52; 1 Thess 4:16). Only Christians, the church, await the Second Coming, and so Daniel's very specific wording in Daniel 12:12 once again further affirms the presence of the church on Earth during that entire time, for he describes the "blessed people" as those who wait for and reach day 1,335.

This again is an affirmation that during that entire time of the Great Tribulation, which begins with the abomination of desolation, the church is on the Earth; otherwise it is impossible to wait for and reach that day unless you have already gone through the previous 1,335 days. The fact that Daniel specifically describes those who wait for, and reach, day 1,335 as being blessed clearly affirms that he is talking about believers, about the church, for only the believers, the church, will wait for the Second Coming—everyone else will hate it and dread it. Only the church will be blessed when that event happens, while everyone else, those who took the mark of the Beast, will be terrified by it (Rev 6:15–17). As a result, we can understand that day 1,335—1,335 days after the setting up of the abomination of desolation—is the very day of the Second Coming, the very day that Jesus will descend to Earth.

A THIEF IN THE NIGHT

Since Seal 6/Trumpet 6/Bowls 6 and 7 are *over* at day 1,290 *after* the abomination of desolation, and since the Second Coming will take place on day 1,335 *after* the abomination of desolation, we can see that there is a 45-day period between the *end* of Seal 6 (which includes Trumpet 6/Bowls 6 and 7) and the Second Coming. During that time, the darkness of Seal 5/Trumpet 5/Bowl 5 will remain, for this same darkness is further affirmed as being present in Seal 6 (Matt 24:29; Rev 6:12–13). As a result, when Jesus tells us that he will come like a "thief in the night" (Matt 24:43; 1 Thess 5:2; Rev 3:3, 16:15), the "night" that he is referring to is, in fact, the same darkness upon the world of Seal 5/Seal 6. Jesus comes down to Earth, at the Second Coming, 1,335 days after the abomination of desolation, coming while the darkness of Seal 5 is still upon the Earth.

The church, who has been waiting for that day, waiting for it throughout the entirety of the Great Tribulation, are described as being blessed if they reach that day.

SUMMARY OF THE SEALS/TRUMPETS/BOWLS TIMELINE

As a result, we can understand the three Revelation timelines—the timeline of the Seals, of the Trumpets, and of the Bowls—as follows:

Seals 1–4

span thirty-three years (prepare the world for the coming of the Beast)

Seal 5

lasts seven years

- = first half = the Beast rules the world, three and a half years
- = second half = the Great Tribulation, three and a half years

  - Trumpets 1–4;
  - Trumpet 5 = Bowls 1–5

Seal 6

lasts thirty days

- = Trumpet 6 = Bowls 6 and 7 (fall of Babylon the Great, armies gathered at Armageddon)

Seal 7

= Trumpet 7 (resurrection of believers and the Second Coming)

- forty-five days *after* the end of Seal 6

This is the clear scriptural outline of the timeline of Revelation. Once again, we see that the Seven Seals are the entirety of the judgment, which is why *only* Jesus Christ, the Judge, can open the Seals (John 5:22; Rev 5:1–5). The Trumpets and Bowls are only *details* of that *same* judgment—Trumpets 1–5/Bowls 1–5 being details of the Great Tribulation of Seal 5, and Trumpet 6/Bowls 6 and 7 being the details of the Seal 6 fall of Babylon the Great, and with the resurrection of believers and the Second Coming happening at Seal 7/Trumpet 7, the final Trumpet.

The three timelines are embedded within one another, with the complete, full timeline—the big-picture timeline of the Seven Seals—spanning a total of forty years, and with the three-and-a-half year period of the Trumpets happening in Seal 5 and 6, and with the six-month period of the Bowls happening during Trumpets 5 and 6. The three timelines of Revelation overlap.

FURTHER CONFIRMATION OF THE OVERLAPPING TIMELINES

There is additional confirmation in Revelation itself of the overlapping timelines.

In a number of instances throughout the book of Revelation, there are many incidents that seem to happen *twice*, as follows:

6:14 (Seal 6) – every mountain and island is moved
16:20 (Bowl 7) – every mountain and island is moved

6:17 (Seal 6) – the day of wrath has come
16:14 (Bowl 6) – the day has come

9:14 (Trumpet 6) – events at the Euphrates, and armies
16:12 (Bowl 6) – events at the Euphrates, and armies

14:8 (after Trumpet 6) – "Fallen is Babylon"
18:2 (after Bowl 7) – "Fallen is Babylon"

14:20 – the winepress is trodden
19:15 – the winepress is trodden

11:15–18 (Trumpet 7) – the Second Coming
19:11–21 – the Second Coming

8:5 (Seal 7 opened) – noises, thundering, lightning and earthquake
11:19 (Trumpet 7 sounded) – noises, thundering, lightning and earthquake, and hail
16:18 (Bowl 7 poured) – noises, thundering, lightning and earthquake

Was every island and mountain moved *twice*? Did the day of wrath come *twice*? Did military events happen at the Euphrates *twice*? Did Babylon fall *twice*? Was the winepress trodden *twice*? Does the Second Coming happen *twice*? Do the "noises, thundering, lightning and earthquake" happen *three* times?

No—in each case, all of those events happen only *once* but they are recounted two or three times because they are being recounted across the three timelines, being recounted, in one instance, in the overall forty-year big-picture timeline of the Seven Seals; then again in the three-and-a-half-year timeline of the Trumpets in the Seal 5 Great Tribulation and the Seal 6 fall of Babylon; then again in the five-month timeline of Bowls 1–5, outlining the final five months of the Great Tribulation. *All* three timelines overlap, with the Seven Bowls being included in Trumpets 5 and 6, and with the Trumpets being included in Seal 5 (Trumpets 1–5), in Seal 6 (Trumpet 6), and in Seal 7 (Trumpet 7). The fact that the exact same events are recounted multiple times in Revelation, spread across many different chapters, is only an *affirmation* of the appearance of those exact *same* events in the overlapping timelines.

There is only *one* overall timeline of Revelation, and that is the timeline of the Seven Seals, which is the full timeline representing the entirety of the judgment of Revelation, encompassing a total of forty years. The Trumpets and the Bowls are only *details* of the Seals, primarily details of the Great Tribulation of Seal 5, but also of the Seal 6 fall of Babylon. Revelation first recounts the opening of the Seven Seals, outlining for us the big-picture timeline and bringing us, with the opening of Seal 7, to the point just before the Second Coming.

At that point, Revelation stops and goes back in time to give us the details of the Great Tribulation, as well as the fall of Babylon, recounted through Trumpets 1–6, with the action stopping again with the blast of Trumpet 7, bringing us again to the point just before the Second Coming.

At that point, Revelation stops again and goes back in time to outline in even greater detail the events of the Great Tribulation and the fall of Babylon, recounted through Bowls 1–7, bringing us, with the completion of Bowl 7, once again to the point just before the Second Coming. After going back in time again to give us the details of the fall of Babylon (Rev 17–18), at that point *all* the action of *all* three timelines resumes as *one* timeline, with the action of all three timelines resuming with the Second Coming (Rev 19:11, Seal 7/Trumpet 7). From that point onwards, to the end of the book of Revelation, there is now only the *one* timeline *and* it is presented in chronological order.

The Trumpets and Bowls are only details of Seal 5 and of Seal 6, for it is the Seals alone that are the judgment of God, which is why no one but the Judge, Jesus Christ, can open the Seals, for the Seals are the entirety of the judgment.

11

The Days of Noah

In Matthew 24:37–40, Jesus tells us that in the days preceding the Second Coming the world will be like the "days of Noah."

> As it was in the days of Noah, so it will be at the coming of the Son of Man. For in the days before the flood, people were eating and drinking, marrying and giving in marriage, up to the day Noah entered the ark; and they knew nothing about what would happen until the flood came and took them all away. That is how it will be at the coming of the Son of Man. Two men will be in the field; one will be taken and the other left. (NIV)

Jesus goes on to tell us that in the days of Noah "people were eating and drinking, marrying and giving in marriage, up to the day Noah entered the ark," having no idea of what was about to come. Jesus then describes the flood as coming and as taking them all away, clearly defining for us that to be taken away means to be destroyed, killed.

Why does Jesus tell us that the days preceding the Second Coming will be like the days of Noah? Is it *only* to tell us that people will not be expecting the Second Coming, just as the people of Noah's day were not expecting the flood? That can certainly be a part of his meaning, but there are many other examples in the Bible where major catastrophic events happen and where the people had no idea or expectation as to what was coming—all the plagues of Egypt (Exod 7–11) and the destruction of Sodom and Gomorrah (Gen 19) are such examples. Why does Jesus specifically choose the days of Noah as his example if his intent is to only illustrate not being ready?

There is very good reason to understand that likening the days of Noah to the days preceding the Second Coming is much more than just an illustration of surprise at the coming of a catastrophic event; rather, we can understand that the *state of the world* in the days of Noah itself illustrates the *kind* of world that will exist before the Second Coming, a state of world that existed *only* in the days of Noah and will exist *again* prior to the Second Coming. As a result, the question must be asked—what kind of world existed in the days of Noah?

To begin to understand the answer to that question, it is important to briefly look at the philosophy of Evolution since the Evolution philosophy has very much come to color our view of history.

THE EVOLUTION PHILOSOPHY

In our modern day, we live in an age that has chosen to subscribe to a philosophy called Evolution. Stated briefly, Evolution teaches that life began on its own, as a chemical and/or molecular reaction by accident, with the basic chemical building blocks of life forming in a "primordial soup" on the early Earth, leading to the existence of the most basic single-cell organisms. Evolution teaches that, over time, this single-cell organism changed, or "evolved," into a multi-cell organism, and eventually, over many eons of time, transforming into all the forms of complicated life in existence today, including transforming into human beings. The prime proponent of Evolution was Charles Darwin with the publication of his book *On the Origin of Species* (1859). Since the publication of Darwin's *On the Origin of Species*, the Evolution philosophy has tried to present itself as a scientific fact, and it has come to be accepted as such.

However, at its very core, Evolution is not a science, nor is it a theory; it is in fact nothing more than a philosophy masquerading as science. Some people dismiss Evolution by describing Evolution as being "only a theory," rather than a scientific fact. However, that is incorrect—Evolution does not even qualify as a *scientific* theory— a scientific theory is not just the proposing of an idea; rather, a *scientific theory* is defined in a very specific way. There are three key elements that must be present for something to qualify as a scientific theory.

The first element that must be present in a scientific theory is that the subject of the theory, i.e., the thing that is being talked about, must be either observable or measurable—if you cannot *see* what you are describing or you cannot *measure* it, it is not scientific.

The second element that must be present in a scientific theory is that the subject of the theory must be *testable* by experimentation, and those experiments must be *reproducible* by others. If you cannot *test* what the theory is talking about, it is not a scientific theory.

The third element that must be present in a scientific theory is in fact the most important one—the hypothesis itself must be *falsifiable*; that is, it must have the ability to be proven *false* (not proven true, but proven false). If the hypothesis is not falsifiable, it is not a scientific theory.

The fact is that evolution is not observable or measurable (since it conveniently takes millions of years to happen), it cannot be tested by experimentation (for the same reason), and the hypothesis itself does not have the ability to be proven false. On all three counts of what defines a scientific theory, Evolution does not qualify—as a result, Evolution is not a scientific theory; rather it is only a *philosophy* that masquerades as being scientific.

The very heart of the Evolution philosophy is the teaching that one species of creature will, over time, *evolve* to become another completely new species. Hence, a single-cell organism can, over eons of time, become a horse. But what is the *mechanism* by which such changes in a species would happen?

In the very earliest days of the Evolution philosophy, its proponents taught that *acquired characteristics* could be passed on to offspring and, in that way, over time, a new species would be created. An *acquired characteristic* is simply a physical trait acquired by any creature during the course of its life, which is then passed on to its offspring, who are then born with that acquired, or new, physical trait. A simple example is as follows. A small, frail young man devotes himself to exercise and bodybuilding, turning himself into a big, muscular man—his newfound muscles are his acquired characteristic; he was not born with them, but he *acquired* them through physical training. That man then fathers a son, and he passes on to his son his newly acquired muscular characteristics, and so his son grows up to be a muscular man. This is a clear, and simple, illustration of acquired characteristics as a mechanism of evolution.

However, with the discovery of genes and genetics, Gregor Mendel (ca 1865) showed that it is impossible to pass on acquired characteristics to offspring. As a result, the Evolution philosophy had to try and adapt itself to these new discoveries. Without the passing on of acquired characteristics, the Evolution philosophy had no mechanism to invoke for the evolutionary process to occur. As a result, in having to deal with the fact of genetics, the Evolution philosophy began to teach that the mechanism by which evolution occurs is *genetic* mutation—genes would change, little by little over great spans of time, and, with the passage of enough time and enough accumulation of small genetic changes, one species would transform into a new species. No one had ever seen, or recorded, the emergence of a new species, but the proponents of Evolution were confident that, as time unfolded, evidence would be found to support Evolution and the change of one species into a new species.

However, as the years passed, no such evidence was found. As a result, in its attempt to appear credible, the Evolution philosophy had to try and adapt to the lack of evidence for the philosophy. There are two key ways in which the Evolution philosophy has tried to do this.

The first way that proponents of Evolution tried to make evolution appear credible was as follows. In the early part of the twentieth century, the definition of "species" was changed. Since the entire premise of Evolution is that one *species* of creature will, over time, change, or evolve, into a new *species*, the very definition of "species" is foundational to the Evolution philosophy. The original scientific definition of species was framed by the founder of taxonomy, Carl Linnaeus (1707–1778). The definition of Linnaeus' categorization of living creatures, or "species," was simple and accurate, and was as follows—if two creatures could mate, and produce viable offspring, then those two creatures were the same species. A "viable" offspring means only that the offspring of those two creatures could itself mate and reproduce, versus being sterile. So, for example, a dog and a wolf can mate and produce viable offspring; that is, their offspring can in turn mate and reproduce, and therefore the dog and the wolf are the same species. But a horse and a donkey can also mate, and produce an offspring, a mule, but the mule itself is sterile and cannot reproduce, and therefore the mule is *not* a viable offspring, and therefore the horse and the donkey are two different species. This fundamental definition of being able to mate and produce viable offspring is what defined creatures as being of the same species.

The entire thrust of the Evolution philosophy is that all species in existence have evolved or arisen from other species—one species changed into another species, over time. According to Linnaeus' fundamental definition of "species," if a completely new species arose from a previous, different species, then that *new* species and the *old* species could not mate and produce viable offspring, since the *definition* of being *different* species is that the two creatures cannot produce viable offspring.

The fact is that, throughout the entirety of human history, no one has observed the formation of any new species so defined—no one has ever observed a *new* species arising from an *old* species, resulting in those two species, old and new, being unable to produce viable offspring.

Since Evolution presents itself as scientific, and since science is founded upon observation and testing, the fact that the emergence of a new species has never been observed is a major problem for Evolution Therefore, to address this problem, in the first part of the twentieth century, the definition of "species" was changed—no longer was "species" defined as creatures who can mate together and produce viable offspring; rather, now, with the redefinition of "species," even small differences between creatures that previously were classified as the same species would result in those creatures being classified as two *different* species. As a result, with that redefinition of species, a dog and a wolf are now different species. Therefore, when talking about the origin of dogs, saying that dogs came from the same line as wolves, this is then cited as a *proof* of evolution, since, in the new redefinition of "species," the dog and the wolf are now different species, and so if the species dog came from the species wolf, this is now invoked as a support, or proof, of Evolution The redefinition of "species" now allows proponents of evolution to say that one species has turned, or evolved, into another new species.

Evolution's second attempt to adapt, so as to still appear scientifically credible, was by the creation of the convenient term "microevolution." "Microevolution" is in fact an outgrowth of the redefinition of "species." True evolution is a fish, eventually, turning into a horse, or one species turning into a completely new species, something that has never been observed. The term "microevolution" means only that a species, *within itself*, exhibits small physical changes from one generation to another, regardless of the reason for those changes.

So, for example, people have tried to create experiments using fruit flies to study evolution. The reason that fruit flies are used is because the lifespan of a fruit fly is approximately forty days. This means that in the course of one year we would see nine generations of fruit flies come into being. Many kinds of experiments have been performed on fruit flies to try and observe evolution, and one such experiment involved exposing fruit flies and their offspring, over a period of some generations, to the wind of a fan. After some generations, it was observed that future generations of that fruit fly were generally now having shorter, smaller wings, the reason for this being cited as an "evolutionary" adaptation to being exposed to the wind of the fan. This is now called "microevolution"—small differences within successive generations of the same species arising as an adaptation to environment. However, in fact, that generation of shorter-wing fruit fly is exactly the same genetically as the original generation; it is exactly as much of a perfect fruit fly as the original generation—it is still, in every way, exactly the same species (i.e., there was no evolution of one species into a new species), but, by creating the term "microevolution" and then defining it as very small changes within a species over successive generations, it allows people to claim that they have observed a form of evolution, and then present those observations as scientific proof for the existence of evolution.

But, in fact, it is nothing of the kind—microevolution is *not* evolution; rather it is a contrived fiction, for the very heart of the Evolution philosophy is one species turning into a completely new and different species, not the same species remaining the same species with certain retained characteristics being more or less pronounced (that would be akin to stating that a short man born from a line of tall men is an example of evolution, albeit microevolution, and then arguing that the short man is a different species of human). The fact remains that across the many thousands of generations of fruit flies studied and observed over many decades (that is nine generations per year, for over eighty years, with many such experiments and observations occurring simultaneously throughout the world), the emergence of a truly new species has never been observed.

All that to say that Evolution is not science, nor does it even qualify as a scientific theory; rather it is merely a philosophy that masquerades as science.

DATING TECHNIQUES

One other key element in promoting the Evolution philosophy is dating techniques. Dating techniques are the tools used to determine the age of a thing. There are numerous dating techniques, the most commonly known being carbon-14 (a radiocarbon technique), but there is also potassium-argon, uranium-lead, rubidium-strontium et al (radiometric techniques). All of these are used to date things, whether it is dating organic matter (carbon-14) or non-organic matter (the other radiometric tests).

All dating techniques are based on rates of change. So, for example, we have measured and observed the half-life of carbon-14 (i.e., how long it takes for carbon-12 to turn into carbon-14, the *rate* of change from carbon-12 to carbon-14), just as we have measured and observed the rate of radioactive decay between various elements (e.g., potassium to argon)—*all* dating techniques are based on this *rate* of change. Therefore, if we know the rate of change, and if we can measure the amount of the radiocarbon, or radiometric element, in an object, we can arrive at an age for that object—all of which makes sense.

However, the absolute foundation for all of these dating techniques is an *assumption*, and that assumption is this: in order to apply *any* dating technique, one must first *assume* that the rate of change that we have observed and measured in our twentieth century has *always* been the same throughout the entire history of the Earth. If one does *not* make that *assumption*, then one cannot apply any dating techniques.

The fact is there is *no reason* to believe such an assumption—it is just an arbitrary assumption that says, "If we assume this to be true, then we can say this . . . ," but there is no foundation for the assumption in the first place—it is literally no different than saying, "Let's pretend that this is true . . . ," and then using that pretending to be the foundation of future statements.

To illustrate this approach by way of example, if we were to say, "Let's pretend that 2 + 2 = 9," then that would allow us to say, based on that premise, that 2 + 2 + 7 = 16—this is the essential illustration of the assumptions of dating techniques. All this to say that without the use of the unfounded assumption that the observed rates of change have been constant and the same throughout the Earth's entire existence, dating techniques would have no merit. Yet, the assumption that the observed rates of change have reached equilibrium since the earliest existence of the Earth (i.e., the rates of change that we see and measure now have stayed the same throughout almost the entire history of the Earth) remains foundational in promoting the philosophy of Evolution.

WHAT DOES EVOLUTION HAVE TO DO WITH THE DAYS OF NOAH?

Why are we raising the point of Evolution in the context of Revelation and the days of Noah? The fact is this—although the Evolution philosophy presents itself primarily as a philosophy of the emergence of new species, that same evolutionary *approach* has come to infiltrate our general way of thinking.

For example, many Christians, if asked, would say that they do not believe in the idea of evolution, and yet, if you asked them, "Which civilization was the greatest civilization on Earth?," they would almost all certainly say, "Ours." Why? Because they are in fact subscribing, often unknowingly, to the Evolution philosophy.

The Evolution philosophy, ultimately, does not restrict itself to *just* the evolution of species, but is also applied to history and civilization. The reason people would describe our civilization as the greatest civilization ever is because they believe that civilizations only grow, evolve, get better, or get more advanced over time. By buying into this evolutionary philosophy, one does not even entertain the thought that, in history, there may have been equally advanced, or even more advanced, civilizations on Earth, civilizations that have been destroyed or wiped out. The reason that people do not often entertain even the idea of previously highly advanced civilizations is because they have, subconsciously, bought into the philosophy of Evolution.

And yet, there is a vast amount of artifacts, objects, and fossils that have been discovered, actual physical evidence, that contradict the Evolution philosophy. There are numerous discovered fossils, as well as physical artifacts, that, if Evolution was true, should not exist, but they do exist. Their very existence is witness against the Evolution philosophy. It is not the scope of this book to delve into all the evidence that contradicts the Evolution philosophy, but some compilations and discussions of this physical evidence can be found in *Forbidden Archeology: The Hidden History of the Human Race* (Michael A. Cremo & Richard L. Thompson; Bhaktivedanta Book Publishing; Revised edition January 1, 1998; 952 pages). A more general overview of previous civilizations can be found in *Secrets of the Lost Races: New Discoveries of Advanced Technology in Ancient Civilizations* (Rene Noorbergen, Macmillan, 1977), *We Are not the First* (Andrew Tomas, 1971, G.P. Putnam, rev. 2019), and others

And yet, if it is true that such physical evidence exists, physical evidence that contradicts the Evolution philosophy, showing it to be unfounded, then why don't we hear about this evidence?

In fact, we do hear about it, very often, but we hear about it through the lens of the Evolution philosophy.

So, for example, worked-gold chains have been discovered embedded deep within coal seams, which, based on the presumptive dating techniques applied, give those gold chains an age of millions of years (based on the depth of the coal seam et al.). But the Evolution philosophy teaches that humanity was only still in its very early form of descent from the common ancestor of apes at that time. Therefore, since that primitive, almost ape-like view of humanity must be true (because the Evolution philosophy says so), then if worked-gold chains are discovered deep in a seam of coal, and are dated to be millions of years old, those gold chains could not possibly be the result of human civilization. So, what then could account for the existence of those gold chains dated to an age of millions of years?

This is where the idea that "It must be aliens from another planet visiting Earth in ages long past" comes in. The Evolution philosophy teaches that humanity could not be responsible for such found artifacts, and so an appeal is made to "intelligent life" from elsewhere as being responsible for those artifacts. This idea of aliens visiting Earth in the distant past is commonly repeated throughout our society—sometimes ridiculed, sometimes not—but it is based on the fact of discovered manufactured artifacts whose very existence is incompatible with the Evolution philosophy.

The fact remains that, once you discount the unscientific Evolution philosophy, and the accompanying presumptive dating techniques used to support it, there is no reason to appeal to aliens as the originators of these found artifacts. It was not intelligent alien life from elsewhere that made those ancient artifacts (or that was responsible for the similar incongruous evidence also found in fossils); rather, it was, in fact, a previous *human civilization* that made those artifacts, a civilization that once flourished but has been lost to history, a civilization no longer remembered, a civilization completely and utterly obliterated ("taken away") from the Earth—the civilization of Noah's day.

WHAT DOES THE BIBLE SAY ABOUT HISTORY?

Concerning peoples, civilizations, and ages past, we are very clearly told the following, by God himself, in Ecclesiastes:

> What do people gain from all their labors
> at which they toil under the sun?
> *Generations come and generations go,*
> but the earth remains forever . . . .
> *What has been will be again,*
> *what has been done will be done again;*
> *there is nothing new under the sun.*
> Is there anything of which one can say,
> "Look! This is something new"?
> *It was here already, long ago;*
> *it was here before our time.*
> *No one remembers the former generations,*
> and even those yet to come
> will not be remembered
> by those who follow them. (Eccl 1:3–4, 9–11 NIV)

God here tells us that "there is nothing new under the sun," that "what has been will be again," that if anyone says, "Look! This is something new!," in fact, "It was here already, long ago . . . before our time." It is in that context, in the context of "it was here before our time," that God then talks about the people, or generations, no longer remembered, i.e., a people whom even history does not record.

Is any of this true? Or is God just being poetic? Symbolic? Exaggerating?

No, he is not exaggerating, nor is he being poetic nor symbolic; rather, in these verses, God is making a clear statement of fact. When God, who himself has witnessed all human history, tells us that "there is nothing new under the sun," and that "what has been will be again," and that if anyone says, "Look! This is something new!," in fact,

"It was here already, long ago . . . before our time," he is telling us the truth. If we are to believe God, if we are to believe what he tells us, then we can understand the following—there *truly* is *nothing new* under the sun, *nothing new* on Earth, and if we look at our own society and say of our civilization's accomplishments, "This is something new" or "This has never been before," then, according to God, we are *wrong*, for God himself tells us that anything that we declare as being new or as never having been before in fact is *not* new, and it *was* here before. Either that is a fact or God is a liar or he is ignorant, and God is neither a liar nor ignorant. According to God himself, who has seen and witnessed *all* the ages past, there really, truly, is nothing new on Earth; there is nothing that will come into being, from *any* civilization, that has not been here before, exactly as God tells us in Ecclesiastes.

If God is to be believed, and if this is true, then this includes absolutely *everything* that describes our own civilization—electricity, nuclear power, computers, machinery, medicine, genetics and more. God's statement is a very clear and blanket statement that leaves no room for exceptions—there is nothing of our civilization that is new.

If the great accomplishments of our own civilization are, in fact, *not* new, but were here before, accomplished by a people no longer remembered (Eccl 1:11), then when did the advancements and accomplishments of our civilization, or possibly even greater advancements and accomplishments, exist previously upon Earth?

They existed in Noah's day, accomplished by the people described in Ecclesiastes as the people "no longer remembered," the ones wiped out of history, the people and generations before the flood. The most advanced civilization the world has ever known is not our own civilization, but the civilization of Noah's day, whose advanced remnants we find buried deep in seams of coal, sediment, and rock.

THE WORLD OF NOAH'S DAY—ONE CONTINENT

Too often, due in large part as a result of subconsciously subscribing to the Evolution philosophy, the days of Noah are thought of as being almost primitive, as being a society of farmers, shepherds, small advancements, often considered as even less advanced than many ancient civilizations in the historical record. But is this true? What was the world of Noah's day like?

The first thing we must look at is the physical state of the Earth in Noah's day, and there is no question that, from Genesis 1:9 to Noah's own day, the entire Earth was one continent. We know this from Genesis 1:9–10.

> Then God said, "Let the waters below the heavens be gathered into one place, and let the dry land appear"; and it was so. *And God called the dry land "earth,"* and the gathering of the waters he called "seas"; and God saw that it was good. (NASB)

In this passage, as God is restoring the cursed Earth (cursed as of Gen 1:2), we are told that God gathered the water under the sky to *one* place, so that dry ground appeared. To say that the waters were gathered to *one* place, specifically so that the dry ground would appear, intrinsically implies that the dry ground itself was gathered to *another* one place; that is to say, the dry ground that appeared did so as *one* landmass, or what we would call one "continent." If this is so, then how did the current seven continents form? The current seven continents formed as a result of the flood.

THE FLOODWATERS

The Bible is very clear—the *primary* source of the waters of the flood was *not* rain from the sky; rather it was great reservoirs of water from *within* the Earth.

> In the six hundredth year of Noah's life, in the second month, on the seventeenth day of the month, on that day *all the fountains of the great deep burst open*, and the floodgates of the sky were opened. (Gen 7:11 NASB)

We are told, very clearly in Genesis 7:11 that the first, or primary, source of the water for the flood was the "fountains of the great deep." We are also very clearly told that those fountains "burst," or exploded, open and only then, *afterwards*, "the floodgates of the sky were opened."

What does it mean when it says that the "fountains of the great deep burst open"? It means that the primary source for the water of the flood was from *inside* the Earth, *not* from the sky or the rain—the rain from the sky came *after* the fountains of the great deep burst forth, and, in fact, there is good reason to understand that the floodgates of the sky opening up were the *result* of the enormous force of the water, with its sediment, exploding forth, skyward.

Also, we can understand the term "great deep" as referring to more than just the global ocean, since, with the description of the fountains "bursting" or exploding forth, this strongly suggests that those waters exploded through the *land*, that is, through the one continent. In fact, the geological makeup of the Earth today affirms exactly that scenario.

On any map of the world, it is obvious that when looking at the shapes of the continents around the Atlantic Ocean, they all look like they fit together. In fact, when taking into account the curvature of the Earth, the shape of the continents around the Atlantic Ocean do not quite fit together. However, running right down the middle of the entire Atlantic Ocean, submerged beneath the ocean waters, is the longest mountain chain on Earth—the Mid-Atlantic, or Mid-Oceanic, Ridge, with a total length of approximately forty thousand miles—it encircles the globe (for comparison's sake, the length of the entire Rocky Mountain range is three thousand miles). When looking at an image of the Mid-Atlantic Ridge (search online and see), it is clear that the shape of the Mid-Atlantic Ridge is in fact the same shape as the outlines of the continents on either side of it. When the curvature of the Earth is taken into account, the base of the world's continents *do* fit into the base of the Mid-Atlantic Ridge—it is the Mid-Atlantic Ridge that is the *remnant* of the *divide* of the one original continent.

Furthermore, the rock of the Mid-Atlantic Ridge is basalt rock, which is the same rock as the Earth's crust, while the majority of the world's great mountain ranges are generally granite, or similar, and not basalt. The implication is that the Mid-Atlantic Ridge was the result of an upward thrust of the Earth's crust, pushing upwards through the landmass above, and that thrust upward caused the divide of the landmass, resulting in the current continental plates and continents themselves.

What caused that upward thrust of the Earth's crust? It was the force of water exploding through that land, the "fountains of the great deep" bursting forth from inside the Earth, the release of the waters of the flood.

If this is true, then with such an upward thrust of the Earth's crust, and the creation of the continental plates by way of that thrust, then we would expect to see a resulting elevation of the divided landmass, which uplifted landmass would then begin a slow slide in the opposite direction, that is, towards the Pacific Ocean. That being the case, then, as the plates would slide downwards and eventually collide with the Earth's crust, we would expect this to result in folded mountains, that is, mountains formed by the folding of the continental plates as they grind into the Earth's crust. This means that, with the Mid-Atlantic Ridge being the upward thrust that divided the one continent, we would expect to see the resulting folded mountains on the *opposite* side of that rise, which would place the folded mountains all around the Pacific Ocean. In fact, that is exactly what we see—pretty well all the folded mountains of the world encircle the Pacific Ocean; there are none around the Atlantic: in regard to North America, along virtually the entirety of its Pacific length we see the Rockies; in regard to South America, along virtually its entire Pacific length, we see the Andes; in regard to Asia, we see the Himalayas along the Pacific/Indian Ocean; likewise, along the Pacific coast of Australia we see the Great Dividing Range.

In addition to this, as a result of the folding landmass, as one section of the newly created land plate rises to form the mountains, we would expect a similar, and opposite, reaction on the other side of the plate (as per Newton's laws of motion), which means that, together with the high folded mountains of the world surrounding the Pacific, we would likewise expect the deep ocean canyons to also be located in the Pacific, which is exactly what we see (Marianas Trench et al.).

All this to say that the geography of the Earth perfectly aligns with, and affirms, that the Earth's land mass was at one time a single great continent that was broken up and divided. The Bible explains how this occurred—it was the result of the waters of the flood bursting forth from within the Earth, exploding forth through the landmass with enormous force, and thereby splitting the land mass and dividing it. The crack in the world that is the remnant of that event is the Mid-Atlantic Ridge, the rise into whose base all the continents fit, the crack through which the flood waters burst forth from within the Earth, the primary source of the waters for the flood.

Eventually, over time, the divided continent, and its various continental pieces, began a slow drift apart, drifting to where they are today, becoming the continents of the world. In fact, the Bible affirms this drift in Genesis 10:25.

> Two sons were born to Eber; the name of the one was Peleg, for in his days **the earth was divided**; and his brother's name was Joktan. (NASB)

We are told that in the days of Peleg, who was of the fourth generation born *after* the flood, "the earth was divided." The term "earth" in the Bible *always* refers *only* to the *surface* of the planet (Gen 1:10 NKJV, NASB, ESV, RSV, YLT et al.) *not* to the planet itself—the *planet itself* is always referred to as "the foundations of the Earth" (Ps 82:5; Prov 8:29; Isa 24:18; 40:21, 51:13; Jer 31:37; Mic 6:2). Therefore, we can understand the words "the earth was divided" as meaning that the surface of the Earth was divided—that is, the newly made continental divides, which resulted from the flood, began, in Peleg's day, to drastically separate further apart.

The above outline is not in any way a treatise or study of the geology of the Earth, but rather just a brief overview of the generalities of the Earth's geology from both a physical, observable standpoint as well as a biblical standpoint. The Bible is clear, in Genesis 1:9–10, that the entire land mass of the Earth was once one land mass, one continent, with that one original continent dividing into the continents of today, all by way of the force of the flood, by the release of the waters of the flood from inside the Earth. In today's field of geology, new terminology is used for some of these aspects, as even the term "folded mountains" has in some ways been replaced by newer, more fine-tuned terminology, but though the nuances of terminology may have changed, the fundamental truths remain. The flood created the continents, splitting the one continent of Genesis 1:9–10 by way of the waters bursting forth from within the Earth.

A further affirmation of water being an essential component of the Earth's very creation, and thereby being an affirmation of water being the *essence* of the Earth, is found in 2 Peter 3:5.

> For when they maintain this, it escapes their notice that by the word of God the heavens existed long ago and the earth was formed **out of water** and **by water**. (NASB)

Peter tells us that the Earth was "formed out of water and by water"—*water* is at the very essence of the Earth's creation and of its very nature.

Also, we must remember that the waters of the flood *receded*—to where did they recede? They slowly receded to where they had originally come from—they receded to inside the Earth. As a result, the Earth, to this day, is filled with water (which is why, if you dig down six feet almost anywhere on the planet, you will hit water).

As a result, we can understand clearly that the world of Noah's day was defined as being one great continent.

THE WORLD OF NOAH'S DAY—ONE LANGUAGE, ONE PEOPLE

One very important defining characteristic of the world of Noah's day is that there were no divisions of humanity—there were no differing languages, no divisions of skin color, and therefore no divisions of nations.

The very concept of race does not exist in the Bible. The languages and skin colors of humanity were instituted by God at the tower of Babel, occurring some generations *after* the flood, as an act of God's mercy upon humanity (Gen 11:1–9). Together with the creation of languages at Babel, God also, at that same time, as an act of mercy, marked those language divisions by divisions of skin color. One reason for that was so that as people found themselves speaking different languages, they would have had great fear as to what was going on, especially when they could no longer understand their neighbor. It is for this reason that God also, at that same time, caused the visible division of skin color, so that just as people would have heard each other now speaking many different languages, they would also now see different skin colors, and when those of one skin color would see others having the same appearance or skin color as themselves, they would be drawn to them and would find them to be speaking the same new language—the different skin colors allowed people to find one another. As a result, the skin colors of humanity, occurring at Babel, were a mercy from God that would have helped people find others speaking their own new language.

In the Bible, the differing skin colors of humanity are *never* called "races"—in the Bible, there is only one race, the race of Adam, the one race of humanity, whereas the differing skin colors of peoples are only ever referred to as "nations" (listed in Gen 10, especially 10:32). These nations of humanity seem to be permanent and will continue after the resurrection of humanity, for we are told in Revelation 22:2 that the leaves of the Tree of Life are for the healing of the "nations," that is, for the healing of a divided humanity, yet those nations remain ("nations" here does not refer to countries, but rather to the division of humanity by skin color).

All of this division—the division of languages, the division of nations (skin colors)—occurred at the tower of Babel, a number of generations *after* the flood. In the days of Noah, there were no divisions of humanity, no differing skin colors, and only one language of humanity—the *entire humanity* of Noah's day was all *one* humanity, all speaking *one* language, all being *one* nation, all living on *one* great continent.

SONS OF SETH AND SONS OF CAIN

If this is true, then why does the Bible give us a genealogy of Seth (Adam's son, Gen 5) and Cain (also Adam's son, Gen 4:17–24), all who lived before the flood? Doesn't this show a division of humanity before the flood?

No, it does not. Just because the Bible lists a genealogy does not mean that any such division, or delineation, existed in the world itself. A perfect example of this is the twelve tribes of Israel listed in Revelation 7—*only* the tribes of Judah, Benjamin, and Levi are Jews, while *all* the rest of the tribes of Israel are *not* Jews and have, in fact, been lost to history (but not to God) since about 750 BC. And yet, despite those ten tribes being lost to history since ca. 750 BC, God lists those tribes, and the peoples descended from them, as being present in the days preceding the Second Coming. Does this mean that the descendants from those tribes will recognize themselves as being from those tribes? No, it does not, for those people will *not* recognize their tribal origins—rather, God's listing of the descendants of those lost tribes only means that *God* knows their identity, even if they, and the world, do not. So those tribal divisions as listed in Revelation 7 will not be perceived by anybody in the world, but only by God, and so he lists them as a statement of fact, regardless of whether anyone will recognize it or not.

It is the same with the genealogies listing the children of Seth and Cain—God lists those children as a statement of fact, and the fact is important for two reasons. First, Seth's descendants are listed *only* because they culminate in Noah, through whom the entire humanity will survive and continue to exist. Noah's genealogy is vitally important because it affirms that Noah's humanity was exactly the same as Adam's created humanity—Noah was perfect in his heredity, perfect in his "generations" (Gen 6:9 NKJV); he had exactly the same humanity as did Adam—Adam's humanity continues through Noah, and the genealogy of Seth affirms that. Cain's descendants, on the other hand, are listed to show certain great accomplishments.

The listing of Seth's children, which culminate in Noah, or Cain's children and their great accomplishments, in *no way* means that *any* part of humanity was divided along those lines; there was no Seth/Cain division of humanity. The listing of those genealogies is only God affirming Noah's generations and humanity's accomplishments, and *not* a delineation of humanity. The children of Seth and the children of Cain, for the most part, would not have even been aware of their ancestry, since they were all children of Adam and were all one humanity, just like the 144,000 of Revelation 7 will not know their descent from the lost tribes of Israel. Though the children of Seth, the children of Cain and the 144,000 may not know their ancestry, God knows it, and so he spells it out for *us*, for specific reasons (to affirm Adam's humanity continuing through Noah; to affirm the accomplishments of pre-flood humanity; to affirm the lost tribes of Israel playing their role in the days preceding the Second Coming).

The world of Noah's day was one humanity, one language, one people, with no divisions, all inhabiting one great continent.

THE WORLD OF NOAH'S DAY—GREAT LIFESPANS

One of the other very key defining elements of the days of Noah was the length of human lifespans. It is clear from a reading of Genesis 5 that the average lifespan of people before the flood was far greater than our lifespans today. Adam died at age 930, Seth at age 912, Kenan at 910, and Methuselah at 969, whereas in our day if a man reaches age 90, he is an old man.

How are we to understand such great lifespans? Did the people of Noah's day age at the same *rate* as we do—being old and frail at 90 years of age and then remaining old and frail for the next 800 years? No, rather, in the days of Noah, the *rate* of physical decay as a result of aging was greatly slowed. In fact, we can understand the rate of aging before the flood as differing by a factor of ten.

For example, in the days before the flood, as today, a child would be fully grown at about age 30. In our day, after about age 30, we begin to physically decline and decay so that, by the time we are in our 80s we are old and, to a degree, decrepit. But that is *not* how aging worked before the flood. Prior to the flood, a person was also fully grown at about age 30 but then, upon reaching age 30, that person would physically *remain* at that peak of vigor and power up to their 400s—we can consider a pre-flood man in his 400s to have been the same physically as we are in our 40s. Likewise, a pre-flood man in his 500s would be the equivalent of us in our 50s; a pre-flood man in his 600s would be the same as us in our 60s, and so on. So when Adam died at age 930, he would have been similar to a modern man in his 90s.

Not only were the lifespans before the flood far greater lifespans, but the people were characterized by centuries of strength, vigor and power.

CHILDBEARING AND POPULATION

One very important by-product of such great lifespans was the ability to have many children. God commanded Adam, and his descendants, to "be fruitful and multiply" (Gen 1:22, 28; 8:17, after the flood). It was God's *command* that people multiply.

We must remember that, with the great lifespans of pre-flood man, the childbearing years of women lasted for many centuries—where a modern woman may bear children into her early 40s, if we multiply that by a factor of 10, a pre-flood woman would have been able to bear children well into her 400s. However, especially in light of God's specific command to multiply, and also in light of the fact that pre-flood humanity was so close to the physical perfection of Adam, being only 10 generations removed from Adam by the time of the flood, we can expect that a woman's childbearing years may in fact have lasted much longer, perhaps, for example, even into her

600s. As a result, if a pre-flood woman's childbearing years lasted into her 600s, and if she started to bear children at age 25, then she would have 600 years of childbearing. If she bore one child only every three years (which, in light of God's command to be fruitful and multiply, seems unlikely, with either one child per year, or one child every two years, being more likely) then, in her 600 years of childbearing, one woman could bear a minimum of 200 children, while if she bore one child per year, one woman could bear 600 children. In addition, *each* of *her* children could then in turn bear, or father, 600 children *each*, and likewise for each of *those* children, and so on.

As a result of such vast lifespans, and of the generational proximity to Adam's physical perfection, and as a result of God's specific command to be fruitful and multiply, when we factor in the exponentiality of population growth, it has been estimated that the global population of humanity by the time of the flood would have been anywhere from seven to 10 *billion* people, or more.

INBREEDING

Since Adam and Eve were the father and mother of the entire humanity, then the only people their children could marry and have children with were each other—brothers marrying sisters. If, especially in the first generations of humanity, brothers married sisters and fathered children with them, wouldn't this result in severe genetic and birth defects among the children as a result of inbreeding?

In fact, it would not, the reason being that those first generations were physically so close generationally to Adam's physical perfection that, especially in the earlier generations, there almost certainly would have been no ill effect from inbreeding for generations to come.

THE CAPACITY OF PRE-FLOOD MAN

In addition to the great lifespans before the flood, the Bible also affirms for us the far greater *capacity* of pre-flood man—pre-flood man was far more capable than modern man today. How can we know this? This great capacity of pre-flood man is in fact first illustrated in Adam himself.

We are told in Genesis 2:20 that Adam gave names to *all* the land animals of the world, as well as to *all* the birds of the air. What does this tell us about Adam? It tells us that he had a mind of *vast* capacity. Adam was created by God, and he was God's son (Luke 3:38), perfect in every way—physically perfect, emotionally perfect, intellectually perfect, spiritually perfect, completely without sin, completely and fully indwelt by the Holy Spirit, exactly as was Jesus Christ (who was God's only *begotten* son, whereas Adam was God's *created* son). Adam's intellect was *vast*; it was *perfect*—his intellectual capacity was far beyond that of modern man, and his naming of all things is a small demonstration of his great capacity. Just as the generational proximity to Adam of pre-flood humanity gave that humanity a far greater physical power, strength, and perfection than we have, likewise, that same generational proximity to Adam, the proximity to perfection, gave pre-flood man a far greater *intellectual* capacity and power than we have, and this far greater intellectual capacity of pre-flood man is in fact clearly illustrated in Genesis.

JABAL, JUBAL, AND TUBAL-CAIN

Three examples of the great intellectual capacity of pre-flood man, and of pre-flood man's great accomplishments, are seen in Jabal, Jubal, and Tubal-Cain, described for us in Genesis 4.

In Genesis 4:20 we are told that Jabal, a descendant of Cain, became the father of all who live in tents and have livestock; i.e., Jabal was the *father* of the domestication of animals. Jubal, his brother, was the father of all who play music; i.e., Jubal was the *founder* of music; while Tubal-Cain, brother to both Jubal and Jabal, was the *father* of all who work in bronze and iron; i.e., Tubal-Cain was the father of *all metallurgy*. Jabal, Jubal, and Tubal-Cain were the eighth generation from Adam (Adam inclusive). Comparing this to our own historical understanding of events, we see the following.

In our chronology of history, based as it is on presumptive dating techniques and a degree of circular reasoning, modern humanity is described as appearing ca. 60,000–40,000 years ago, with the domestication of livestock usually placed at ca. 8500 BC (again, this is the timeline as based on presumptive dating techniques, which themselves are based on multiple assumptions). Based on this timeline, it took tens of thousands of years for humanity to domesticate livestock.

Likewise for the discovery of bronze and iron. The general timeline for the Bronze Age is usually listed as ca. 3000 BC to 1200 BC, a period of 1,800 years, with the Bronze Age being followed later by the Iron Age, which is usually placed, depending on the region, as starting from ca. 800 BC to 500 BC. Based on this historical timeline (historical since actual recorded history began ca. 3000 BC with Egypt's Narmer Palette), from the start of the Bronze Age to the start of the Iron Age is a period of approximately 2,200 years.

The domestication of livestock, based on the above timelines, took place over a period of tens of thousands of years, but the Bible tells us that in the pre-flood world it was done by one man, Jabal, in his own lifetime. Likewise, the invention and transition from bronze to iron, based on the above historical timelines, took place over a period of 2,200 years, but the Bible tells us that in the pre-flood world it was all done by one man, Tubal-Cain, in his own lifetime. Likewise for the discovery of the art of music—that was also done by one man, Jubal, in his own lifetime.

If we conflate these two timelines, and their achievements—the historical timeline for the domestication of animals, and the historical timeline for the development of metallurgy—and compare the achievement of those timelines with those same achievements as outlined in the Genesis 4 timeline of pre-flood man, we see that what took us 2,200 years to invent and develop, at least in regard to historical metallurgy, was accomplished by *one* man *in his own lifetime.* Likewise, what took us tens of thousands of years to accomplish, in regard to the domestication of animals, was also accomplished by *one* man *in his own lifetime.* In each case, *one man*, in his own lifetime, accomplished what took us thousands of years and many generations to accomplish. What does this say about the intellectual *capacity* of pre-flood man? It was vast, and the reason for that is that pre-flood man was so much closer to Adam's intellectual perfection.

CAIN AND HIS CITY

This same great capacity of pre-flood man is seen in Cain himself, who is described in Genesis 4:17 as building a city and naming it Enoch, after his son.

This verse tells us that Cain, *on his own*, built a *city* (and, especially when understood in the light of Jabal, Jubal, and Tubal-Cain, this does *not* imply that Cain merely *oversaw* the building of a city; rather, it means exactly what it says, that Cain *himself* built the city). What kind of capacity and strength does it take for one man to build a city? It is a great capacity, both intellectual and physical, and it is a capacity that Cain possessed, as did pre-flood man in general. Again, the reason for the great physical and intellectual capacity of pre-flood man was the generational closeness to Adam's physical and intellectual perfection.

NOAH AND THE ARK

Another very clear example of the great physical and intellectual capacity of pre-flood man is the building of Noah's ark. In Genesis 6:13–22, God tells specifically *Noah* to build an ark, and we are given the dimensions of that ark (Gen 6:15)—and it was a vast structure. We are also told in 6:22 that it was specifically *Noah* (not Noah and his sons) who built the ark. We also know that the ark was well built, for it survived the flood. What kind of physical strength and intellectual capacity does it take for one man to build such a vast structure? It was a vast strength and capacity, a strength and capacity that Noah possessed by virtue of being only ten generations removed from Adam's perfection.

These are some biblical examples of the great capacity of pre-flood man—a physical and intellectual capacity far greater than our own, a power and capacity that could flourish over individual lifetimes, which lifetimes lasted almost a thousand years.

THE EXPONENTIAL GROWTH OF KNOWLEDGE

The growth of knowledge is exactly analogous to population growth—it is an exponential growth; that is to say, as it starts to increase, at one point in that increase, it explodes.

Imagine individual lifespans lasting almost a thousand years, and then imagine that applied to the last thousand years of our own history. In the last thousand years, for example, in the realm of science, the following figures have lived: Newton, Copernicus, Galileo, Faraday, Einstein, Kepler et al. Each of these people lived normal lifespans (i.e., normal as per our measure), lifespans of seventy to eighty years of age, and, for the most part, they lived in *successive* generations. Isaac Newton, the greatest scientific mind in recorded history, died at age eighty-four in 1727—imagine what Isaac Newton could have accomplished if he lived to be nine hundred years old? Likewise, Einstein died at age seventy-six in 1955—again, imagine what Einstein could have accomplished if he lived to be nine hundred years old? And then imagine what *both* Newton *and* Einstein would have accomplished if they were alive *together* at the *same time*—it is an astounding thought, and yet that was the reality of the pre-flood world. In the pre-flood world, a pre-flood "Newton" would be so far greater in his mental capacity than our historical Newton, as would a pre-flood "Einstein" be so far greater in his mental capacity than our historical Einstein, *and* they would have lived *simultaneously*—what we imagine as an incredible thought scenario for our days was the reality of the pre-flood world. This same astounding contemporary collaboration of lives and great genius in the pre-flood world would have applied to every field of human endeavour—music, literature, the arts, government, science, architecture et al. That was the world of Noah's day.

Also remember that, in addition to the great physical and intellectual capacity of pre-flood Man, and in addition to the great lifespans, as well the simultaneous living of multiple great geniuses in all fields throughout those great lifespans, the entire humanity had *one* language, was *one* people, and inhabited *one* continent—there were no divisions of languages, skin colors, or oceans. This meant that knowledge could be shared with ease, with no barrier of language or geography, which meant that the great and exponential increase of knowledge, or civilization, of the pre-flood world was heightened to an even greater, and incredible, degree.

With all of these factors being true—*one* language, *one* people, *one* continent, multiple contemporary great geniuses of great capacity with lifespans lasting almost one thousand years—it seems like there would have been nothing that pre-flood man could not accomplish.

In fact, God himself affirms exactly this in Genesis 11:5–7, speaking of a time only a few generations *after the* flood.

> But the LORD came down to see the city and the tower the people were building. The LORD said, "If as one people speaking the same language they have

begun to do this, then nothing they plan to do will be impossible for them. Come, let us go down and confuse their language so they will not understand each other." (NIV)

God himself tells us that the people who were building the tower of Babel were a people who were all speaking the same one language (which would have been the same one language as humanity spoke before the flood). God then tells us that, as a people speaking *one* language, *nothing* would be impossible for them to accomplish—God specifically tells us that great human accomplishment is predicated on the foundation of humanity speaking one language. The speaking of one language was the reality of the pre-flood world. If the people of Nimrod's day, a few generations *after* the flood, were accomplishing a great thing *because* they spoke one language, then the people before the flood could also accomplish truly great things as well, since they were an entire humanity speaking one language. Just as God himself tells us that, by speaking one language, the people building the tower of Babel could accomplish anything, likewise, we can understand that humanity before the flood, speaking one language, could accomplish anything.

THE LAST ONE THOUSAND YEARS

When we look at the last one thousand years of our own history, what do we see? In the year 1000 AD we see a medieval world, a world of tradesmen and craftsmen, a world of farmers and agriculture, a world of horses and carts, a world with very minimal scientific understanding in the areas of physics, chemistry, biology, medicine, and astronomy—in fact, we would, in many ways, describe the world of one thousand years ago as a backward and superstitious society.

Fast forward one thousand years to our own day: we have a world where man has walked on the moon; we have a global society that operates on electricity; we have nuclear power, a society run on machines; we perform genetic modifications on living things; we have a globally computerized society, a great medical knowledge whereby we can even transplant a living heart from one person to another—*all* of that has happened in only the last *one hundred* years, and is a superb illustration of the *exponential* nature of the growth of knowledge. The entirety of the above accomplishments, the accomplishments of our civilization, have happened over the course of the last one thousand years—and yet, in the pre-flood world, that *entire* timeframe is only the lifespan of *one* man, *one* generation.

THE MOST ADVANCED CIVILIZATION

The point of all of this is as follows—there is good reason to understand that the civilization of Noah's day was the greatest, most technologically advanced civilization this world has ever known; it was a civilization that far exceeded our own, populated by a people of far greater physical and intellectual capacity, all speaking one language, all living on one vast continent, with lifespans of 900 years and more. We, in our own civilization, are only now *beginning* to reach that same previous level of civilization. The many advanced, yet ancient, technological artifacts discovered throughout the world, over decades, and even centuries, are the remnants of that civilization—those are artifacts that were made by *human* civilization, not by alien beings.

Based on God's own declaration to us in Ecclesiastes 1:9–11 that there is "nothing new under the sun," and if we believe him to be telling us the truth, then we can understand the following—if we have air travel and, yes, space travel, so did the people of Noah's day; if we have great medical knowledge, so did the people of Noah's day; if we can perform genetic manipulation, so could the people of Noah's day—this is what God means when he tells us in Ecclesiastes that there is nothing new under the sun. As God very clearly tells us, if we think that there is something new on this Earth, some thing or some accomplishment that we think has never been here before, we are wrong; it is not new—it was here long ago, done by a people no longer remembered. The people no longer remembered are the people of Noah's day, the people before the flood, the people wiped out by the flood, and their accomplishments far exceeded our own.

WHAT DEFINED THE IMMEDIATE DAYS BEFORE THE FLOOD

In addition to being the most advanced civilization that this world has ever known, the Bible tells us that the immediate pre-flood world, i.e., the world during the actual days of Noah's lifespan, was defined by one very specific thing, and, in fact, it is this one specific thing that was the reason for the flood.

> When human beings began to increase in number on the earth and daughters were born to them, the sons of God saw that the daughters of humans were beautiful, and they married any of them they chose. Then the LORD said, "My Spirit will not contend with humans forever, for they are mortal; their days will be a hundred and twenty years." The *Nephilim* were on the earth in those days—and also afterward—when the sons of God went to the daughters of humans and had children by them. They were the heroes of old, men of renown. (Gen 6:1–4 NIV)

Who, or what, were the Nephilim?

12

The Nephilim

THERE IS VERY GOOD reason to understand that the world of Noah's day was the most advanced civilization this world has ever known, the most advanced in science, technology, arts, construction, medicine, engineering, and across all fields of human endeavor. As result, God is completely accurate when he tells us in Ecclesiastes that there is "nothing new under the sun," and that if we think that there is something new in the world, something that has not been here before, we are wrong, it was here before. It is in that context that God mentions the people no longer remembered, the people before the flood (Eccl 1:9–11).

However, as great as was the advancement of the pre-flood civilization, its advancement, in and of itself, is not what *defined* the days of Noah—the days of Noah were defined by the sons of God going to human women and having offspring with them.

> When human beings began to increase in number on the earth and daughters were born to them, the sons of God saw that the daughters of humans were beautiful, and they married any of them they chose. Then the LORD said, "My Spirit will not contend with humans forever, for they are mortal; their days will be a hundred and twenty years." The Nephilim were on the earth in those days—and also afterward—when the sons of God went to the daughters of humans and had children by them. They were the heroes of old, men of renown. (Gen 6:1–4 NIV)

SONS OF GOD

Throughout the entire Old Testament, the term "sons of God" (*bene Elohim*) refers solely and exclusively to angelic beings—it *never* refers to human beings. This is clearly seen in Job:

> Now there was a day when the **sons of God** came to present themselves before the Lord, and Satan also came among them. (1:6 NASB)

> One day the **angels** came to present themselves before the Lord, and Satan also came with them. (1:6 NIV)

> Again, there was a day when the **sons of God** came to present themselves before the Lord, and Satan also came among them to present himself before the Lord. (2:1 NASB)

> On another day the **angels** came to present themselves before the Lord, and Satan also came with them to present himself before him. (2:1 NIV)

> When the morning stars sang together
> And all the **sons of God** shouted for joy? (38:7 NASB)

> while the morning stars sang together
> and all the **angels** shouted for joy? (38:7 NIV)

Apart from the passage in Genesis 6:1–4, the above instances in Job are the *only* passages in the *entire* Old Testament where the term "sons of God" (Hebrew *bene elohim*) is used, and they are, unquestionably, solely and exclusively a reference to angelic beings.

Likewise, when the passage in Genesis 6:1–4 uses that exact same term, *bene Elohim*, "sons of God," it is also referring *only* to angelic beings. As a result, we can read Genesis 6:1–4 as follows:

> When human beings began to increase in number on the earth and daughters were born to them, *angelic beings* saw that the daughters of humans were beautiful, and they married any of them they chose. Then the Lord said, "My Spirit will not contend with humans forever, for they are mortal; their days will be a hundred and twenty years." The Nephilim were on the earth in those days—and also afterward—when *angelic beings* went to the daughters of humans and had children by them. They [their children] were the heroes of old, men of renown.

The above is the accurate and very clear meaning of that passage.

If this is true, then why, in almost all translations, is *bene Elohim* in Genesis 6:1–4 left translated as "sons of God" rather than as "angels" or "angelic beings"? It is because of Cyril of Alexandria.

CYRIL OF ALEXANDRIA

Cyril of Alexandria was a fifth-century church leader (ca. 376–444) who was an influential voice in the early church. One of his many collected writings was his response to the Roman emperor Julian the Apostate's (361–363) mockery of Christianity, part of which centered around Genesis 6:1–4. The Roman Empire became a Christian empire with the conversion of the emperor Constantine (306–337), but after Julian became emperor, he publicly rejected Christianity, writing extensively against it, and tried to bring Rome back to its pagan roots, hence Julian's historical designation as "Julian the Apostate." In Julian's writings, he attacked and mocked Christianity from various angles, and in regard to Genesis 6:1–4 Julian specifically mocked the idea of angelic beings impregnating human women and having offspring with them (and yet, the very paganism to which Julian wanted to return echoes exactly this same idea; e.g., Zeus, or Jupiter, has sex with a human woman and the offspring is the demigod Hercules).

Cyril of Alexandria wrote extensively against Julian's written attacks on Christianity, with Cyril's writings in that regard collectively known as *Contra Julianum*, or *Against Julian*. One of the points that Cyril addresses is Julian's mockery of Genesis 6:1–4. In Cyril's response, he states, and subsequently teaches, that the term "sons of God" in Genesis 6:1–4 refers *only* to the *godly* line of Seth (i.e., Adam's son), while the phrase "daughters of men/humans" refers *only* to the daughters of the *ungodly* line of Cain (Adam's son who murdered his brother Abel). It was in the fifth century that Cyril came up with this idea and, since Cyril of Alexandria was an influential voice in the early church, that idea, that teaching, began to spread over time. As a result, to this day, seminaries still often teach that Genesis 6:1–4 is to be understood as saying that the godly line of Seth married, or intermingled with, the ungodly line of Cain.

However, there is not one shred of truth to this idea, and the very idea completely contradicts Scripture—Cyril of Alexandria may have been an influential (but also controversial) voice in the early church, but he was completely wrong in this teaching.

Read Genesis 6:1–4 yourself, just as is, and ask yourself what possible connection, by either reference or implication, does *any* of that passage have to Seth or Cain—the answer is none. Read it especially in light of the passages in Job, where the Bible clearly shows that the term "sons of God" means exclusively angelic beings. Read it also again from the standpoint that no human being between Adam and Jesus Christ is called a "son of God"—*no one*, ever, in the Old Testament calls God "Father," because God is *only* a Father to humanity if that specific human being was created (not born) by God, as was Adam (Luke 3:38), or if God *begot* that specific human being, as he did Jesus Christ (Heb 1:5l 5:5) or if God *adopted* any specific human being as his son/child, as he has Christians (Rom 8:15, 23; 9:4; Gal 4:5; Eph 1:5)—*only* if God has *created* you, or has *begotten* you, or has *adopted* you is God your Father. As a result, only Adam (the created son of God), Jesus Christ (the begotten Son of God), and Christians (the adopted sons of God) call God "Father." In fact, in John 8:44, Jesus specifically tells the Pharisees that they are of their "father, the devil." Angels were created by God, as was Adam (Ps 148:1–5), and so, as a result, angels *are* "sons of God," being, like Adam, *created* sons of God. It is inescapable that Genesis 6:1–4 *specifically* tells us that it was the "sons of God" who came to "human women" and took them as wives (that is, had sexual union with them), and those women then bore offspring, which were the result of that union, and the Bible calls those offspring "Nephilim."

It is for this reason, the reason of Cyril of Alexandria's teaching, that, across almost every single Bible translation, the term "sons of God" is kept rather than being translated as "angelic being"—by keeping the term "sons of God," the Bible translators will not take a stance on interpretation, but will just translate it *exactly* as it is written—*bene Elohim*, "sons of God," leaving it to the reader to investigate and decide.

To say that the term "sons of God" refers to the godly line of Seth and that the "daughters of men" refers to the ungodly line of Cain is no different than me saying that the term "sons of God" refers to Jedi Knights and that the term "daughters of men" refers to Sith Lords—there is just as much reason to adopt the Jedi Knights-and-Sith Lords interpretation as there is to adopt Cyril's Seth-and-Cain interpretation—none; each interpretation is equally nonsense fantasy. The idea that the term "sons of God" means the godly line of Seth and that the term "daughters of men" refers to the ungodly line of Cain is baseless and unbiblical and is nothing more than Cyril of Alexandria grasping at straws to refute the mockery of Julian the Apostate—instead of holding to biblical truth, Cyril invented a nonsense based on fantasy. There is nothing godly about Seth, Adam's son, nor is there anything particularly ungodly about Cain's descendants—in the Old Testament, the term "sons of God" means, *always*, solely and exclusively, *angelic beings*.

THE GODLY LINE OF SETH

For no reason whatsoever, Cyril of Alexandria decided that Seth (Adam's son) and Seth's children were godly. The reason he tries to make this look reasonable is because Noah is descended from Seth. Yet, what are we told about Noah?

> But Noah found favor in the eyes of the LORD. (Gen 6:8 NIV)

We are told that *Noah* found favor in the eyes of God, and the clear meaning of this, especially in light of the preceding verse, is that among *all* the inhabitants on the Earth of that day, *only* Noah found favor in the eyes of God. However, Noah's grandfather Methuselah (Gen 5:21–27) was alive during this exact same time, and Methuselah, just like Noah, was descended from Seth (5:1–21). This means that, since *only* Noah found favor in the eyes of God, and since Methuselah was in fact alive during that entire time (Methuselah actually died just before the flood came), Methuselah, a son of Seth, did *not* find favor in God's eyes.

Likewise, we are told the following about Enoch, Methuselah's father, Noah's great-grandfather:

> When Enoch had lived 65 years, he became the father of Methuselah. After he became the father of Methuselah, Enoch walked faithfully with God 300 years and had other sons and daughters. Altogether, Enoch lived a total of 365 years.

Enoch walked faithfully with God; then he was no more, because God took him away. (5:21–24 NIV)

The Bible goes *out of its way* to tell us that Enoch, who was a son of Seth, "walked with God." Why would the Bible make a point to do this? The reason the Bible goes out of its way to describe someone as having walked with God is because it was unusual, and exceptional, in that whole time, for *anyone* to walk with God. Since *none* of Enoch's fathers (all of whom were also sons of Seth) are described as walking with God, and since the Bible goes out of its way to tell us that Enoch *did* walk with God, the conclusion is very clear—Enoch walked with God, but his fathers did not, and this is further affirmed when we are told in 6:8 that *only* Noah found favor in God's eyes, but Methuselah did not.

From all of this, we see very clearly that being a son of Seth has *nothing* to do with being godly; in fact, of the descendants of Seth listed in Genesis 5, *only* Enoch and Noah are actually *highlighted* as having a heart for God, which means, by implication, that none of the rest of Seth's sons had a heart for God, or walked with him, or found favor in his eyes. All that to say that any idea, or teaching, that calls Seth's line "godly" is completely baseless and is, in fact, in contradiction to the Bible's clear teaching—there is nothing godly about Seth or his children.

THE TOWER OF BABEL

Prior to the flood, the whole humanity was *one* people, living on *one* vast continent and speaking *one* language—there were *no divisions* of humanity. The division of humanity happened *only* at the tower of Babel, a number of generations *after* the flood (Gen 11:1–9). It was at the tower of Babel that humanity was divided in regard to language and skin color, and that division of humanity is *never* referred to in the Bible as "races" of humanity; rather, these divisions of humanity are always and only ever referred to as "nations."

As a result, we know that in the days of Noah there were no nations or divisions of humanity, so any teaching that states that there *were* divisions of humanity *before* the flood is in contradiction to the clear teaching of the Bible. To teach that there was a division of humanity into the "sons of Seth" and the "daughters of Cain" lines is in complete contradiction to the clear teaching of Scripture—the divisions of humanity happened at the tower of Babel, a number of generations *after* the flood, and did *not* exist in Noah's day.

Once again, on all counts, Cyril of Alexandria's teaching on this is unbiblical. The "sons of God" of Genesis 6:1–4 are angelic beings, and the "daughters of men" are exactly what it says they are—human women. Genesis 6:1–4 tells us that angelic beings (fallen angelic beings) went to human women, impregnated them, and had offspring with them, with those offspring being called "Nephilim." Within six verses of *that* event, God says he will wipe all life off of the face of the Earth, but Noah finds favor in his eyes. The flood did *not* come because people were *bad*; the flood came because fallen angelic beings had offspring with human women, which resulted in a *corruption* of humanity—that is, by way of the offspring of that union, it resulted in a humanity that was now no longer the same humanity as God had created in Adam—humanity had *corrupted* itself.

PERFECT IN HIS GENERATIONS

In Genesis 6:9, we are told some information about Noah—and here is a common translation of that verse:

> This is the account of Noah and his family. Noah was a righteous man, blameless among the people of his time, and he walked faithfully with God. (NIV)

In this translation, as well as others, Noah is described as being a "righteous man" and as being "blameless." However, that is a wrong translation—Noah was *not* blameless (in fact he was found drunk and naked after the flood; Gen 9:20–27). The correct and accurate translation is much more specific, and is as follows:

> This is the genealogy of Noah. Noah was a just man, *perfect in his generations.* Noah walked with God. (NKJV)

Here, in this translation (as well as others, including the YLT), Noah is *not* described as "righteous" or "blameless"; rather he is described as "just" and as "perfect in his generations." It is important to note that just prior to this, in Genesis 5, we are given the first detailed genealogy in the Bible, and it is the genealogy of *Noah*. Why is this genealogy important? And why is it given? It is given because humanity will continue with Noah, and this genealogy makes very clear that Noah had the exact same humanity as did Adam. As a result of the Genesis 5 genealogy of Noah, we know, for a fact, that Noah's descendants, which is all subsequent humanity, will have the exact same humanity as was created by God in Adam.

The term "perfect in his generations" is a very specific, and almost strange, term—what does it mean, and why is it used here? Why does it say "generations" and not "generation"? The meaning of the phrase "perfect in his generations" is this—it means that Noah was perfect in his *heredity*, perfect in his *ancestry,* perfect in his *humanity*, and it is not by coincidence that that specific phrase is used of Noah almost immediately after his genealogy is given. The genealogy of Noah *affirms* that he was *perfect in his heredity*.

This is an extremely important point, for it is a clear affirmation that Noah's humanity was the exact same humanity as created by God in Adam. That phrase "perfect in his generations" refers only to Noah's heredity as being fully, completely, and perfectly *human*, as being an *uncorrupted* humanity, in contrast to what was happening throughout the world of Noah's day, where that very *humanity*, that is, the *physical* human nature as created by God in Adam, was being *corrupted*, becoming something *other* than what God had created in Adam.

In fact, that corruption was not restricted only to humanity, for we are told in Genesis 6:12,

> So God looked upon the earth, and indeed it was corrupt; for *all flesh* had *corrupted* their way on the earth. (NKJV)

Here we are told not only that all *people* had corrupted their "way," but that "all flesh" had corrupted its way—this includes animals, which is why God specifically also *includes* the destruction of animal life as part of the destruction of the flood (Gen 6:7).

What was this corruption? *How* did humanity, and then all animal flesh, corrupt itself? The initial corruption of humanity began with the sons of God going to human women and having offspring with them, and those offspring were the Nephilim.

THE NEPHILIM

The offspring of the union of the sons of God with the daughters of men are referred to as "Nephilim." The name Nephilim means "fallen ones," and we are told the following:

> The Nephilim were on the earth in those days—and also afterward—when the sons of God went to the daughters of humans and had children by them. They were the heroes of old, men of renown. (Gen 6:4 NIV)

It is the clear sense of this passage that the Nephilim, who are mentioned specifically in the context of the sons of God going to the daughters of men and having children by them, are in fact the *offspring* of that union—the Nephilim are the offspring of the sons of God and the daughters of men. Their very name, Nephilim, or "fallen ones," denotes their nature—they are born as the "fallen ones" because they are the offspring of the fallen sons of God, of fallen angelic beings.

We are also told that the Nephilim were "heroes of old, men of renown"—those offspring were exceptional; they stood out from among other people. In some translations they are also described as follows:

> There were *giants* on the earth in those days, and also afterward, when the sons of God came in to the daughters of men and they bore children to them. Those were the mighty men who were of old, men of renown. (6:4 NKJV)

Here, Nephilim is translated as "giants," and this does, in fact, mean to be of great stature. We are also told an extremely interesting point—we are told that those *giants* (Nephilim) were "on the earth in those days, and *also afterward*"; that is, we are told that the giants/Nephilim were again on the Earth sometime *after* the flood.

If the Nephilim were on the Earth after the flood, does the Bible mention them again? In fact it does, and that description can give us a much greater understanding of the nature of the Nephilim of Noah's day.

NEPHILIM IN THE PROMISED LAND

When Israel entered the promised land, the land of Canaan, after the exodus, Joshua sent spies to scope out the land. The promised land was the land given by God, to Israel, to be their own possession. After the spies went to spy out the land and its people, they returned and gave this report to Joshua:

> But the men who had gone up with him said, "We can't attack those people; they are stronger than we are." And they spread among the Israelites a bad report about the land they had explored. They said, "The land we explored devours those living in it. All the people we saw there are of *great size*. We saw *the Nephilim* there (the descendants of Anak come from the Nephilim). *We seemed like grasshoppers in our own eyes, and we looked the same to them.*" (Num 13:31–33 NIV)

The Israelite spies reported that, in the land of Canaan, in the promised land, they saw people of "great size," i.e., they saw giants. They then specifically described those people as "Nephilim" and, just to make it absolutely clear what they meant by describing those people as giants, we are told specifically that those people were of such great stature that the Israelites seemed to be the size of grasshoppers next to them. There is no question—the Nephilim of Numbers 13:31–34 are clearly described as physical *giants*, people of far greater stature than normal human beings.

We are then also told another extremely strange, yet interesting, detail about that land and its people.

> When they reached the Valley of Eshkol, they cut off a branch bearing a single cluster of grapes. Two of them carried it on a pole between them, along with some pomegranates and figs. (Num 13:23 NIV)

Those same spies that went to explore the promised land, and who came back with the report about the Nephilim, also, while they were spying out the land, came across a valley within which were growing some grapes. We are told that they cut off *one* "single cluster of grapes," and that they then put that single cluster of grapes on a pole and that pole was then *carried*, with the single cluster of grapes, by *two men.*

We have all seen a single cluster of grapes—a single cluster of grapes can fit easily into the palm of any hand. Here though, in this valley, in the land of the Nephilim, a single cluster of grapes was so huge that it had to be put onto a pole, and then that pole, with that single cluster of grapes hanging from it, was so heavy and so large, that it had to be carried by two men (the implication is that the pole with the cluster of grapes was carried on the shoulders of two men)—this single cluster of grapes would had to have weighed at least in the *hundreds* of pounds. How could this be? That is *not* how God created grapes. What was going on? The gigantic size of that single cluster of grapes is inextricably tied to the land of the Nephilim, the land of extraordinary *giants*—it is a clear implication that the abnormal and gigantic size of those grapes is *because* of the giant Nephilim. These Nephilim of Numbers 13:31–33 are the same Nephilim referred to in Genesis 6:4 as being on the Earth "afterwards." Those Nephilim, in the promised land, are not normal human beings; they are something strange, a different humanity than what God had created, just as their grapes are different, in their nature, from what God had created.

The Nephilim of Numbers 13:31–33 are then also connected to Anak and his sons. We are told that Anak's sons are in fact *descendants* of those same Nephilim, which tells us that Anak would have also been one of those same promised land Nephilim, or descended from them.

The Anakites, or Anakim, are mentioned throughout the Old Testament, and are in the promised land (Deut 1:28; 2:10, 21; and 9:2, where they are also described as being of great size; Josh 11:21–22; 14:12, 15, 15:13–14; 21:11; Judg 1:20). Also, a close study of the tribes whom Israel encountered in the promised land reveals that a number of tribes are described as being of great, abnormal stature—as being a people of giants. These include Rephaites, who in Deuteronomy 2:11 are equated with the Anakites; also Joshua 12:4 and 13:12 tells us that the last king of the Rephaites was Og of Bashan; the Horites (Deut 2:22); Zamzummites (Deut 2:20, also equated with the Rephaites); the Amorites, described as being as tall as cedar trees (Amos 2:9), and others. All of these tribes who were inhabiting the promised land upon Israel's arrival there are described as abnormally large in stature.

We are told a very specific detail about Og, the king of Bashan, who is described as being one of the last of the Rephaites.

> Og king of Bashan was the last of the Rephaites. His *bed* was decorated with iron and was more than *nine cubits long* and *four cubits wide*. It is still in Rabbah of the Ammonites." (Deut 3:11 NIV)

The Bible goes out of its way to tell us the *size* of Og's bed—his bed is described as being "nine cubits long and four cubits wide"—this is approximately thirteen to fourteen feet long and six feet wide. Why would the Bible go out of its way to tell us this detail? The implication is clear—if Og's *bed* was thirteen to fourteen feet long, it is because *Og himself* was about that same size—Og, of the Rephaim, was a physical giant, as were all the other Nephilim and Nephilim-descended tribes.

GOD'S COMMAND TO KILL EVERYONE

It is in this context that we encounter a scenario that has caused much confusion among Christians, and has led non-Christians to describe God as a bloodthirsty murderous monster.

In the Old Testament, when Israel was conquering the peoples of the promised land, God had commanded Israel to kill *everyone* from those occupying tribes—to kill *all* men, women, and children (Num 21:2–3; Deut 20:17; Josh 6:21). For this reason, some people describe God as being a bloody, merciless God—but is this true?

In fact, it is not true. On the contrary, God's command to Israel to kill every one of the peoples of those tribes was in fact God's *mercy* and compassion on *humanity*. How can this be so? It is because the tribes on whom God's judgment was being cast were all *Nephilim* tribes, peoples and tribes who were the result of the same fallen angel–human union as Genesis 6:1–4—God was telling Israel to wipe out that *corruption* of *humanity*, for the Nephilim were not humanity as was created by God.

As Israel went ahead and killed the peoples of those Nephilim tribes, we are told that Israel did *not* wipe out *all* of those Nephilim descendants, and that a remnant of those Nephilim tribes survived, with that surviving remnant fleeing to Gath, Gaza, and Ashdod.

> No Anakites were left in Israelite territory; only in Gaza, Gath and Ashdod did any survive. (Josh 11:22 NIV)

Nephilim descendants survived in Gaza, Gath, and Ashdod. Why is this significant? It is significant because approximately five hundred or so years later we encounter a descendant of those same giants/Nephilim.

> A champion named Goliath, who was from Gath, came out of the Philistine camp. His height was six cubits and a span. (1 Sam 17:4 NIV)

Goliath was a giant, described as being "six cubits and a span" in height, which is approximately ten feet tall, and he comes from *Gath*—Goliath is a watered-down descendant of the Anakite survivors, who, for almost five centuries, intermarried with normal women and so each successive generation had a more watered-down Nephilim aspect, which was there nonetheless. So, where Og of Bashan, who was alive in Joshua's day, is described, by implication, as being approximately thirteen to fourteen feet tall (Deut 3:11), Goliath is only approximately ten feet tall. Goliath was a watered-down Nephilim descendant.

The land of Canaan, the promised land that was to be given to Israel by God, was inhabited by Nephilim and by Nephilim descendants. *Why* was this so? The reason that the promised land was inhabited by Nephilim and by Nephilim descendants can be traced back to Noah.

THE CURSE OF NOAH

We must remember that before the flood *only* Noah found favor in the eyes of God; this means that neither Noah's wife, nor his sons, nor his sons' wives found favor with God. We must also remember that the days of Noah, as a result of the Nephilim corruption, was a world of extreme sexual immorality, a sexual immorality that resulted in a union of humanity with fallen angelic beings.

After the flood, a strange scene is recounted for us.

> The sons of Noah who came out of the ark were Shem, Ham and Japheth. (Ham was the father of Canaan.) These were the three sons of Noah, and from them came the people who were scattered over the whole earth. Noah, a man of the soil, proceeded to plant a vineyard. When he drank some of its wine, he became drunk and lay uncovered inside his tent. Ham, the father of Canaan, saw his father naked and told his two brothers outside. But Shem and Japheth took a garment and laid it across their shoulders; then they walked in backward and covered their father's naked body. Their faces were turned the other way so that they would not see their father naked. When Noah awoke from his wine and found out what his youngest son had done to him, he said,
>
> "Cursed be Canaan!
> The lowest of slaves
> will he be to his brothers."
> He also said,
> "Praise be to the Lord, the God of Shem!
> May Canaan be the slave of Shem.
> May God extend Japheth's territory;
> may Japheth live in the tents of Shem,
> and may Canaan be the slave of Japheth." (Gen 9:18–27 NIV)

Sometime after the flood, Noah planted a vineyard, grew some grapes, made some wine, drank it, got drunk, and fell unconscious in his tent. Some people try and say that Noah was naïve, and that he accidentally made wine—that he didn't know what it was—and accidentally got drunk. This is both foolish and impossible. Noah, as with all people before the flood, was not a stupid man—he alone, single-handedly, built the ark. Also, making wine is a lengthy and involved process, usually taking a minimum of six months—you cannot make wine by accident. Noah knew exactly what he was doing—he knew what he was doing when he first planted his vineyard and then nurtured the grapes to grow; he knew it when he crushed the grapes, fermented them, and purified the juice to eventually make wine; and he knew it when he drank too much of that wine. Noah did not make wine by accident, nor did he get drunk by accident.

While Noah was unconscious in his tent, and also naked, his youngest son, Ham, entered into the tent and found his unconscious, naked father. We are then told that

Ham went out and told his brothers, Shem and Japheth. Shem and Japheth then took a garment and walked into Noah's tent *backwards*, so that they would not see his nakedness, and then they covered him with the garment. We are then told that Noah awoke, found out what Ham had "done to him," and then proceeded to curse, not Ham, but Ham's *son*, Canaan.

Does any of this make sense? Why would Noah be so enraged at his son Ham that he cursed Ham's *son*, Canaan, Noah's own grandson? He then goes on to *bless* Shem and Japheth. Is there anything normal about Noah's reaction, if all as that happened is that Ham saw his father unconscious and naked in his tent? No, this is not a normal reaction—if that is all that happened. However, we have very good reason to understand that something far worse occurred when Ham entered into Noah's tent and found him there unconscious and naked, and that is implied in the very specific way the incident is described.

> When Noah awoke from his wine and found out what his youngest son had done *to* him, he said, "Cursed be Canaan!" (Gen 9:24–25 NIV)

First, how did Noah find out what went on in the tent while he was unconscious and naked? There is only one way—Shem and Japheth told him. What did they tell him? They would have told Noah what Ham had told them.

It is in that context that we are told that Noah had found out what his youngest son had "done *to* him." If all that Ham did was see his father naked, and then go outside of the tent to tell his brothers that their father was naked, we would be told, "When Noah had found out what his youngest son had *done*," but, instead, we are told that Noah had found out what his youngest son had "done *to* him"—why this specific language?

It is because this specific language is accurate. When Ham came into his father's tent, and found him there, naked and unconscious, Ham did something *to* his naked and unconscious father—the very strong, almost inescapable, implication is that Ham entered his father's tent, found him naked and unconscious, and did sexual things to his unconscious and naked father. Once we understand this, then every aspect of the story makes perfect sense. Ham went into his father's tent, found him naked and unconscious, did sexual things to his naked and unconscious father, and then went out to tell his brothers—what did he tell his brothers? We can understand that Ham went out to his brothers to tell them that their father was naked and unconscious inside the tent, and that he did sexual things to their naked and unconscious father, and they also, Shem and Japheth, could go in and do the same. It is for that reason that Shem and Japheth were utterly disgusted and took a garment and walked backwards into their naked father's tent, so that there was not even a hint of what Ham was suggesting—they, Shem and Japheth, not only would *not* do to Noah what their brother Ham had done, but they would not even look upon the sight of their naked father, and this is exactly how it plays out. Later, when Noah recovered, Shem and Japheth told

Noah what Ham had done *to* him, and now Noah's reaction is completely understandable—he is livid with anger, so much so that he pronounces a curse.

But why did Noah curse Ham's *son*, and not Ham himself? It is because Noah wanted Ham to know what it would be like to have a degenerate son—just as Noah had a degenerate son in Ham, likewise, he wanted Ham to have a degenerate son in Canaan, and that is what happened. The curse that Noah pronounced upon *Canaan* was a curse that was the result of gross sexual sin.

The promised land was the land of Canaan, the son of Ham, the one whom Noah had cursed. Ever since the curse of Noah upon Canaan, gross sexual immorality is repeatedly tied in to the land of Canaan—much earlier, in the days of Abraham, both Sodom and Gomorrah were located in the land of Canaan (Gen 10:19), with each city being a city of extreme sexual sin. Likewise, by the time of Israel's exodus, in the land of Canaan, there was the second irruption of Nephilim, the "afterwards" spoken of in Genesis 6:4—the Nephilim in the promised land were, like the Nephilim of Genesis 6:1-4, the offspring of the union of fallen angelic beings and human women—the most vile sexual perversion—again, all in the land of Canaan.

The land of Canaan was the breeding ground of enormous sexual sin of every kind—why? The reason that the land of Canaan was the breeding ground of great sexual sin is because that was the manifestation of the curse of Noah, pronounced upon Canaan as a result of his father Ham's gross sexual sin against his own father.

NEPHILIM IN THE DAYS OF NOAH

By Noah's day, the Nephilim corruption was rampant, a spreading of the union of fallen angelic beings with human women, resulting in an actual physical corruption of humanity, a humanity that was now becoming something other than how God had created it in Adam. Noah, however, was untainted by that physical Nephilim corruption, and it is for this reason that Noah himself is described as being "perfect in his generations" (Gen 6:9 NKJV)—Noah, the one through whom all humanity would continue, was perfect, uncorrupted, in his *humanity*, in his *heredity*, in his human *ancestry*.

When the Nephilim were on the Earth in Noah's day, what were they doing? Did they just live as normal human beings, despite being a corrupted humanity? The Bible only tells us that these Nephilim offspring were giants, that they were "great" and that they had "renown"—obviously, then, the Nephilim had some great influence over pre-flood humanity.

The Bible gives only that very general information of the Nephilim of Genesis 6:1-4, while giving us more detailed information on the Nephilim of the promised land in Numbers 13. There is an extrabiblical book, the book of Enoch, non-canonical, whose entire content deals exclusively with the details of these Nephilim, how they came to be, who they were and what they did, and it is interesting to review its contents in light of what the Bible says.

THE BOOK OF ENOCH

The book of Enoch is a hard book to understand—hard to understand in that it is not part of Scripture, and yet *one* verse from that book *is* Scripture, for we are told in the book of Jude,

> Now Enoch, the seventh from Adam, prophesied about these men also, saying, "Behold, the Lord comes with ten thousands of His saints, to execute judgment on all, to convict all who are ungodly among them of all their ungodly deeds which they have committed in an ungodly way, and of all the harsh things which ungodly sinners have spoken against Him." (Jude 14–15 NIV)

The book of Jude makes clear that the Enoch that is being talked about is the same Enoch of Genesis 5:21, Noah's great-grandfather, the one who is described as "walking with God" (Gen 5:24). The quote of Enoch in the book of Jude—"Behold, the Lord comes with ten thousands of His saints . . . "—is in fact from the book of Enoch. So, what do we make of the book of Enoch? Is it Scripture, or is it not? If it were Scripture, it would be included in the canon of the Bible, for the Holy Spirit would have made sure of that, so the fact that it is not included in the canon of Scripture tells us that we cannot approach it as Scripture, *but* we know for a fact that at least *one* verse from the book of Enoch *is* Scripture—that is as much as we can say. With that in mind, we can approach the book of Enoch at least as a sort of historical/anecdotal book, though not as Scripture.

The entire book of Enoch is a detailed account of the sons of God of Genesis 6:1–4 going to human women and having offspring by them. Enoch is very clear that these are angelic beings uniting with human women. He tells us that there were two hundred of these angelic beings that went to human women, and that their captain's name was Samyaza, and that they lusted after women's hair (see also 1 Cor 11:9–10). The book of Enoch tells us that the offspring of that union between angelic beings and human women was the Nephilim. Enoch then describes for us the height, the stature, of those Nephilim offspring, telling us that those Nephilim were three thousand *ells* in height. Enoch then tells us that those Nephilim instructed humanity in many areas of knowledge, giving instruction in the knowledge of science, arts, beauty, and the occult.

Enoch was the seventh generation from Adam (including Adam), and this explosion in human knowledge in the eighth generation of Adam is borne out by Scripture, which tells us that the domestication of livestock, the discovery of the art of music, and the discovery of all metallurgy, including bronze and iron, all happened in the eighth generation of Adam (Gen 4:19–22). This coincides with the timeline of the life of Enoch. If we piece these things together, we can conclude that the original pre-flood Nephilim irruption would have occurred in the days of Enoch, the seventh generation of Adam, with the following eighth generation—the generation of Jabal, Jubal, and Tubal-Cain—experiencing an explosion of knowledge. As a result, based on this scenario, we can see that by Noah's day, by the tenth generation from Adam, this explosion of knowledge would have reached great heights, especially when considering that the lifespan of a pre-flood generation was almost one thousand years.

THE JUDGMENT OF THE SONS OF GOD OF GENESIS 6

How could the sons of God, angelic beings, go to human women and have offspring with them? How could God allow such a thing? The fact is that this was *not* something that was allowed; the fallen angels who did this crossed a line, and there were severe consequences for those angelic beings.

In the Bible, there are three domains that are located *inside* the Earth. The first domain is called the "Realm of the Dead," in Hebrew called *Sheol*, in Greek called *Hades*. The Realm of the Dead is the place where all people who had ever lived and died, from Adam to Jesus Christ, went to after they died, and, in fact, that is also where Jesus himself was for the three days that he was dead (Job 26:6; Ps 16:10; Prov 9:18, Isa 14:19, et al.). The Realm of the Dead is located inside the Earth, specifically beneath the floors of the oceans (Job 26:5).

The second domain inside the Earth, deeper down than the Realm of the Dead, is a place the Bible calls the "Pit" or the "Abyss" (Pss 28:1; 30:9; 55:23; 88:4; Isa 14:15; 38:18; Luke 8:31; Rev 9:1–2, 11; 11:7; 17:8; 20:1). The Pit, or the Abyss, is the place to which the angels who rebelled in heaven were cast—the rebel angels were cast down to the *Earth* (Ezek 28:17; Rev 12:7–9), *inside* the Earth, into the Pit, or the Abyss. The Pit is a place of imprisonment; it is a place of chains and darkness, and it is *only* for the fallen rebel angels. All the rebel angels, together with Satan, were cast into the Pit when they were originally cast out of heaven, but Satan was allowed out of the Pit so as to tempt Adam in Eden. When Adam sinned, the dominion to the Earth that was given by God to Adam was then given by Adam to Satan—upon his fall, Adam gave the authority of the Earth and everything in it to Satan (Luke 4:5–7). Upon Adam's fall, not only did Satan become the rightful lord, or ruler, of Earth (John 12:31), but *all* the fallen angels that had been cast into the Pit, inside the Earth, were now also released, to inhabit the Earth, with Satan, with their earthly base of operations to be located in the earthly sky (Eph 2:2; 6:12). Reference to fallen angels having previously been in the Pit is found in the Gospel of Luke.

In Luke 8:26–33, a demon possessed man was brought before Jesus, and Jesus asked the demons possessing the man for their name, and they replied that their name was "Legion," for they were many (that is, there were many demons inhabiting, or possessing, that man). Then, immediately upon telling Jesus their name, those demons *begged* Jesus to *not* send them to the Abyss.

> And they begged Jesus repeatedly not to order them to go into the Abyss."
> (Luke 8:31 NIV)

Why were they so scared of being cast into the Abyss? It is because they were there before; it was the place of their previous imprisonment, a place of chains and darkness, the place to which they were cast when they were originally cast out of heaven. The Pit, as a place of imprisonment for the fallen angels, was not a good place, and so those demons *begged* Jesus not to send them back to the Pit, and Jesus granted their request—he was merciful to demons.

The third domain inside the Earth is located at the very heart of the Earth, deepest down, and it is called the "Lake of Fire" (Matt 25:41; Rev 20:14–15)—this is the place that is commonly called "hell," and it is inside the Earth, at the heart of the Earth. After the judgment to come, the Realm of the Dead (Hades) and, by implication, the Pit, both of which are located inside the Earth, will collapse down into that Lake of Fire, also inside the Earth (Rev 20:14).

It is very important to understand that *no one* has *ever* been in the Lake of Fire, in hell, and *no one* is there right now—no human being has ever been there or is there now, no fallen angel has ever been there or is there now, and Satan has never been there, and he is not there now; the Lake of Fire is totally empty, no one has ever been there, and the very first beings to be cast into the Lake of Fire will be the Beast of Revelation and his False Prophet (Rev 19:20). Satan will not be thrown into the Lake of Fire until much later after that, over a thousand years *after* the Second Coming (Rev 20:10). Satan, and *all* the fallen angels, have only ever been in either heaven or Earth or in the Abyss/Pit within the Earth.

The Pit, or the Abyss, was the place of imprisonment for all the fallen angels, including Satan, upon being cast out of heaven and until the fall of Adam. Upon Adam's fall, Satan was given dominion of the Earth and, as a result, every fallen angel imprisoned in the Pit, inside the Earth, was then released to be free, with Satan, upon the Earth. However, the Pit remained in place, even though it was then empty. But it did not remain empty. The "sons of God" of Genesis 6:1–4, having gone to human women, impregnating them and having offspring with them, grossly violated their restrictions in regard to human beings, and they were judged for it, and their judgment was to be thrown back into the Pit, to be kept in chains and darkness until the judgment. The sons of God of Genesis 6:1–4 are now the only inhabitants of the Pit.

How do we know this?

Peter tells us the following:

> After being made alive, he went and made proclamation to *the imprisoned spirits*— to those who were *disobedient long ago* when God waited patiently *in*

the days of Noah while the ark was being built. In it only a few people, eight in all, were saved through water (1 Pet 3:19-20 NIV)

Peter tells us that during the three days that Jesus was dead, while he was in the Realm of the Dead, he made "proclamation to the *imprisoned spirits*," and he tells us that these spirits were the spirits who were "disobedient long ago," spirits who were disobedient "in the days of Noah." The disobedient and imprisoned spirits referred to in 1 Peter 3:19-20 are the very same sons of God of Genesis 6:1-4—they were thrown into the prison of the Pit as judgment for what they had done.

We are also told the following in Jude:

> And the angels who did not *keep their positions* of authority but *abandoned their proper dwelling*—these he has kept in darkness, bound with everlasting chains for judgment on the great Day. *In a similar way*, Sodom and Gomorrah and the surrounding towns gave themselves up to *sexual immorality* and *perversion*. They serve as an example of those who suffer the punishment of eternal fire. (Jude 6-7 NIV)

Jude tells us that there were "angels who did not keep their [proper] positions" but abandoned their proper place—that is, those angels went where they were not supposed to go. As a result of what they did, those same angels are now in chains and in darkness, imprisoned, awaiting judgment. Then, very importantly, Jude *immediately* connects the actions of those imprisoned angels with the *sexual sin* of Sodom and Gomorrah—Jude *specifically* connects those angels leaving their proper positions of authority with sexual sin. The reason Jude does this is to make clear that the act of the imprisoned angels abandoning their proper positions and going where they were not allowed to go is to be understood *in the same way* as Sodom and Gomorrah giving themselves up to *sexual* perversion—the angels abandoning their proper *dwelling*, their proper "position," is equated, in this context of Sodom and Gomorrah, with sexual sin.

The clear point is this—those imprisoned angels went where they were not supposed to go; they went to human women, had sexual union with them, and fathered offspring with them—they committed an extraordinary sexual sin, and, as a result, they were bound in chains and darkness, thrown into prison, the prison of the Pit, the Abyss. Those imprisoned angels of Jude 6-7 are the same "sons of God" of Genesis 6:1-4, as well as being the same "imprisoned spirits" of 1 Peter 3:19-20. The punishment, or judgment, upon the angelic beings that went to human women and had sexual union with them, fathering offspring with them, was to be cast into the Pit, the Abyss, in chains and darkness.

It is extremely important to understand that Satan was *not* among those sons of God/fallen angels of Genesis 6:1-4 who went to human women. Satan would have known, as would have all the fallen angels known, that to go and have union with human women would be a great violation of the restrictions placed upon them in regard to humanity (just as, in a similar way, the enemy is not allowed to physically harm a human being unless allowed to by the free will of that person)—there are strict limits as to how the enemy can engage with human beings. Satan absolutely would have known this, and he also would have known that to cross that line would result in severe consequences. As a result, though the idea of the sons of God going to human woman was almost certainly Satan's idea, he himself did not do it; he got others to do it, because he knew there would be a big price to pay.

As a result, we can understand from Scripture that the fallen angelic beings of Genesis 6:1–4, the sons of God, who had sexual union and offspring with human women, were bound in chains and thrown into the Pit, the Abyss, as judgment for what they had done, and they are there still, awaiting the judgment to come, as outlined in Revelation. Also, in Revelation, in the days preceding the Second Coming, in the days that will be like the days of Noah, the Pit is described as being opened and its inhabitants released (Rev 9:1–11).

THE PHYSICAL STATURE OF THE NEPHILIM

It is true that in both Genesis 6:4 as well as Numbers 13:31–33, as well as the many other passages that describe the Nephilim tribes of the promised land, the Nephilim are described as physical giants. But, do they *necessarily* have to present as physical giants?

The answer is no—a Nephilim offspring, the offspring of an angel/human union, can also appear to be of normal human stature, and that point is best illustrated by the Incarnation itself.

Jesus Christ is God's *only* begotten Son (Heb 1:5, 5:5), the result of God physically *impregnating* a human woman, so as to reproduce himself in his offspring, which reproduction would be inextricably joined and united, forever, with the woman's reproduction of herself—that is the Incarnation We could easily expect that Almighty God's only begotten Son might be one million feet tall and outshine all the suns of the universe, but that was not the case. In fact, Isaiah tells us the following:

> He grew up before him like a tender shoot,
> and like a root out of dry ground.
> *He had no beauty or majesty to attract us to him,*
> *nothing in his appearance that we should desire him.* (Isa 53:2 NIV)

We are specifically told in Isaiah that there was nothing exceptional about Jesus' physical appearance—he did not possess any extraordinary "beauty or majesty," and there was nothing in his appearance that would have drawn us to him—he would, in fact, have had the appearance of an ordinary man.

Likewise, if the only begotten Son of God, the result of Almighty God impregnating a human woman and reproducing himself in her womb, was born having the appearance of an ordinary man, then any offspring of an angelic being and a human woman—a far lesser union than the union of God with a human woman—can likewise have the appearance of an ordinary man; such an offspring does not necessarily, in any way, have to appear as a gigantic being of exceptional stature. As a result, we can understand that a Nephilim offspring may, just like God's only begotten Son, have the appearance of an ordinary man.

WHAT SPIRIT ANIMATED THE NEPHILIM?

The Nephilim were the offspring of the union of fallen angelic beings with human women. Yet, upon their birth, what kind of spirit was it that that gave them *life*? Were they made alive by a new spirit, or soul, as created by God? That would be impossible, for the following reasons.

Since the Nephilim were *not* part of God's created order but were the result of the fallen sons of God committing an extraordinary sin, crossing a forbidden line, then it is reasonable to understand that the spirit that would have given life to a Nephilim was *not* a newly created, God-made, life-giving spirit, as is a human soul. If that is the case, then what, or how, did the offspring of the sons of God have life?

It is very possible, or even likely, that the Nephilim were in fact inhabited, or indwelt, made alive, by the same fallen angelic beings that fathered them. In fact, some people have pointed to demon possession as an example of how fallen spirits *seek* to inhabit flesh, saying that the Nephilim offspring was an attempt by those fallen angelic beings to father their own flesh so as to, themselves, inhabit that flesh.

There are some intriguing verses in Young's Literal Translation that have been cited as an example of this very thing, verses speaking about the Rephaim, one of the Nephilim tribes of the promised land.

> The Rephaim are formed, Beneath the waters, also their inhabitants. (Job 26:5 YLT)

> To the dead dost Thou do wonders? Do Rephaim rise? do they thank Thee? Selah. (Ps 88:10 YLT)

> Dead—they live not, Rephaim, they rise not, Therefore Thou hast inspected and dost destroy them, Yea, thou destroyest all their memory. (Isa 26:14 YLT)

Job 26:5 tells us that the Rephaim are "formed, beneath the waters"—the immediate connotation of "beneath the waters" is that it is a reference to the Realm of the Dead, or possibly the still-deeper Pit, or Abyss—is this verse telling us that the *spirit* that would have inhabited, or given life to, a Rephaim was a spirit from the Pit?

Likewise, both Psalm 88:10 and Isaiah 26:14 tell us that the Rephaim "rise not"—this seems to be telling us that the Rephaim, a Nephilim tribe, do *not* share in the resurrection, and yet *all* human beings will be resurrected, both Christians and non-Christians—*everyone* (1 Thess 4:16; Rev 20:11–15). Since all human beings, Christian or not, *will be* resurrected, then how is it that the Rephaim, one of the Nephilim tribes of the promised land, will *not* be resurrected? Is it because a human *spirit* or *soul* does not indwell a Rephaim body, but rather a fallen spirit, a spirit that at one time was in the Pit, a fallen angelic being? People have pointed to these verses, which teach that the Rephaim will not be resurrected, as support that the Rephaim, who were Nephilim descendants, were inhabited, or made alive, by the indwelling of fallen angelic beings.

NOTHING NEW UNDER THE SUN—GENETICS

If God is actually telling us the truth in Ecclesiastes 1 that there is, in fact, "nothing new under the sun," and that whatever we think of as being new was in fact already here long ago, done by a people no longer remembered, then that would include, and apply to, every aspect of human endeavor. This would include the entire realm of science, technology, and medicine—if our age and world is involved in something and is accomplishing something that we think is unique to our age, something that is new upon the Earth (e.g., a heart transplant), God tells us that it is *not* new, that it was here before, long ago, done by a people no longer remembered—the people before the flood. If this is true, and if God is telling us the truth, then this also applies to every aspect of genetics.

In the realm of modern genetics, our world is right now engaging in genetic combinations of humans and animals—any online search for modern "chimeras" will lead you to articles outlining these current practices. One of the most current of these genetic combinations of human and animal DNA is genetic modifications of a monkey brain with human DNA. In our own day we are seeing human and animal DNA being genetically combined. If Ecclesiastes is actually true, then we are not the first to do this—it was already done before, done by the pre-flood world.

If this is true, then we must more carefully consider the very specific language of Genesis 6, which tell us that "all *flesh*" had "corrupted" itself (Gen 6:11–12)—the term "all flesh" includes *both* animal and human. This is very specifically talking about *flesh*, about physicality, *not* morality or a state of heart. *How* was all *animal* flesh corrupted? *How* was all *human* flesh corrupted? Was it by the genetic combining of human and animal DNA, as our own world is right now starting to do? There is good biblical reason to think so.

MAN'S CHANGING DIET

When God created Adam, he told Adam that his food would be seed-bearing fruit (Gen 1:29), while the animals were given the "plants of the field" or every "green plant" for food (1:30). However, after Adam had sinned, God changed man's diet—now, after the fall, God tells Adam that he too will eat the plants of the field for food, as do the animals (3:18). After the flood, God once again changes man's diet, telling Noah that, from now on, he, and all humanity, will *eat animals* (9:2–4).

Why does God, *after* the flood, command Noah, and humanity, to eat animals? The reason for it is certainly a response to events before the flood. There is good reason to understand that God's command to Noah to eat animals is connected to the pre-flood corruption of all flesh, the corruption of all human flesh as well as the corruption of all animal flesh. In fact, it is completely in line with the idea that prior to the flood humanity had begun, just as we have now also begun, to genetically combine itself with animals, a combining of human and animal DNA, so that the resulting humanity and animals were no longer as God had created them, but rather had now *corrupted* themselves, in their very natures, to be something other than what God had created. As a result, God tells Noah, and humanity, to *eat* animals so that humanity would never come to consider animals as being equal to human beings. God's command in this regard is in line with the idea of a pre-flood human/animal corruption, which in itself affirms Ecclesiastes 1 and its truth, in regard to our own day, that there is "nothing new under the sun."

(An interesting possibility to consider: if this is the case, and if pre-flood man did, as we are doing now, combine human and animal genetics so as to create hybrid creatures, then, in the example of the genetic combination of human and monkey DNA of our own day, if this practice were to continue to unfold and expand, then what kind of creature would result from the human-monkey genetic manipulation? A strange human-monkey hybrid? If so, would such a human-monkey hybrid be any different in its physicality than an Australopithecus, a seeming human-ape fossil, described as a human evolutionary ancestor? If that is the case, then in light of the fact that there is "nothing new under the sun," might we not then consider the Australopithecus fossils to be examples of the *result* of a similar genetic human-monkey DNA manipulation rather than an evolutionary ancestor? It is a profound thought).

SUMMARY OF THE NEPHILIM TIMELINE AND INFLUENCE

Based on all of this, we can conclude the following. The sons of God, fallen angelic beings, went to human women, had sexual union with them ("marriage"), and had offspring by them, the Nephilim, in the seventh generation of Adam, the days of Enoch. This event, together with the great capacity of pre-flood man, ultimately led to a great and extremely advanced civilization, more advanced than our own, greatly advanced in science, technology, arts, medicine, and more. This would eventually have led to genetic manipulation of both humanity and animals, ultimately resulting in the corruption, or dirtying, of human and animal natures, a combining of human and animal DNA, which is occurring right now in our own day in a preliminary way. It is for this reason that Noah is described as "perfect in his generations" (Gen 6:9 NKJV), or perfect in his human heredity and ancestry, remaining uncorrupted, and so the humanity that continues through Noah would be just as perfectly human as was he. This was the reason for the flood—not that people were bad, but that humanity was becoming other than how God had created it.

JESUS AND THE DAYS OF NOAH

It is with all of that in mind that we approach Matthew 24:36–44, where Jesus describes the days, and the world, preceding his Second Coming as being "like the days of Noah." How do we now understand this? Is this just a moral statement? Merely a statement to illustrate surprise? No, it is much more. We can understand it as follows.

The world prior to the Second Coming, in its advancement and character, will come to approximate the world before the flood, the world of Noah's day. The world of Noah's day was defined by there being only one vast continent, one language, so that all humanity could communicate easily with one another. There were no nations, nor divisions of skin color or appearance, so the whole world was one humanity. As a result of all of this, there was nothing that that world could not accomplish (Gen 11:6). Such a civilization, when combined with the great lifespans and enormous capacity of pre-flood man, both a physical and intellectual capacity resulting from being only ten generations removed from the perfection of Adam, could accomplish astounding things, and so they did.

The division of humanity into languages, skin colors, and nations was accomplished by God at the tower of Babel (Gen 11:1–9), and the world has been divided ever since. For the first time since the tower of Babel, our society, today, is overcoming those divisions—and we are doing it by means of technology. The divisions of oceans and continents, the result of the flood, remain, but we have overcome that with the technology of flight; the division of languages remains, but we have also overcome that with technology, where we now have translation software that allows us to speak to anybody, anywhere, in any language, and instantaneously converse with one another and share ideas and thoughts. As a result of all of this, we are now beginning to achieve a level of civilization not seen since before the flood, not seen since the days of Noah, and yet, by the propagation of the Evolution philosophy, we are blinded to this truth.

For the first time since the division of the tower of Babel, and since the days of Noah, we are now, in or own day, becoming one humanity, one people, speaking one language, all accomplished through the means of technology. As a result, we too can fulfill God's own word in that regard—nothing will now be impossible for us to achieve (Gen 11:6). In every regard, we are now becoming like the days of Noah.

THE NEPHILIM IN OUR OWN DAY

If this is true, and since one of the very key and defining elements of the days of Noah was the Nephilim and their presence upon the Earth, then what does that mean for our own day? If our own day is now coming to be like the days of Noah, should we not expect to see a Nephilim presence here in our time as well? If so, how would this look? How would this be manifest? Here is something to consider.

The enemy is not stupid, and the enemy lies and deceives, and intentionally disguises himself, for we are told,

> And no wonder, for Satan himself masquerades as an angel of light. It is not surprising, then, if his servants also masquerade as servants of righteousness. Their end will be what their actions deserve." (2 Cor 11:14–15 NIV)

We are told that Satan can disguise himself to be something other than what he is, and that his servants (other fallen angelic beings) can do the same. With this in mind, we can approach the presentation of the enemy, in regard to coming to human women, as happening in a disguised sort of way. It would be virtually ridiculous to think that a fallen angelic being would come undisguised to a woman and declare himself to be a demonic being who wants to impregnate her. Rather, we would expect any such being to come in a disguised approach—coming as something like a "god" who has chosen the woman to procreate a new race with him, a disguised approach that appeals to pride and vanity. Or perhaps, especially when the indoctrinated angle of Evolution is available, such beings may disguise themselves as coming from other parts of the galaxy in order to help us, humanity, "evolve" to our next evolutionary level, and these "higher beings" would be our "guides" to help us achieve that. And what kind of "higher beings" would they present as? Obviously, they would present as beings who themselves have already evolved to that next level, including a level of technological evolution. In fact, would these fallen angelic beings present themselves to humanity as aliens, coming from other parts of the galaxy to help us in our human evolution?

Of course, we have all heard about UFOs and "alien abductions"; this is a common thing in our day, with such reports being sometimes embraced, often ridiculed. But they are reported nonetheless. It is interesting to note that in a great many of the so-called alien abductions that are reported throughout world, the "aliens" who encounter people often talk to people about God, telling the people that humanity is on its own evolutionary road that will see us come to realize that we ourselves are, in fact, God, and those aliens are here to help us get there. These same aliens also, according to many reports, often talk specifically about Jesus Christ, saying that he is only one of a number of "masters" throughout human history who came to help us along the road of our evolution to "self-realization."

In addition to talking to people about God and Jesus Christ, these same aliens, in many instances, are described as having sexual union with human women. This has become a common narrative of our world, where even Hollywood movies and TV shows actually romanticize such human-alien sexual unions (e.g., *The Shape of Water*). Often, such accounts are subject to ridicule, while at other times they are not, and more increasingly they are not.

So, what would a modern, twenty-first-century Nephilim incursion look like? Would it come in the guise of "aliens," and would these "alien comings" be openly and publicly discussed, while being simultaneously ridiculed and dismissed, especially by the church? Just an observation—something to consider.

THE NEPHILIM AND THE BEAST

Revelation makes some very clear connections between the Beast, the nature of the Beast, and the Pit, which seems to very much indicate a Nephilim character to the Beast. Furthermore, Genesis 3 inarguably teaches this truth, for when God curses the serpent, he says,

> And I will put enmity
> between you and the woman,
> and between your offspring and hers;
> he will crush your head,
> and you will strike his heel. (Gen 3:15 NIV)

Here God talks about the *seed* of the woman, the "offspring" of the woman—the seed of the woman is unquestionably Jesus Christ. In that same breath, God also talks about the seed of the serpent—who or what, is the seed of the serpent, the *offspring* of the serpent? It is the Beast of Revelation.

13

The Nature of the Beast

The central human character of Revelation is the man commonly called the "antichrist"; however, in Revelation he is never referred to as the "antichrist," he is only ever called the "Beast."

The term "antichrist" occurs only four times in the entire Bible, and in every case it is found in the letters of the apostle John. Three of those references to the antichrist are just general references—one being a reference to the "spirit of antichrist" (1 John 4:3), two references being a reference to any person who is a liar and deceiver by way of denying Jesus Christ (1 John 2:22; 2 John 1:7), and only one reference is to an "antichrist" who is "coming" (1 John 2:18), and even that reference also includes other people whom John calls "antichrists," people who were alive in John's own day in the first century AD. All that to say that the term "antichrist" occurs only a few times in the entire Bible, always in the letters of John, and in all but one of those times it is used as a general term to describe someone, or some people, who deny Jesus Christ. It is important to note that this same John, who uses the term "antichrist" four times in his letters, is also the one who wrote Revelation, and yet in Revelation John never uses the term "antichrist"—why is that? Is it because that term is not necessarily the correct term? Instead, in Revelation, the person who is commonly called the "antichrist" is always and only called the "Beast."

ANTICHRIST

There is a general, and very serious, misconception that surrounds the word "antichrist" as it is applied to the Beast, and it is this—people start to think that this man, when he appears, will come onto the world's stage and say, "I am the antichrist," and that the world will look at that man and say, "Look! It's the antichrist—let's go worship him!" That is a completely wrong understanding. It is fundamental to understand that this man will *not* come onto the world's stage and declare that he is the antichrist, nor will the world look at him and say "Look! It's the antichrist!"; rather, he will come onto the world's stage and say, "I am Christ," and the world will look at him and say, "Look! It's Christ—he has returned! It's the Second Coming!" This man will present himself to the world as Christ returned, and the world will look at him and declare him to be Christ returned—he will be the ultimate *false* Christ, and his appearing on the world's stage will be a great and exceedingly powerful deception (Matt 24:22–24)—it is essential that we understand that. Since that man is virtually never called the "antichrist" in the Bible, we will refer to him here as he is referred to in Revelation—as the *Beast*. Everything about that man's life, every detail of his life and of his being, will seek to emulate Jesus Christ, including his birth.

THE SEED OF THE SERPENT

Jesus Christ is the only begotten Son of God (Heb 1:5 NKJV), the offspring of God and of a human woman (Luke 1:26–37)—God physically impregnated a human woman in order to father his son (Matt 1:18). If the Beast is seeking to emulate every aspect of Jesus Christ, in order to set himself up as the ultimate false Christ, then we would expect that his very conception and birth would seek to emulate the conception and birth of Jesus Christ, and, in fact, that is exactly what we see.

The very first prophecy in the Bible occurs in Genesis 3.

> So the Lord God said to the serpent:
> "Because you have done this,
> You are cursed more than all cattle,
> And more than every beast of the field;
> On your belly you shall go,
> And you shall eat dust
> All the days of your life. And I will put enmity
> Between you and the woman,
> And between *your seed* and *her Seed*;
> He shall bruise your head,
> And you shall bruise His heel." (Gen 3:14–15 NKJV)

This same passage is translated in the NIV as follows:

> So the Lord God said to the serpent, "Because you have done this,
> "Cursed are you above all livestock
> and all wild animals!
> You will crawl on your belly
> and you will eat dust
> all the days of your life.
> And I will put enmity
> between you and the woman,
> and between *your offspring* and *hers*;

> he will crush your head,
> and you will strike his heel."

In this prophecy, God talks about the seed of the serpent and the Seed of the woman—there is no question that the term "seed" means "offspring." What is the Seed of the woman? There is no question that the Seed of the woman is Jesus Christ—the church has always understood it this way, over the entire two-thousand-year history of the church.

What kind of a Seed was Jesus Christ? Was he only symbolic? Is he only a metaphor, a poetic symbol? Or was he an actual, physical, flesh-and-blood human being? The Bible is extremely clear—Jesus Christ, the Seed of the woman, was *not* just a symbol, nor a metaphor, nor a poetic device; rather, he was, without question, a physical, flesh-and-blood *man* (Luke 24:39; 1 John 4:2; 2 John 1:7).

The Seed of the woman and the seed of the serpent are spoken of by God in the same breath—in fact, in this prophecy they are inextricably connected. Since this is the case, and since we know, for a fact, that the Seed of the woman is not a symbolic statement, nor a poetic metaphor, but an actual physical, flesh-and-blood *offspring* of the woman, therefore we can know, with certainty, that the seed of the serpent must, likewise, be just as physical as the flesh-and-blood Seed of the woman. It is impossible to say that the seed of the serpent is only symbolic but that the Seed of the woman is not, since these two seeds are literally spoken of in exactly the same breath. So, if the Seed of the woman is a flesh-and-blood *offspring* of the woman, likewise, the seed of the serpent must also be the physical, flesh-and-blood *offspring* of the serpent—there is no other interpretation.

So, who is the serpent?

THE SERPENT

The Bible clearly tells us the identity of the serpent.

> The great dragon was hurled down—that ancient *serpent* called *the devil*, or *Satan*, who leads the whole world astray. He was hurled to the earth, and his angels with him. (Rev 12:9 NIV)

> He seized the dragon, that ancient *serpent*, who is *the devil*, or *Satan*, and bound him for a thousand years. (Rev 20:2 NIV)

The Bible is very clear—the serpent is Satan, the devil.

Since Satan is the serpent, then how do we understand Genesis 3:14–15, and the serpent's seed? There is only one possible way to understand it—just as God physically impregnated a human woman and begot his own Son, likewise, Satan will physically impregnate a human woman and beget his own offspring—it is an attempt by Satan to emulate God by begetting his own offspring. This means that the Beast will be a Nephilim offspring, the offspring of a "son of God," Satan, and a human woman.

Jesus specifically tells us that in the days preceding his Second Coming the world will be like the days of Noah (Matt 24:37–39). As discussed, this is not merely a moral statement, but a description of the state of the world, the state of civilization and its advancement, prior to his Second Coming. Also, the defining characteristic of the days of Noah was the sons of God fathering offspring with human women; these offspring were called the Nephilim. Likewise, if the days preceding the Second Coming will in fact be like the days of Noah, then, in addition to the great advancement of the day, there would also have to be the Nephilim element present, and, in fact, with the seed of the serpent that is exactly what we see—the Beast is a Nephilim offspring of Satan.

SATAN AND THE NEPHILIM

We have seen, and know for a fact, that the original sons of God going to human women (Gen 6:1–4) did *not* include Satan—he himself did not go to any human woman and have offspring with her. We know this since the sons of God who did do that have all been thrown into the Pit, a prison of chains and darkness, to await the judgment (1 Pet 3:19–20; Jude 6–7). Satan is *not* in prison; rather, he is free to roam and rule upon the Earth, with his base of operations being in the earthly sky (Job 1:7; Luke 4:5–7; Eph 2:2). Satan, though certainly the author of the *idea* of the sons of God going to human women, did not *himself* do that, since he would have known that that is forbidden and would result in a great punishment upon those who did that.

However, in the days prior to the Second Coming, that will change, and Satan *will* go and do what he has never done before— impregnate a human woman so as to father his own offspring. Why would he do that? The Bible tells us,

> Therefore rejoice, O heavens, and you who dwell in them! Woe to the inhabitants of the earth and the sea! For the devil has come down to you, having great wrath, because he knows that he has a short time. (Rev 12:12 NKJV)

The Bible tells us that in the days prior to the Second Coming Satan will know that his time is short, and so he will be *desperate* and full of "great wrath." It is in his *desperation* and in his *wrath* that Satan goes and does what he has never done before— it is a vain grasping at straws to try to avoid the inevitable.

SATAN'S JUDGMENT

After Jesus returns at the Second Coming, we are told of Satan's fate.

> Then I saw an angel coming down from heaven, having the key to the bottomless pit and a great chain in his hand. He laid hold of the dragon, that serpent of old, who is the Devil and Satan, and bound him for a thousand years; and he

cast him into the bottomless pit, and shut him up, and set a seal on him, so that he should deceive the nations no more till the thousand years were finished. But after these things he must be released for a little while. (Rev 20:1–3 NKJV)

We know that the judgment on the sons of God of Genesis 6 was to be thrown into the Pit, the Abyss, in chains, the punishment for their going to human women and having sexual union with them. If Satan was to also go to a human woman and have sexual union with her, as the sons of God had done in Genesis 6, we would expect that Satan would also suffer the same judgment as was suffered by the sons of God in Genesis 6, and, in fact, that is exactly what we see. After the Second Coming, Satan is taken, bound in chains, and cast into the Pit, or the Abyss—Satan suffers the *exact* same judgment as the sons of God of Genesis 6. Why? For the same reason—he fathered a Nephilim offspring with a human woman. It is very important to understand that Satan is *not* being thrown into the Lake of Fire, commonly called "hell," but into the *Pit*. After a thousand years of being imprisoned in the Pit, Satan will be released and will once again, for a time, be free upon the Earth.

The fact that the Bible clearly prophesies about the seed of the serpent, Satan, and does so in the same breath as it prophesies about Jesus Christ, the seed of a woman; the fact that Satan is thrown to Earth and is desperate and in great wrath because he knows his time is short; the fact that Satan is always trying to emulate God; the fact that Jesus specifically tells us the days prior to his Second Coming will be like the days of Noah, which were defined by the presence of the Nephilim; the fact that, at the Second Coming, Satan suffers the exact same judgment as the sons of God of Genesis 6, being chained and thrown into the Pit, leads to only one inescapable conclusion—Satan fathers his own Nephilim offspring through a human woman.

Who is that offspring? It is the Beast of Revelation.

THE SPIRIT OF THE BEAST

As with the Nephilim of Genesis 6, what sort of soul, or spirit, would inhabit, animate, or give life to a Nephilim offspring? Since only God can create life, and since Nephilim offspring are in every way contrary to God's will, so much so that any angelic being that engages in such an act suffers immediate judgment and imprisonment, it is reasonable to conclude that the spirit inhabiting, or giving life to, a Nephilim offspring is *not* a spirit created by God for that purpose. Rather, it seems the only reasonable conclusion in regard to what sort of spirit would live in a Nephilim offspring is that it is one of the fallen angels, one of the "sons of God" themselves.

Does this mean that Satan will inhabit the Beast, or that the Beast will be the incarnation of Satan?

We know that Satan is *not* the one who will inhabit the Beast, for the Bible tells us that there is a *distinction* between the Beast and Satan.

> Now *the beast* which I saw was like a leopard, his feet were like the feet of a bear, and his mouth like the mouth of a lion. The *dragon* gave *him* his power, his throne, and great authority. (Rev 13:2 NKJV)

> So they worshiped *the dragon* who *gave authority to the beast*; and they worshiped the beast, saying, "Who is like the beast? Who is able to make war with him? (Rev 13:4 NKJV)

> He laid hold of the *dragon*, that serpent of old, who is *the Devil and Satan*, and bound him for a thousand years; (Rev 20:2 NKJV)

The Bible is very clear—the Beast is *given* rule and authority by *Satan*, the "dragon." Since Satan is the one giving authority and rule to the Beast, it is very clear that the Beast is *not* Satan and is not inhabited by Satan, nor is he possessed by him, nor is the Beast the incarnation of Satan—the Beast is clearly distinct from Satan.

That being the case, then who, or what, inhabits the Beast and makes him alive?

THE SON OF PERDITION

The Beast has many names throughout the Bible—in Revelation he is called the "Beast," but elsewhere in the Bible he is called by many different names, including the "man of lawlessness" (2 Thess 2:3), the "little horn" (Dan 7:8), the "worthless shepherd" (Zech 11:17), and many more. One of the names of the Beast found in Scripture is the "son of destruction" (2 Thess 2:3).

The Hebrew word for "destruction" is *abad*, also figured *abaddon*. With that in mind, we read Revelation 9:11:

> And they had as king over them the angel of the bottomless *pit*, whose name in Hebrew is *Abaddon*, but in Greek he has the name Apollyon. (NKJV)

We are told here that imprisoned within the Pit is a fallen angelic being described as the "king" over the other fallen angels in the Pit, and that fallen angel's name is given, in Hebrew, as *Abaddon*, which means "destruction"—in Greek his name is given as *Apollyon*, which means "destroyer."

We are also told the following about the Pit in the days prior to the Second Coming:

> Then the fifth angel sounded: And I saw a star fallen from heaven to the earth. To him was given the key to the bottomless pit. And he opened the bottomless pit, and smoke arose out of the pit like the smoke of a great furnace. So, the sun and the air were darkened because of the smoke of the pit. Then out of the smoke locusts came upon the earth. And to them was given power, as the scorpions of the earth have power. (Rev 9:1–3 NKJV)

We are told that a fallen angelic being was given the key to the Pit, and that the Pit is opened, and out of the Pit rises great smoke, which darkens the sun, and out of that smoke come beings that are described as looking like locusts and having the power of scorpions (and these are the same beings who, in 9:11, are described as having Abaddon as their king). So the Pit is *opened* prior to the Second Coming *and* the inhabitants of the Pit are *released* upon the Earth.

This can only mean that the same fallen angelic beings of Noah's day, the ones who went to human women and fathered the Nephilim and who have been imprisoned in the Pit since that time (1 Pet 3:19; Jude 6–7), will be set *free* upon the Earth. Since one of those angelic beings is specifically named—Abaddon—we can conclude that Abaddon is among those beings released from the Pit. The name Abaddon means "destruction." With that in mind, we look at one of the names of the Beast—"son of destruction" (2 Thess 2:3).

There is very strong reason to understand that the Beast will be a Nephilim offspring of Satan himself, but the Beast will *not* be the incarnation of Satan, *nor* will the Beast be inhabited by Satan. As a Nephilim offspring, there must be some spirit that will give life to him. Since he is specifically called the "son of destruction" (2 Thess 2:3), and since a powerful fallen angelic being is released from the Pit, whose name is Abaddon, whose name means "destruction," is it possible that *Abaddon* is the spirit that indwells the Beast? There is very good reason to believe so.

We are told the following about the Beast:

> When they finish their testimony, *the beast that ascends out of the bottomless pit* will make war against them, overcome them, and kill them. (Rev 11:7 NKJV)

> *The beast* that you saw was, and is not, and *will ascend out of the bottomless pit* and go to perdition. (Rev 17:8 NKJV)

The Bible specifically tells us that the Beast will "ascend out of the bottomless pit"—that is the same Pit of Jude 6–7, as well as the same place of 1 Peter 3:19—the Pit is *only* for angelic beings; it is *never* connected to *any* human being. And yet, the Beast is also specifically called a "man."

> Don't let anyone deceive you in any way, for that day will not come until the rebellion occurs and the *man of lawlessness* is revealed, the man doomed to destruction. (2 Thess 2:3 NIV)

So, the Beast is specifically described as being a man, and yet is also described as ascending out of the Pit, a place where *only* fallen angelic beings have been cast. How can this be? Is this not a contradiction? No, it is not; rather, it is a more detailed account of events.

As a Nephilim offspring, the Beast *will* be a man, but his soul/spirit will be a fallen angelic spirit inhabiting that human body. Since the Beast is described as ascending out of the Pit, the place of imprisonment of the fallen angels/sons of God of Noah's day, and since the Beast is also called the "son of destruction," and since the fallen angel Abaddon is described as coming out of the Pit, and the name Abaddon means "destruction," there is good reason to understand that it is the fallen angel, Abaddon, who ascends out of the Pit, who indwells and makes alive the Beast.

This is further affirmed when we look at the description of the Beast as described in Revelation 17:8, where the Beast is referred to as the Beast that "was, and is not, and will ascend out of the bottomless pit . . . " John wrote this around 94-96 AD, and he is describing a Beast that existed *before* his own time, and yet *during his time* was not there, but that same Beast *will ascend* out of the Pit thousands of years later—this cannot be a human being. So, what is John describing? That description perfectly fits a fallen angel, as follows.

First, the Beast is described as ascending out of the Pit, a place of *imprisonment* for fallen angelic beings, and so the Beast who ascends out of the Pit must be a fallen angelic being. Then, for the Beast to be described first as one who "was" means that at one time that fallen angel originally was *not* in the Pit, was *not* imprisoned. Then, to be described as one who "is not" means that during John's day that fallen angel currently *was* in the Pit, having been cast there in the days of Noah as judgment for his actions. To then be described as "will ascend . . . " means that that same fallen angel, currently imprisoned in the Pit, will be *released* in the days before the Second Coming. As a result, we can understand the Revelation 17:8 reference to the Beast as a reference to the *spirit* that makes the Beast, Satan's offspring, *alive*, and that spirit is a fallen angel from the Pit, almost certainly the fallen angel named as king in the Pit and as being released from the Pit—Abaddon.

THE SEA

In addition, the Beast is also described as rising "out of the sea."

> And I saw a beast coming out of the sea. (Rev 13:1 NIV)

Here the Beast rises out of the sea, and yet in 11:7 and 17:8 the Beast ascends from the Pit—is this not a contradiction? No, it is not; rather it is two ways of saying the same thing.

As discussed, in the Bible, the sea always and only represents *judgment*—the sea absolutely does *not* represent peoples and nations—the "waters" of Revelation 17:15, which *do* represent peoples and nations, are rivers, *not* seas or oceans; seas and oceans always represent judgment. We know that inside the Earth there are three realms—the Realm of the Dead (Sheol/Hades), the Pit/Abyss, and the Lake of Fire. We know that the Realm of the Dead is located not only inside the Earth but, more specifically, *beneath* the floors of the *oceans* (Job 26:5). The reason for that is that the Realm of the Dead (Hades/Sheol) is *under judgment*, and so it is located beneath the judgment of oceans. This is also why in Revelation 20:13 we are told that the "sea gave up the dead that were in it," and, in that same breath, we are told that Hades (the Realm of the Dead) gave up its dead—in fact, this is the same thing—Hades, the Realm of the Dead, is located beneath the floors of the seas (Job 26:5), and so when the sea gives up its dead it is referring to the Realm of the Dead, and the mention of Hades giving up its dead, in that same breath, is just an *affirmation* that the sea giving up its dead and Hades giving up its dead is the same thing. All of this is just further affirmation of the sea as representing judgment.

Likewise, the Pit/Abyss is also inside the Earth (Rev 9:1), but deeper down than the Realm of the Dead, with the Lake of Fire being at the very heart of the Earth, deepest down of all (which is why in Revelation 20:14 Hades, the Realm of the Dead, is described as being "thrown into," or collapsing down into, the Lake of Fire—the Lake of Fire is located deeper down in the Earth than Hades). There is no question that if the Realm of the Dead is located beneath the *judgment* of the seas/oceans, the same *must* be true of the Pit. This is affirmed in Genesis 1:2, where we see a description of the cursed Earth, immersed in total darkness and covered by a global ocean—that global ocean was the judgment upon the Earth for the rebel angels being cast out of heaven down *into* (or under) the Earth (Phil 2:10; Rev 5:3, 13; 12:9). Therefore, when the Beast is described as ascending out of the Pit, and then is *also* described as rising from the sea, this is saying the same thing—the Pit is located beneath the floors of the oceans, and so when the Beast (that is, the spirit that gives life to the Beast, Abaddon) ascends out of the Pit, he is also, in fact, rising from the sea, for in ascending from the Pit he is also rising from beneath the place of judgment, the sea. These two descriptions are saying exactly the same thing, and from the fact that the Beast is described as rising out of the sea, and with the sea always and only representing judgment, and with that same Beast also ascending out of the Pit, we can understand that the spirit that indwells the Beast is a fallen angelic being that rises from, ascends out of, is set free from, the Pit, and his name is Abaddon—all of these things hold together, across many scriptures.

THE EMULATION OF GOD

It has always been Satan's desire to be *like* God (Isa 14:14)—Satan didn't *hate* God; he *envied* him. As a result, when Satan is thrown to the Earth, in great wrath, because he knows his time is short (Rev 12:12), in his desperation he tries, in his final moment, to emulate God in the grandest way possible—by fathering his own begotten son, which is the Beast. The reason there is a "seed" of the serpent is because there is a "Seed" of the woman—it is, once again, Satan trying to be like God.

THE CONCEPTION OF THE BEAST

There is no question that the Beast is conceived, and *born*, during Seal 1 of Revelation.

Jesus clearly explains to us what defines Seal 1—it is the apostasy of the church (Matt 24:4–5), which is also affirmed by Paul (2 Thess 2:1–3) and by Peter (1 Pet 4:17); this is inarguable. However, within the context of the rebellion, or apostasy, of the church, we are given the image of a rider on a white horse, who wears a crown, who has a bow, and who rides out to conquer (Rev 6:1–2). The rider of Seal 1 is certainly representing a false *Christianity*, but, *simultaneous with that*, there is a second layer of meaning to the image of that rider—there is no question that this rider is *also* a pale image of the *real* Rider on a White Horse, Jesus Christ at the Second Coming (Rev 19:11–16). Paul, in 2 Thessalonians 2:1–3, specifically tells us that the Beast (the man of sin, son of destruction) will *not* come to power, or be revealed to the world, until *after* the church abandons Jesus Christ. So, we know that the apostasy of the church, false Christianity, happens first. Since we know, from Jesus' own words in Matthew 24:4–5, that Seal 1 is defined by the church abandoning Jesus Christ by embracing false and deceptive teachings, then it is *impossible* that the Beast comes to power in Seal 1—he certainly does *not* (in fact, the Beast comes to power in Seal 5). So, if the Beast does *not* come to power in Seal 1, then, in addition to the rider of Seal 1 being the force of a false Christianity, how can we also understand the rider as simultaneously having the secondary meaning of a false Christ?

It is because the secondary meaning of the rider being the false Christ is that the Beast, the false Christ, is *born* in Seal 1; he is *born* during that time of apostasy. When he *grows up*, then that *same* Beast will go out conquering and to conquer (and he will almost certainly be thirty-three years of age when he comes to power). This is how we can understand the secondary meaning of the image of the rider in Seal 1—it is a description and affirmation of the *birth* of the Beast.

Also, the fact that the rider of Seal 1 is described as having a bow but no arrows can also be understood as an affirmation of that same secondary fact. The *primary* meaning of the rider of Seal 1 is that it represents a false Christianity, the apostasy of the church (Matt 24:4–5; 2 Thess 2:1–3; 1 Pet 4:17; Rev 2–3)—as such, we can understand that the arrows that will be fired from the bow described in Seal 1 will be the flaming arrows of lies and deception that come from Satan, the father of lies (Eph 6:16). However, in regard to the secondary meaning of the rider of Seal 1, being a simultaneous representation of the false Christ, the fact that the false Christ is represented *in Seal* 1 as having a bow but *no arrows* can also be understood to mean that, at the time of Seal 1, that false Christ has *no power*. The secondary representation of the rider of Seal 1 as a false Christ with no power can be understood as a further affirmation that in Seal 1 the Beast is only *born*, having no power *yet*, but he will come to power later (in Seal 5).

Also, in addition to this, it is fitting, almost poetic, that the Beast is born during the time that the church is abandoning Jesus Christ and is prostituting itself.

THE SIGN OF HIS BIRTH

Since everything about the Beast, and about Satan, is a total emulation of God and of Jesus Christ, and since the very birth of Jesus Christ was signified in the heavens by the star of Bethlehem, we can expect that the birth of the Beast would also be accompanied by a celestial sign (especially since God himself tells us that one of the purposes of celestial objects is to act as signs of important events on Earth; Gen 1:14).

However, it's important to remember that when such a celestial sign does appear, almost nobody will understand it or recognize it for what it signifies, just as with the star of Bethlehem. The star of Bethlehem was a heavenly sign that signified the birth of Jesus Christ (Matt 2:2, 9), and yet, to the people of the world it would only have been a curious object in the sky—no one, apart from the three wise men of the East, would have had any idea that the star signified the birth of Incarnate God. Likewise, whatever celestial sign will accompany the birth of the Beast, it will certainly be a sign that people will see, will know, and will even talk about, but almost nobody will recognize it for its significance.

Also, since everything about the Beast will be the emulation of Jesus Christ and will be part of the great deception that the Beast *is* Jesus Christ returned, we can expect the birth of the Beast to occur on or around December 25. Of course, the December 25 date may or may not be an accurate date for the birth of Jesus Christ, but it is the date selected as the date to honor and celebrate his birth, and for the Beast's, and Satan's, purposes, that's all that matters. If the world celebrates the birth of Jesus Christ as December 25, and then if the Beast would also be born on Earth on or around that same date, it only makes for a much stronger connection and claim for the Beast as being Christ returned. As a result, we can reasonably expect the Beast to be born in December, on or around December 25, and with that birth accompanied by some sort of celestial sign.

However, prior to his birth, the Beast must first be conceived. It is almost inconceivable that the very *conception* of the Beast would not *also* happen during Seal 1; in fact, it is extremely likely that his very conception is connected directly with the very *opening* of Seal 1. If that is so, and if the Beast will be born on or around December 25, then that means the conception of the Beast must take place in March of that same year. As a result, should we expect some sort of sign of the times to mark the *conception* of the Beast? There was no sign accompanying Jesus' conception, though there was the Annunciation to Mary, by Gabriel, that she will become pregnant. At the very least, in regard to Jesus' conception, there was no *heavenly* or *celestial* sign accompanying the conception of Jesus Christ, but only one accompanying his birth.

As a result, it is reasonable to expect the same for the Beast—a heavenly, or celestial, sign that marks his birth, but not a celestial sign that marks his conception.

However, it is possible that the conception of the Beast may be marked by other earthly, *non-celestial* signs or events, especially since the Beast is the result of the desperation and wrath of the enemy, who knows that his time is short (Rev 12:12). It is very possible for Satan, as the ruler of this world (Luke 4:5–7; John 12:31; 16:11), to maneuver the world (people, nations) in some way to signify that event—the conception of the Beast.

THE ETHNIC ORIGIN OF THE BEAST

Although the Beast will be the seed of the serpent, the offspring of Satan, he will also be the son of a *human* woman. As a result, the Beast *will* have an ethnic, human origin. It is almost certain that in regard to his ethnic origin, the Beast, on his mother's side, will be of the tribe of Dan. This means, without a doubt, that the Beast will *not* be Jewish.

As discussed, there are twelve full tribes of Israel, with the tribe of Joseph being divided into the two half-tribes of Ephraim and Manasseh. With that division of the tribe of Joseph, there are thirteen tribes of Israel. The one nation, Israel, split into two nations during the reign of Rehoboam, Solomon's son, with three tribes—the tribes of Judah, Benjamin, and, ultimately, Levi—becoming the southern kingdom of Judah, with Jerusalem as its capital. The remaining ten tribes became the northern kingdom of Israel, with Samaria as its capital. Ever since that split of Israel into two nations, God has kept that distinction, especially in regard to *prophecy*. *Only* the tribes of the nation Judah are Jews—in fact, the very word "Jew" comes from the name Judah. All the other ten tribes of the northern kingdom of Israel are *not* Jews. Those ten tribes have been lost to history (but not to God) since the Assyrian captivity of ca. 750 BC, and there is good reason to believe that the lost ten tribes of Israel are, in fact, ancestors of many of the nations of the Western world. To the world, the peoples of those lost ten tribes of Israel would all be *Gentiles*. The tribe of Dan is one of those ten lost tribes; therefore, if the Beast has an ethnic origin from the tribe of Dan, he would be a *Gentile*, and definitely *not* Jewish.

THE TRIBE OF DAN

There are two very good reasons to believe that the ethnic origin of the Beast is the tribe of Dan.

The first is found in Revelation 7:3–8. In these verses, which is a description of the first half of Seal 5, we are told that God has set aside 144,000 servants to proclaim his gospel throughout the world, during the same time that the Beast rules the Earth in power. Then follows a list of the twelve tribes of Israel—including the three tribes that make up the Jews (Judah, Benjamin, Levi) as well as all the remaining tribes that are Gentile (non-Jewish) tribes, and there are 12,000 people set aside from each tribe. What is striking among that list of the tribes of Israel is that *one* of the tribes of Israel is *not* listed there—the tribe of Dan. Why is the tribe of Dan not listed there? *Why* are there *not* 12,000 from the tribe of *Dan* sealed to preach the gospel to the world? Is it because the tribe of Dan is the tribe of the Beast (which no one in the world will even know or recognize; only God will know that origin)? The answer is almost certainly yes—and that is further affirmed by Genesis 49.

In Genesis 49:1–28, Jacob, the father of the twelve tribes, says to his sons that he will now tell them what will befall each of them, and their descendants, in the *last days*.

> And Jacob called his sons and said, "Gather together, that I may tell you what shall befall you in the *last days*" (49:1 NKJV)

The moment we come across the term "last days" we know, without a doubt, that it is a reference to the days before the Second Coming.

In a number of translations, when the translators add headings to sections of Scripture (and none of those headings are part of Scripture; they are only the translators added headings for ease of reference), this section, Genesis 49:1–28, is often headed as "Jacob Blesses His Sons." However, that is an absolutely incorrect heading. As we read what Jacob actually says to his sons, together with the fact that he *begins* his words with, "Gather together, that I may tell you what *shall befall you* in the *last days*," we see, without any doubt, that what follows is *not* a blessing, but rather is a *prophecy*. Genesis 49:1–28 is Jacob *prophesying* about his sons, and their descendants, prophesying about what will become of them in the days before the Second Coming, in the "last days."

Here is what Jacob prophesies about Dan:

> Dan shall judge his people,
> As one of the tribes of Israel.
> Dan shall be a serpent in the way,
> A horned viper in the path,
> That bites the horse's heels,
> So that its rider falls backward.
> For Your salvation I wait, Lord." (49:16–18 NASB)

In this prophecy, specifically concerning the (lost) tribe of Dan in the last days, the days preceding the Second Coming, we are told that "Dan shall judge his people," that is, Dan will bring *judgment*. Dan is then described as being a "serpent" by the way, or by the path or roadside, described as being a "viper," and we are told that Dan, as this serpent, will "bite the horse's heels, So that its rider falls backward." What does this mean?

These words have a striking similarity to Genesis 3:14–15, when God says to the *serpent*,

> And I will put enmity
> Between you and the woman,
> And between your seed and her Seed;
> He shall bruise your head,
> And *you shall bruise His heel.* (NKJV)

In Genesis 49:16–18, the tribe of Dan is described as a *serpent*, and, as a serpent, Dan *bites the heels* of the horse. This is very similar to the Genesis 3:14–15 passage, also about the *serpent*, where that serpent is described as bruising the heel of the Seed of the woman. So, in both passages, we are told of a serpent harming one's heel. We know without a doubt that the Seed of the woman in Genesis 3:14–15 is Jesus Christ. Who, or what, then is the horse and its *rider* of Genesis 49:16–18?

There is good reason to understand that this is the same horse and rider of Revelation 19:11, which is Jesus Christ at the Second Coming. If the serpent, Dan, strikes at the heel of the horse upon which the Seed of the Woman is riding, and causes the Seed of the woman to fall backwards, this fulfills *both* Genesis 3:14–15 *and* Genesis 49:16–18. We know that the seed of the serpent is in fact the Beast, and so it is the Beast who bruises the heel of Jesus Christ. Likewise, if, *in the last days*, it is the *serpent* who bites at the *heel* of the horse on which sits Jesus Christ, and this serpent is *Dan* or *of Dan*, we then have a complete connection between Genesis 3:14–15 and Genesis 49:16–18, and the connection is this—the serpent of Genesis 3:14–15, who bruises the heel of Jesus Christ, is the Beast; likewise, the serpent who bites at the heels of the horse in Genesis 49:16–18, the horse upon which Jesus Christ rides, is also the Beast, who is from the tribe of *Dan*. Since the Beast is from the tribe of Dan, it also perfectly fulfills Jacob's opening words in his prophecy about Dan—that Dan will be a *judge* upon his people, that he will in fact *bring judgment*—and there is no question that the Beast absolutely brings catastrophic judgment.

Also, Jacob's final words about Dan in his prophecy sound ominous.

> I have waited for your salvation, O LORD!

This is also translated as,

> I look for your deliverance, LORD (Gen 49:18 NIV)

The NIV translation gives the true sense of the words—Jacob ends his prophecy about Dan with a plea, a longing, for "deliverance." Why is Jacob asking for deliverance in his prophecy about Dan during the last days? It is because the Beast will be from the tribe of Dan and he will bring global judgment upon the Earth. Also, because he is the seed of the serpent, he himself, in his nature, will be of the same *nature* as the serpent, and so it is accurate to also describe the Beast as being a serpent.

When we put all of this together—Genesis 49:16–18; Genesis 3:14–15; and Revelation 7:3–8—it is almost certain that the ethnic human origin of the Beast, on his mother's side, will be the tribe of Dan; he will be a Gentile, and *not* a Jew.

We must remember that almost no one in the world will recognize the Beast as being from the tribe of Dan, since Dan has been lost to history since ca. 750 BC—lost to history, but not lost to God. There may be one human indication to the Beast's descent from the tribe of Dan, and that would be in his human mother's maiden last name. Dan had a habit of adding its name to any location in which they settled; likewise, the presence of any form of "dan" in one's last name could be an indication of a descent from the tribe of Dan. So, if the mother of the Beast has any of "dan," "don," "din," "dun," or "den" as part of her last name, it could be an indication of the Beast's descent from Dan. Apart from that one possible clue, only God will know the Beast's descent from Dan—to the world the Beast will be a Gentile.

THE NAMES OF THE BEAST

Throughout the Bible, the Beast is mentioned many times, by many different names. As with all names in the Bible, names have meaning, with the meaning of that name bringing an insight into the person who carries that name.

In the Old Testament, there are twenty-three different names for the Beast, as well as three descriptors of the Beast, while in the New Testament there are six different names for the Beast. Here is a listing of those names and descriptors, with a note for each one as to what meaning each name might carry.

Twenty-Three Names from the Old Testament

Adversary (Ps 74:8–10; Amos 3:11)

The Beast is against God.

Assyrian (Isa 10:5, 12; Mic 5:5)

One possible meaning is a reference to the original Assyrian captivity of the ten lost tribes, where the Assyrian is the one who "takes captive" God's people.

Wicked One (Ps 10:2, 10:4; Nah 1:15)

Wickedness is his nature.

Bloody and Deceitful Man (Ps 5:6 NKJV)

He persecutes and kills.

Cruel One (Jer 30:14)

He has cruelty and hatred in his heart towards humanity.

Evil Man (Ps 10:15)

His nature is evil.

Worthless (or Idol/Idle) Shepherd (Zech 11:16–17)

He is the false shepherd, a "worthless shepherd," a false Christ, in contrast to the "good shepherd," Jesus Christ.

King of Princes (Hos 8:10)

He rules over other leaders—he is the king of princes.

King of Babylon (Isa 14:3–11)

The nation Babylon (Babylon the Great) is his initial power base; he comes to power by way of being leader of the nation Babylon.

Little Horn (Dan 7:8–11, 7:21–26, 8:9–12, 8:23–25)

The horn represents being a king, a ruler, but he is a "little" horn, meaning his rule is very brief (only three and a half years).

Man of the Earth (Ps 10:18)

Both a man of worldly honor, as well as, ultimately, a man of dust, destroyed.

Mighty Man (Ps 52:1)

He is a mighty, or powerful, man on the Earth, a ruler.

Prince That Shall Come (Dan 9:26)

A reference to him being not only the false Christ, but also, to the Jews, their (false) Messiah

Prince of Tyre (Ezek 28:2–10)

He is a human ruler who rules by the power of Satan (see Ezek 28:11–19)

Wicked Prince of Israel (Ezek 21:25–27)

"Israel" refers to the ten lost tribes of the northern kingdom, who, to the world, are gentiles, and so he is a leader and ruler among them, and being of the tribe of Dan, he is of Israel.

Proud Man (Hab 2:5)

He is arrogant and proud, honoring himself.

Seed of the Serpent (Gen 3:15)

He is the physical offspring of Satan and a human woman.

Spoiler, Destroyer (Isa 16:4–5)

He destroys (also see the Greek version of the name Abaddon, which is Apollyon, which means "destroyer"—Rev 9:11 NIV).

Vile Person (Dan 11:21)

He is contemptible and evil in every regard.

Violent Man (Ps 140:11)

He is a man of violence and destruction.

Willful King ("will do according to his own will," Dan 11:36)

He will have absolute rule and absolute corruption.

A Fierce Looking King/King of Fierce Countenance (Dan 8:23)

He will have a fierce, menacing appearance.

The King of the North (Dan 11:40)

He has dominion over the North, which does *not* mean that he is *from* there, but only that the North is a part of his dominion (just like Queen Elizabeth is Queen of Canada, but she is neither Canadian nor is she from Canada, Canada is just one of her dominions; likewise with the Beast being the King of the North—the North described here will be just one of his dominions, and not necessarily the place of his origin).

Descriptive Verses

Destroyer of the nations (Jer 4:7)

He is conqueror of many nations.

Judge among/over many Nations (Ps 110:6)

He rules over many nations.

Head of the Northern Army (Joel 2:20)

He is king of the "northern army."

6 Names from the New Testament

Antichrist (1 John 2:18, 22)

The *false* Christ.

Beast (Rev 11:7, 13)

"Beast" represents both a king and his kingdom, an enemy of God, also carries the connotation that, as the unnatural offspring of Satan, he is more beast than human.

Lawless One (2 Thess 2:8)

He regards no law, he acts as a law unto himself.

Man of Sin (2 Thess 2:3)

Sin is his very nature, his very essence.

One who comes in his own name (John 5:43)

The false Messiah for the Jews.

Son of Perdition/Destruction (2 Thess 2:3)

Son of Abaddon ("destruction") denotes that the fallen angel from the Pit, Abaddon, indwells him and animates him.

Each of these names tell us something about the Beast, about his nature, about his character and his position. Although he is commonly called the "antichrist," in fact that reference appears only *once* in the Bible (1 John 2:18) and is not his primary description or his primary name in the Bible. As a result, it is a mistake to refer to him primarily as the "antichrist." The name by which he is called more than any other name is his name in Revelation—he is called the Beast; that, more than anything, is his primary name, his ultimate description.

THE PEOPLE OF THE PRINCE TO COME

Among the numerous names of the Beast throughout the Bible, as listed above, there is one verse that seems to speak to the ethnic origin of the Beast, and it is found in Daniel 9:26.

> And after the sixty-two weeks Messiah shall be cut off, but not for Himself; and *the people of the prince who is to come* shall destroy the city and the sanctuary. The end of it shall be with a flood, and till the end of the war desolations are determined. (9:26 NKJV)

In this verse, the "prince who is to come" is certainly the Beast, but he is described here in the context of "the *people of* the prince who is to come." This verse is clearly understood as a prophecy about the destruction of Jerusalem and the temple in 70 AD by Rome. Since the destroyers of the temple are referred to in this prophecy as "the people of the prince who is to come," and since the "prince who is to come" is the Beast, does that not then mean that the Beast will be of the same ethnic origin as those who destroyed the temple in 70 AD; i.e., will he not be Roman?

This does not necessarily mean, in any way, that the Beast will be Roman—but it is almost certain that he will be of the tribe of Dan, as discussed. How then are we to understand this verse? We can understand it in light of the lost tribes of Israel, and their descendants.

First, it is a historical fact that Roman legions, in the reign of Vespasian, conquered Judea, sacked Jerusalem, and destroyed the temple in 70 AD. But who were the people who *actually* comprised those legions? Rome was a great empire, stretching from Britain in the northwest, to the northern and eastern reaches of modern Europe, and also south to Egypt, Carthage, and Africa, and to the Middle East. The Roman Empire comprised a vast territory, and *all* of that territory belonged to Rome, as did all of the inhabitants of those territories. This also means that the Roman legions were also comprised of all the various peoples that made up the Roman Empire—they may have all been *citizens* of the Roman Empire, but the great majority of those citizens were not themselves Roman.

As previously discussed, there is good reason to understand that the lost tribes of Israel, after the Assyrian captivity of ca. 750 BC, eventually came to be the ancestors of many of the peoples of Europe. If true, then many of the citizens of the Roman Empire at the time that Vespasian conquered Judea would have had descent from any one of the lost tribes, though their ethnic identities by that time would have been lost, even to themselves (but not to God). As a result, we can understand that in regard to the legions involved in the conquest of Judea and Jerusalem in 70 AD, those legions may have been peopled by descendants of the lost tribes, in particular of the tribe of Dan. With that in mind, when we encounter the phrase "the people of the prince who to come" in regard to the people who destroyed Jerusalem and conquered Judea, this then can be perfectly in line with the Beast's origin as being from the tribe of Dan, rather than being Roman.

Also, in addition, and specifically in regard to the conquest of Judea and Jerusalem, and also in regard to Jacob's prophecy over Dan as one who will bring judgment upon his people (Gen 49:16–18), we can understand the destruction of Jerusalem, the conquest of Judea, and the destruction of the temple during that same conquest as very much being a judgment upon Jacob's descendants. If the legions who carried out that conquest were in fact descendants of the tribe of Dan, then this also is perfectly in line with Jacob's prophecy over Dan.

As a result, the phrase "the people of the prince who is to come" does not necessarily mean that the Beast will be Roman; rather it can easily be an affirmation of his origin as being from the tribe of Dan.

THE DESIRE OF WOMEN

Another verse that is often referred to in discussion about the Beast and his character is also found in Daniel.

> He shall regard neither the God of his fathers nor the desire of women, nor regard any god; for he shall exalt himself above them all. (11:37 NKJV)

This verse is often invoked to support the idea that the Beast will be a Jew and that he will be homosexual.

Why is this verse invoked to support the idea that the Beast will be a Jew? It is because of the phrase "God of his fathers."

The "fathers" referred to here are Abraham, Isaac, and Jacob—the fathers of the nation Israel. However, as we have already seen, Israel was comprised, ultimately, of thirteen tribes, and only *three* of those tribes—the tribes of Judah, Benjamin, and Levi—are Jews, while the other ten tribes, the great majority of tribes, are *not* Jews; rather, to the world they are *Gentiles*. And yet, Abraham, Isaac, and Jacob are fathers to *all* thirteen tribes—not just the three tribes that constitute the Jews, but also the other ten tribes who are *not* Jews. This includes the tribe of Dan, which is *not* one of the Jewish tribes. So the phrase "God of his fathers," in its reference to Abraham, Isaac, and Jacob, does not mean that the Beast will be Jewish, for he can come from any one of the other ten non-Jewish tribes and still be fully descended from Abraham, Isaac, and Jacob, and thereby Abraham, Isaac, and Jacob would still be his fathers. It is almost certain that the Beast will be of the tribe of Dan, and therefore will not be Jewish; yet, by being from the non-Jewish tribe of Dan, he will still have Abraham, Isaac, and Jacob as his fathers.

The other part of that verse that is invoked in regard to the Beast is that he will have no regard for "the desire of women." It is for this reason that people teach that the Beast will be homosexual, but this is absolutely *not* what this verse is saying.

Put very simply, the phrase "the desire of women" refers specifically to Jesus Christ—*Jesus Christ* is the desire of women.

What does that mean? It means that any woman, anywhere, but especially any woman of Israel, would very much *desire* to be the mother of God, and *that* is how we are to understand the word "desire"—it is not a meaning of sexual desire; rather, its meaning is of *maternal* desire.

This fact is made clear in other translations of Daniel 11:37.

> He will show no regard for the gods of his ancestors or for *the one desired by women*, nor will he regard any god, but will exalt himself above them all. (NIV)

> He shall give no heed to the gods of his fathers, or to *the one beloved by women*; he shall not give heed to any other god, for he shall magnify himself above all. (RSV)

> He shall pay no attention to the gods of his fathers, or to *the one beloved by women*. He shall not pay attention to any other god, for he shall magnify himself above all. (ESV)

In each of these translations (and others), the phrase "the desire of women" is translated as "the *one* desired by women" or "the *one* beloved by women"—this is the clear sense and meaning of the verse. "The one desired by women" is Jesus Christ, because any woman would desire to be the mother of God.

Also, the fact that being the mother of the Incarnate God is the greatest blessing that could be conferred on any woman is affirmed by Elizabeth when she greets the pregnant Mary.

> Then she spoke out with a loud voice and said, "*Blessed are you among women, and blessed is the fruit of your womb!*" (Luke 1:42 NKJV)

And also by the angel at the Annunciation to Mary.

> And having come in, the angel said to her, "Rejoice, highly favored one, the Lord is with you; *blessed are you among women*!" (Luke 1:28 NKJV)

To be the mother of the living and Incarnate God is a blessing that elevates the mother above all other women, and to be such a mother, and to have such an offspring, would be the "desire" of any woman—and so the phrase "the desire of women" refers specifically to the person of Jesus Christ.

Also, to understand "the desire of women" as being a reference to Jesus Christ fits perfectly with the entire context of the words that both precede and then follow that phrase. The phrase "the desire of women" is *preceded* by "He shall regard neither the God of his fathers . . . " and is followed by "nor regard any god," telling us that the Beast shall exalt himself above all gods. If the phrase "the desire of women" meant that the Beast will be homosexual, then the verse would be speaking as follows:

> He shall not regard the God of his fathers, he will be homosexual, and he will not regard any god; for he shall exalt himself above them all.

So the verse begins with talking about regarding God and it ends with talking about regarding God and of exalting oneself above all gods—what possible place does any talk of the Beast being homosexual have in that context? If the phrase "the desire of women" meant that the Beast will be homosexual, then it would be a complete non-sequitur in that verse, completely out of context with the full and clear meaning of every other part of that verse.

If, on the other hand, the phrase "the desire of women" refers to Jesus Christ, then we can read it as follows:

> He shall regard neither the God of his fathers, nor Jesus Christ, and he will not regard any god; for he shall exalt himself above them all.

When we understand that the phrase "the desire of women" does, in fact, refer to Jesus Christ, then every aspect of this verse makes complete sense and has one clear meaning—the entire verse is talking about the Beast not regarding any god but himself, and that includes not regarding the God of his fathers, not regarding Jesus Christ, not regarding *any* god. That is the clear meaning of the verse.

As a result, Daniel 11:37 in no way supports the idea that the Beast will be Jewish or homosexual.

CONCLUSION

Putting all this together, we can conclude the following. Satan impregnates a human woman and she bears him his offspring (the "seed" of the serpent, Gen 3:14–15). By being the offspring of a fallen angelic being (Satan) and a human woman, that offspring is a Nephilim offspring. As a Nephilim offspring, that offspring is given life by way of being inhabited by a preexisting fallen angelic being, a being who at one time was free, but who was, in the apostle John's day, imprisoned in the Pit, and who will one day be released from the Pit to inhabit and give life to that offspring. That fallen angelic being who will be released from the Pit to give life to the Beast seems certainly to be the fallen angel named in Revelation 9:11—Abaddon.

This is the nature of the Beast—a man who will be the offspring of Satan and a human woman, animated by the indwelling of a fallen angelic being who ascends out of the Pit, and that man, that son of Satan, will be the ruler of the world.

14

THE RULE OF THE BEAST

SEALS 1–4 ENCOMPASS A period of thirty-three years and set the world's stage for the coming of the Beast. The Beast comes to power in Seal 5, and his entire three-and-a-half-year rule, as well as the entire three-and-a-half-year Tribulation that follows, is all in Seal 5. Jesus makes this clear for us in his description of the Seven Seals in Matthew 24.

JESUS' DESCRIPTION OF SEAL 5 IN MATTHEW 24

In Matthew 24:3–31, Jesus outlines for us the Seven Seals of Revelation, in order, and with descriptions. Matthew 24:4–8 outlines Seals 1–4, while 24:29–32 outlines Seals 6 and 7. For each of Seals 1, 2, 3, 4, 6, and 7, Jesus spends about a verse (or less) talking about each of those Seals. But for Seal 5, which he describes in 24:9–28, Jesus spends *twenty* verses describing that Seal in detail. Here is how Jesus describes the Seven Seals of Revelation in Matthew 24.

Seal 1, described in Matthew 24:4–5, describes the apostasy of the church, with the church corrupting itself by its embrace of false teachings, which come by way of false Christian teachers. Also, together with Jesus' description of Seal 1 in Matthew 24:4–5, we can conclude from Revelation 6:1–2 that the Beast is conceived and born as a human baby during Seal 1.

Seal 2, described in Matthew 24:6–7, is global war. We know it will be a global war, rather than a localized war, because Jesus says of the war that "nation will rise against nation, and kingdom will rise against kingdom"—it will be a war of multiple nations and multiple kingdoms, not just a local or regional war. Also, when taken together with the Revelation 6:4 description of Seal 2—"Its rider was given power to take peace *from the earth*"—which describes peace being taken *from the Earth*, it is certain that Seal 2, and the parallel passage of Matthew 24:6–7, are describing a global war.

Seal 3, described by Jesus in only four words in Matthew 24:7—"there will be famines"—is global famine, as is also specifically outlined in the parallel passage of Revelation 6:5–6, describing that same global famine.

Seal 4 is global death resulting from the global war, the global famine, and from disease, with that disease described by Jesus in Matthew 24:7 as "pestilences" (NKJV, YLT) and described in the Revelation 6:8 description of Seal 4 as death "by the wild beasts of the earth," which is diseases, or pestilences, spread to people via wild animals.

Also, we know from Revelation 6:8 that one quarter of humanity will die during Seals 2–4.

Also, Jesus makes an important side comment immediately *after* he describes Seal 4, telling us that what he has just described (i.e., Seals 1–4) are only the "*beginning of birth pains*" (Matt 24:8 NIV, NASB, ESV). Why does Jesus make this comment here, immediately after his description of Seal 4?

The reason Jesus makes that comment immediately after his description of Seal 4 is to affirm that Seals 1–4 are only the *beginning* of what is to come, with the fullness of what is to come to be revealed in Seal 5—this is also affirmed by the fact that Jesus spends only a verse or less in his Matthew 24 description of Seals 1–4, as well as Seals 6 and 7, but he spends twenty verses on his description of Seal 5. As a result, we can understand the phrase "beginning of birth pains" to mean that Seals 1–4 *set the stage* for what is to come in Seal 5.

What will come in Seal 5?

The Beast will appear on the world's stage in Seal 5, and his entire rule, including his persecution of the church, will be in Seal 5. Also in Seal 5 will be the *entire* Great Tribulation. As a result, we can understand Seals 1–4 as preparing the world for the appearing of the Beast and for his rule.

It is in his twenty-verse description of Seal 5 that Jesus describes for us the entire seven-year period of Daniel 9:26–27. It is in that context, in the context of that seven-year period of Daniel, that Jesus tells us that if anyone says "Look! There is the Christ!" (Matt 24:23), we are *not* to believe it; he tells us of "false prophets" being present during that same time, false prophets who will be deceiving many (Matt 24:11); he tells us that the church will turn away from faith (Matt 24:10), which will be the *culmination* of the prostitution and apostasy described in Matthew 24:4–5 and the Seal 1 description of Revelation 6:2 (which is the same apostasy and rebellion described in 2 Thessalonians 2:3). Jesus also tells us that at the start of Seal 5 the church will be persecuted and put to death (Matt 24:9; also Rev 13:7; 17:6, all contrary to the rapture teaching). Continuing with his description of Seal 5, Jesus tells us, in a specific reference to Daniel 9:26–27, that the Great Tribulation will occur during the time of Seal 5 (Matt 24:21). *All* of those events are included in Jesus' description of *Seal 5*.

What is also very important is that when Jesus begins to tell us of the events of Seal 6, he begins with these words:

> *Immediately after the tribulation of those days* the sun will be darkened, and the moon will not give its light; the stars will fall from heaven, and the powers of the heavens will be shaken. (Matt 24:29 NKJV)

Jesus is very clear—as he begins to describe Seal 6, starting at Matthew 24:29, he tells us that the Seal 6 events will occur *after* the Tribulation is *over*. As he continues to describe the events that occur *after* the Tribulation, he uses almost the exact same language as Revelation 6:12 does in its description of Seal 6.

> behold, there was a great earthquake; and the sun became black as sackcloth of hair, and the moon became like blood. And the stars of heaven fell to the earth . . . (Rev 6:12–13 NKJV)

In both Matthew 24:29 and in Revelation 6:1–13, the sun is "darkened," "black as sackcloth"; "the moon will not give its light," "becoming like blood"; "the stars will fall from heaven" (from the sky) "to the Earth." The descriptions of Seal 6 in Matthew 24:29 and Revelation 6:12 are identical—they are a description of the same event. The Matthew 24:29 description of Seal 6 is the companion passage to the Revelation 6:12–13 description of Seal 6.

As a result, based on Jesus' own words as he begins to describe Seal 6 in Matthew 24:29, it is inarguable that the entire Tribulation is *over* by the *end* of Seal 5—this is a fact, and is Jesus' own word on the subject. The entire three-and-a-half-year rule of the Beast, as well as the entire three-and-a-half-year Tribulation, occur in Seal 5. The events of Seal 5 are huge events, and Seals 1–4 are just the preparation of those Seal 5 events, and so Seals 1–4 are described as the "beginning of birth pains."

To summarize, the key events of Seal 5, as based on Matthew 24:9–28 as well the book of Revelation, are as follows—the Beast appears on the world's stage and rises to power; he will be proclaimed as Christ returned; false prophets (and one pre-eminent False Prophet) will flourish and deceive the world; the church, which is on Earth in all of its fullness and totality, will be persecuted, overcome, and put to death; the Great Tribulation, in its entirety, will occur during that time—*all* of these are the events of Seal 5.

So how, in the preparatory context of Seals 1–4, does the Beast appear on the world's stage and rise to power?

THE BEAST APPEARS ON THE WORLD'S STAGE

As Jesus tells us in Matthew 24:8, the events of Seals 1–4 are only the "*beginning* of birth pains," that is, the events of Seals 1–4 set the stage, or prepare the world, for the coming of the Beast. What are the events that set the stage for the coming of the Beast?

They are the events of Seals 1–4—first, the prostitution and apostasy of the church of Seal 1 (Matt 24:5; 1 Pet 4:17; Rev 2–3, 6:1–2), followed by the global war of Seal 2 (Matt 24:6; Rev 6:3–4), with the global famine of Seal 3 opened sometime after

Seal 2 is opened but then being simultaneous with it (Matt 24:7; Rev 6:5–6). From these events, and from the pestilence and disease of Seal 4, there will be global death, with one quarter of the human population dying as a result of those events (Matt 24:7; Rev 6:7–8).

These are the events that Jesus describes as being the "beginning of birth pains," and they are described as the "beginning" because their purpose is to set the world's stage for the rise of the Beast. The Beast appears on the world's stage with the opening of Seal 5. In what context does he first appear on the world's stage? What will he do? The answer is found in Daniel.

THE BEAST COMES TO POWER BY BRINGING PEACE

The world, by the end of Seal 4, is in a terrible state. Thirty-three years after Seal 1 has been opened, which begins with the apostasy of the church, and which then leads to the global war, together with the global famine and global disease, one quarter of the world's population will have died. It will be a hopeless time, a time of great despair. While the global war is still happening, in the midst of the global famine and the global death, the Beast will appear on the world's stage, and he will be thirty-three years of age.

The Bible tells us that the Beast comes onto the world's stage seemingly out of nowhere, and with few supporters.

> with only a few people he will rise to power. (Dan 11:23 NIV)

Prior to coming upon the world's stage, the Beast will be virtually unknown, and only a very few people will know who he is and will support him. Yet he will appear, a completely unknown individual, right when Seal 5 is opened, and Daniel tells us that when he appears, it is to make a "covenant," and that covenant will be a covenant "with many," and it will be a covenant of peace.

> He will confirm a *covenant with many* for one "seven." In the middle of the "seven" he will put an end to sacrifice and offering. And at the temple he will set up an abomination that causes desolation, until the end that is decreed is poured out on him. (Dan 9:27 NKJV)

> And in his place shall arise a vile person, to whom they will not give the honor of royalty; but *he shall come in peaceably*, and seize the kingdom by intrigue. (Dan 11:21 NKJV)

Daniel tells us that the Beast will make a "covenant with many" for a period of "one 'seven.'" He also tells us that when he comes, i.e., when he appears on the world's stage, he will come "peaceably," or *with peace*. What does this mean?

We know that the Beast appears on the world stage with the opening of Seal 5, in the midst of the devastation of the global famine, global pestilence and death, and the global war. We are to understand the covenant and his coming peaceably in the context of that global war, the global war of Seal 2.

The Beast will appear on the world's stage as a peacemaker, appearing in the midst of the global war, and he will succeed in bringing peace by bringing that war to an end. We can understand the covenant referred to in Daniel as being a treaty, and we can understand his coming peaceably as him bringing a treaty (covenant) of peace. We can also understand the phrase "covenant with *many*" as meaning that the covenant of peace, or peace treaty, that he will negotiate will be a treaty with the many nations of the world who were involved in the global war (the very same nations that rise against nations and kingdoms that rise against kingdoms as described by Jesus in Matthew 24:6–7). The Beast will appear on the world's stage, out of nowhere, in the midst of the devastating global war, and he will bring peace.

Also, with an end to that war, he will bring an end to the global famine, the global disease, and the related global death. He will be hailed as the savior of humanity.

HOW DOES THE BEAST COME TO SUCH A PROMINENT POSITION?

In the midst of the global war of Seal 2, the Beast seemingly appears on the world's stage out of nowhere and with very few supporters. How can he come to such a prominent global position if he is virtually unknown? We are told the following in Daniel:

> In the latter part of their reign, when rebels have become completely wicked, a fierce-looking king, a *master of intrigue*, will arise. (8:23 NIV)

Daniel describes the Beast as a "master of *intrigue*," and we are told in this context that he "will arise." As a result, we can understand that the Beast, though virtually unknown and with only a very small group of supporters, will *maneuver* himself, through intrigue, through scheming and plotting, into a position of global prominence at just the right time to bring peace and an end to the global war.

THE WAR OF SEAL 2 IS NOT ARMAGEDDON

The global war of Seal 2 will be seen by the world, and even by many Christians, as the final war, the end, Armageddon. It is the Beast who will come in the midst of "Armageddon" and bring peace to the world, being hailed as savior. It is in this context, in the context of the global war of Seal 2, which people will believe to be Armageddon, that the deadly nature of the false rapture teaching will be revealed. It is with the rise of the Beast and his bringing global peace to the world that the ticking time bomb that is the rapture will go off. What does that mean, and how will it happen?

In Matthew 24:6–7, when Jesus is talking about the global war of Seal 2, he adds this side comment—"but the end is not yet." Why does he say that, in the context of the global war of Seal 2? It is because the people who are on the Earth at that time, who are in the midst of that devastating global war, will believe that war to be Armageddon, the final battle; they will believe that war to be "the end." It is for that reason that Jesus makes a point to say that that war is *not* "the end," the war of Seal 2 is *not* Armageddon, because most of the world will think that it is.

Included in that camp will be the church. The church will be fully present upon the Earth during that entire time—the church will *not* be removed from the Earth in any way whatsoever, in accordance with Jesus' own clearly stated will (John 17:15). As a result, those Christians who were taught that there *will* be a rapture, but who then find themselves in the middle of the global war of Seal 2, will be dismayed, especially in light of the fact that they, like the rest of the world, will think that Seal 2 war to be Armageddon. As a result, those Christians will be shocked and surprised to find themselves on the Earth, in the midst of those events, when they were taught that they would be supernaturally removed off the face of the Earth so as to be spared from going through those events.

Jesus himself affirms the full presence of the church on Earth at the time the Beast appears when he tells us, in his opening words describing Seal 5,

> Then they will deliver you up to tribulation and kill you, and you will be hated by all nations for My name's sake." (Matt 24:9 NKJV)

Jesus is here talking about the church at the start of *Seal* 5, when the Beast comes to power, and Jesus is clear—the church will not only be fully present upon the Earth during that time, but it will be persecuted and put to death. As a result, since the church is fully present upon the Earth at Seal 5, it is most certainly present upon the Earth through Seals 2–4.

Those Christians who were believing in the false teaching of the rapture will come to understand only then, in the midst of the global war of Seal 2, that they were taught a lie.

As a result of that realization, those same Christians, while still in the midst of that global war, will also start to question *what else* they were taught that was a lie. Ultimately, that will lead to those Christians questioning what the Second Coming of Christ will *really* look like when he comes to bring peace at Armageddon.

It is in context of *that* questioning that the Beast will appear. He will appear in the midst of that global war, which will be seen by the world, and by much of the church, as Armageddon, and *he* will bring peace to the world by bringing that global war, "Armageddon," to an end. As a result, those same Christians who had come to realize that they were taught a lie in regard to a rapture will now see this man appear on the world's stage, in the midst of "Armageddon," bringing global peace, and so they will ask, "Who is this man?"

Those same Christians will know that in the Bible it is *Jesus* who appears at Armageddon to bring an end that war, and who brings global peace. Since the war of Seal 2 will be considered, even by many Christians, to be Armageddon, then when the

Beast appears in the midst of that war and brings peace, those very same Christians, who will now be questioning the Second Coming, will then ask if he, *the Beast*, is *Christ returned*. With the events that follow—which is the fake death and fake resurrection of the Beast, as well as the False Prophet, a great Christian leader, declaring to the world that the Beast *is* Christ returned—those same Christians will truly wonder if the Beast is Christ returned.

This will be an unfathomable deception upon the whole world, and even upon Christians, and so will be fulfilled the words of Jesus Christ when he speaks of exactly these things.

> For false christs and false prophets will rise and show great signs and wonders to *deceive*, if possible, *even the elect*. (Matt 24:24 NKJV)

Jesus tells us that the deception of that time, the deception of the Beast and the false prophets, will be so great that, if it were possible, *even Christians* will be deceived to worship the Beast, to worship him as Christ returned. However, because Jesus uses the words "if possible," many believe that it will *not* be possible, and that the elect will *not* be deceived. Be that as it may, the deception of that time will be so enormous, so overwhelming, that even if Christians are, ultimately, *not* deceived, they will be right on the very knife's edge of being deceived.

The foundation of that deception, in regard to Christians—the deception that the Beast is Christ returned—will be the lie of the rapture, the false teaching that teaches that Christians will not be on Earth during that time. That deception will be in place just prior to the Beast's appearing.

WHY IS HE CALLED THE "BEAST"

This man who appears on the world's stage in the midst of the global war and brings the global peace is referred to throughout the Bible by many different names, but in the book of Revelation, and more than any other name throughout the Bible, he is referred to exclusively as the "Beast." Why is he called the "Beast"? What kind of a beast might he be? We are given a very clear description of the Beast in Revelation 13:1–2.

> Then I stood on the sand of the sea. And I saw a beast rising up out of the sea, having seven heads and ten horns, and on his horns ten crowns, and on his heads a blasphemous name. Now the beast which I saw was like a leopard, his feet were like the feet of a bear, and his mouth like the mouth of a lion. The dragon gave him his power, his throne, and great authority. (NKJV)

Revelation 13:1–2 describes a very strange Beast, unlike any beast that actually exists. It is a Beast that is "like a leopard," but has the "feet of a bear," the "mouth of a lion," and "seven heads and ten horns." What do we make of this Beast? It is obviously symbolic, and, as with all symbols in the Bible, that symbolism conveys meaning. How do we understand the symbolism of this very strange Beast? It is explained for us in Daniel 7, in conjunction with Daniel 2.

In Daniel 7:1–8, Daniel describes having a vision of a lion, a bear, a leopard with four heads and a monstrous beast of iron with ten horns. In 7:15–28, the angel explains to Daniel the meaning of those beasts, telling him that those beasts are kingdoms and kings (7:17, 23). How can a symbol represent *both* a kingdom *and* a king? When the king is the sole and absolute ruler of his kingdom, when the king is answerable to no one, when the very word, will, or whim of the king is the law of the kingdom, in that case the king and the kingdom are one and the same, for, in that case, the will and whim of the king defines everything about the kingdom—the king *is* the kingdom.

We know from Daniel 2:27–45, which is a parallel image and prophecy to 7:15–28, that those four beasts of Daniel 7, the four kings/kingdoms, are the Babylonian (lion), Persian (bear), Greek (leopard with four heads), and Roman (beast of iron) empires, all of which were ruled by absolute rulers. Daniel's four beasts, taken together, have a total of "seven heads and ten horns."

Daniel's four beasts, together, are exactly like the Beast that rises from the sea in Revelation 13.

The Beast of Revelation 13 is an amalgamation of Daniel's four beasts, having the feet of a bear (Persian Empire), the mouth of a lion (Babylonian Empire), being like a leopard (with four heads, Alexander's Greek empire), and having the ten horns of Daniel's fourth beast (the beast of iron, the Roman Empire). Also, the seven heads of the beast in Revelation 13 are in fact the same seven heads of Daniel's four beasts—one head of a lion, one head of a bear, four heads of a leopard, and one head of the iron beast with ten horns—so the Beast of Revelation 13 is the combination of Daniel's four beasts.

What does this tell us about the Beast of Revelation?

We can understand that, just as Daniel's four beasts each represented a kingdom/empire, likewise, the Beast of Revelation also represents a kingdom/empire. Since the Beast of Revelation is a combination of Daniel's four beasts, we can understand the coming kingdom of the Beast to also be a combination of the qualities of the Babylonian, Persian, Greek, and Roman Empires. We can understand the combined qualities of those four ancient empires in the following ways.

Like the Babylonian Empire, the Beast's empire will have enormous wealth; like the Persian Empire, his empire will rule over many nations and kingdoms and be vast; like Alexander the Great's Greek empire, his empire will be an unstoppable military force (Rev 13:4); like the Roman Empire, his empire will be ruthless and powerful. It is in these ways that the kingdom/empire of the Beast will be the combination of those four previous great empires, and that meaning is conveyed to us specifically through the use of beast imagery.

Also, one other thing that we can know for a certainty is that, as in Daniel 7:17, the Beast and his kingdom will be one and the same—he will be the absolute ruler of his empire; his will and whim will be law, and he will be accountable to no one. All of this is contained in the imagery of the Beast that rises from the sea in Revelation 13:1–2.

One other possible additional layer of meaning conveyed by the beast imagery is as follows. To describe someone as a "beast" carries with it the implication of being something less than human. It is a certainty that the Beast will be the seed (or offspring) of the serpent, of Satan, and thereby a Nephilim offspring of Satan, the union of human and angelic natures. Is it possible that, in light of that fact, he is called the "Beast" so as to convey his corrupted humanity, a humanity corrupted by its union with the fallen angelic nature? It is a possibility worth considering.

THE EMULATION OF CHRIST—DEATH AND RESURRECTION

The Beast will be the seed of the serpent, the offspring of Satan and a human woman, indwelt, inhabited, and animated by a fallen angelic being. He will also be the ultimate false Christ. As the ultimate false Christ, the Beast will, in every possible way, emulate the real Christ, the Lord Jesus Christ, and this is especially true in regard to death and resurrection. Here is what we are told:

> And I saw one of his heads *as if* it had been mortally wounded, and his deadly wound was healed. And *all the world marveled* and followed the beast. (Rev 13:3 NKJV; also see 13:12, 14)

In the imagery of the Beast, the Beast has seven heads, and this passage tells us that *one* of his heads *appeared* to be "*mortally* wounded." How do we understand this? We can understand it as follows.

After the Beast comes onto the world's stage, and after he brings global peace, he will *appear* to be *killed*, almost certainly by means of some sort of assassination. It is important to note that the Bible describes this one head looking only "*as if* it had been mortally wounded," meaning that the Beast will only *appear* to have been killed, but, in reality, he will *not* have been killed, but will have been only *wounded*. But the world will not know that—to the world, the Beast will have been killed, and the world will be witness to that assassination.

But then, sometime after he appears to have been killed, the Beast will be seen to be alive again, which is described by the phrase "his deadly wound was healed." The entire world will see this and we are told that, specifically as a result of the Beast's wound being healed, the whole world will marvel, or be astonished, at this, and the whole world will, *for that reason*, follow the Beast.

What do we make of this?

This apparent death and resurrection of the Beast is the ultimate emulation of Christ, for, in the eyes of the world, the Beast will appear to have been killed and *resurrected*. It is this apparent resurrection that convinces the world that the Beast is Christ returned.

This "resurrection" of the Beast is what *defines* the Beast to the world. In Revelation 13:3–14 we are told, three times across only twelve verses, that the Beast had the "deadly wound" that "was healed" (13:3, 12, 14). The Beast's "resurrection" is mentioned repeatedly, three times, within only twelve verses—it is a clear emphasis of that one event coming to *define* the Beast. We are specifically told in 13:3 that it is this very fact—the Beast receiving a seemingly deadly wound and then being healed from that wound—that causes the world to "marvel" at the Beast, causes the world to be "filled with wonder" (NIV), "amazed" (NASB), "astonished" (LEB). The Beast suffering that apparent death wound, and then being healed from it, as an emulation of the death and resurrection of Jesus Christ, will be a proclamation to the world that the Beast *is* Christ, and, for *that* reason, the world will be amazed and the world will follow the Beast, and worship him.

Why will the world *worship* the Beast?

The Beast comes at the height of "Armageddon" (in truth, only the global war of Seal 2); he ends that war, brings global peace, and simultaneously ends the global famine and disease. He is then apparently killed and resurrected. In the Bible, it is Jesus Christ who actually comes at Armageddon, who ends that war and brings global peace. Also, it is Jesus Christ who is put death and is then resurrected. For all of these reasons, and more, the Beast will appear to be, in every way, Christ returned—the world will see the Beast as the Second Coming of Christ and will worship the Beast as Christ returned.

THE WOUNDS OF THE BEAST

What will the apparent death wound of the Beast look like? Where will this wound be? Since Revelation 13:3 specifically describes a *head* as having the wound, does this mean that apparent death wound of the Beast will be a head wound?

The apparent death wound of the Beast is described for us in Zechariah 11:17.

> "Woe to the *worthless shepherd*,
> Who leaves the flock!
> *A sword shall be against his arm*
> *And against his right eye;*
> His *arm* shall completely wither,
> And his *right eye* shall be totally blinded." (NKJV)

The term "worthless shepherd" is one of the names of the Beast and is a total contrast to Jesus Christ, who is called the "good shepherd" (John 10:11, 14)—the "good shepherd" is the real Christ; the "worthless shepherd" is the false Christ. In this passage from Zechariah, we are given a description of the wounds of the worthless shepherd, the wounds of the Beast. He is described as being "totally blinded" in his "right eye" (a head wound), and as having a "completely wither[ed]," or useless, arm—this is a description of the seemingly mortal, or deadly, wound that the Beast suffers in Revelation 13.

Zechariah tells us specifically that it is the Beast's "*right* eye" that is totally blinded, and, although it doesn't tell us which arm has been wounded and made worthless, we can conclude that it is in fact his *right* arm—this is almost certainly the case, as is evidenced in Revelation when it tells us where the people of the world put the mark of the Beast—they will put the mark of the Beast either on their forehead (i.e., above their right eye) or on their *right* arm (Rev 13:16). Revelation 13:6 tells us, very specifically, that it is the *right* arm. When taken together with Zechariah 11:17, we can understand that it is his *right* arm that is completely withered or wounded. As a result, we can conclude that the apparent death wound suffered by the Beast in Revelation 13:2 is to his head (his "right eye") and to his right arm.

Based on the fact that the Beast's right eye is totally blinded, and that his right arm will be made useless, we can conclude that whatever blow it is that he will receive, which will be witnessed by the world and considered to be his death blow, that blow will come upon the right side of his body—he will receive his seemingly deadly wound(s) on his right side.

THE EMULATION OF CHRIST—THE AGE OF THE BEAST

The apparent death and resurrection of the Beast will be a powerful and vivid emulation of the death and resurrection of Jesus Christ, and, as a result of his "resurrection," the whole world will declare him to be Christ returned. Since everything about the Beast is a total emulation of Christ, and since Jesus Christ died at age thirty-three, it is almost certain that, in accordance with the Beast's total emulation of Christ, the Beast will also be thirty-three years of age at the time that he receives his apparent death wound and is apparently resurrected, so as to even more so identify himself with Jesus Christ.

Since we know that the Beast will be born in Seal 1, conceived almost certainly with the very opening of Seal 1, and since we know that the Beast comes to power with the opening of Seal 5, and since there is very strong reason to understand that he will be thirty-three years of age at the time of his apparent death and resurrection, we can therefore conclude that Seals 1–4—the time from the birth of the Beast to his coming to power in Seal 5—encompass a period of thirty-three years.

Also, once the Beast comes to power at age thirty-three, he will rule for only three and a half years, which rule will then be followed by the three and half years of Tribulation, giving us a total of seven years from the time that the Beast comes to power to the end of the Great Tribulation. We can therefore know that the events of the Seven Seals, the *entirety* of the events of Revelation 6–19, encompass a total of forty years—the thirty-three years of Seals 1–4 plus the seven years of the Beast's rule and the Great Tribulation.

HOW LONG WILL THE BEAST BE APPARENTLY DEAD?

After the Beast receives his apparent death wound, how long will it be before he is seen to be alive again, seen to be resurrected?

The Bible doesn't tell us that detail, but it is still possible to come to a reasonable conclusion. Since the Beast will, in absolutely every way, be emulating Jesus Christ, there is very good reason to believe that from the time that he has his apparent death wound to the time that he is seen as being resurrected there will be a period of three days. Why would we think this? It is because Jesus Christ was resurrected after being dead for three days (Matt 12:40; 27:63), and since the Beast will ty to emulate Jesus Christ in every way so as to show to the world that he is, indeed, the Second Coming of Christ, there is good reason to believe that he will also be apparently dead for three days.

THE AUTHORITY OF THE DRAGON

We're also told the following about the Beast:

> The dragon gave him his power, his throne, and great authority. (Rev 13:4 NKJV)

The dragon is Satan (Rev 12:9), and so we are told that it will be Satan who will give to the Beast (Satan's own seed) *Satan's* own power, *Satan's* own throne and *Satan's* great authority. This in fact is exactly the same power, throne, and authority that Satan offered to Jesus Christ.

> The devil led him up to a high place and showed him in an instant all the kingdoms of the world. And he said to him, "I will give you all their authority and splendor; it has been given to me, and I can give it to anyone I want to. If you worship me, it will all be yours." (Luke 4:5–7 NKJV)

Satan offered to Jesus all the kingdoms of the world, all their authority and all their splendor, and Jesus said "no." It is the exact same power, throne, and authority that Jesus refused that Satan will give to the Beast.

How did Satan come to have such authority? He tells Jesus that all that authority, and all the world's kingdoms, have been *given* to him—who gave it to him? Adam gave it to him.

When God created Adam, he gave to Adam dominion over all the Earth and over all life upon the Earth (Gen 1:26). Under Adam's dominion, all animals, including lions, tigers, and all others, ate the plants of the field (Gen 1:30)—there was no such thing as a meat eater or carnivore. But when Adam sinned, not only did the physical sinful nature take up residence within him, in his blood, and then, from him, in Eve; but Adam also, at that same time, by his sinning, *gave away* his God-given dominion of the Earth to Satan—and this is what Satan is referring to in Luke 4:5–7; it was *Adam* who gave Satan all the kingdoms of the world and all their authority.

Also, it is as a result of the world now being under Satan's dominion that death came also to animals and plants, and animals began to kill and eat one another, and plants became poisonous etc., because Satan's dominion is a dominion of death (Heb 2:14). However, Jesus Christ, the second Adam, never sinned, and by never sinning, and by having no sin within himself (since he did not have a human father), Jesus *took back* that dominion to the Earth, taking it back not at the cross but by never sinning in his life, and so Jesus tells us, prior to going to the cross.

> Now is the time for judgment on this world; now *the prince of this world will be driven out.* (John 12:3 NKJV)

What does it mean that "the prince of this world will be driven out"? It is referring to the fact that Jesus, upon his resurrection (which will be the full affirmation of his sinless self), is *taking back* the dominion of the Earth, the same dominion that Adam gave to Satan—upon his resurrection, that dominion will now be Jesus' dominion. But he will not *claim* or *take up* that dominion until the Second Coming, and, in fact, that's *why* there is a Second Coming—the Second Coming happens because it is the Lord Jesus Christ returning to Earth to claim his dominion of the Earth, the dominion that he took back from Satan by having lived a sinless life.

This change of dominion is beautifully illustrated for us in Isaiah 65.

> The wolf and the lamb will feed together,
> and the lion will eat straw like the ox (65:25 NKJV)

This is a description of the world *after* the Second Coming, and we see that animals will then be as they were created to be, as they were when they were under Adam's original dominion—lions will once again eat plants, and wolves will play and eat plants with lambs. The reason for this is that after the Second Coming the dominion of the Earth is now the dominion of Jesus Christ, the dominion of life, and is no longer under Satan's dominion, the dominion of death.

However, even though since the resurrection the dominion of the Earth, and the authority of the whole world, belongs to Jesus Christ, he has not yet returned to claim that dominion; so, for the time being, that same authority continues to be exercised by Satan, until the Second Coming. As a result, until the Second Coming, Satan still *exercises* that authority, and it is *that* authority, *that* power, *that* throne, that he gives to the Beast.

This is also illustrated in Ezekiel 28:1–19, which describes a human "prince of Tyre," a man who claims to be "god" (28:1–10), but then we are told about the non-human, angelic "king of Tyre," Satan—the *real* ruler behind the human "prince of

Tyre" (28:11–19), the real power, authority, and throne behind Tyre. This is, in fact, an account of the Beast and Satan, an account of the same scenario as is described for us in Revelation 13:2—the human ruler of Ezekiel 28:1–10 is the Beast, whom the world will consider as a king, and who will claim to be God (2 Thess 2:4), but behind him is the real ruler, Satan, the dragon, who gives the power, throne, and authority to the Beast.

It is in this context that we are also told very clearly in Revelation 13:7 that the Beast will have great authority and will rule over all the nations of the world—his dragon-given authority will be complete.

A GREAT MOUTH

One of the clear characteristics of the Beast is that he is exceedingly boastful and utterly blasphemous, for we are told,

> And he was given a mouth speaking great things and blasphemies, and he was given authority to continue for forty-two months. Then he opened his mouth in blasphemy against God, to blaspheme His name, His tabernacle, and those who dwell in heaven. (Rev 13:5–6 NKJV)

> Then the king shall do according to his own will: he shall exalt and magnify himself above every god, shall speak blasphemies against the God of gods, and shall prosper till the wrath has been accomplished; for what has been determined shall be done. He shall regard neither the God of his fathers nor the desire of women, nor regard any god; for he shall exalt himself above them all. But in their place, he shall honor a god of fortresses; and a god which his fathers did not know he shall honor with gold and silver, with precious stones and pleasant things. Thus he shall act against the strongest fortresses with a foreign god, which he shall acknowledge, and advance its glory; and he shall cause them to rule over many, and divide the land for gain. (Dan 11:36–39 NKJV)

We are told very clearly that the Beast will boast greatly, that he will "exalt" himself, even exalting himself above God (since he will say to the world that he is Christ returned, and therefore he will claim to actually be God). He will also "blaspheme"—or curse and demean and insult—the living God. He will have a great, self-exalting, blasphemous mouth, and the world will hear him, and the world will believe him.

WAR ON THE CHURCH

In Revelation 13:7, we are told the following about the Beast:

> It was granted to him to *make war with the saints* and to *overcome them*. And authority was given him over every tribe, tongue, and nation. (NKJV)

The Bible is very clear—the Beast will make war on the church, in the same way that Hitler made war on the Jews, and the Beast will overcome the church. This is an astounding statement.

In the two-thousand-year history of the church, such a thing has never happened. Empires, kingdoms, and nations have tried, repeatedly, to destroy the church—whether it be the Roman Empire or modern-day Communism—but, in every instance, the church has only grown and flourished even more. But here the Beast will, in fact, *succeed* in crushing the church. Remember that to the world he will be presented as Christ returned and the world will worship him as the returned and resurrected Christ. The real church, though, will of course still be fully on the Earth during that same time, and the real church will *not* follow the Beast, nor worship him. The world will see the real church refusing to follow or worship the Beast, and the world will then also see the Beast "make war with," or persecute and put to death, the true church, and the world will see the Beast *succeed* in *defeating* the true church of Jesus Christ. In the eyes of the world, if the church is indeed the *real* church who follows the *real* Jesus Christ, then, as history has always shown, that church, those people, *cannot* be defeated or overcome. So, when the Beast goes to war against the church, against the real church, which follows the real Jesus Christ, and he *defeats* them and *overcomes* them, that will even *further affirm* and *prove* to the world that the *Beast* is the real Christ, and that the overcome, defeated church was a *false* church. As Jesus says in Matthew 24:24, the deception of that time will be immense.

THE SECOND BEAST—THE BEAST OF THE EARTH

There is a second human character that is central to the rule of the Beast, and he is referred to as a "*second* beast," described as follows:

> Then I saw a second beast, coming out of the earth. It had two horns like a lamb, but it spoke like a dragon. It exercised all the authority of the first beast on its behalf, and made the earth and its inhabitants worship the first beast, whose fatal wound had been healed. And it performed great signs, even causing fire to come down from heaven to the earth in full view of the people. Because of the signs it was given power to perform on behalf of the first beast, it deceived the inhabitants of the earth. It ordered them to set up an image in honor of the beast who was wounded by the sword and yet lived. The second beast was given power to give breath to the image of the first beast, so that the image could speak and cause all who refused to worship the image to be killed. It also forced all people, great and small, rich and poor, free and slave, to receive a mark on their right hands or on their foreheads, so that they could not buy or sell unless they had the mark, which is the name of the beast or the number of its name.

> This calls for wisdom. Let the person who has insight calculate the number of the beast, for it is the number of a man. That number is 666. (Rev 13:11–18 NIV)

John here describes a "second beast," but this one, unlike the first Beast, comes up from the *Earth*, whereas the first Beast rose from the sea. What does this mean?

Often, in writings on the book of Revelation, people say that the sea represents peoples, and they base that on Revelation 17:15, where the angel explains to John that the "waters" upon which the Prostitute sits are "many peoples." However, those "waters" of Revelation 17:15 are *not* the sea; rather, they are rivers—*rivers* may represent peoples, but the *sea* always represents *only* judgment.

Also, those same commentaries, in incorrectly describing the sea as representing peoples, also often say that the sea represents specifically *Gentile* peoples, based on the idea that the sea being referred to in that imagery is specifically the Mediterranean Sea. There is no basis in the Bible, whatsoever, to come to that conclusion. Again, the sea always and only represents God's *judgment*; it never represents peoples.

In that same context, where people equate the symbol of the sea with Gentile peoples, they then, conversely, equate the Earth with Israel. As a result, they conclude that the Beast of Revelation 13:1, which rises out of the sea, is a Gentile, but the "second beast" of Revelation 13:11, which rises from the Earth, is a Jew. Just as equating the symbol of the sea to mean peoples or Gentiles has no biblical basis, likewise, there is no biblical reason whatsoever to equate the Earth with Israel.

As previously discussed in some detail, the sea always and only represents God's judgment, and, as discussed, there is very strong reason to understand that to rise from the sea means to rise from judgment, meaning that the spirit that animates the Beast, the spirit that gives life to the seed of the serpent, is a fallen angelic being who ascends from the Pit. Since the Pit is within the Earth, *beneath* the seas, beneath the *judgment* of the seas (Job 26:5; Rev 9:11; 11:7; 17:8), to rise from the sea equates to rising from the Pit, rising from judgment. It is from that perspective that we can also come to understand what it means for the second beast to come from the Earth.

The key to understanding the beast from the Earth is in Genesis.

> And the LORD God formed man of the dust of the ground, and breathed into his nostrils the breath of life; and man became a living being. (Gen 2:7 NKJV)

The Bible is very clear—*man* is made from the Earth; *human beings* are made from the Earth. This is how we can understand the beast from the Earth.

Where the first Beast rises from the sea, we can understand that rising from the sea as denoting the *nature* of that Beast, namely, that, as the seed of the serpent (Gen 3:14–15), he is a Nephilim offspring, the offspring of Satan and a human woman, and, as such, that offspring is animated by a fallen angelic being who was released from/ascended from the Pit, or the Abyss (Rev 11:7; 17:8). Since the Pit/Abyss is located inside the Earth, beneath the judgment waters of the seas/oceans (Job 26:5), we can understand the description of rising from the sea to denote ascending from the Pit (Rev 11:17; 17:8), thereby also denoting the Nephilim nature of that seed of the serpent.

Likewise, when the second beast is described as "coming out of the earth," we can understand that description as *also* denoting the nature of the second beast, and we can understand it as follows. Since the second beast comes out of the Earth, we can understand that the second beast is *not* a Nephilim offspring; rather that second beast is *fully human*, a *man*, since being made from the "dust of the earth" is what *defines* the physical nature of *man* (Gen 2:7).

As a result, we can understand that the second beast is a normal man, fully human, and not a Nephilim offspring.

THE SECOND BEAST—THE FALSE PROPHET

As Revelation unfolds, we are given more information about this second beast, and in fact this second beast as specifically named as the False Prophet (Rev 16:13; 19:20; 20:10). We must remember that *all* of these events occur during Seal 5, and in Jesus' description of Seal 5 in Matthew 24:9-28, he also makes specific reference to "false prophets" (24:11) as well as to a "false Christ" (24:23). Though there will be various false prophets during that time, there will be one preeminent False Prophet who will be guiding all things—Jesus' reference to the false Christ in Matthew 24:23-26 is in fact a reference to the first Beast, while his reference to false prophets in 24:11 and 24:24 include reference to the second beast, the False Prophet.

What is the purpose of the False Prophet?

The Bible tells us very clearly—the False Prophet, the second beast, will exercise all the authority of the first Beast, on his behalf, and it is the False Prophet who will deceive and force the world to *worship* the Beast (Rev 13:12).

Also, the False Prophet will perform actual miracles, for all the world to see, to *prove* that what he says about the Beast is true, and the world will be deceived (Rev 13:13-14).

We are also told that there will be an image of the Beast that will be set up by the False Prophet (which almost certainly will be a *statue*, not a holographic image, since it is almost certainly a parallel reference to Daniel 3:1-7). We are told that the False Prophet will be able to "give breath" to that image, to that statue, so that it can speak. That *speaking statue* will then command all people to *worship the statue*, and all who refuse to worship the statue will be put to death (Rev 13:15; exactly as Nebuchadnezzar commanded all people to worship his statue, and all who refused were to be put to death, Dan 3:1-7). We are also told that this False Prophet will cause all people to receive a mark on either their forehead or right arm (the same places where the Beast had his wounds, Zech 11:17), which would allow them to participate in the economic life of the world (Rev 13:16-17). The False Prophet, in every way, serves the Beast.

What else do we know about the False Prophet?

TWO HORNS LIKE A LAMB

In John's description of the second beast that comes up out of the Earth, he tells us that this second beast, the False Prophet, has "two horns" and is "like a lamb," but "spoke like a dragon" (Rev 13:11). What does it mean to say that he is "like a lamb"?

Throughout the Bible, "lamb" is a reference to Jesus Christ, who himself is "the Lamb of God" (John 1:29; Rev 5–6; 7:9–10; 7:14; 12:11). Therefore, to say that this second beast was "like a lamb" would almost certainly mean that this second beast will be seen, by the world, as a Christian.

But this second beast is also described as having two horns. The passage itself describes those horns as being "two horns like a lamb," relating the symbolism of a lamb and horns together, being presented as *one* image. However, those two *elements* of that one image *also* stand as independent descriptions of the second beast. As mentioned, the symbol of a lamb is almost certainly a reference to the fact that the second beast, the False Prophet, is seen as a Christian. What then do the two horns represent? The Beast, which rises from the sea in Revelation 13:1, is described as having *ten* horns, but this second beast, the False Prophet, is described as having only *two* horns. How do we understand this?

As discussed previously, throughout the Bible the image of horns always represents rule and authority (Dan 7:24; 8:3–21). It is in this context that we are to understand the two horns of the second beast. The two horns represent the fact that this "Christian" man will, first and foremost, be a great Christian *leader*; he will be in a position of *authority,* for the two horns represent authority, or rule.

What does he rule over? Does the second beast rule over a nation? A kingdom? Something else? We don't know, but we can conclude from the fact that this man is, above all, a False Prophet, a man who will do miracles, a man who is "like a lamb," seen as a Christian, that his sphere of authority, his sphere of rule, will most likely be a *religious* rule; he will be in a position of *religious* authority, rather than exercising rule or authority over nations.

Also, since there are *two* horns, we can conclude that he has authority over *two* religious spheres.

For example, if a high-profile Christian leader, such as the pope, who has authority over the sphere of the Roman Catholic Church, also became, through whatever means, the head of the Orthodox Church, healing the one-thousand-year rift between the two denominations, and the Orthodox Church came to consider the pope as their head as well, this then would be an example of a prominent Christian leader having authority over two religious spheres. Or it may be that the leader of one of the major Christian denominations comes to be hailed by Muslims as the leader of Islam as well, in which case, again, a prominent Christian leader would come to have authority over two religious spheres. We cannot say what those two religious spheres will be, but we have very good reason to understand that this second beast, the False Prophet, will be a prominent Christian leader, with a high visibility on the world's stage (someone like the pope or a Billy Graham, someone of that stature), and that man will come to be the head of two major religious spheres, having authority over them. This is what the two horns of the second beast represent.

SPEAKS LIKE A DRAGON

We are also told, in the description of the second beast, that the False Prophet, though looking "like a lamb," will in fact speak "like a dragon" (Rev 13:11). The dragon is Satan, the devil (12:9). To say that the second beast speaks like a dragon means that, although to the world he will be seen as a great, prominent Christian leader, in truth he will be a liar, a great deceiver, and he will be of Satan, a satanic wolf in sheep's clothing.

This is also further affirmed by the fact that this False Prophet will "exercise all the authority of the first beast in his presence" (13:12). What is this authority that the False Prophet will exercise? It is the authority of Satan, for the only authority that the Beast has is the authority, throne, and power that was *given to him* by Satan (13:2). Therefore, when we are told that the False Prophet exercises *all* the authority of the Beast, it means that the False Prophet is exercising the authority of Satan, the dragon, which is why the False Prophet is also described in 13:11 as speaking like a dragon.

WHAT IS THE ROLE OF THE FALSE PROPHET?

The entire role of the False Prophet is to make people worship the Beast, to worship the Beast as God. The Beast will be presented to the world as Christ returned, and his fake death and resurrection will be the pivotal point in the world recognizing him as Christ returned. It is in that context that we must remember that the False Prophet will himself be a prominent Christian leader, but he will be a deceiver, for he will actually be of Satan. His preeminent role on the world's stage will be to get the world to worship the Beast.

As a result, we can easily understand that after the Beast's fake death and resurrection, the False Prophet, a great and prominent Christian leader on the world's stage, will point to the (falsely) resurrected Beast and will himself testify, to the world, that the Beast *is* Christ returned—the world will hear that declaration come from a very prominent and renowned Christian leader.

In addition to his public declaration that the Beast is Christ returned, in order to *prove* that what he is saying is true, the False Prophet will then, before the eyes of the whole world, perform *actual* miracles, and the Bible tells us what kind of miracles he will perform—the False Prophet, in full view of the world, will make fire come down from heaven (the sky) to Earth (13:13); he will also do other signs, as Revelation 13:13 also makes clear, but the fire from the sky will be among the most profound, and the most impactful. So, the world will see a (falsely) killed and resurrected Beast, and the world will be amazed and astonished at his resurrection; they will then see a great Christian leader proclaim the "resurrected" Beast as Christ returned, and they will then watch that same Christian leader perform actual miracles to prove the truth of his proclamation. The world will then believe that the Beast is Christ returned, and the world will worship the Beast. We must remember that the Beast will be worshiped *as Christ returned*—the world will believe that the Beast is the Second Coming of Christ and will worship him as Christ. Taken all together, this will be an *immense* deception, so powerful that, if possible, even true Christians would be deceived to worship the Beast (Matt 24:24).

THE IMAGE OF THE BEAST

One of the key accomplishments of the False Prophet is that he will make an "image of the Beast."

> And he deceives those who dwell on the earth by those signs which he was granted to do in the sight of the beast, telling those who dwell on the earth to make an image to the beast who was wounded by the sword and lived. He was granted power to give breath to the image of the beast, that the image of the beast should both speak and cause as many as would not worship the image of the beast to be killed. (Rev 13:14–15 NKJV)

What is this "image of the Beast"? Some have said it will be a holographic projection of the Beast; some have said that it will be a robot; while others say it will be a statue. There is good reason to understand that the image of the Beast will be a statue, for the following reasons.

There is a striking similarity between the description of this image of the Beast and the statue of King Nebuchadnezzar in Daniel.

> King Nebuchadnezzar made an image of gold, sixty cubits high and six cubits wide, and set it up on the plain of Dura in the province of Babylon. He then summoned the satraps, prefects, governors, advisers, treasurers, judges, magistrates and all the other provincial officials to come to the dedication of the image he had set up. So the satraps, prefects, governors, advisers, treasurers, judges, magistrates and all the other provincial officials assembled for the dedication of the image that King Nebuchadnezzar had set up, and they stood before it. Then the herald loudly proclaimed, "Nations and peoples of every language, this is what you are commanded to do: As soon as you hear the sound of the horn, flute, zither, lyre, harp, pipe and all kinds of music, you must fall down and worship the image of gold that King Nebuchadnezzar has

set up. Whoever does not fall down and worship will immediately be thrown into a blazing furnace." (Dan 3:1–6 NIV)

Daniel 3 describes for us a statue, an "image," of gold made by King Nebuchadnezzar, and once that statue was erected, a royal decree was issued ordering all people of the kingdom to "fall down and worship" the statue, and those who would not fall down in worship of that statue would be put to death. This is an almost exact parallel to Revelation 13:14–15 and the image made by the False Prophet. The False Prophet makes an image of the Beast, and everyone is commanded to worship that image, and those who do not worship that image of the Beast will be put to death. Just as the image erected by King Nebuchadnezzar was a statue, especially in light of the striking parallels between Daniel 3:1–6 and Revelation 13:14–15, there is good reason to understand that the image of the Beast made by the False Prophet will also be a statue.

Also, in the Ten Commandments, the Second Commandment is as follows:

> You shall not make for yourself a carved image—any likeness of anything that is in heaven above, or that is in the earth beneath, or that is in the water under the earth; you shall not bow down to them nor serve them. For I, the LORD your God, am a jealous God" (Deut 5:8–9 NKJV)

The image referred to in the Second Commandment is a "carved image," or "graven [engraved] image"—this is a statue. Since God specifically is speaking of a statue in the Second Commandment, and since Daniel 3:1–6, as a striking parallel to Revelation 13:14–15, is also speaking of a statue, we have good reason to understand that the image of the Beast of Revelation 13:14–15 will also be a statue.

But we are told more—not only will the False Prophet cause an image of the Beast to be made, but he will also "give breath" to that image, he will make that image alive, so that the statue/image can, itself, "speak."

Young's literal translation translates that as follows:

> and there was given to it to *give a spirit* to the image of the beast, that also the image of the beast may speak . . . " (Rev 13:15 YLT)

The YLT translates "give breath" as "give a spirit"—the clear meaning of this is that the image, the statue, will seem to be *alive*.

We must remember that all of this will be part of the great miraculous wonders that will be performed by the False Prophet in order to deceive the world. If this image of the Beast were only a holograph, or a televised image, there would be nothing miraculous about any of that—any sort of electronic image is exceedingly commonplace in the world, and there would be nothing wondrous about a speaking electronic image. Also, when the Bible refers to it specifically as giving "breath" or giving a "spirit" to that image, it truly means that there will be *life* given to that image (exactly as when God gives life to man by *breathing* into him the "breath of life," Genesis 2:7). When we understand the image of the Beast as being a statue, and when we understand that statue as being given a spirit or breath so as to make it, at least appear, alive, then this would be a great wonder, another miraculous sign performed by the False Prophet. Since it is the role of the False Prophet to deceive the world by way of signs and wonders, we can understand the image of the Beast as being one of those great signs and wonders. In fact, the description of the False Prophet making the image of the Beast and then giving it breath is given in the exact same sentence that tells us that the False Prophet will perform signs that will deceive the world.

> And he *deceives those who dwell on the earth by those signs* which he was granted to do in the sight of the beast, *telling those who dwell on the earth to make an image to the beast* who was wounded by the sword and lived. He was granted power to give breath to the image of the beast, that the image of the beast should both speak . . . " (Rev 13:14–15 NKJV)

As a result, we can clearly understand that this image of the Beast is at the very heart of the miraculous signs performed by the False Prophet.

Also, in regard to giving that image breath, we are told that the False Prophet "was granted power" to do so. This in itself emphasizes that the giving of breath to the image of the Beast will be no ordinary thing; rather, *supernatural power* will be given the False Prophet so as to enable him to give breath to that image—giving breath to the image of the Beast will be a miraculous sign, a great wonder in full view of the world, and will be one of the great ways in which the world will be deceived to worship the Beast.

Also, we are very clearly told that when the image of the Beast begins to speak, it will be the *statue* of the Beast that will command the world to worship the *statue*. Based on this verse, we can understand that it is not the False Prophet, nor the Beast, that will force the world to worship the Beast, but it will be the *statue* of the Beast that will force the world to worship the image/statue of the Beast, and thereby worship the Beast.

Again, this will be a miraculous wonder, and the world will be amazed, and many will worship the image and the Beast. All of this is the work of the False Prophet.

THE MARK OF THE BEAST

We are told one other thing about the False Prophet.

> He causes all, both small and great, rich and poor, free and slave, to receive a mark on their right hand or on their foreheads, and that no one may buy or sell except one who has the mark or the name of the beast, or the number of his name. (Rev 13:16–17 NKJV)

The False Prophet will devise a system whereby if anyone wishes to participate in the economic life of the world, they must first receive the "mark or name of the beast." This will be discussed in detail later, but it is important to note here that it is the False

Prophet who creates and implements this. Also, since we are told about receiving the mark of the Beast immediately after, and in the context of, worshiping the image of the Beast, the implication is that the only way to get that mark is to worship the image of the Beast.

In every respect, we see that everything that the False Prophet will do he will do so as to bring worship to the Beast.

THE EMULATION OF THE TRINITY

It has been pointed out that with the three characters of the dragon, the Beast, and the False Prophet, the enemy is mimicking, or emulating, the Trinity, where Satan, the dragon, emulates the Father, where the Beast (the seed of the serpent) emulates the Son, and where the False Prophet emulates the Holy Spirit. Just as the Holy Spirit works on people's hearts so as to lead them to Jesus Christ, the False Prophet, though only a man, will do all that he can to force people to worship the Beast.

THE TEN HORNS

In the imagery of the Beast that rises from the sea, we have seen that that Beast is the combination of the four beasts of Daniel 7, and that the seven heads of the Beast that rises from the sea are the same as the seven heads of Daniel's four beasts. Also part of that same imagery are ten horns. In addition to the seven heads, that Beast that rises from the sea has ten horns. In fact, these are the *same* ten horns as Daniel's fourth beast.

> After this I saw in the night visions, and behold, a fourth beast, dreadful and terrible, exceedingly strong. It had huge iron teeth; it was devouring, breaking in pieces, and trampling the residue with its feet. It was different from all the beasts that were before it, and it had ten horns. I was considering the horns, and there was another horn, a little one, coming up among them, before whom three of the first horns were plucked out by the roots. And there, in this horn, were eyes like the eyes of a man, and a mouth speaking pompous words. (Dan 7:7–8 NKJV)

This fourth beast of Daniel has ten horns. We are also told, as Daniel watched this vision, that a "little" horn, an eleventh horn, sprang up before those ten horns, and, as a result of that little eleventh horn, "three of the first [ten] horns were plucked out by the roots." We are also told that this little horn had "eyes like the eyes of a man," and had a "mouth speaking pompous [arrogant] words."

Just as the Beast in Revelation 13:1 is an assemblage of only *parts* of Daniel's four beasts (the *body* of a leopard, the *feet* of a bear, the *mouth* of a lion, all only *parts* of the leopard, bear, and lion of Daniel's beasts), likewise, the *part* of Daniel's fourth beast that is included in the Revelation 13:1 imagery is the part of the head with ten horns—the ten horns of 13:1 are from Daniel's fourth beast. If we are to understand the ten horns of the Beast in Revelation 13:1, that understanding will come only from Daniel 7, and, in fact, the ten horns are specifically explained for us by the angel in Daniel 7:24–25.

> The ten horns are ten kings
> Who shall arise from this kingdom.
> And another shall rise after them;
> He shall be different from the first ones,
> And shall subdue three kings.
> He shall speak pompous words against the Most High,
> Shall persecute the saints of the Most High,
> And shall intend to change times and law.
> Then the saints shall be given into his hand
> For a time and times and half a time. (NKJV)

We are specifically told that the ten horns of Daniel's fourth beast are "ten kings," ten earthly rulers. As a result, we can understand the ten horns of the Beast in Revelation 13:1 as being those same ten kings, or ten earthly rulers.

What then is the little eleventh horn?

The eleventh horn is, in fact, the Beast of Revelation. He is described as having the eyes of a man (he is an individual person) and a boastful, pompous mouth who speaks against the Most High (blasphemy) and who will persecute the church, the saints. This arrogant, boastful, blaspheming mouth is a defining characteristic of the Beast, as we have already seen (Dan 11:36–39; Rev 13:5–6). The reason the Beast is here described as a "little" horn is that his reign will be very brief, and in fact we are told here that his entire reign, his time of unopposed, absolute rule, will last only three and a half years ("a time and times and half a time," also 1,260 days or 42 months, Rev 13:5; 11:3, 12; 12:6).

It is in this context that we must also refer to Daniel 2, which is a parallel vision to the beasts of Daniel 7. In Daniel 2, Daniel tells Nebuchadnezzar his dream and interprets it for him, and then goes on to describe a statue comprised of four distinct sections—a head of gold, a chest and arms of silver, a belly and thighs of bronze, and legs of iron, but also, as a fifth element, feet (and, by extension, the toes; see Dan 2:41) of iron and clay (2:31–34). As Daniel explains the meaning of this image, and of the dream, as he progresses through the image of the statue, progressing through future history, it is clear that he comes to the time preceding the Second Coming, the same time as described in the book of Revelation (Dan 2:44)—this is the time of the feet and of the ten toes.

In his explanation of the dream and of its imagery, Daniel refers to the ten toes of the feet of the statue as "kings" (2:44) and talks about events that happen in "the days of these kings," telling us that in the days of those ten kings God will set up his everlasting kingdom on Earth. God's everlasting kingdom on Earth is set up by Jesus Christ at his Second Coming; therefore, we know, without any doubt, that the days of these kings, the ten kings represented by the ten toes, are the days that precede the Second Coming, the same time period as described in Revelation. The ten horns of the Beast that rises from the sea in Revelation 13:1 are the same as the ten horns of Daniel's fourth beast in Daniel 7, which are the same as the ten toes of Daniel 2:41–44. So we can understand that the ten horns of the Beast of Revelation 13:1 are ten kings that will be ruling the Earth in the days that precede the Second Coming.

What is the nature of those ten kings?

IRON AND CLAY—MINGLE WITH THE SEED OF MEN

There is a very intriguing and unique description given by Daniel in his description of the ten toes. The feet of that statue of Daniel 2, and the ten toes of those feet, are described as being a mix of iron and clay.

> Whereas you saw the feet and toes, partly of potter's clay and partly of iron, the kingdom shall be divided; yet the strength of the iron shall be in it, just as you saw the iron mixed with ceramic clay. And as the toes of the feet were partly of iron and partly of clay, so the kingdom shall be partly strong and partly fragile. As you saw iron mixed with ceramic clay, they will mingle with the seed of men; but they will not adhere to one another, just as iron does not mix with clay. (Dan 2:41–43 NKJV)

Daniel explains for us the meaning of this iron-clay mixing. He tells us that iron and clay do *not* mix, and if you try to mix iron and clay, they will not hold together, and the mixture will be weak. As a result, Daniel tells us that that final kingdom, the one on Earth prior to the Second Coming, will be a divided kingdom—it will still retain the great strength of iron, but the mixing with clay will weaken it, and so that kingdom, which is the kingdom of the Beast, will be *both* strong and fragile.

It is in that context that Daniel then tells us the following:

> As you saw iron mixed with ceramic clay, they will *mingle with the seed of men*; but they will not adhere to one another, just as iron does not mix with clay. (Dan 2:43)

In describing those ten kings, as represented by the imagery of the ten toes, Daniel tells us that those ten kings will be like the mixing of iron and clay, and then he specifically connects that with the "seed of men." What does that mean? The term "seed of men" means human offspring. Why does Daniel talk to us about human offspring and a mingling "with the seed of men" in the same context as iron and clay not mixing, and then telling us, after referencing the mingling with the seed of men, that that mingling, that mixing, will *not* adhere?

Here is that same verse in Young's Literal Translation:

Because thou hast seen iron mixed with miry clay, *they are mixing themselves with the seed of men*: and they are not adhering one with another, even as iron is not mixed with clay."

Young's Literal Translation very clearly tells us that those ten kings, as represented by the ten toes of iron and clay, are "mixing *themselves*" with the "seed of men." This very clearly sounds like a mixing of something that is *not* of the seed of men with the seed of men—there is no other accurate way to understand this.

That being the case, what does it mean for those ten kings to be a mixing of something that is not of the seed of man with the seed of man?

In fact, it is an affirmation that those ten kings themselves, the ten toes of Daniel 2 and the ten horns of Revelation 13:1, will be, like the Beast, Nephilim offspring, the union of two natures, two natures that are not meant to mingle, natures that will not adhere—those ten kings will be the product of the union of fallen angelic beings with human women, exactly as in Genesis 6:2–3 and 3:14–15. This is also a further affirmation of Jesus' own words in Matthew 24:37, where he tells us that the days preceding the Second Coming will be like the "days of Noah"—the days of Noah were defined by the Nephilim of Genesis 6:2–4. Just as iron and clay cannot adhere to one another, likewise the angelic nature cannot adhere to the human nature.

THE TEN KINGS GIVE THE BEAST THEIR POWER

What is the purpose of the ten kings in Revelation? The Bible explains it for us clearly.

> The ten horns which you saw are ten kings who have received no kingdom as yet, but they receive authority for one hour as kings with the beast. These are of one mind, and they will give their power and authority to the beast. (Rev 17:12–13 NKJV)

The angel affirms that the ten horns of the Beast in Revelation 13:1 are, in fact, ten kings, in exact accordance with Daniel 2:41–44. Those ten kings, like the Beast, will come to power for only a very brief time, described here as being for only "one hour." But most importantly, we are told that these ten kings will be "of one mind" and that "they will give their power and authority to the beast." Those ten kings will come to power around the time, and almost certainly just before, the Beast comes to actual rule (the actual rule of the Beast will commence only after his fake death and resurrection). It is important to remember that the Beast comes upon the world's stage and brings the global peace *before* his fake death and resurrection. There is very good reason to understand that, as part of the Beast's global peace plan, he divides the world into ten regions (none of which currently exist), and that those ten kings will be the rulers of those ten regions, and so those ten kings will come to power only at *that* time, as a result of the global peace instituted by the Beast. This means that when the Beast is fake assassinated and fake resurrected, those ten kings will *already* be in power, and only just so, and all as a result of the Beast's covenant of peace (Dan 9:27).

We can understand the Beast's creation of the ten regions of global rule in the same way as the events that occurred in the aftermath of World War I and World War II. In both cases, the global war led to the creation of an attempt at global government—in the case of WWI, it was the creation of the League of Nations; in the case of WWII, it was the creation of the United Nations. In both cases, those two global organizations were each the result of a world war, and each was an attempt at global governance, and both have failed. It is in that context that we can understand the Beast's negotiated peace covenant. He also, in the aftermath of World War III, the war of Seal 2, will implement a reorganization of the world so as to ostensibly (as with the League of Nations and the United Nations) prevent such a global war from happening again. It is that reorganization of the world that will result in the creation of the ten kingdoms, or ten regions, upon the Earth, which will each be ruled by one of the ten kings. This global peace covenant, and the ensuing division of the world into ten regions, is accomplished by the Beast *before* his fake death and resurrection.

We are told that the ten kings who will rule those ten regions will be "of one mind," and it is possible that, since those ten kings will almost certainly be Nephilim offspring themselves, the fallen angelic spirits that animate them will coordinate so as to institute, in full, the plan of the dragon. As a result, when the Beast has his fake resurrection and is proclaimed as Christ returned, at that point those ten kings will *give* the Beast the authority of their ten regions, and since the entire world will at that time, and as a result of the Beast's global peace, be divided into those ten regions, this means that in giving the Beast their power and authority those ten kings will be giving the Beast authority over the whole world.

THREE KINGS SUBDUED

However, when Daniel describes for us these same ten horns, he tells us the following:

> The ten horns are ten kings
> Who shall arise from this kingdom.
> And another shall rise after them;
> He shall be different from the first ones,
> And *shall subdue three kings*. (Dan 7:24 NKJV)

We are told in Revelation 17:12–13 that the ten kings "are of one mind" and "give their power and authority to the Beast," and yet in Daniel 7:24 we are told that of those same ten kings, three of them are "subdued," or conquered, by the Beast. Is this not a contradiction? No, it is not; rather it's a fleshing out of the whole picture, and we can understand it as follows.

Based on Revelation 17:12–13 and on Daniel 7:24, here is what we can conclude. The ten kings come to power very briefly, for "one hour," as a result of the Beast's global peace covenant—the brevity of the rule of the ten kings is exactly in line with the brevity of the reign of the Beast (the little horn of Daniel 7:20), and so the ten kings are described as coming to power at about the same time as the little horn, the Beast. Since those ten kings *give* the Beast their power and authority (Rev 17:12–13), we know, for a fact, that they come to power just *before* the Beast's fake death and resurrection. As a result of Daniel's description of the ten toes as being iron and clay, and then likening the mixing of iron and clay to the mixing of the seed of men with something other than the seed of men, we can understand those same ten kings as being, themselves, Nephilim offspring, like the Beast himself. It is for this reason that the ten kings are given the authority over the ten regions of the world created by the Beast when he brings the global peace, and it is for this reason that those ten kings are all "of one mind"—they are all of one mind because they are all of a similar spirit. We know, for a fact, that after the Beast's fake resurrection *all* ten kings will give the Beast their power, and so, as a result, he will rule over all the world. However, based on Daniel 7:24, we can also conclude that *after* the ten kings *initially* give the Beast their power, three of them will change their minds and will try and hold on to their kingdoms and authority, and it will be in response to *that* that the Beast then subdues, or conquers, those three kings and their kingdoms/regions.

This scenario perfectly accommodates both Revelation 17:12–13 and Daniel 7:24. It also is a fulfillment of Daniel's words in Daniel 2:41–43, where he describes the mixing of iron and clay, all in connection with the mixing of the seed of men, as being *weak* and as making for a divided kingdom (Dan 2:41). The above scenario of events perfectly accommodates every aspect of all of those verses.

HOW LONG DOES THE BEAST RULE?

We know, for a fact, that from the time that the Beast brings the global peace to the time of the Second Coming is a period of seven years (not necessarily *exactly* seven years, i.e., maybe not exactly to the day, but, in general, seven years overall). This *entire* seven-year period is *all* in Seal 5. Very often, people describe the Beast as actually *ruling* for the entirety of these seven years, but that is not correct. The fact is that the Beast will rule as an absolute, unopposed ruler for only three and a half years (42 months, 1,260 days, "a time, times and half a time"). This is affirmed by a number of verses.

> And he was given a mouth speaking great things and blasphemies, and he was given authority to continue for *forty-two months*. (Rev 13:5 NKJV)

> He shall speak pompous words against the Most High, Shall persecute the saints of the Most High, And shall intend to change times and law. Then the

> saints shall be given into his hand For *a time and times and half a time.* (Dan 7:25 NKJV)

> Then I heard the man clothed in linen, who was above the waters of the river, when he held up his right hand and his left hand to heaven, and swore by Him who lives forever, that it shall be for a *time, times, and half a time*; and when the power of the holy people has been completely shattered, all these things shall be finished. (Dan 12:7 NKJV)

> And I will give power to my two witnesses, and they will prophesy *one thousand two hundred and sixty days*, clothed in sackcloth. (Rev 11:3 NKJV)

> Then the woman fled into the wilderness, where she has a place prepared by God, that they should feed her there *one thousand two hundred and sixty days.* (Rev 12:6 NKJV)

> He will confirm a covenant with many for one "seven." In *the middle of the "seven"* he will put an end to sacrifice and offering. And at the temple he will set up an *abomination that causes desolation*, until the end that is decreed is poured out on him. (Dan 9:27 NIV)

We are told, very clearly, that the Beast will be given authority for only forty-two months (Rev 13:5), or three and a half years. It is also while he rules as absolute ruler for those three and a half years that he will persecute the church, and we are specifically told that the time of the persecution of the church will last only 1,260 days, during which same time the Two Witnesses will preach against the Beast, on the world's stage, from Jerusalem, and expose him for what he is (Rev 11:3).

The Beast does *not* rule for seven years, but only for half that time, for three and a half years. What happens at the three-and-a-half-year point to change that? *Why* does he not rule for the whole seven years?

Daniel 9:27 specifically tells us that the seven-year period *begins* with the establishment of the covenant of peace, and then he tells us that at the midpoint of that seven-year period the Beast "will set up an abomination that causes desolation." Remember, this is *all* happening during Seal 5, and when Jesus describes for us the events of Seal 5 in Matthew 24, he specifically refers to this same verse from Daniel, and explains to us what it means.

> "Therefore when you see the 'abomination of desolation,' spoken of by Daniel the prophet, standing in the holy place" (whoever reads, let him understand), "then let those who are in Judea flee to the mountains. Let him who is on the housetop not go down to take anything out of his house. And let him who is in the field not go back to get his clothes. But woe to those who are pregnant and to those who are nursing babies in those days! And pray that your flight may not be in winter or on the Sabbath. For then there will be great tribulation, such as has not been since the beginning of the world until this time, no, nor

ever shall be. And unless those days were shortened, no flesh would be saved; but for the elect's sake those days will be shortened." (Matt 24:15–22 NKJV)

Jesus tells us that when the "abomination of desolation," as spoken of in Daniel 9:27, is set up, *that* is the specific event that will unleash the Great Tribulation. That Great Tribulation will last for the remaining three and a half years of the seven-year period, and the details of the Tribulation are described by Trumpets 1–5 and Bowls 1–5 (with the Bowls 1–5 all being part of Trumpet 5)—*all* of that, the Trumpets and Bowls, the *entire* Great Tribulation, occurs in Seal 5 (Matt 24:29; Rev 6:12–13).

What is the abomination of desolation that the Beast will set up and that unleashes the Great Tribulation?

THE ABOMINATION OF DESOLATION

In Daniel 9:27, in talking about the abomination of desolation, Daniel specifically tells us that it will be set up at (or in) the temple, and that is a reference to the Jewish temple in Jerusalem. The temple was originally built by Solomon, was destroyed, and then later rebuilt after the Babylonian exile. That rebuilt temple was the temple from which Jesus drove out the moneychangers and in which, at age twelve, he was teaching the elders of the Jews (Mark 11:15; Luke 2:41–49). That temple, the rebuilt temple of Jesus' day, was itself destroyed in 70 AD by the Roman conquest of Judea, by Vespasian, and it has not existed for two thousand years. The reason that God had the temple destroyed in 70 AD was the following—since the sacrifice of Jesus upon the cross, and with his resurrection, God would not allow any more sacrifices for sin, for to do so would be a defamation of Jesus' once-and-for-all accomplishment upon the cross, where he took upon himself the sin of Adam, the sin of the world, bringing it to conclusion in his death, and so destroying the power of sin and thereby removing the obstacle that prevents us from knowing God's love and forgiveness (see *What Happened on the Cross*, Wipf & Stock 2020). The fact that Daniel specifically tells us that the Beast will set up the abomination of desolation in the temple can therefore only mean that the temple, having been destroyed by Vespasian in 70 AD, will be rebuilt again in the time preceding the Second Coming.

So, what exactly is the abomination of desolation that gets set up in the rebuilt temple? The Bible tells us,

> Let no one deceive you by any means; for that Day will not come unless the falling away comes first, and the man of sin is revealed, the son of perdition, who opposes and exalts himself above all that is called God or that is worshiped, so that *he sits as God in the temple of God*, showing himself that *he is God*. (2 Thess 2:3–4 NKJV)

This is a description of the Beast and of what he will do. Once again, Paul describes the Beast as one who "exalts himself above all that is called God," as a blasphemous boaster. Paul then tells us that the Beast will go into the temple (i.e., the still-to-be-rebuilt temple) and will *sit* in the temple and thereby proclaim himself as the living Almighty God. There is no question that the Beast will, in fact, sit in the very holy of holies, the very heart of the temple, where, in the Old Testament, only the high priest could enter once a year to meet with God—no one else, ever, was allowed in the holy of holies (Exod 30:10; Lev 16:2; Heb 9:7). By that act, by setting up his own throne in the holy of holies of the rebuilt temple, the Beast will proclaim himself as God Almighty. That act is an act of "abomination" and an act of "desolation"—it is an "abomination" because it is an exceedingly great offence, and it is a "desolation" because it is an act of exceeding sacrilege—the abomination of desolation is the Beast enthroning himself in the holy of holies of the rebuilt temple, and thereby proclaiming himself to be God. That happens three and a half years into the reign of the Beast, and *that* is the event that unleashes the Great Tribulation.

WHY DOES THAT ACT UNLEASH THE TRIBULATION?

Why is the act of sitting enthroned in the rebuilt temple the act that unleashes the wrath of the Tribulation?

It is because in enthroning himself in the holy of holies of the rebuilt temple, the Beast is, in fact, taking the seat of Jesus' throne, the throne of David, upon which the Lord Jesus Christ will sit after the Second Coming, enthroned as the King of the world.

When Jesus returns at the Second Coming, as the "King of kings and Lord of lords" (Rev 19:16), and after he destroys the armies at Armageddon, he will sit enthroned in Jerusalem and rule the world, as King, from Jerusalem (Zech 14:1–21). From where in Jerusalem will Jesus rule? He will rule from that same rebuilt temple, seated on *his* throne, which itself will be *located in the holy of holies*. This is why when the Beast sets up his throne in the holy of holies, in the rebuilt temple, he is, in fact, usurping Jesus' own earthly throne. As a result, it is that act of usurpation of Jesus' very own throne that unleashes the wrath of the Tribulation.

WHEN IS THE TEMPLE REBUILT?

It is virtually certain that it is the Beast himself who will cause the temple to be rebuilt in Jerusalem, and it is that fact, above all others, that will cause the Jews to hail the Beast as Messiah. Jesus himself tells us,

> I have come in My Father's name, and you do not receive Me; if another comes *in his own name*, him *you will receive*. (John 5:43 NKJV)

Jesus here tells us that the Jews will reject him, and yet a time will come when "another" will come "in his own name" and *that* person the Jews "will receive." This means that when Jesus, the true Messiah, came, he was rejected, but another false

Messiah will come, and him the Jews will accept. This one who will "come in his own name" is the Beast, the false Christ, the false Messiah—he will not only be the false Christ to the world, but he will also be the false Messiah to the Jews.

Also, it is important to remember that the Beast comes upon the world's stage as the bringer of peace, and that will certainly mean bringing peace to the Middle East, as well as to the whole world. By bringing peace to the Middle East, he will accomplish what no else has yet accomplished, and so, especially in light of his fake death and resurrection, and even just in regard to his bringing of peace to the Middle East, the Jews will hail him as Messiah.

Furthermore, as part of that peace, and since he himself will be the ruler of the world, it is the Beast himself who will cause the Jews to rebuild their temple in Jerusalem, which will even further affirm him to the Jews as Messiah.

The rebuilding of the temple is witness to the fact that Judah, the Jews, will be participating in the Beast's "covenant with many," a covenant that is also described in the Bible as the "covenant with death."

THE COVENANT WITH DEATH

The fact of the Jews (Judah) participation in the Beast's global peace covenant, the same covenant of peace that will result in the rebuilding of the temple and in the Jews hailing the Beast as Messiah, is further affirmed in Isaiah.

> Because you have said, "*We have made a covenant with death*,
> And with Sheol we are in agreement.
> When the *overflowing scourge* passes through,
> It will not come to us,
> For *we have made lies our refuge*,
> And under falsehood we have hidden ourselves."
> Therefore thus says the Lord God:
> "Behold, I lay in Zion a stone for a foundation,
> A tried stone, a precious cornerstone, a sure foundation;
> Whoever believes will not act hastily.
> Also I will make justice the measuring line,
> And righteousness the plummet;
> The hail will sweep away the refuge of lies,
> And the waters will overflow the hiding place.
> *Your covenant with death will be annulled*,
> And *your agreement with Sheol* will not stand;
> When *the overflowing scourge* passes through,
> Then you will be trampled down by it. (Isa 28:15–18 NKJV)

This passage is a prophecy about Jerusalem (Isa 27:13), and therefore is a prophecy over Judah and the Jews. In this passage, the people of Jerusalem, the Jews, are described as making a "covenant with death," as making "lies our refuge," having confidence in that covenant and in those lies to protect them from any harm that might come. All of this is further described as taking place during an "overflowing scourge."

What is the "covenant with death"? It is, in fact, the same "covenant with many" of the Beast. Furthermore, the overwhelming scourge described here are the same events described in Zechariah 14:1–15, which are the same events as described in Revelation—the armies of the world gathered against Jerusalem as those armies gather at Armageddon in the days preceding the Second Coming. This passage in Isaiah is an affirmation that Judah, the Jews, enter into the Beast's "covenant with many" (Dan 9:27), accepting him, the Beast, the one who "comes in his own name" (John 5:43) as their Messiah. The reason the Jews will accept the Beast as Messiah is because it is almost certain that, as part of his "covenant with many," the same "covenant with death" that will be entered into by the Jews, it will be the Beast who will cause the temple to be rebuilt, and so the Jews will hail him as Messiah.

It is almost certain that the decree to begin rebuilding the temple will happen at the very outset of the Beast coming to power, soon after his fake resurrection, and it is virtually certain that it will take three and a half years for the temple to be rebuilt. How can we know that it will take three and a half years to rebuild the temple?

THREE AND HALF YEARS TO REBUILD THE TEMPLE

We must remember that the reason the temple was destroyed in the first place, in 70 AD, was because God would no longer allow any sacrifice for sin to take place, as that would be a defamation of the sacrifice of Jesus upon the cross. With that in mind, Daniel specifically tells us,

> But in the middle of the week he shall bring an end to sacrifice and offering."
> (Dan 9:27 NKJV)

From this, we can know, for a certainty, that in the rebuilt temple the Jews will once again *begin* to offer the Old Testament sacrifices to God, for we are told that, at the three-and-half-year point of the rule of the Beast, the Beast himself will put *an end* to that sacrifice in the temple.

Since the very reason that God had the temple destroyed in the first place was to ensure that there would no longer be any sacrifice for sin offered in the temple, as that would be a defamation of the sacrifice of the cross, it is inconceivable that God would allow any renewed sacrifices for sin to occur at the rebuilt temple, as those renewed sacrifices for sin would, in themselves, be an offense to God as they would be a defamation of the sacrifice of the cross. It is for that reason that we can conclude that the sacrifices and offerings that are ended by the Beast in Daniel 9:27 must only have *just begun* to be performed, just as the rebuilt temple was completed. Since we know that the Beast puts an end to those sacrifices at the three-and-a-half-year point of his rule, and since there is good reason to understand that it is the Beast who causes the rebuilding of the temple, we can therefore conclude that the temple itself comes to completion at about that same three-and-a-half-year point.

It is the Beast who causes the temple to be rebuilt, affirming him as Messiah to the Jews, and it is the Beast who, at the three-and-a-half-year point of his rule, is in Jerusalem, where he puts an almost immediate end to the daily sacrifices that were just beginning to be performed in the rebuilt temple. Upon putting an end to the daily sacrifices that were just beginning to be performed, the Beast will then enthrone himself in the temple, in the holy of holies, thereby usurping the throne of the returning Jesus Christ and unleashing the Tribulation. As a result, we know that at the three-and-half-year point into his rule the Beast will be in Jerusalem.

Prior to the events at the temple, and happening almost at the very start of the Beast's reign, the False Prophet will institute a system designed to ensure worship of the Beast, and it is a system based on the mark of the Beast.

15

THE MARK OF THE BEAST

OF ALL THE IMAGERY, symbols, topics, and prophecies in the book of Revelation, probably nothing is so well known, or referred to as often, as the mark of the Beast. The mark of the Beast is found in many movies, video games, music (especially metal music), books, even fashion—it is probably the single most well-known fact of Revelation.

So, what is the mark of the Beast?

> He causes all, both small and great, rich and poor, free and slave, to receive a mark on their right hand or on their foreheads, and that no one may buy or sell except one who has the mark or the name of the beast, or the number of his name. Here is wisdom. Let him who has understanding calculate the number of the beast, for it is the number of a man: His number is 666. (Rev 13:16–18 NKJV)

We are told here that the False Prophet, *not* the Beast, is the one who will cause people throughout the world "to receive a mark on their right hand or on their foreheads." We are told that in order to participate in the economy of the world, one must have that mark—unless one has that mark, they cannot buy or sell.

We are then told that this mark is, in fact, the very *name* of the Beast, or rather, it is the *number* of his name. We are then exhorted to apply wisdom to understand this, and are told that, if we have understanding, we can "*calculate* the number of the Beast," and that the number of the Beast "is the number of *a* man," and that number is 666.

From this one passage, people have created many scenarios. First, they imagine that the people of the world will have the actual Arabic numerals 666 emblazoned on their forehead or right hand. They create scenarios that describe the number of the Beast as the *means* by which you buy or sell, or that it is some sort of microchip implant. Others use the number 666 to try to identify, or prophesy, individuals on Earth who may, right now, be candidates for the Beast. The fact is, there is nothing biblical about any of these scenarios.

WHY THE RIGHT HAND OR FOREHEAD?

The Bible is very clear and specific—the mark of the Beast will be placed *only* on a person's *right* hand *or* on their *forehead*. Why?

People have come up with all kinds of non-biblical ideas to explain this. One of the most common is the idea that the mark of the Beast will be a personal ID chip, containing all of the person's personal information, including all of their financial information, much like a glorified, or enhanced, debit card. In this scenario, a person will have to actually *use* that chip to enact a transaction to either buy or sell something. Embedded into that person's unique *personal* ID chip, or PIN number, will be the number 666. In this scenario, since the ID chip contains all of a person's personal and financial information, then, in order to prevent it from being lost or stolen, that chip will be physically *implanted* into a person's body. The question then arises as to how such an implanted chip will be powered. The answer usually given is that it will be powered by body heat. At that point, the statement is made that two areas of the highest body heat in the human body are the right hand or arm and the forehead. Therefore, according to this scenario, the ID chip will be implanted into a person's right hand or forehead because that is how the chip can be powered.

From virtually every angle, there is nothing biblical about any of this, and, in fact, in many ways it contradicts what the Bible actually tells us.

THE NUMBER OF HIS NAME

One very paramount point to understand is that the number of the Beast is, plain and simple, exactly what the Bible tells us that it is—it is the number of the *name* of the Beast.

As we all know, for any type of technological commerce to take place, *each* person must have their *own* unique card number, account, and associated PIN number. If seven billion people in the world all had the *same* number, it would be impossible to distinguish any one transaction from any other transaction—it is a completely impossible scenario. Rather, in order for this idea to be even remotely workable, *every* person would have to have *their own number*, a number different from anyone else's number. As a result, proponents of the implanted chip idea say that each person will indeed have their own unique microchip number, but embedded *within* that unique number will be the digits 666. So, for example, if a person's unique PIN number is 123456789012345, then, according to the scenario outlined above, their own unique PIN might be modified to be 1234567-666-89012345. So, each person will still have their *own* number, but that number will also have some connection with the three digits 666.

This is absolutely *not* what the Bible says about the number of the Beast.

First and foremost, the Bible does *not* say that everybody gets their *own* number—we are very clearly told that there is only *one* number, and that *all* people will get that *same* number, and that number is *not* just a number that is *possessed* by any one person; rather that number is solely and exclusively the number of one person's *name*. That number will be the *Beast's* number. Also, that number, in its *totality*, will *only* be the number of the *name* of the Beast. So 666 will be the *entire* number, and it will be the number of the *name* of the Beast. Therefore, any teaching that says people will each get *their own* number, and that each number will be a uniquely different number, but just contains three 6s within it, is in contradiction to the clear teaching of the Bible. There will be only *one* number, the *same* number for everyone, and that number will be 666—that will be the *entire* number, and it will only have one meaning; it will be the name of the Beast.

HOW CAN A NUMBER BE A NAME?

How can the number 666 be the *name* of the Beast? We can understand it as follows.

In English, and other languages, numbers are represented as distinct numerals. For example, the numbers of the English language are in fact Arabic *numerals*. But many languages—for example, Latin, Greek, and Hebrew—do *not* have numbers represented by numerals; rather they use *letters* of their own *alphabet* to *also* represent numbers. Probably the best-known example of this is Roman numerals.

In Latin, the language of ancient Rome, certain Roman letters also doubled as numbers. So, for example, the Roman letter V was also the number 5, while the Roman letter X was also the number 10. Likewise, an I was a 1, L was 50, C was 100, D was 500, and M was 1000. From these alphabet numbers the Romans could devise every number. For example, the number 25 would be written XXV, while the number 90 would be written XC, and so on. So, in those languages, the same letters that were used to spell words were also used for numbers.

As such, it is possible to take a name and *convert* that name to its *number equivalent*, since the letters that spell that name *also* represent numbers.

As an example, if we take the name Vic (short for Victor), and, using Roman numerals, convert it to its number equivalent, we will get the following:

V = 5
I = 1
C = 100

If we then add up the numbers that those letters represent, we will have: 5 + 1 + 100 = 106. Therefore, *the number of the name Vic is* 106.

This is exactly what it means to say that *the number of the name of the Beast is 666*. If we take the name of the Beast, and *convert* it to its *number equivalent*, it will add up to 666. Hebrew, like Latin or Greek, is one of the languages where numbers are also represented by letters of the alphabet. Therefore, in regard to calculating the number of the name of the Beast, many people understand it as taking the name of the Beast and first converting his name to Hebrew, and then taking the number equivalents of those Hebrew letters that spell his name and then adding up those numbers. When those Hebrew letter-numbers are added up, the number of the name of the Beast will add up to 666.

Whether or not it will be necessary to first convert the name of the Beast to either Hebrew or Greek (the language of the New Testament), regardless of how we would approach it, the letters of his name will have number equivalents and, when added up according to their number equivalents, the letters of his name will add up to 666.

NERO

It is in this context that we must consider Nero.

Nero was one of the early Roman emperors, and it is a fact of history that when you take the full name of the Roman emperor Nero and convert the letters of his name to their number equivalents, they add up to 666. This is important as it tells us something of the Beast.

The Roman emperor Nero (54–68 AD) is almost universally considered to have been a true monster, having even ordered the murder of his own mother. As a Roman emperor, Nero was an absolute ruler with total power and authority. Also, one very important historical fact to keep in mind when looking at Nero, especially as it relates to Revelation, and for the purpose of insight into the Beast, is this—Nero was the first persecutor of Christians.

In 64 AD a great fire erupted in Rome, causing great destruction to the city, even completely destroying three of the fourteen districts of the city, and greatly damaging seven other districts. In many ancient sources (Pliny the Elder, Suetonius, Cassius Dio) it is reported that Nero himself was suspected of actually starting that fire. Why would Nero, the Roman emperor, want to start a fire to destroy his great city? In these same sources we are told that Nero had an idea that he would rebuild Rome as a new city, Neropolis. True or not, there is much suspicion in ancient sources around Nero and the cause of that fire, and that suspicion is from ancient Roman historians.

However, regardless of how the great fire of Rome actually started, someone had to be blamed, and it was Nero who selected a new "Jewish" sect upon whom he would cast blame—Nero blamed Christians for starting that fire. The usual Roman punishment for arson was to take the arsonist and burn them alive, and, as a result, many Christians, by Nero's order, were arrested and burned alive as human torches, while others were fed alive to wild animals (lions, tigers, et al.), to be torn apart, while others were crucified. It was a concerted persecution of Christians in 64 AD, the first ever persecution of Christians. In fact, it was during that persecution of Nero that the apostles Peter and Paul were killed. As a result, Nero has come down in history as the first persecutor of Christians, and the number of *his* name adds up to 666.

Just as the Beast of Revelation 13:1 is an amalgamation of parts of the four beasts of Daniel, and, as a result, can give us a prophetic insight into the coming kingdom of the Beast, the fact that the number of the name of the Beast will be 666, as was the number of Nero's name, likewise makes a strong prophetic connection between the Beast and Nero. We can understand this as a prophetic connection, as follows—by looking at Nero, we can gain some insights into the Beast. We can consider the Roman emperor Nero as being a *prophetic picture* of the Beast to come.

In what way is the Roman emperor Nero a prophetic picture of the Beast to come? There are two key ways in which Nero paints a picture of the coming Beast.

First, Nero, as a Roman emperor, was an absolute ruler. Therefore, like Nero, the Beast will be an absolute ruler—his word will be law, and he will rule unopposed.

Second, Nero was a persecutor of Christians, the very *first* persecutor of Christians. This means that in the annals of Christian persecution Nero holds an eminent position. Therefore, like Nero, the Beast will be a persecutor of Christians (Matt 24:9; Rev 13:7; 17:6). However, the Beast will not be *just* a persecutor of Christians, but, like Nero, the Beast will hold a special position in the annals of Christian persecution. Where Nero was the very *first* persecutor of Christians, the Beast will be the *greatest* persecutor of Christians. In fact, not only will the Beast persecute the church, but he will actually overcome and defeat the church (Rev 13:7).

It is because the number of the name of Nero is the same as the number of the name of the Beast that we can understand Nero as being a prophetic picture of the Beast to come. Just as 666 was the number of Nero's actual name (in some parts of the empire, Nero's name had a slightly different spelling, so, based on that spelling, the number of Nero's name is 616, rather than 666, as is attested by some manuscripts of Revelation), there is no question that 666 will also, in actual fact, be the number of the *name* of the Beast.

THIS CALLS FOR WISDOM AND UNDERSTANDING

> This calls for wisdom. Let the person who has insight calculate the number of the beast, for it is the number of a man. That number is 666. (Rev 13:18 NIV)

We are specifically told that to calculate the number of the Beast will require both wisdom and insight. What does that mean?

We are clearly told that the number of the name of the Beast must be *calculated*, which means that just to see his name, just to look at it, will not make it apparent that the number of his name is 666. This is further affirmed by the injunction that in order to make that calculation both wisdom and insight will be required. This is to say, once again, that it will *not* be apparent that 666 is the number of the name of the Beast—in fact, if someone does not have wisdom and insight then, according to Revelation 13:18, they will not be able to calculate the number of the Beast.

This is an important point to make, for there is always someone who is trying to calculate the number of the Beast in the most simplistic, superficial ways where no wisdom or insight is required.

For example, US presidents are always on people's lists when trying to identify a candidate that will be the Beast, and one of the greatest US presidents of the twentieth century was Ronald Reagan. Ronald Reagan's full name was Ronald Wilson Reagan. There were a number of people in the 1980s who noticed that each of Reagan's three names was comprised of six letters: Ronald is six letters, Wilson is six letters, and Reagan is six letters. As a result, there were people identifying Ronald Reagan as the Beast solely for the reason that he had three names and each name had six letters. This is an example of an exceedingly simplistic approach to the number 666, an approach that in no way involves either wisdom or insight.

All that to say that we must beware, and cautious, of those kinds of approaches. The fact is that to calculate the number of the Beast will not be something obvious, but rather it will involve, as the Bible says, wisdom and insight.

PREDICTING A CANDIDATE

As with the Ronald Reagan example above, people are always trying, in some way, to identify an existing candidate on the world's stage, in advance, as being a possible candidate for the Beast of Revelation. Usually they try to identify, or predict, this by seeing if that person's name, according to whatever method they're using, adds up to 666.

It is virtually certain that we cannot use 666 to try and identify, or predict, in advance, any individual who might become the Beast—that's not how it works. At the very most, that identification of the Beast, of his name as adding up to 666, will only be possible *after* the Beast is *already* on the world's stage, *after* he brings the global peace, and, most importantly, *after* his fake resurrection—but by then those very events themselves will testify to the identity of the Beast, since no one else on Earth will have a globally witnessed resurrection. What we can probably expect is that once the Beast is in power, the Holy Spirit only *then* will reveal how to calculate the number of his name, revealing it at least to the church. It will be only then, by means of that insight and wisdom, that such a calculation will only *affirm* what will already be apparent on the world's stage.

WHY THE RIGHT HAND AND FOREHEAD?

We are very clearly and specifically told that the number of the Beast will be received by people on either their right hand or on their forehead. Why?

The Bible itself gives us the reason why—the reason that people receive the number of the Beast, the number of his *name*, on their forehead or right arm is to *honor* the Beast, to commemorate his "death" wounds and to thereby identify with him.

The Beast will bring peace to the world after the great devastation of the Seal 2 global war, the Seal 3 global famine, and the Seal 4 global death from the war, famine, pestilence, and disease. He will come "peaceably" (Dan 11:21, 24) and will make a "covenant with many" (Dan 9:27)—this is the global peace that he will negotiate and institute. One of the key features of his global covenant of peace is that he will divide the world into ten governmental regions (Dan 2:41–44; Rev 17:12–13). Once that is accomplished, the world will rejoice, and then, in the midst of having just brought that global peace, the Beast will be "fatally" wounded before the eyes of the world and will be proclaimed dead (Rev 13:3, 14). He will be "fatally" wounded on the right side of his body, losing his right eye and his arm, which will be almost certainly his right arm (Zech 11:17; Rev 13:16). The world will mourn greatly, and then, most likely three days after witnessing his "death," the Beast will be seen alive, and the world will rejoice over his "resurrection."

In their exuberance at the Beast's resurrection, and after the False Prophet institutes the system of receiving the mark of the Beast in order to participate in the global economy, the world will receive the mark of the Beast upon their own bodies, receiving it on the same places where the Beast suffered his "fatal" wounds—on their right arm or their forehead.

To take the number of the Beast is nothing more than to *identify* with the Beast; it will be done as a sign of *devotion* to him, and the reason the mark of his name will be taken on either the right hand or forehead is because, in order to identify with the Beast, to honor the sacrifice of his life for the global peace, people will take the mark on the same parts of the body where the Beast, the supposed savior, suffered his "fatal" wounds, as is explained for us in Zechariah 11:17.

> Woe to the worthless shepherd,
> Who leaves the flock!
> A sword shall be against *his arm*
> And against *his right eye*;
> *His arm* shall completely wither,
> And *his right eye* shall be totally blinded. (NKJV)

The "worthless shepherd" is the Beast, the false Christ, a contrast to the "good shepherd," Jesus Christ (John 10:11–14). We are told, very clearly, in Zechariah 11:17 that the Beast suffers terrible wounds to "his right eye" and to "his arm," and, as discussed earlier, it is almost certain that arm that is wounded is his right arm. These are the same "mortal" wound(s) received by the Beast as described in Revelation 13, the wounds that lead the world to believe that the Beast has been killed (Rev 13:3, 13:11, 14), from which "mortal" wound he will be "healed," so that the world will hail him as resurrected. This will affirm him, to the world, as Christ returned.

The places upon their bodies where people will take the mark of the Beast are the same places where the Beast suffered his wounds—his wounds, as per Zechariah 11:17, were to his right eye and to his (right) arm. It will not be possible for people to take the mark directly on one's eye, so, as a result, instead of taking the mark directly on the right eye, people will place the mark just *above* their right eye, which will place the mark on their forehead. They can also take the mark upon their right arm, which is the other place where the Beast suffered his "mortal" wound.

To take the mark of the Beast on one's right arm or hand, or on one's forehead above the right eye, is to *commemorate* the *sacrifice* of the Beast, to commemorate the *wounds* that led to his "death," the sacrifice of himself in service of bringing peace to humanity, from which "death" he was "resurrected." To take the mark of the Beast is nothing more than to identify with him, to honor him, to commemorate his wounds—it is only a sign of devotion.

If a Christian were to do a similar thing in honor of Jesus Christ, it would be like taking an oval tattoo mark on the palms of your hands and on the tops of your feet, to signify the nail wounds of the cross. In so doing, the Christian would be honoring Jesus Christ, celebrating and commemorating his sacrifice and showing their devotion to him as their Savior. It is in exactly that same way that people will take the mark of the Beast and take it on the same spots where he suffered his wounds, as outlined in Zechariah 11:17—to celebrate and commemorate his sacrifice and to show their devotion to him as their savior.

WHAT WILL THE MARK LOOK LIKE?

The Bible very clearly tells us that the mark of the Beast will be 666, but what will that 666 look like?

Very often, when people depict the mark of the Beast on someone, they usually show the three Arabic numerals 666 emblazoned in the center of one's forehead (which, as we have just seen, will not be accurate, since the spot on the forehead where that mark will be placed will almost certainly be *above the right eye*, above the place where Beast suffered his wound, not the center of the forehead). However, it is almost certain that people will *not* be walking around with the blatant Arabic numerals 666 on their bodies, as Satan is much more clever than that. The 666 mark will, at the very least, almost certainly be a *stylization* of that number, and there can be literally hundreds of ways that could look—below are only two examples of a stylized Arabic numerals 666.

The Mark of the Beast

It is also possible that, rather than Arabic numerals, 666 can be stylized in Greek letters, Hebrew letters, or Latin letters, as follows:

DCLXVI

There are so many ways to stylize 666 that it will not be apparent as to what it actually is. However it will be stylized, it will be subtle and effective, and also deceptive, but people will know that it is the mark of his *name*, even if they don't recognize it as the Arabic numerals 666.

HOW DOES ONE GET THE MARK OF THE BEAST?

How will one go about securing the mark of the Beast upon one's forehead or right arm/hand?

It seems clear that the only way to get the mark is to worship *the image* of the Beast, which is to worship the Beast himself, as is affirmed by the following verses in Revelation:

> He was granted power to give breath to the image of the beast, that the image of the beast should both speak and cause as many as would not worship the image of the beast to be killed. He causes all, both small and great, rich and poor, free and slave, to receive a mark on their right hand or on their foreheads, and that no one may buy or sell except one who has the mark or the name of the beast, or the number of his name. (13:15-17 NKJV)

> Then a third angel followed them, saying with a loud voice, "If anyone worships the beast and his image, and receives his mark on his forehead or on his hand, he himself shall also drink of the wine of the wrath of God, which is poured out full strength into the cup of His indignation. He shall be tormented with fire and brimstone in the presence of the holy angels and in the presence of the Lamb. And the smoke of their torment ascends forever and ever; and they have no rest day or night, who worship the beast and his image, and whoever receives the mark of his name." (14:9-11 NKJV)

> So the first went and poured out his bowl upon the earth, and a foul and loathsome sore came upon the men who had the mark of the beast and those who worshiped his image. (16:2 NKJV)

> Then the beast was captured, and with him the false prophet who worked signs in his presence, by which he deceived those who received the mark of the beast and those who worshiped his image. (19:20 NKJV)

In every instance, receiving the mark of the Beast is connected with the worship of his image. It is almost certain that the only way to receive the mark of the Beast is to worship his image, the image/statue of the Beast that will be erected and animated by the False Prophet.

The entire system of receiving the mark of the Beast is designed and instituted by the False Prophet for one reason only—to cause the world to worship and follow the Beast—and the mark of the Beast will represent that you are a follower and worshiper of the Beast.

WHAT ARE THE CONSEQUENCES OF RECEIVING THE MARK?

To receive the mark of the Beast will be no small thing, for it will have enormous and catastrophic consequences. The Bible is very clear—all those who receive the mark of the Beast are declaring themselves as belonging to him (just as cattle are branded by their owner) and, in so doing, those people will suffer condemnation in the Lake of Fire, commonly called "hell."

> . . . If anyone worships the beast and his image, and receives his mark on his forehead or on his hand, he himself shall also drink of the wine of the wrath of God, which is poured out full strength into the cup of his indignation. He shall be tormented with fire and brimstone in the presence of the holy angels and in the presence of the Lamb. And the smoke of their torment ascends forever and ever; and they have no rest day or night, who worship the beast and his image, and whoever receives the mark of his name. (Rev 14:9–11 NKJV)

To take the mark of the Beast is to be doomed.

WHAT IS THE MARK?—A CHIP? A TATTOO?

As previously discussed, it is virtually certain that the mark will not, in any way, be any sort of technological chip. In fact, there is very good biblical reason to understand that the mark will, in fact, be a tattoo—nothing more than a mark of ink upon skin. What biblical support is there for that?

We are told the following in Leviticus:

> You shall not make any cuttings in your flesh for the dead, *nor tattoo any marks* on you: I am the LORD." (19:28 NKJV)

Why does God expressly command us to *not* take any tattoo marks upon our bodies?

On the one hand, it can certainly be because, since we are created in God's "image" and "likeness" (Genesis 1:26, and "likeness" means that we physically *look* like him), by marking up our bodies with the markings of any sort of tattoo, we are in fact defacing the likeness of God.

However, in the context of the mark of the Beast, there seems to be a much more profound reason that God tells us *not* to take tattoos upon our bodies, and it is for this reason—if we start to put marks on our bodies, tattoo or otherwise, it will start to *condition* us to *accept* marks upon our bodies. Eventually, a day will come when people will be faced with the choice of taking the mark of the Beast or not, and if people have already gotten used to marking their bodies with tattoos, then it would be no big deal to take just another mark, the mark of the Beast, upon themselves, especially when that mark is to honor the supposed savior of the world.

Also, it is noteworthy that in Leviticus 19:28 God specifically refers to a tattoo as "marks," which, in its very language, denotes some sort of similarity, or connection, to the "mark" of the Beast.

As a result, when God tells us in Leviticus 19:28 to not take any tattoo "marks" upon our bodies, he is in fact being merciful, warning us so as to protect us from the coming mark of the Beast. As discussed, to take the mark of the Beast is to ensure one's own destruction, and God does *not* want *anyone* to be destroyed (1 Tim 2:3–4; 2 Pet 3:9).

As a result of God's explicit command, or warning, in Leviticus 19:28, to not take tattoo "marks" upon our bodies, and since we know that the Beast will have a "mark" that people *will* take upon their bodies, there is good reason to understand that the mark of the Beast will, in fact, be a tattoo, ink on skin, and nothing more.

BUYING AND SELLING

We are very clearly told that in order to participate in the economy of the world, one must have the mark of the Beast.

> It also forced all people, great and small, rich and poor, free and slave, to receive a mark on their right hands or on their foreheads, so that they could not buy or sell unless they had the mark, which is the name of the beast or the number of its name. (Rev 13:16–17 NIV)

We are told that during the reign of the Beast if anyone wants to buy or sell anything, they can only do so if they have the mark of the Beast. What does that mean?

People often say that the mark of the Beast is in fact the *means* by which the buying and selling transactions are completed, that the mark is like a microchip version of a debit card through which one would buy and sell. But, as already discussed, that would be impossible, since everyone would have to have their own singular, unique, and distinct number in order for that to be possible—i.e., each person would need to have *their* own number. In reality, though, people will have only the *one* number, the *same* number, the number of *his* name, the one number 666. So how then are we to understand having the number and being able to buy and sell? We can understand it as follows.

The mark of the Beast will *not* be the *means* by which people buy and sell, for the reasons outlined above, as that would be impossible and would require billions of unique numbers; rather, the mark of the Beast will only be a *sign* of devotion to the Beast and of *belonging* to his kingdom—it will be a sign of belonging to his *system*.

A very similar, yet opposite, thing existed in Nazi Germany that illustrates the principle of the mark.

In Nazi Germany, Jews were singled out from among the population and were forced to wear a mark. In their case, they were forced to wear a yellow star of David, large and clearly visible, on the outside of their clothes. That was their mark. Why were the Jews forced to wear the mark of the star of David? For one reason only—to *identify* that they were Jews, nothing more. What was the reason the Nazis wanted them identified to the rest of the population? Simply this—if someone was a Jew, they had virtually no rights, and any non-Jew would be in their right to refuse to do business with a Jew. So, in that case, the yellow star of David was a mark that said, "I don't have to do business with you."

The mark of the Beast will be exactly this same kind of thing, but from the opposite end. In the reign of the Beast, if someone has the mark of the Beast, that will signify that they *belong* to the kingdom of the Beast, that they *belong* to the system of his kingdom. By belonging to the system of the Beast, then when a shop owner sees a customer come in, and the customer has the mark of the Beast, the shop owner can recognize, and know right away, "I can do business with you," and then the customer buys however they want, and pays however they want—cash, credit, crypto, barter, or whatever, a normal transaction. So, the mark itself is not, in any way, the *means* by which the *transaction* will be done; rather, having the mark is only to *identify* that someone can do business with you.

Likewise, in that system, if someone comes into a store and does *not* have the mark, the shop owner can say, "I *can't* do business with you," and so, by *not* having the mark of the Beast, you cannot buy or sell, because you don't *belong*. So the mark of the Beast only signifies that you belong, and, by belonging, people can do business with you, whether buying or selling.

NOT EVERYONE WILL WORSHIP THE BEAST

Often, we hear people teach that every human being on the planet will worship the Beast, but that is not true. In fact, we are specifically told in Revelation 20:4,

> I saw thrones on which were seated those who had been given authority to judge. And I saw the souls of those who had been beheaded because of their testimony about Jesus and because of the word of God. *They had not worshiped the beast or its image and had not received its mark* on their foreheads or their hands. They came to life and reigned with Christ a thousand years. (NIV)

There will certainly be people on Earth who will *not* worship the Beast, and this will include not only Christians and the church, but non-Christians as well (which we will see when we look at the judgment of Jesus in Matthew 25:31–46 and Zechariah 14:16–18). Many of those people, probably most of them, who do not worship the Beast or receive his mark will be put to death by the False Prophet for not worshiping the Beast, but many will escape and will not be put to death—they will find a way to avoid capture, find a way to eat, buy, and sell without the mark of the Beast (that is, buy and sell and eat outside of his system).

If this is true, and not everyone will worship the Beast and take the number of his name, then how to do we understand the following?

> It also forced *all people*, great and small, rich and poor, free and slave, to receive a mark on their right hands or on their foreheads (Rev 13:16 NIV)

> *All inhabitants of the earth* will worship the beast—whose names *have not* been written in the Lamb's book of life, the Lamb who was slain from the creation of the world." (Rev 13:8 NIV)

From the two verses above, it seems like everyone on Earth will worship the Beast; however, Revelation 13:8 qualifies that when it tells us that will only apply to those "whose names have not been written in the Lamb's Book of Life." We will see that is not only a reference to Christians but to non-Christians as well, for, as we shall see, the sheep of Matthew 25:31–46, together with the goats, are *all* non-Christians— the sheep are the non-Christians who *do not* take the mark of the Beast, while the goats are the non-Christians who *do* take the mark of the Beast. We will also see that many, if not all, of those non-Christian sheep help Christians during the time of the Beast's great persecution of the church, and, as a result of helping a "righteous person," those non-Christians will get the same reward as the righteous man.

> Anyone who welcomes you welcomes me, and anyone who welcomes me welcomes the one who sent me. Whoever welcomes a prophet as a prophet will receive a prophet's reward, and *whoever welcomes a righteous person* as a righteous person *will receive a righteous person's reward*. And if anyone gives even a cup of cold water to one of these little ones who is my disciple, truly I tell you, that person will certainly not lose their reward. (Matt 10:41–42 NIV)

If anyone helps a "righteous person"—helps a Christian—that person "will receive a righteous person's reward"; that is to say, they will receive the same reward as the Christian. What reward does the Christian receive? The Christian inherits the kingdom. Therefore, for any non-Christian (the "sheep" of Matthew 25:31–46) that helps a Christian in that time of persecution, they will receive the same reward as the Christian—they will inherit the kingdom of Jesus Christ (also affirmed in Isaiah 65:17–25).

Though the Beast will rule the world during his three-and-a-half-year reign, and though the Beast will be celebrated and worshiped as Christ returned, his kingdom will have both weakness and division (Dan 2:41–43; 7:24; Rev 16:12), and not all will follow the Beast.

GOD'S MERCY

During the three-and-a-half-year reign of the Beast, during the time of the great persecution of the church (Matt 24:9), God does not abandon the world; rather he shows the world great mercy and speaks to it the voice of truth.

During the three-and-a-half-year reign of the Beast, God will have Two Witnesses in Jerusalem who will be exposing the Beast, to the world, for the liar that he is. God will also have, during that same time, 144,000 preachers of truth sent out into the whole world, into the kingdom of the Beast, to proclaim the true gospel.

16

THE TWO WITNESSES AND THE 144,000

GOD LOVES THE WORLD (John 3:16) and he never abandons humanity; rather, he redeems humanity. Whether in the midst of judgment or on the eve of impending judgment, God is present with humanity, speaking truth to humanity so as to encourage people to turn to him, for it is his clearly stated will that he wants *all* people to come to him and have salvation (1 Tim 2:3–4; 2 Pet 3:9).

It will be no different during the three-and-a-half-year reign of the Beast, which occurs during the first half of Seal 5. The church, in all of its fullness, is completely present upon the Earth during that time (Matt 24:9; John 17:15; Rev 13:7, 10; 16:6), and during that same time the Beast will persecute, and overcome, the church (Rev 13:7). But also, during that same three-and-a-half-year reign of the Beast, the time of the persecution of the church, God will have other voices of truth in addition to his church, proclaiming truth to the world, proclaiming the gospel and exposing the Beast for the liar that he is. There will be two preeminent men upon the Earth during that time who will do exactly this, and they are described in Revelation as the "Two Witnesses."

THE TWO WITNESSES

The Two Witnesses are described in Revelation 11.

> Then I was given a reed like a measuring rod. And the angel stood, saying, "Rise and measure the temple of God, the altar, and those who worship there. But leave out the court which is outside the temple, and do not measure it, for it has been given to the Gentiles. And they will tread the holy city underfoot for forty-two months. And I will give power to my two witnesses, and they will prophesy one thousand two hundred and sixty days, clothed in sackcloth." These are the two olive trees and the two lampstands standing before the God of the earth. And if anyone wants to harm them, fire proceeds from their

mouth and devours their enemies. And if anyone wants to harm them, he must be killed in this manner. These have power to shut heaven, so that no rain falls in the days of their prophecy; and they have power over waters to turn them to blood, and to strike the earth with all plagues, as often as they desire. When they finish their testimony, the beast that ascends out of the bottomless pit will make war against them, overcome them, and kill them. And their dead bodies will lie in the street of the great city which spiritually is called Sodom and Egypt, where also our Lord was crucified. Then those from the peoples, tribes, tongues, and nations will see their dead bodies three and a half days, and not allow their dead bodies to be put into graves. And those who dwell on the earth will rejoice over them, make merry, and send gifts to one another, because these two prophets tormented those who dwell on the earth. Now after the three and a half days the breath of life from God entered them, and they stood on their feet, and great fear fell on those who saw them. And they heard a loud voice from heaven saying to them, "Come up here." And they ascended to heaven in a cloud, and their enemies saw them. In the same hour there was a great earthquake, and a tenth of the city fell. In the earthquake seven thousand people were killed, and the rest were afraid and gave glory to the God of heaven. (Rev 11:1–13 NIV)

In this passage, the angel tells John to measure the temple in Jerusalem, but to *not* measure the court *outside* the temple, saying that what is outside the temple will be given over to the Gentiles to trample, or tread, over that land for forty-two months, which is three and a half years. This three and a half years is the same three and a half years of the reign of the Beast, which is why God describes Jerusalem as being given to the Gentiles, for during that three-and-a-half-year period Jerusalem will be ruled by the Beast and his kingdom.

God then tells us that during that same three-and-a-half-year period he will have Two Witnesses to whom he will give power, and the Two Witnesses will prophesy to the world for 1,260 days, which is also three and a half years—so the 1,260 days during which the Two Witnesses will prophesy is the same as the forty-two months of the Gentile rule of Jerusalem, which is the same as the three-and-a-half-year rule of the Beast. From the verses that follow, we know that these Two Witnesses will be located in Jerusalem, preaching truth and prophesying to the world from Jerusalem (Rev 11:8). This is why the account of the Two Witnesses begins with John being told to measure the temple in Jerusalem, for all the events around the Two Witnesses will take place in Jerusalem.

We are also told that no one on Earth can harm the Two Witnesses, the implication being that people will try to harm them, for we are told that if anyone does try to harm them, fire will proceed from the mouth of the Witnesses and kill those trying to harm them (Rev 11:5). We are also told that the Two Witnesses will be given power to shut the sky so that no rain falls and will also have power to turn the waters to blood *and* bring all kinds of plagues upon the Earth (Rev 11:6).

WHAT IS THE PURPOSE OF THE TWO WITNESSES?

First and foremost, we must understand that these two men are, in fact, *witnesses*, and they are witnesses *to God*, which means that these two men will be *testifying* to the world about *God* and will be proclaiming his truth to the world, for all the world to hear. As these events will be taking place in the modern age, we can know that the entire world will see and hear the Two Witnesses—they will be on TV, on radio, on the internet; the *entire world* will know of them and will hear what they will be saying.

It is also very important to understand that the Two Witnesses will be proclaiming God's truth *during* the three-and-a-half-year reign of the Beast. So, the world that will be hearing their message will be the world that is under the rule of the Beast, the world that is his kingdom, the world that is worshiping the Beast, that is taking upon themselves the mark of the Beast so that they can identify as belonging to his kingdom, and thereby participate in the economy of the world.

As a result, for those devotees of the Beast, for those who have his mark, which will be a great many people on Earth, those people will hate the Two Witnesses, for the Two Witnesses will be exposing the Beast for what he is. Whereas the world will be worshiping the Beast as Christ returned, the Witnesses will be exposing the Beast as a liar, proclaiming to the world that the Beast is *not* Christ returned. To the Jews in Jerusalem who will be rebuilding the temple as per the Beast's command, and who will therefore be accepting the Beast as Messiah, the Two Witnesses will be proclaiming to the Jews and to the world that the Beast is *not* the Messiah. To the whole world, the Two Witnesses will be proclaiming Jesus Christ as *yet* to come and will be proclaiming to the world the true gospel, and they will be calling on all the inhabitants of the Earth to repent, to turn away from the Beast and to believe in Jesus Christ, who is yet to come.

The world, of course, will, at first, consider these two men to be lunatics—the Beast will have brought world peace, a flourishing economy, will have been "killed" and "resurrected" in full view of the world, proclaimed by a great Christian leader (the False Prophet) as Christ returned, with that same Christian leader performing miracles in full view of the world to prove that what he is saying about the Beast as Christ returned is true. The Beast will also be overcoming the true church, who will not be bowing to him, and, by the Beast overcoming the true church, the world will see that as further proof that the Beast is Christ returned. It is in that context that the Two Witnesses come upon the world's stage. They will come onto the world's stage in Jerusalem, and they will be proclaiming to the world that *everything* about the Beast, including his "death" and "resurrection," is a lie, and they will also be exposing the False Prophet as a liar, and the whole world will hear the words and message of the

Two Witnesses. The False Prophet of course will slander and demean the Two Witnesses in every way possible, and, most likely, will continue to perform miracles for the world to see, since it is by his performance of such miracles that he deceived the world to believe his testimony about the Beast (Rev 13:13-14). However, the Two Witnesses will then, themselves, perform miracles for the whole world to see—they can prevent the rain from coming and, together with that, can turn the waters to blood, which means the Two Witnesses can affect the world's supply of drinking water, and, as such, can bring distress to the world.

Once the Two Witnesses begin to demonstrate the power that they have been given to exercise, the world will take notice and there will be fear. In addition to the prevention of rain from the sky and turning the waters into blood, the Two Witnesses can, at their own discretion, cause other plagues to come upon the world. Again, the world will see this, and the world will fear them.

It will also certainly be in this context that people will try to kill the Two Witnesses, who will be blamed for bringing suffering upon the world, in contrast to the peace and prosperity that was brought by the Beast. The world will see people try to kill the Two Witnesses, and they will see, on TV, online, and through any and every other means, that when anyone tries to kill the Two Witnesses, fire will come out of the mouths of the Witnesses and those people looking to do harm to the Two Witnesses will die as a result. The world will see that the Two Witnesses are untouchable, and the world will have fear.

What is the purpose of shutting the sky from raining, of turning waters to blood, of bringing plagues as often as one desires? Isn't this evil?

No, this is *not* evil; rather, those are acts of love and mercy. We must remember that the Two Witnesses are addressing an entire world that has been deceived by the Beast and the False Prophet, who themselves will be performing miraculous signs in order to deceive the world (Rev 13:13-14), and so the Two Witnesses will counter those deceiving signs with demonstrations of God's power, and the signs that the Two Witnesses will do—shutting the sky from raining, turning the waters into blood, bringing plagues—will *not* be reproducible by the False Prophet. The very nature of the powers that will be demonstrated by the Two Witnesses will bear witness to the world that the Witnesses are of God.

It is also for this same reason that the Two Witnesses will be untouchable, and also the reason why anyone who wants to harm them will be killed by fire coming from their mouths. When the world sees fire coming from the mouths of the Two Witnesses against anyone who wants to harm them, the world will see, and know, that this is of God, for no one, anywhere, can produce fire from their mouths, and neither will the False Prophet be able to do so. Once again, the very means by which the Witnesses will deal with those trying to harm them will be, in their very nature, unreproducible by anyone, including the False Prophet, and so will testify to the world that the Witnesses are from God.

In light of all of this, in light of the clear demonstration of the power of the Two Witnesses, it will be impossible for the world to ignore the Witnesses and, as a result, it will be impossible for the world to not hear their message, their proclamation of the truth. It is for *that* reason, for the reason of ensuring that the entire world *will* hear the truth in the time of complete lies and deception, that God will give his Two Witnesses the power that he will—it is because of his love and mercy for the world that God will make sure that his message of truth cannot be ignored, for God loves the world.

WHO ARE THE TWO WITNESSES?

Of course, the Bible does not tell us anything about the personal identity of the Two Witnesses, but, because of the description of their powers, people often propose candidates as to the identity of the Two Witnesses, and it's usually the same two candidates, as follows.

Since the Witnesses are specifically described as having the power to shut the sky so that it doesn't rain, and as having the power to turn the waters into blood, people often say that the Two Witnesses will be Elijah and Moses. Why?

In the Old Testament, the prophet Elijah also shut the sky so that it didn't rain (1 Kgs 17:1–7; Jas 5:17). Also, one of the plagues that God brought upon Egypt through Moses was to turn the Nile, and the waters of Egypt, into blood (Exod 7:14–25). For those reasons alone, some people propose that the Two Witnesses are Elijah and Moses. However, this is impossible and is based on nothing biblical, and, in fact, such an idea contradicts the very clear teaching of the Bible.

First, both Moses and Elijah *died*, and so they cannot die a second time (Heb 9:27)—the Bible is clear, people can only die *once*. The death of Moses is specifically outlined in Deuteronomy 34:5 and in Jude 9, but, for Elijah, some people teach that Elijah did not die, and that is based on the account of Elijah being taken up *into heaven* (2 Kgs 2:11). Usually, people teach that Elijah was taken up into heaven on a chariot of fire, which of course he was not, for the Bible specifically tells us that the chariot of fire came only to *separate* Elijah and Elisha, and it was the whirlwind, or tornado, *not* the chariot of fire, that came and took Elijah.

It is certainly true that Elijah was taken by the whirlwind *into* heaven, but the "heaven" being talked about is *not* the heaven where God established his throne; rather, it is only the earthly sky—the whirlwind came and lifted Elijah up into the air (and the wording used specifically does say "into" heaven, as in "lifted up into," which also denotes the sky), and it carried him away and placed him down somewhere else, *on Earth*.

We know that Elijah was placed down onto the Earth, by the whirlwind, at another location, and that he did *not* die and was *not* taken up to the "third heaven" (2 Cor 12:2), the place where God temporarily established his throne, for seven years later, seven years *after* the whirlwind takes Elijah up into the sky and carries him away,

Elijah writes and sends a letter to the king of Judah, King Jehoram (2 Chr 21:12–20). This letter was written and sent by Elijah seven years *after* Elijah was taken up into the sky.

Now, of course, for those who teach that Elijah was lifted up to the third heaven, this presents a huge problem, so, to still try and hold on to the idea that Elijah was in fact taken up into the third heaven, where God has his throne, and still explain how a letter can come from Elijah seven years after the fact, those same people say that Elijah wrote that letter *prophetically* before he was taken up, and so he wrote that letter years earlier—however, that still, in no way, explains how such a letter was sent seven years later.

The fact is that Elijah was *not* carried up to the third heaven, the place where God temporarily put his throne, but instead Elijah was only lifted up by the whirlwind into the *sky*, and transported to another location, *on Earth*, and put down—and we know this as an inarguable certainty from the following:

> *No one has ascended to heaven* but He who came down from heaven, that is, the Son of Man who is in heaven. (John 3:13 NKJV)

The Bible is very clear—*no human being* ascended to God's heaven (the third heaven) before Jesus Christ ascended to heaven, and Jesus Christ ascended to heaven forty days *after* his resurrection. That is the end of the discussion—we can be absolutely certain, from John 3:13, that Elijah absolutely did *not* ascend to God's heaven. As a result, and based on the fact of the letter that was sent seven years after Elijah was taken up by the whirlwind, we can know that Elijah was only lifted up into the sky and transported *away from Elisha*, but the "mantle," or cloak, of Elijah *remained*—why is this significant?

It was God's will for Elijah to end his prophetic ministry and for Elisha, Elijah's servant scribe, to take up that same ministry. However, when Elijah says to Elisha that he (Elijah) will be taken away *from him*, Elisha adamantly says that he, Elisha, will *never* leave Elijah, that he will always remain Elijah's servant (2 Kgs 2:1–6). It is in *that* context, as Elijah and Elisha were walking, that, first, a chariot of fire came to *separate* Elisha from Elijah (2 Kgs 2:11); then, the whirlwind came and lifted Elijah away, taking him up into *the sky* (2 Kgs 2:11); and then, after Elijah was removed, the chariot of fire left but Elijah's prophetic *mantle* remained behind. At that point, Elisha, now without Elijah, takes up Elijah's mantle, puts it on, and takes up Elijah's prophetic ministry (2 Kgs 2:13). The *reason* that all of this happened was very simple—Elisha refused to leave Elijah, despite God's clearly stated will, so God just took Elijah away from Elisha so that Elisha would have no choice but to take up Elijah's mantle and continue the prophetic ministry—that is the *only* reason the events of the chariot of fire and the whirlwind occurred. Elijah himself, after being lifted up into the sky by the whirlwind, was transported by that same whirlwind to be put down somewhere else, *away from Elisha*, and then, seven years later, Elijah writes and sends his letter to King Jehoram. Later, when his time came, Elijah died, like everyone else.

All that to say that any argument that proposes one of the Two Witnesses is Elijah, basing that on the idea that Elijah never died, but was taken up into God's heaven, is a completely baseless argument—Elijah is absolutely *not* one of the Two Witnesses, nor is Moses, for both Elijah and Moses died, and a man can only die *once* (Heb 9:27).

As a result, all as we can say in regard to the identity of the Two Witnesses is that the Two Witnesses will be two men who will be raised by God at that specific time, for the specific purpose of being his Witnesses to the world during the reign of the Beast, and those two men will be given *similar* powers as were given by God to Moses and Elijah. That is the full extent of what we can say about the identity of the Two Witnesses.

THE DEATH OF THE TWO WITNESSES

The Two Witnesses will be untouchable; no one will be able to harm them, though some will try, for much of the world will wish them dead. We are told that the Witnesses will prophesy, exercising the authority of God and proclaiming his truth to the world for 1,260 days, for three and a half years, and then, after that three-and-a-half-year period is over, we are told that they will finish their testimony. At that point we are told that after three and a half years of the Two Witnesses proclaiming truth to the world, and being untouchable during that entire time, the Beast himself will personally go to Jerusalem to confront the Witnesses. With the entire world watching—on television, online, and via any and every other means—the Beast will come against the Two Witnesses and will, in full view of the world, kill them. The Beast will accomplish what no one else on Earth was able to do—he will bring harm, and death, to the Two Witnesses.

The death of the Two Witnesses will bring euphoria to the world. The Witnesses will be killed in Jerusalem, and their bodies will lie, unburied, in the street, lying where they were killed, and their bodies will lie in the streets of Jerusalem for three and a half days, and through that whole time the world will see and watch their dead bodies as they lie in the streets of Jerusalem (Rev 11:9–11). In fact, we are told that it will be the people of the world themselves who will not allow the bodies of the Two Witnesses to be buried; rather, the world will want their bodies to suffer the indignity of just lying dead in the street. The world, in its euphoria over the death of those two "tormentors," will celebrate on a global scale, turning the celebration of the death of the Witnesses into their new Christmas, for we are told that the world will celebrate the death of the Witnesses by exchanging gifts with one another (Rev 11:1)—it will be a time of great celebration.

Moreover, having watched the Beast accomplish what no one else could do, namely, killing the Two Witnesses, the world will be even more convinced that the Beast is Christ returned, unstoppable and unopposable.

The bodies of the Two Witnesses will lie in the streets of Jerusalem for three and a half days, during which entire time the whole world will be watching them on television, online, and via any other media, all while they exchange gifts in celebration of their death. However, after three and a half days, in full view of the entire world, a voice will be heard, from heaven, saying in a loud voice, "Come up here," and at that point the bodies of the two dead Witnesses will resurrect, in full view of the world, and the Two Witnesses will rise from the dead, as the whole world is watching. The resurrected Witnesses will ascend into the sky, into a cloud, to heaven. This will be seen by the entire world while the world is celebrating the death of the Witnesses and exchanging gifts in that celebration.

We are told that upon the ascension of the Two Witnesses, a great earthquake will strike Jerusalem and one tenth of the city will be destroyed and seven thousand people will die. We are then told that the *rest* of the people in Jerusalem, those who are not killed by the earthquake, will be afraid by what they had seen and heard, and that *all* those people will give glory to the living God (Rev 11:13). The fact that all the people that remain alive in Jerusalem turn to God and give him glory is another strong affirmation that during the reign of the Beast there will still be many people who will be non-Christians and who will *not* take the mark of the Beast.

THE TIMELINE OF THOSE EVENTS

With the death of the Two Witnesses we see, for a fact, that the Beast is himself, personally, *in Jerusalem* at the three-and-a-half-year point into his reign. This is important, for, as we have already seen, it is at the three-and-a-half-year point into his reign that the Beast goes to the newly rebuilt temple, *in Jerusalem*, where he stops the newly commenced daily sacrifice, enters the temple, goes into the holy of holies, and sets up his own throne there, in the holy of holies of the rebuilt temple, the abomination of desolation. All of these events align. As a result, we can understand the timeline of those events as follows.

At the start of his reign, the Beast, as part of the global peace negotiated by him, and after his fake death and resurrection, will allow the Jews to begin to rebuild the temple in Jerusalem, which will cause the Jews to hail him as Messiah. The temple will be completed right at about the three-and-a-half-year point into the reign of the Beast and, at that point, the Jews will just begin to offer up the daily sacrifice, as they did in the Old Testament.

During the three and a half years that the temple is being rebuilt, the Two Witnesses will also be in Jerusalem proclaiming God's truth to the world and exposing the Beast and the False Prophet for the liars that they are. The Two Witnesses will be untouchable and no one will be able to harm them. At the three-and-a-half-year point of the Beast's reign, right at the time that the rebuilding of the temple has just been completed and the daily sacrifice is just recommencing, the Beast will himself go to Jerusalem to confront the Two Witnesses and will kill them, and the whole world will celebrate. This then places the Beast in Jerusalem at the three-and-a-half-year point into his reign. After the Two Witnesses have been killed, most likely during the three and a half days that they are dead and lying in the street, the Beast, who is already in Jerusalem, will then go to the newly rebuilt temple in Jerusalem, stop the just-commencing daily sacrifice, and enthrone *himself* in that same temple, thereby proclaiming himself as the Living God (2 Thess 2:4).

It is very likely that the Beast will enthrone himself in the rebuilt temple *before* the resurrection of the Two Witnesses, riding the euphoria of the world, who are not only celebrating the death of the Witnesses, but are also celebrating the only one who was capable of killing them, the Beast. It is very reasonable to conclude that, as part of that global euphoria and worldwide celebration over the death of the Two Witnesses, the Beast enthrones himself in the temple.

It is then at that point, after the Beast has enthroned himself in the temple, that the voice is heard from heaven calling the Witnesses to come up, at which point the great earthquake hits Jerusalem and seven thousand people die as a result.

It is very reasonable to understand that as being the sequence of events, for, as we have already seen, it is the event of the Beast enthroning himself in the temple, the abomination of desolation, that triggers the Great Tribulation (Matt 24:15–21). As a result, we can understand that after the act of abomination by the Beast, the Two Witnesses are *then* resurrected, and a great earthquake hits Jerusalem and many people die—all while the Beast is still in Jerusalem and enthroned in the holy of holies. The resurrection of the Two Witnesses, as well as the ensuing earthquake, will signify the turning point in the reign of the Beast—the resurrection of the Witnesses, and the ensuing earthquake, can be seen as the official launch of the Tribulation.

THREE AND A HALF DAYS

It is interesting to note that the bodies of the Two Witnesses will lie in the streets of Jerusalem for three and a half *days*, and that their death and resurrection will come three and a half *years* into the reign of the Beast—this cannot be coincidence. What would be the significance of this? We can understand it as follows.

The reason the bodies of the Two Witnesses will lie dead in the streets of Jerusalem for three and a half *days* is because each day will be representing a year of the reign of the Beast. Just as those events will occur three and a half *years* into his reign, so the bodies of the Two Witnesses will lie dead in the street for three and a half *days*, so three and a half *days* represents the three and a half *years* of the Beast's rule. With the resurrection of the Two Witnesses after the three and a half days, whereby their resurrection demonstrates God's power as overcoming the power of the Beast, this signifies the end of the three-and-a-half-year rule of the Beast, signifying that now the power of God will overcome the reign of the Beast upon the Earth. The resurrection of the Two Witnesses occurs just after the Beast's act of abomination, and so their resurrection is a declaration of God's power, to be manifest fully in the Great Tribulation, which will begin immediately after the resurrection of the Two Witnesses. It is also important to note that, in that demonstration of God's power as manifest in the resurrection of the Two Witnesses, all the people in Jerusalem who survive the great earthquake will give glory to God (Rev 11:13)—the miraculous demonstration of God's power leads to faith.

This understanding of a day representing a year is also completely in line with Daniel's description of the entire seven-year period as being a period of seven days, again, a day for a year (Dan 9:24–27).

The Beast ruled unopposed for three and a half years, and so the Two Witnesses lie dead for three and a half days, after which they are resurrected, a witness to God and his power and a witness to the end of the reign of the Beast.

Also, just as the Beast ruled for three and a half years, now there will be Tribulation for that equal time—the duration of the Tribulation that will now come upon the world will be equal in duration to the reign of the Beast.

Also, just as the rule of the Beast was based upon the world's witness of his fake resurrection, likewise, with the Two Witnesses, the world will now see a *real* resurrection, and the world will be astonished, amazed, and afraid. Just as the fake resurrection of the Beast began his reign, so the real resurrection of the Two Witnesses begins God's reclamation of the Earth and the institution of his dominion, the kingdom of Jesus Christ, which dominion he won back by his sinless life, the second Adam redeeming what the first Adam had given away.

THE 144,000

During that same three-and-a-half-year reign of the Beast, the same three and a half years during which the Two Witnesses will be proclaiming God and his truth to the world, God will also have 144,000 people who will also be proclaiming his truth to the entire world—they will be preaching the gospel to the world. The 144,000 are outlined for us in Revelation 7.

> After this I saw four angels standing at the four corners of the earth, holding back the four winds of the earth to prevent any wind from blowing on the land or on the sea or on any tree. Then I saw another angel coming up from the east, having the seal of the living God. He called out in a loud voice to the four angels who had been given power to harm the land and the sea: "Do not harm the land or the sea or the trees until we put a seal on the foreheads of

the servants of our God." Then I heard the number of those who were sealed: 144,000 from all the tribes of Israel.

> From the tribe of Judah 12,000 were sealed,
> from the tribe of Reuben 12,000,
> from the tribe of Gad 12,000,
> from the tribe of Asher 12,000,
> from the tribe of Naphtali 12,000,
> from the tribe of Manasseh 12,000,
> from the tribe of Simeon 12,000,
> from the tribe of Levi 12,000,
> from the tribe of Issachar 12,000,
> from the tribe of Zebulun 12,000,
> from the tribe of Joseph 12,000,
> from the tribe of Benjamin 12,000. (7:1–8 NIV)

These same 144,000 are also mentioned in Revelation 14.

> Then I looked, and behold, a Lamb standing on Mount Zion, and with Him one hundred and forty-four thousand, having His Father's name written on their foreheads. And I heard a voice from heaven, like the voice of many waters, and like the voice of loud thunder. And I heard the sound of harpists playing their harps. They sang as it were a new song before the throne, before the four living creatures, and the elders; and no one could learn that song except the hundred and forty-four thousand who were redeemed from the earth. These are the ones who were not defiled with women, for they are virgins. These are the ones who follow the Lamb wherever He goes. These were redeemed from among men, being firstfruits to God and to the Lamb. And in their mouth was found no deceit, for they are without fault before the throne of God. (14:1–5 NKJV)

Who are these 144,000?

The Bible makes it very clear that the 144,000 are 12,000 from each of the 12 tribes of Israel, and then lists each of those tribes for us. What is striking here is that one tribe of Israel is *not* on that list, the tribe of Dan (the half-tribe of Ephraim is designated here as the tribe of Joseph, while the half-tribe of Manasseh is listed separately). Why is Dan missing from this list? Why are there not 12,000 from the tribe of *Dan* that are part of this number?

It is because Dan is the tribe of the Beast, on his mother's side, and the Beast, as a descendant of Dan, brings judgment upon the world, in fulfillment of Jacob's prophecy over his sons (Gen 49:16–18).

Also, it is very important to remember that *only* 36,000 of these 144,000 *are Jews*—the 12,000 each from the tribes of Judah, Levi, and Benjamin—*all* the rest, in the eyes of the world, are *Gentiles*.

It is also important to remember that the identity of the 108,000 non-Jews, that is, their Israelite tribal identity, will be known only to God. The ten lost tribes of Israel have been lost to history since ca. 750 BC, but not lost to God—*we* have no idea who they are or where they are (and, in fact, as previously discussed, there is good reason to understand that the ten lost tribes are in fact the ancestors of much of the Western, or European, nations), but God knows exactly who's who. So, of the 144,000 listed here, 108,000 will in no way, by the world, be identified as being from a tribe of Israel—to the world, those 108,000 will be Gentiles.

THEY ARE SEALED

We are also told that these 144,000 will be "sealed," on their forehead, so as to separate them from the rest of humanity (Rev 7:3–8), and they will be sealed on their foreheads with the seal of God. It's important to understand that the seal upon their foreheads will not be visible to anybody—the seal will be visible only to God and angelic beings (including fallen angelic beings). It's also important to note that they will be sealed on their *foreheads*, which is one of the places where people will take the mark of the Beast. So, whereas people take the mark of the Beast upon their foreheads, these 144,000 will take the mark of God upon their foreheads.

WHAT DO THESE 144,000 DO?

It is striking to note that immediately after we are told about the 144,000, we are told the following:

> After these things I looked, and behold, a great multitude which no one could number, of all nations, tribes, peoples, and tongues, standing before the throne and before the Lamb, clothed with white robes, with palm branches in their hands, and crying out with a loud voice, saying, "Salvation *belongs* to our God who sits on the throne, and to the Lamb!" (Rev 7:9–10 NKJV)

Immediately *after* we are told about the 144,000, we are told of a "great multitude" of people who belong to Christ, surrounding his throne and worshiping him, and we are told, very specifically, that *those* are people who have "*come out of* the Great Tribulation," who survived the reign of the Beast, and who came to faith during his three-and-a-half-year reign.

> These are the ones who come out of the great tribulation, and washed their robes and made them white in the blood of the Lamb. Therefore they are before the throne of God, and serve Him day and night in His temple. And He who sits on the throne will dwell among them. (Rev 14:14–15 NKJV)

There is good reason to understand that the 144,000 who were mentioned immediately before this scene were in fact *responsible* for the proclamation of the gospel during the reign of the Beast, resulting in many people coming to believe in the Lord Jesus Christ. In fact, this is perfectly in line with Jesus' own words as he describes for us Seal 5, when he tells us,

> And this gospel of the kingdom will be preached in all the world as a witness to all the nations, and then the end will come. (Matt 24:14 NKJV)

Jesus tells us that during Seal 5, during the reign of the Beast, *the gospel will be preached* throughout all the world. There is very good reason to understand that when Jesus says this, he is specifically talking about the three-and-a-half-year reign of the Beast, the time that *precedes* the Tribulation, since, starting with the very *next* verse, 24:15, Jesus begins to describe the Tribulation, which implies that the Tribulation itself comes *after* the gospel is preached throughout the whole world.

When we put all this together—the 144,000 sealed people, sealed unto God and separated out for him, the description immediately afterwards of those who have come out of the Tribulation with salvation, Jesus' own words that the gospel will be preached throughout the whole world, almost certainly referring to the time that *precedes* the Tribulation—we can conclude the following: the 144,000 people, sealed by God and separated out for him, are in fact preachers of the gospel, the very ones who will fulfill Jesus' own words of Matthew 24:15 by preaching the gospel throughout all the Earth, to all nations, and many will come to faith.

Also, we must remember that this will be during the three-and-a-half-year reign of the Beast, the exact same time period that the Two Witnesses will be proclaiming truth to the world from Jerusalem, exposing the Beast and the False Prophet as liars.

Taken together—the two Witnesses in Jerusalem *and* the 144,000 upon the Earth preaching the gospel, simultaneous with one another—this shows the immense love and mercy of God, where he does *not* abandon the people of the world, but proclaims truth to the whole world, for all the world to hear, and deeply and incessantly calls out to the world to come to him, and many will.

So, we can conclude that the 144,000 are God's special preachers, powerful preachers of the gospel, 36,000 of whom will be Jews, 108,000 of whom will, to the world, be Gentiles, and these are the ones who will fulfill Jesus' words of Matthew 24:15.

MERCY AND LOVE

Both the Two Witnesses and the 144,000 will be present in the world during the three-and-a-half-year reign of the Beast. The Beast, together with the False Prophet, will be the greatest of deceivers, perpetrating the greatest deception, deceiving the world. But God does not abandon the world; rather, he loves the world, so, for that reason, during that same time of great deception and complete persecution of the church, God will have his two untouchable Witnesses proclaiming the truth to the world for all the world to hear, and the world will hear. He will also have the 144,000, simultaneous with the Two Witnesses, preaching the gospel to all the nations of the world, and the world will hear the gospel.

After the three-and-a-half-year reign of the Beast, the Two Witnesses are killed by the Beast in Jerusalem, upon whose death the Beast enters the rebuilt temple in Jerusalem and enthrones himself in the holy of holies in the temple. Then, in full view of all the world, the Two Witnesses are resurrected, and great fear grips the world, and many people will believe. It is with that event that the Great Tribulation is unleashed.

17

The Great Tribulation

The term "Great Tribulation" comes from Jesus himself, in his description of the events of Seal 5 (Matt 24:21). It is also from Jesus' own words that we know, for a certainty, that the entire Great Tribulation takes place during Seal 5, for when Jesus begins to describe the events of Seal 6, he begins with these words:

> Immediately *after* the tribulation of those days . . . " (Matt 24:29 NKJV)

As a result, from Jesus' own words, we know, without question, that the *entire* Great Tribulation occurs during Seal 5.

We also know, from both Daniel and Jesus, that the Great Tribulation will last for three and a half years. Daniel tells us that at the midpoint of the seven-year period the "abomination" that "makes desolate" will occur (Dan 9:27). Jesus himself tells us that it is this same "abomination of desolation" spoken of by Daniel that triggers the start of the Great Tribulation (Matt 24:15). As a result, since we know from Daniel that the abomination of desolation happens at the midpoint of the seven-year period, at the three-and-a-half-year point, and since we know from Jesus that it is that same abomination of desolation that triggers the start of the Great Tribulation, then we can know that the Great Tribulation will last for the final three and a half years of the seven-year period—the first three and a half years of that seven-year period is the reign of the Beast, while the second three and a half years of that seven-year period is the Great Tribulation. In one sense, we can understand the three-and-a-half-year duration of the Great Tribulation as being a response in equal measure to the three-and-a-half-year reign of the Beast.

We have also seen that at the three-and-a-half-year point into his reign, the Beast will be in Jerusalem, where he will kill the Two Witnesses. Upon the death of the Two Witnesses, the world will be euphoric in its celebration of their deaths and will give all honor and worship to the Beast, the savior of the world.

At that same time that the Beast will be in Jerusalem, at the three-and-a-half-year point of his reign, the rebuilt temple in Jerusalem will have just been completed and the Old Testament daily sacrifice will have just begun to be implemented in the temple. After the Beast has killed the Two Witnesses, in the midst of the world's euphoria over their deaths, and while he is already in Jerusalem, the Beast will go to the rebuilt temple, stop the daily sacrifice (Dan 9:27), go into the holy of holies and there enthrone himself, thereby proclaiming himself to be Almighty God (2 Thess 2:4). His act of enthroning of himself in the rebuilt temple is the abomination of desolation, and that is the event that triggers the Great Tribulation.

It is also at this time, just after the Beast enthrones himself in the temple, that the Two Witnesses, in full view of the world, will be resurrected. The resurrection of the Two Witnesses will mark the beginning of the Tribulation.

WHY WILL THERE BE SUCH TERRIBLE TRIBULATION?

Jesus himself tells us that the Great Tribulation will be unlike any time ever before in the history of the world, and will never be equaled again for its devastation, telling us that if he did not return at the Second Coming, no life would be left on Earth (Matt 24:22).

Why would God allow such terrible devastation? Does God delight in death and destruction?

God does *not* delight in death and destruction; rather, in his infinite love for all humanity (John 3:16), he wants *all* people to come to salvation and be in fellowship with him (1 Tim 2:3–4; 2 Pet 3:9). If this is so, what then is the purpose of the Tribulation? There are at least two purposes.

A NEW DOMINION

Jesus himself, in describing Seals 1–4, describes Seals 1–4 as the "beginning of birth pains" (Matt 24:8 NIV). Seal 5, the reign of the Beast and the entire Great Tribulation, is the full intensity of those birth pains, followed by Seal 6, the fall of the nation Babylon the Great, and finally Seal 7, the resurrection of all believers and the Second Coming. What is actually being born? As discussed, the "birth pains" will result in the birth of a new dominion.

How do we understand the birth of a new dominion? What dominion are we talking about? We can understand it as follows.

When God created man, he gave him dominion over the Earth and over everything upon it (Gen 1:26)—Adam was the rightful lord and ruler of the Earth. But when Adam fell, then, upon his fall, he gave that same dominion to Satan (Luke 4:5–7), who, ever since, has been the rightful lord of this Earth. Satan's rightful lordship of the Earth, given to him by Adam, remained until Jesus Christ reclaimed that same dominion by his sinless life (John 12:31, 16:11)—Jesus Christ never sinned, and he had no sin within him, and so, by never sinning, he defeated sin and Satan, and in so doing he, the second Adam (1 Cor 15:45), reclaimed the dominion of the Earth, the same dominion given to Satan by Adam. As a result, ever since the resurrection, Jesus Christ is now the rightful ruler of the Earth, for he took back the dominion to the Earth that Adam gave away.

Since the resurrection, Satan is now on Earth *illegally*, and the reason for the Second Coming is that the Lord Jesus Christ is returning to Earth to *claim* his dominion, to sit as Lord and King over all the Earth, in his everlasting kingdom, here on the everlasting, redeemed Earth. The Great Tribulation is Jesus coming to claim what is now rightfully his, and Satan desperately trying to hold on to what is no longer his (Rev 12:12). The thing that is being born is the new dominion, the everlasting dominion of Jesus Christ on Earth, while the Great Tribulation is the final birth pains that will lead to the new dominion.

Although Satan is now illegally on the Earth, a usurper and no longer the rightful lord, having lost the dominion to the Lord Jesus Christ, he will not want to let go of his dominion, and he will be both desperate and have great wrath (Rev 12:12). Since Satan will seek to hold on to what is now no longer his, God will take that dominion by force, for that dominion of the Earth now rightfully, and righteously, belongs to the Lord Jesus Christ.

We can understand it in exactly the same way as Pharaoh refusing to let Israel go from Egypt.

Pharaoh had enslaved Israel, though he had no right to do so—Israel belonged to God; they were his people, but Pharaoh subjugated them and refused to let them go. God sent Moses to tell Pharaoh, "Let my people go" (Exod 5:1), yet *Pharaoh* repeatedly *hardened his own* heart (Exod 7:13–14, 22; 8:15, 32), and he refused to let them go, in full disobedience to God's command. It was only *after* Pharaoh, of his own free will, repeatedly (four times) hardened his own heart that God *gave him over* to the hardness of his heart, which the Bible describes as "the LORD hardened Pharaoh's heart" (Exod 9:12). After hardening Pharaoh's heart on that fifth occasion, Pharaoh once again had the chance to obey God, but once he again he hardened *his own* heart (Exod 9:34). God then, in response to Pharaoh hardening his heart, gave Pharaoh over *again* to the self-chosen hardness of his heart, again described as God hardening Pharaoh's heart (Exod 10:1).

All this to say that Pharaoh refused to obey God and let Israel go, even though he had no right to keep Israel as slaves. In response to Pharaoh's refusal to obey God, in response to his usurpation of God's authority, God sent the plagues upon Egypt, a show of force whereby God, by force, would accomplish his will, since Pharaoh refused to listen to and obey God.

It is in exactly this same way that we can understand the events of the Tribulation. Satan, like Pharaoh, is refusing to obey God, refusing to let go of a dominion that, since the resurrection, is no longer his. As a result, just like the plagues in Egypt, God will take what is rightfully his with righteous force. It is also interesting to note that many of the devastating events of the Tribulation are parallel to the plagues of Egypt.

Also, just as Israel was in Egypt throughout all the plagues but were not harmed by them, for the plagues harmed *only* the Egyptians, likewise the church will be on the Earth during the entirety of the Tribulation but, like the Israelites in Egypt, the Tribulation events will harm *only* the Beast and those who have his mark and will *not* fall upon or harm the church, for the church will be protected from those events (Rev 3:10; 12:14–16).

A DEMONSTRATION OF GOD

The second purpose of the Great Tribulation is that it will be an absolutely unquestionable witness to God himself. Remember that for three and a half years a false Christ has been on the Earth, being worshiped as Christ returned, persecuting the church and overcoming it, and causing great evil, and great deception, throughout the Earth. With the Great Tribulation, God will show to the world *his* power, not for the sake of vanity, but for the sake of love and mercy—by this demonstration of *God's* power, the world will see, and *know*, that the Beast is *not* Christ returned, that he is in fact a *false* Christ, a liar and a deceiver. The nature and scope of the events of the Tribulation will be so great that no one, anywhere, will ascribe them to any human origin—people throughout the entire world will *know*, for a certainty, that it is *God himself* who is author of those great events. In fact, we are specifically told this in the description of Seal 6, which immediately follows the Tribulation of Seal 5.

> Then the kings of the earth, the princes, the generals, the rich, the mighty, and everyone else, both slave and free, hid in caves and among the rocks of the mountains. They called to the mountains and the rocks, "Fall on us and hide us from the face of him who sits on the throne and from the wrath of the Lamb! For the great day of their wrath has come, and who can withstand it?" (Rev 6:15–17 NIV)

After the Great Tribulation, people will *know* that what they have just experienced, the events of the Great Tribulation, were from God and from the Lamb—they will know it without any doubt. They will *know* that what they have just experienced is from the *real* Christ, the Lord Jesus Christ, and the *expression* of that wrath is the events of the Tribulation.

It is for this reason that the events of the Tribulation will be so great, will be so colossal, that it will be impossible to ascribe them to a human origin; they will be so great that they can only be of divine origin, and therefore those same colossal events will be witness to God himself.

Also, due to the colossal scale of those events, those events will shake the world out of the great deception thrown upon it by the Beast and the False Prophet—those events will make it absolutely clear that the Beast is *not* Christ returned, and that the *real* Christ is now about to come.

God will shake the world out of its deception in the most unmistakable way, and he will do that because he loves all people and he wants all people to come to him, to believe and to have salvation (1 Tim 2:3–4). The enormity of the Tribulation events will be the unmistakable demonstration of his power, a power that will utterly destroy the pretended power of the Beast, a power that will destroy the deception upon the world.

As people witness and live through those events, there will be fear, but that fear will be to encourage people who were previously ignoring God, and who were being deceived, to come to God, to turn to him. This is exactly the same as when fear gripped the people in Jerusalem after the Two Witnesses were resurrected, which resulted in *all* the surviving people in Jerusalem turning to God, believing in him and giving him glory (Rev 11:13).

The ultimate purpose of the Great Tribulation is to shake the world out of its deception, to turn people to God, and to take the dominion that, since the resurrection, now rightfully belongs to the Lord Jesus Christ.

THE PROTECTION OF THE CHURCH

Throughout the entire forty-year period of Revelation, the church, in all of its fullness, remains on the Earth. During the three-and-a-half-year reign of the Beast, which constitutes the first half of Seal 5, the church will be greatly persecuted and overcome (Matt 24:9; Rev 6:9–11; 13:7). But during the next three and a half years, during the second half of Seal 5, the time of the Great Tribulation, the church, though fully present upon the Earth, will be *protected* from those events, exactly as Israel was protected in Egypt during the ten plagues.

During the Great Tribulation, we are told that God will have a place of refuge, in the wilderness, for his church.

> The woman was given the two wings of a great eagle, so that she might fly to *the place prepared for her in the wilderness*, where she would be *taken care of for a time, times and half a time*, out of the serpent's reach. Then from his mouth the serpent spewed water like a river, to overtake the woman and sweep her away with the torrent. But the earth helped the woman by opening its mouth and swallowing the river that the dragon had spewed out of his mouth. (Rev 12:14–16 NIV)

The "woman" here is the church, and we are told, very specifically, that the woman will be taken to a "place prepared for her in the wilderness," to be "taken care of" for three and a half years ("a time, times and half a time"). This three-and-a-half-year period is the time of the Great Tribulation, and Revelation 12:14–16 is an affirmation that God will protect his church during that time, just as he protected Israel in Egypt during the time of the plagues.

This place of protection in the wilderness is also referred to by Jesus in his letter to the angel of the church in Philadelphia.

> Since you have kept my command to endure patiently, *I will also keep you from the hour of trial* that is going to come on the whole world to test the inhabitants of the earth. (Rev 3:10 NIV)

This "keep you from the hour of trial" is, of course, in no way a reference to any rapture, since, as discussed, the rapture teaching is a false teaching, the invention of John Darby. In fact, this reference to being kept from the hour of trial means that God will *protect* his church, *on Earth*, from that trial, exactly as is also spelled out for us in Revelation 12:14–16.

We are also told, very clearly, that the devastating events of the Tribulation will *only* come upon those who have the mark of the Beast.

> The first angel went and poured out his bowl on the land, and ugly, festering sores broke out *on the people who had the mark of the beast* and worshiped its image. (Rev 16:2 NIV)

> A third angel followed them and said in a loud voice: "If anyone worships the beast and its image *and receives its mark on their forehead or on their hand, they, too, will drink the wine of God's fury*, which has been poured full strength into the cup of his wrath." (Rev 14:9–10 NIV)

> They were told not to harm the grass of the earth or any plant or tree, but *only those people* who *did not* have the seal of God on their foreheads. (Rev 9:4 NIV)

> The fifth angel poured out his bowl *on the throne of the beast*, and *its kingdom* was plunged into darkness. (Rev 16:10 NIV)

The Bible is very clear—just as in Egypt *only* the Egyptians suffered the plagues, while Israel, though in Egypt, was *protected* from those same plagues, likewise, during the Great Tribulation, *only* those who have the mark of the Beast and are part of his kingdom will suffer the devastations of the Tribulation, while the church, though in the world, will be protected from those same events during that time, protected in a place prepared in the wilderness (Rev 12:14–16). The church is on Earth through the entirety of the events of Revelation, with Seal 1 itself being *defined* by the prostitution and apostasy of the church (Matt 24:4; 2 Thess 2:3), with the judgment of Revelation actually *beginning* with the church in Seal 1 (1 Pet 4:17). During the first half of Seal 5, which is the Beast's three-and-a-half-year reign, the church will be persecuted and overcome (Rev 13:7), but during the second half of Seal 5, during the time of the three-and-a-half-year Great Tribulation, the remaining church will be protected from those devastating events.

THE EVENTS OF THE GREAT TRIBULATION

The Great Tribulation, in its entirety, occurs in the second half of Seal 5. The Trumpets and Bowls listed in Revelation are only *details* of the Seal 5 judgment. In regard to the Great Tribulation, Trumpets 1–5, and then Bowls 1–5, are the *entire* details of the Great Tribulation, and they all occur during the second half of Seal 5.

After the Two Witnesses are resurrected, after the Beast has enthroned himself in the temple (2 Thess 2:4), which act is the abomination of desolation, Trumpet 1 sounds and releases a devastation upon the Earth—hail mixed with fire (just as one of the plagues of Egypt—Exod 9:23 NKJV, NASB, ESV) and with blood. As a result of Trumpet 1, one third of the Earth, the trees, and the grass are burned up (Rev 8:7).

Trumpet 2 releases something like a mountain that is thrown into the sea, blazing like a torch, falling from the sky, turning a third of the sea to blood as a result (similar to another one of the plagues of Egypt, Exod 7:17). As a result of Trumpet 2, a third of the sea creatures will die, and a third of the ships at sea will be destroyed (Rev 8:8–9).

With the sounding of Trumpet 3, a great star named Wormwood, also blazing like a torch, falls from the sky, and a third of the world's rivers and freshwater turn bitter and become undrinkable, and many people die (Rev 8:10–11).

As Trumpet 4 sounds, a third of the sun, the moon, and the stars are struck dark, so that a third of the day will be darkness (Rev 8:12, also similar to one of the plagues of Egypt, Exod 10:21).

At that point, before the sounding of Trumpet 5, something different happens—the action stops, and an angel makes an announcement to the world that something terrible is now about to come.

> As I watched, I heard an eagle that was flying in midair call out in a loud voice: "Woe! Woe! Woe to the inhabitants of the earth, because of the trumpet blasts about to be sounded by the other three angels!" (Rev 8:13 NIV)

The angel declares that great woe is now about to come "to the inhabitants of the earth," which will be announced by the remaining three Trumpets. Why does the angel make this declaration now, in advance of the sounding of Trumpet 5?

The reason the angel makes this declaration now, in advance of the sounding of Trumpet 5, is because, with the sounding of Trumpet 5, the Bowls will now be poured out. The Bowls are part of the Trumpet 5 events, which itself is part of the Seal 5 judgment. And so we see that as we get closer to the event of the Second Coming, closer to the birth of the new dominion, the frequency and intensity of the judgment events greatly increases. This is the perfect fulfillment of Jesus' own words of Matthew 24:8, where he describes the events that precede the Second Coming as "birth pains"—the frequency and intensity of the pains increases as the birth nears.

With the sounding of Trumpet 5 the Pit is opened and vile beings are released from the Pit to torment *only* those who do not belong to God (Rev 9:4, i.e., the church is protected). Those vile beings coming out of the Pit are described as looking like locusts with women's hair and with tails and stingers like scorpions, and having as their king Abaddon, the angel of the Pit (9:11). We are told that those afflicted people will seek death but will not be able to find it (9:6). We are also told that the beings released by Trumpet 5 will torment those who do not belong to God for a total of *five months* (9:5). Why is this five months significant? It is significant because the sounding of Trumpet 5 releases the Bowl events, and Bowls 1–5 are poured out during Trumpet 5, during the five months duration of Trumpet 5. We can therefore understand this as *one Bowl* poured out *per month* for a period of *five months*—once again, the frequency and intensity of the pains greatly increases as the birth nears, and this is evidenced by the pouring of Bowls 1–5 during Trumpet 5, and is also why the angel in 8:13 declares great woe to the world, in advance of the sounding of Trumpet 5—Trumpet 5 releases the Bowls.

BOWLS 1–5

Once Trumpet 5 sounds, Bowl 1 is poured out, and Bowl 1 releases "foul and loathsome" soars upon *only* those who have the mark of the Beast (Rev 16:2 NKJV). These foul and loathsome soars seem similar to what was described for Trumpet 5.

> They were not allowed to kill them but only to torture them for five months. And the agony they suffered was like that of the sting of a scorpion when it strikes. During those days people will seek death but will not find it; they will long to die, but death will elude them. (Trumpet 5, Rev 9:5–6 NIV)

> The first angel went and poured out his bowl on the land, and ugly, festering sores broke out on the people who had the mark of the beast and worshiped its image. (Bowl 1, Rev 16:2 NIV)

The torment inflicted on the people who do not belong to God, in Trumpet 5, is inflicted by the "sting" of the "locusts." There is a strong implication here, with the use of the word "sting" in the context of a scorpion strike, and also by the very clear statement that those tormented people will seek physical death for *relief* of the pain of those stings, that this is a description of *physical* pain. This is completely in line with the very physical sores of Bowl 1 inflicted only on those who have the mark of the Beast. Taken together, we can understand the foul and loathsome sores of Bowl 1 as being *the same affliction* as the pain resulting from the Trumpet 5 sting of the locusts—they are one and the same thing, with the Bowl 1 description being just a more detailed description of that same event. The sounding of Trumpet 5 releases the pouring of Bowl 1—that is month 1 of Trumpet 5's five-month duration.

Thirty days later, after Bowl 1 is poured out, Bowl 2 is poured out upon the seas/oceans of the world, and the seas/oceans become blood and *all* living things in the oceans die (Rev 16:3). That is month 2 of Trumpet 5.

Thirty days after that, Bowl 3 is poured and all the world's fresh water become blood (16:4-7). That is month 3 of Trumpet 5.

Thirty days after Bowl 3 is poured, Bowl 4 is poured out upon the sun, and the sun will make the Earth incredibly hot, scorching *only* the people who have the mark of the Beast (9:8-9). That is month 4 of Trumpet 5.

Thirty days after the sun's scorching heat is unleashed, Bowl 5 is poured out, poured out upon the throne of the Beast and upon his kingdom, and the world is plunged into darkness, and *only* those who have the mark of the Beast will suffer great pain (16:10-11). That is month 5 of Trumpet 5, the final Bowl of the Tribulation.

With the pouring of Bowl 5, released as the last of the Bowls of Trumpet 5, in the fifth and final month of Trumpet 5's duration, the Great Tribulation is *over*. After the pouring of Bowl 5, *after* the Tribulation events (which events are the great devastations upon the Earth) are *finished*, then Seal 6 is opened and Trumpet 6 sounds. The sounding of Trumpet 6 releases Bowls 6 and 7, and the pouring of Bowls 6 and 7 results in the fall of the nation Babylon the Great.

The fall of Babylon the Great is *not* part of the Tribulation, for the Tribulation is the colossal devastation of the Earth itself, and the Tribulation is over with the end of Seal 5. The fall of Babylon the Great happens *after* the Great Tribulation, occurring in Seal 6 (Matt 24:29; Rev 6:12-13), which sees the sounding of Trumpet 6 and the pouring of Bowls 6 and 7.

THE GREAT TRIBULATION ENDS WITH DARKNESS

Bowl 5, of Trumpet 5, is the final event of the Great Tribulation, and it leaves the world plunged into darkness. The Great Tribulation ends 1,260 days, 42 months—"a time, times and half a time"—after the Beast enthrones himself in the holy of holies in the rebuilt temple (Rev 12:6, 14; Dan 9:27). That darkness of Bowl 5 will *remain* upon the Earth until the Second Coming (which, as we will see, will occur 1,335 days after the Beast enthrones himself in the rebuilt temple, Daniel 12:12).

Seal 5 is over with the end of the Great Tribulation, and it *ends* with darkness upon the Earth. This is specifically affirmed by Jesus himself in his description of Seal 6.

> Immediately after the tribulation of those days *the sun will be darkened*, and *the moon will not give its light; the stars will fall from heaven*, and the powers of the heavens *will be shaken*. (Matt 24:29 NKJV)

Compare Jesus' description to the description of Seal 6 in Revelation.

> I looked when He opened the sixth seal, and behold, there was *a great earthquake*; and *the sun became black as sackcloth* of hair, and *the moon became like blood*. And *the stars of heaven fell to the earth*, as a fig tree drops its late figs when it is shaken by a mighty wind. (Rev 6:12–13 NKJV)

The Lord Jesus, in Matthew 24:29, is describing the exact same events as are being described in Revelation 6:12–13, the description of Seal 6. As a result, we know, with certainty, that when Seal 5 and the Great Tribulation are over, the world will be a place of *darkness*. This darkness will last until the Second Coming, which will happen seventy-five days after the end of Seal 5 (Dan 12:12). In fact, when Jesus describes himself coming at the Second Coming like a "thief *in the night*," the night he is referring to is this *same* darkness of Bowl 5. Jesus Christ will return at his Second Coming, in Seal 7, coming suddenly in the *darkness* of that same *night*, the darkness at the end of Seal 5, the darkness that remains upon the whole world (1 Thess 5:2; 2 Pet 3:10; Rev 16:15).

At the end of the Great Tribulation, the Beast's entire kingdom, the whole world, will have experienced great devastation and will be left in darkness, and the whole world, all people, will *know* that *all* of those events were from the hand of God himself, and not the result of any human agency (Rev 6:15–17).

Jesus tells us that immediately after the Great Tribulation, immediately after Seal 5 *ends*, Seal 6 will be opened (Matt 24:29). Seal 6, which results in the sounding of Trumpet 6 and the pouring of Bowls 6 and 7, is the fall of the great nation, the power base of the Beast, the greatest of all prostitutes, the nation symbolically described as Babylon the Great.

18

SEAL 6—THE FALL OF BABYLON THE GREAT

WITH THE END OF Seal 5, the Great Tribulation is over and the reign of the Beast is ended. There is only one more global event to take place before the Second Coming, and that is the fall of Babylon the Great.

Jesus tells us that immediately after the Great Tribulation, which is immediately after the end of Seal 5, Seal 6 is opened (Matt 24:29; Rev 6:12–13). The *entirety* of Seal 6 is the fall of Babylon the Great. When the Judge, Jesus Christ (John 5:22; Rev 5:1–7), opens Seal 6, Trumpet 6 sounds and the sounding of Trumpet 6 results in the pouring of Bowls 6 and 7. In fact, the description of the events of Trumpet 6 is almost identical to the description of the events of Bowl 6.

> Then the sixth angel sounded: And I heard a voice from the four horns of the golden altar which is before God, saying to the sixth angel who had the trumpet, "Release the four angels who are bound at **the great river Euphrates**." So the four angels, who had been prepared for the hour and day and month and year, were released to kill a third of mankind. Now the number of **the army of the horsemen** was **two hundred million**; I heard the number of them. And thus I saw the horses in the vision: those who sat on them had breastplates of fiery red, hyacinth blue, and sulfur yellow; and the heads of the horses were like the heads of lions; and out of their mouths came fire, smoke, and brimstone. By these three plagues a third of mankind was killed—by the fire and the smoke and the brimstone which came out of their mouths. For their power is in their mouth and in their tails; for their tails are like serpents, having heads; and with them they do harm. (Trumpet 6, Rev 9:13–19 NKJV)

> Then the sixth angel poured out his bowl on *the great river Euphrates*, and its water was dried up, so that the way of *the kings from the east* might be prepared. And I saw three unclean spirits like frogs coming out of the mouth of the dragon, out of the mouth of the beast, and out of the mouth of the false prophet. For they are spirits of demons, performing signs, which go out to the

kings of the earth and of the whole world, to *gather them to the battle* of that great day of God Almighty. "Behold, I am coming as a thief. Blessed is he who watches, and keeps his garments, lest he walk naked and they see his shame." And they gathered them together to the place called in Hebrew, Armageddon. (Bowl 6, Rev 16:12–16 NKJV)

Both Trumpet 6 and Bowl 6 describe events at the great river Euphrates, and both Trumpet 6 and Bowl 6 describe *military* events related to that. With Trumpet 6 we see that angels who were bound at the Euphrates are released. In Bowl 6 we see that the river Euphrates dries up. In Trumpet 6 we see that a great army numbering 200 million is coming, and their coming is related to the events at the Euphrates River. In Bowl 6 we are told that the drying up of the water of the Euphrates was to prepare the way for the "kings from the east," and the coming of those kings of the east is related to being gathered for battle on the great day of God Almighty.

Do events at the Euphrates happen twice? Do military maneuvers happen at the Euphrates twice? Are the kings of the east and the army of 200 million two different armies? No, in fact, *all* of this is a description of the *same* event. When Trumpet 6 sounds, Bowl 6 is poured as part of Trumpet 6, and the description of the events described after the sounding of Trumpet 6 in Revelation 9:13–19 is an overall description of events, while the Bowl 6 description of Revelation 16:12–16 just gives us more details of those *same* events.

In regard to the army of 200 million and the kings of the east, these are the same people. There are only two nations on Earth that can gather an army of 200 million—China and India, and, of those two nations, China is by far the stronger military. Also, China, of course, is directly east of the Euphrates, whereas India is both east and south. There is very good reason to understand that the kings of the east, the army of 200 million, is the military of China. Again, Trumpet 6 and Bowl 6 are describing the same events. We are further told in Trumpet 6 that a third of humanity will die from the battles that will come, in which the army of 200 million will fight, and we are also told in Bowl 6 that, as an added detail, that same army, as well as all the other armies of the world engaged in that battle, will be gathered, eventually, to Armageddon.

It is during this same time, the time period *after* the Great Tribulation and yet *before* the Second Coming, that the great nation, Babylon the Great, falls and is destroyed. Trumpets 1–5 are the entire Great Tribulation, with Bowls 1–5 being poured during Trumpet 5. Trumpet 7 is the last Trumpet and announces the resurrection of all believers *and* the Second Coming. As a result, the fall of Babylon the Great occurs during Trumpet 6, with those details given by Bowls 6 and 7.

We know, with certainty, that the fall of Babylon the great will be accomplished by worldly armies, for we are specifically told,

And the ten horns which you saw on the beast, *these will hate the harlot, make her desolate and naked, eat her flesh and burn her with fire.* For *God has put it into their hearts to fulfill His purpose*, to be of one mind, and to give their kingdom to the beast, until the words of God are fulfilled. And the woman whom you saw is that great city which reigns over the kings of the earth. (Rev 17:16–18 NKJV)

We are told that the Beast and the other ten kings ("ten horns") of the world will hate Babylon the Great and destroy her, will make her desolate, will burn her, and they will do so because God "put it into their hearts" to do this, so that *they* will accomplish his will in regard to Babylon the Great. The destruction of Babylon the Great will be through *human* agency, as inspired by God; it will be a *military* destruction, not a supernatural divine destruction, and it will happen during Seal 6/Trumpet 6, immediately *after* the Great Tribulation, while the world is in darkness. Those same military events that will result in the destruction of Babylon the Great, as described in Revelation 17:16–18, are the same military events described in Trumpet 6 and Bowl 6 and involve the kings of the east and, eventually, the armies of the world. Seal 6, during which Trumpet 6 sounds and then Bowls 6 and 7 are poured, is the destruction of the nation Babylon the Great.

So who, or what, is Babylon the Great?

BABYLON THE GREAT IS A NATION

Books on Revelation often describe Babylon the Great as being a religious system, based solely on the fact that Babylon the Great is described as a prostitute, based on the understanding that a prostitute in the Bible represents false religion. As previously discussed, the symbol of the prostitute in the Bible *never* represents false religion; rather, it *only* ever represents a *nation*, but not just any nation, rather a very specific kind of nation—a nation that came into existence as a nation unto God and then, later, turned away from him.

Throughout the Bible, and throughout all human history, there has only ever been one such nation that came into existence as a nation unto God, coming into existence as his nation, and that nation was Israel. However, in the reign of Solomon's son Rehoboam, the one nation Israel split into *two* separate nations—the nations of Judah and Israel. Of all the nations that have ever come into existence in Asia, Europe, and Africa, *only* Judah and Israel came into existence as nations unto God. It is only when Judah or Israel turned their backs on God that God then described those *nations* as prostitutes.

> Then Gideon made it into an ephod and set it up in his city, Ophrah. And all Israel played the harlot with it there. It became a snare to Gideon and to his house. (Judg 8:27 NKJV)

And they were unfaithful to the God of their fathers, and played the harlot after the gods of the peoples of the land, whom God had destroyed before them. (1 Chr 5:25 NKJV)

For indeed, those who are far from You shall perish;
You have destroyed all those who desert You for harlotry. (Ps 73:27 NKJV)

How the faithful city has become a harlot! (Isa 1:21 NKJV)

For of old I have broken your yoke and burst your bonds;
And you said, "I will not transgress,"
When on every high hill and under every green tree
You lay down, playing the harlot. (Jer 2:20 NKJV)

Lift up your eyes to the desolate heights and see:
Where have you not lain with men?
By the road you have sat for them
Like an Arabian in the wilderness;
And you have polluted the land
With your harlotries and your wickedness. (Jer 3:2 NKJV)

"You shall call Me, 'My Father,'
And not turn away from Me."
Surely, as a wife treacherously departs from her husband,
So have you dealt treacherously with Me,
O house of Israel," says the LORD." (Jer 3:20 NKJV)

The LORD said also to me in the days of Josiah the king: "Have you seen what backsliding Israel has done? She has gone up on every high mountain and under every green tree, and there played the harlot." (Jer 3:6 NKJV)

There are many similar verses throughout the Old Testament, and they are all verses that talk about Israel and Judah, describing those two *nations* as either prostitutes or as unfaithful wives, because they, being God's nations, turned away from God and followed false gods.

So, it is not the following of false gods that defines the prostitute, but rather the prostitute is defined by *who* is following the false gods—*only* a *nation* that came into existence as a nation unto God, as his nation, can be the prostitute, because such a nation was *his* nation, and, by following other gods, God's nation prostitutes itself by way of its faithlessness to God. Only Israel and Judah are called prostitutes, for only Israel and Judah, throughout the history of the world until the 1500s, came into existence as God's nations. Of course, Babylon the Great, in Revelation, is *also* called the Prostitute.

However, if *only* Judah and Israel, in the Old Testament, are called prostitutes unto God, then how do we understand the pagan *city of Tyre* being described as committing fornication?

> And it shall be, at the end of seventy years, that the LORD will deal with Tyre. She will return to her hire, and **commit fornication with all the kingdoms of the world on the face of the earth.** (Isa 23:17 NKJV)

How can this be, if only Israel and Judah can be described as prostitutes? Like the symbolism of the name Babylon, and as previously discussed, the name Tyre (and Ninevah, Nahum 3:3–4) is *also* used *symbolically* to represent that same city/nation, Babylon the Great, of Revelation 17, and, in fact, the wording used to describe Tyre in Isaiah 23:17 is almost identical to the wording used to describe Babylon the Great in Revelation 17.

> Come, I will show you the judgment of the great harlot who sits on many waters, with whom *the kings of the earth committed fornication*, and *the inhabitants of the earth* were made *drunk with the wine of her fornication.* (Rev 17:1–2 NKJV)

Just as Tyre, in Isaiah 23:17, is described as committing "fornication with all the kingdoms of the world," so is Babylon the Great described as having "committed fornication" with the "kings of the earth." These two passages are describing the same nation, the nation Babylon the Great of Revelation 17, being referred to symbolically in one instance, in Revelation 17, as Babylon, and referred to symbolically in another instance, in Isaiah 23:17, as Tyre.

But if Israel and Judah are the only nations that came into existence unto God, as his nations, and then, in turning away from him, are described as prostitutes, then how can Babylon the Great/Tyre be described as a prostitute?

It is true that Israel and Judah were the only nations in recorded human history that came into existence as nations born unto God, however, that changed in the 1500s with the nations that came into existence in the New World.

IDENTIFYING BABYLON THE GREAT

In all of Asia, Europe, and Africa, no nation, other than Israel and Judah, came into existence as a nation unto God, with the exception of Vatican City, which came into existence in 1929 by way of the Lateran Treaty. However, *all* the nations of North America, South and Central America, and Australia came into existence as *Christian* nations, being founded as *nations unto God*. As a result, if *any* of the nations of the New World turned away from God and abandoned him, *they* could accurately and biblically be described as a prostitute, while, apart from Vatican City, no other nation in Europe, Asia, or Africa could ever be described as a prostitute, because no nation in Asia, Europe, or Africa came into existence as a nation unto God.

We are also told, very clearly and specifically, that Babylon the Great is the city that rules over the Earth.

> And the woman whom you saw is **that great city** which reigns over the kings of the earth. (Rev 17:18 NKJV)

We are told that Babylon the Great is a "city"; it is *not* a religion, nor is it any sort of religious *system*—it is a city that rules the Earth.

We must also understand that just as the symbol of the Beast can be both a kingdom and a king (Dan 7:17, 23), likewise, a *city* can also be a *nation*, when that city is the capital, or heart, of the nation.

For example, Rome was a city, and that city had a vast empire, and yet, throughout history, when people refer to that *entire* empire, comprised of many nations, and stretching over centuries, they simply call it Rome, after the city that ruled the empire.

Likewise with Babylon the Great. Babylon the Great is described, very specifically, as the "city" that "reigns over the kings of the earth," but, as with Rome, if that city is the capital, or heart, of the nation, then Babylon the Great equally represents *both* the city *and* the nation, just as the beasts in Daniel 7 equally represent both kings and kingdoms. So, the name Babylon the Great represents *both* the city *and* the nation of which it is the heart, and which nation reigns over the Earth in both power and wealth.

As a result, we can know, with certainty, that Babylon the Great is *not* a false religion, nor is it *any* sort of *religious system*—Babylon the Great is a *nation* that came into existence as a nation unto God and then turned away from him, and for that reason it is called the "Prostitute."

Babylon the Great, however, is called more than just a prostitute—it is called the "Mother of Prostitutes and of the Abominations of the Earth." Why is called "mother"?

As previously discussed, the term "mother" here does *not* mean the *originator*; rather it means only the *greatest*. In calling Babylon the Great the "Mother of Prostitutes," it only means that Babylon the Great is the *greatest* of all prostitutes, which is to say that of all the nations that have ever come into existence unto God, from Israel and Judah, to all the nations of the New World, *none* of them will have so totally and utterly turned away from God as will Babylon the Great—Babylon's abandonment of God will be epic and total. It is for that reason that Babylon is called the "Mother of Prostitutes," for Babylon the Great will be the greatest of all prostitutes that have ever been.

Babylon the Great is a nation that came into existence, from its very inception, as a nation unto God, coming into existence as his nation. Since we know that Babylon the Great is neither Israel nor Judah, then we can know, for a fact, that Babylon the

Great came into existence as a *Christian* nation, for there is no other way that a nation can be described as coming into existence as God's nation.

What else do we know about the nation Babylon the Great?

THE WEALTH OF BABYLON THE GREAT

The symbol of Babylon, as previously discussed, always denotes great wealth and great power, and also great corruption. In fact, the wealth of Babylon the Great is described as being enormous, for it is described as the wealthiest nation on Earth.

> And **the merchants of the earth will weep and mourn** over her, for **no one buys their merchandise** anymore: merchandise of gold and silver, precious stones and pearls, fine linen and purple, silk and scarlet, every kind of citron wood, every kind of object of ivory, every kind of object of most precious wood, bronze, iron, and marble; and cinnamon and incense, fragrant oil and frankincense, wine and oil, fine flour and wheat, cattle and sheep, horses and chariots, and bodies and souls of men. The fruit that your soul longed for has gone from you, and all **the things which are rich and splendid** have gone from you, and you shall find them no more at all. The **merchants** of these things, **who became rich by her**, will stand at a distance for fear of her torment, weeping and wailing, and saying, "Alas, alas, **that great city** that was clothed in fine linen, purple, and scarlet, and adorned with gold and precious stones and pearls! For in one hour **such great riches** came to nothing." Every shipmaster, all who travel by ship, sailors, and as many as trade on the sea, stood at a distance and cried out when they saw the smoke of her burning, saying, "What is like this great city?" (Rev 18:11–18 NKJV)

> For *your merchants were the great men of the earth*, for by your sorcery all the nations were deceived. (Rev 18:23 NKJV)

We are told that the merchants of the Earth will weep and mourn over the fall of the nation Babylon the Great, and we are given an extensive list of the kinds of merchandise that Babylon deals in, including human beings (in modern terms, human trafficking). Babylon is described as being adorned with "all the things that are rich and splendid," and we are told that the merchants of the world, all who dealt with Babylon, became rich by their trading with Babylon. We are told once again in Revelation 18:16 that Babylon is a *city*, not a religion or a religious system, and in 18:17 we are once again told of Babylon's "great riches." We are also told in 18:23 that those same merchants who grew rich by trading with Babylon were the "great men of the earth."

The description given here is of the preeminent economic power on Earth—Babylon is the greatest, richest, and most economically important nation on Earth; it is at the very heart of the world's economy, its very foundation, and all who trade with Babylon, all who do business with Babylon, grow very rich.

We are also told, by very clear implication, that Babylon has seacoasts, for 18:17–18 describes for us how all the shipmasters and their crews stand at a distance as they watch Babylon's destruction. These same shipmasters and crew are in fact the same merchants described in 18:15, who are also described as standing far off, at a distance, as they watch Babylon's destruction. As a result, because of the importance of ships in Babylon's worldwide trading power, we can know that much of Babylon's worldwide economic trade is done by sea, by ships. As a result, we can understand that the nation Babylon the Great is on coastal waters, by the sea.

THE SEACOASTS OF BABYLON THE GREAT

The seacoasts of Babylon are in fact described in other prophecies.

> The sea has come up over Babylon;
> **She is covered with the multitude of its waves.** (Jer 51:42 NKJV)

> You **who live by many waters** and **are rich** in treasures, your end has come, the time for you to be destroyed. (Jer 51:13 NKJV)

> Therefore thus says the Lord: "Behold, I will plead your case and take vengeance for you. I will *dry up her sea* and make her springs dry." (Jer 51:36 NKJV)

Jeremiah 51 is a prophecy about Babylon; in fact, it is a prophecy about the same Babylon the Great of Revelation 17 and 18. Jeremiah repeatedly tells us that those who live in Babylon live by "many waters and are rich"; we are told that the sea will cover Babylon with the "multitude of its waves"; we are told that God "will dry up her sea," speaking specifically of Babylon's sea. As a result of all of this, and especially when taken together with the very clear descriptions of Babylon the Great in Revelation 18, we can know that Babylon is a nation with many sea and ocean coasts.

THE MILITARY MIGHT OF BABYLON THE GREAT

In his prophecy about the coming destruction of Babylon, which is the same Babylon the Great of Revelation 17 and 18, Jeremiah also tells us,

> How *the hammer of the whole earth* has been cut apart and broken!
> How *Babylon* has become a desolation among the nations! (Jer 50:23 NKJV)

Babylon is described as the "hammer of the whole earth." To be described as a hammer means that Babylon has great military might. Also, Babylon is described as the "hammer of the *whole earth*"; it is *not* described as a *local* power, or a *regional* power, but, very specifically as "*the* hammer of the *whole earth*"—the military might of Babylon is *global*, and since it is very specifically described as "*the* hammer," not "*a* hammer," we can know that, as a global military power, Babylon will have no rival.

BABYLON HAS A MOTHER COUNTRY

In his prophecy about the destruction of Babylon, Jeremiah tells us the following:

> *your mother* will be greatly ashamed;
> *she who gave you birth* will be disgraced.
> She will be the least of the *nations*—
> a wilderness, a dry land, a desert. (Jer 50:12 NIV)

This is part of Jeremiah's prophecy about the destruction of Babylon, the same Babylon the Great of Revelation 17. Jeremiah tells us that, during that time of Babylon's destruction, Babylon's "mother" will be ashamed of Babylon, that "she who gave you birth will be disgraced." This same "mother" is described as a "nation." The meaning of this is clear—the nation Babylon the Great will have a mother nation, for Babylon itself will be the offspring of another nation, and, during the coming destruction of Babylon the Great, that same mother nation will be on the Earth and will witness Babylon the Great's destruction.

This description is in perfect accord with the fact that Babylon the Great is a nation of the New World, born of a mother nation, born as a nation that came into existence as a Christian nation. When later that same Babylon turns its back on God, it is described as the "Prostitute." All of this together affirms that the nation that will be Babylon the Great is a Christian nation of the New World.

In trying to identify the nation that is symbolically called "Babylon the Great," that candidate nation must meet *all* of the characteristics outlined for Babylon—not just some, but *all*. The nation that is described as Babylon the Great *must* be a nation that came into existence as a *Christian nation*, and therefore it must be either a nation of the New World or it must be Vatican City, since Vatican City is the *only* nation, apart from Israel and Judah, in Europe, Asia, or Africa that came into existence as a Christian nation. It must be the *greatest economic power* on Earth. It must have *many seacoasts* and do *much trade* by way of sea and shipping. It must be the *greatest military power* on Earth. It must have *a mother country* on Earth, simultaneous with its own existence. The nation that is Babylon the Great must meet *all* of these criteria.

Based on these criteria, what are the possible nation candidates for Babylon the Great?

POSSIBLE NATION CANDIDATES

The only nation in Europe, Asia, or Africa that can be considered as a candidate for Babylon the Great is Vatican City. Vatican City is a nation-state and was founded as an independent nation only in 1929 by way of the Lateran Treaty. Vatican City came into existence as a Christian nation, a nation unto God, which is an essential requirement of any candidate for Babylon the Great. Of all the requirements that must be met by any potential nation candidate for Babylon the Great, this is the *only* requirement that is met by Vatican City. Vatican City *did* come into existence as a nation unto God, as a Christian nation, but it is *not*, even remotely, any sort of great economic power; it is not, in any way, a military power; it does *not* have seacoasts, and it is *not* the product of a mother country. As a result, we can know, with certainty, that Vatican City *cannot*, in any way, be a candidate for Babylon the Great.

The only other possible candidates for Babylon the Great are the nations of the New World—the nations of North America, South and Central America, and Australia, for those nations are the *only* other nations on Earth that came into existence as Christian nations. They all came into existence as nations unto God *and* they *all* have a mother country on Earth simultaneous with themselves—*all* the nations of the New World meet those two criteria.

In regard to the other criteria, Babylon the Great must have many seacoasts (Jer 51:13). Of the nations in the New World, Australia certainly meets that criterion, for Australia is surrounded on all sides by ocean waters. Also, both Canada and the United States meet that criterion, being surrounded on three sides by ocean waters, as well as having additional coasts from bays along those same seacoasts. Mexico also fits that description, for it has ocean waters on two sides as well as additional seacoasts along its western peninsula. Of the nations of South America, all except one nation have only one seacoast—Brazil has two coasts, while the other South American nations have one. Since Jeremiah 51:13 describes Babylon the Great as having "many waters," or "many coasts," there is good reason to understand that this means more than one or two seacoasts. As a result, based on Babylon having many coasts, the only nations of the New World that fit that description are Australia, Canada, the United States, and Mexico.

The other criterion that must be met by any candidate for Babylon the Great is the economic criterion—Babylon the Great is the greatest economic power on Earth. In regard to the economic power and wealth of the potential candidates of Mexico, Australia, Canada, and the United States, we see the following:

- Mexico's GDP is $2.715 trillion[1]
- Australia's GDP is $1.416 trillion[2]
- Canada's GDP is $1.979 trillion[3]
- the United States' GDP is $20.807 trillion[4]

One of the other key criteria that must be met by any potential candidate for Babylon the Great is the military criterion—Babylon the great is the "hammer of the whole earth" (Jer 50:23), the greatest military power in the world. In regard to the

1. https://en.wikipedia.org/wiki/Mexico.
2. https://en.wikipedia.org/wiki/Australia.
3. https://en.wikipedia.org/wiki/Canada.
4. https://en.wikipedia.org/wiki/United_States.

military might of the potential candidates of Mexico, Australia, Canada, and the United States, of those four New World candidates, only the United States has a military of any global import—in fact, the United States military is the most powerful military on Earth.

When we consider all of these criteria together, as they apply to the possible nation candidates for Babylon the Great—the criteria of coming into existence as a Christian nation unto God, of having a mother country on Earth simultaneous with itself, of having many seacoasts, of being the greatest economic power on Earth, of being the greatest military power on Earth—there is only one nation that fits *all* of these criteria, and that is the United States.

THE UNITED STATES

There is very good reason, perhaps even an inarguable reason, to understand that the United States is the nation that will become Babylon the Great. It's also very important to understand that the United States currently is certainly *not* Babylon the Great, but it would *become* Babylon the Great.

A perfect illustration of this is Germany in the early twentieth century. Germany, in the first part of the twentieth century, was, together with France, Britain, and Spain, one of the great European kingdoms, but by the late 1930s that European kingdom had turned into the Nazi monster—Germany of the late 1930s was a completely different nation than Germany in 1900—the Germany of 1900 *became* the monster of the late 1930s, and that is exactly how it will be with Babylon the Great.

If the United States becomes Babylon the Great, for which there is good reason to believe that it will, then that will happen *over time*, just as it did with Germany's transformation into the Nazi monster—the United States of that future time will be a completely different nation than it was in its history. It's important to understand that in regard to Babylon the Great, that nation will *become* Babylon the Great, transformed over time into the great Prostitute.

IN GOD WE TRUST

The United States is often considered as the greatest of Christian nations—greatest in faith, greatest in missionary zeal, and as having a powerful biblical foundation. Its Christian faith is at the very heart of the nation, as openly declared in its Declaration of Independence and, even more so, on its coinage, with the motto "In God We Trust." With that motto, the United States is declaring its Christian faithfulness to the world. Babylon the Great will have been, at one time, the greatest of Christian nations, which is why, when it abandons God, and turns its back on him, it will be the greatest of prostitutes, the "Mother of Prostitutes."

WHY DOES BABYLON FALL?

One of the names of the Beast is "king of Babylon" (Isa 14:3–8), which is interchangeable with "prince of Tyre" (Ezek 28:2). Also, in Revelation 17, we are told that Babylon the Great "rides" the Beast, which denotes the nation Babylon as having *control* over the Beast. Also, just as we are told that the Beast will be the great persecutor and murderer of the church (Rev 13:7; 20:4), likewise, Babylon the Great is described as being "drunk with the blood of God's holy people."

> I saw that the woman was drunk with the blood of God's holy people, the blood of those who bore testimony to Jesus. (Rev 17:6 NKJV)

We are also told that after the Great Tribulation the Beast will hate Babylon and destroy her (Rev 17:16–17).

From this we can conclude the following. The nation Babylon the Great is the initial power base of the Beast; it is the platform that launches him onto the world's stage, and, after his fake resurrection, if not sooner, he becomes ruler of that nation, and so is referred to as the "king of Babylon." It is Babylon the Great, and its global powerbase, that enables the Beast to become the world ruler, and so Babylon the Great "rides" the Beast.

Also, since the Beast is the greatest persecutor and murderer of the church in history, and since the nation Babylon is described as being "drunk with the blood of God's holy people," we can conclude that the Beast, as king of Babylon, will use Babylon's wealth, power, and all of its resources to persecute and kill the church, and as a result *both* the Beast and Babylon the Great are persecutors and murderers of the church.

Also, since Babylon is described as riding the Beast, which implies Babylon ruling over the Beast to some degree, or having some rein over him, it is understandable *why* the Beast will hate Babylon, for he wants no rein, no accountability, over his power, and so he will seek, and accomplish, the destruction of Babylon the Great.

Since Babylon is the foundation of the Beast's power, and since the nation Babylon is at the very heart of the persecutions, abominations, and bloodshed upon the Earth, all as a result of a complete abandonment of God to an epic degree, Babylon will fall, and its entire destruction will occur in Seal 6, after the Great Tribulation is over.

HOW LONG DOES SEAL 6 LAST?

We know, from Daniel 9:27 and from Matthew 24:9–28, that from the time that the Beast comes to power to the time that the Great Tribulation is over will be a period of seven years. We also know that the first three and a half years of that seven-year period is the reign of the Beast, and the second three and a half years of that seven-year period is the Great Tribulation. We also know that the three and a half years of the Great

Tribulation is also very specifically spelled out for us as being a period of 1,260 days (Dan 7:25; 12:7; Rev 12:6). So we know that from the time that the Beast seats himself in the temple of God, proclaiming himself to be God (the abomination of desolation, Matt 24:15; Dan 9:27), which is the event which triggers the Great Tribulation, to the *end* of the Great Tribulation, will be a total timeframe of 1,260 days. The end of the Great Tribulation is also the end of Seal 5; therefore we can understand that Seal 5 ends 1,260 days *after* the Beast abolishes the daily sacrifice at the rebuilt temple and seats himself in the rebuilt temple of God.

It is in that context that we read the following in Daniel:

> From the time that the daily sacrifice is abolished and the abomination that causes desolation is set up, there will be 1,290 *days*. Blessed is the one who waits for and reaches the end of the 1,335 days. (Dan 12:11–12 NIV)

As previously discussed, the 1,290 days referred to by Daniel, which is an additional 30 days after the end of the Great Tribulation and Seal 5, brings us to the end of the Seal 6 fall of Babylon the Great – Babylon the Great falls in the 30 days after the end of the Great Tribulation, and so we can understand that Seal 6 lasts for a total of 30 days, concluding on day 1,290 after the abomination of desolation.

Though the Great Tribulation will be over, the fall of Babylon the Great will still be a great and powerful fall, and it will be a military destruction, in contrast to the enormous devastation of the Earth in the Seal 5 Great Tribulation. The armies that will cause the fall of Babylon the Great will themselves then continue to be gathered at Armageddon. So the destruction of Babylon the Great, though on the heels of the Great Tribulation, will still be a dark and impactful event, though not the global devastation of the Tribulation, and so Daniel includes that event in his 1,290 days description.

BOWL 7

After the fall of Babylon the Great, and still part of Seal 6/Trumpet 6, Bowl 7 is poured out.

> The seventh angel poured out his bowl into the air, and out of the temple came a loud voice from the throne, saying, "It is done!" Then there came *flashes of lightning, rumblings, peals of thunder* and *a severe earthquake.* No earthquake like it has ever occurred since mankind has been on earth, so tremendous was the quake. The great city split into three parts, and the cities of the nations collapsed. God remembered Babylon the Great and gave her the cup filled with the wine of the fury of his wrath. *Every island fled away and the mountains could not be found. From the sky huge hailstones,* each weighing about a hundred pounds, fell on people. And they cursed God on account of the plague of hail, because the plague was so terrible. (Bowl 7, Rev 16:17–21 NKJV)

Compare the description of Bowl 7 to the description of Seal 6.

> I looked when He opened the sixth seal, and behold, there was *a great earthquake*; and the sun became black as sackcloth of hair, and the moon became like blood. And *the stars of heaven fell to the earth*, as a fig tree drops its late figs when it is shaken by a mighty wind. Then the sky receded as a scroll when it is rolled up, and *every mountain and island was moved out of its place*. And the kings of the earth, the great men, the rich men, the commanders, the mighty men, every slave and every free man, hid themselves in the caves and in the rocks of the mountains, and said to the mountains and rocks, "Fall on us and hide us from the face of Him who sits on the throne and from the wrath of the Lamb! For the great day of His wrath has come, and who is able to stand? (Seal 6, Rev 6:12–17 NKJV)

Trumpet 6, and with it Bowls 6 and 7, all belong to the thirty-day time period of Seal 6. The description of Bowl 7 in 16:17–21 is the same description as the events of Seal 6 in 6:12–17—both Bowl 7 and Seal 6 are described as having a great earthquake, with the Bowl 7 description giving us more details as to its scale and scope; both Bowl 7 and Seal 6 tell us that every island and mountain was moved out of its place; the event described in Seal 6 as the stars of heaven falling to Earth (also Matt 24:29) is described in Bowl 7 as huge hailstones falling from the sky. The Bowl 7 description is the exact same event as is described in the Seal 6 description but giving more detail—the "stars" that fall from the sky are in fact huge hailstones falling from the sky, weighing about a hundred pounds each. With the pouring out of Bowl 7, which is poured after the fall of Babylon the Great, the events of Seal 6 are over.

SEAL 7

After Jesus finishes describing Seal 6 (Matt 24:29), the fall of Babylon the Great, he continues to describe Seal 7. As Jesus describes for us the events of Seal 7 in Matthew 24:30–31, together with telling us of his return to Earth, he also tells us that, at that same time, he will "gather together his elect."

> Then the sign of the Son of Man will appear in heaven, and then all the tribes of the earth will mourn, and *they will see the Son of Man coming on the clouds of heaven* with power and great glory. And He will send His angels *with a great sound of a trumpet*, and they will *gather together His elect* from the four winds, from one end of heaven to the other. (Matt 24:30–31 NKJV)

The gathering of the elect, the event that happens in Seal 7 just before Jesus descends to Earth, while he is still in the sky, is the resurrection of *all* believers.

19

SEAL 7—THE RESURRECTION OF BELIEVERS

THE FINAL EVENT THAT *precedes* the Second Coming is the resurrection of *all* believers. That resurrection happens during Seal 7, as does the Second Coming, but the resurrection happens first.

WHY RESURRECTION?

The resurrection of Jesus Christ, and of all people, is a foundational truth of the Christian faith. Why is there a resurrection? For a detailed understanding of that question, see *What Happened on the Cross* (Wipf & Stock, 2020), but the following is a brief overview.

God is a redeemer; he is not a destroyer. God does not destroy and then recreate his own creation; rather, he redeems it, in totality—this includes not only humanity, but the physical universe as well (Col 1:15–20; Rom 8:19–22).

Our sinful nature is a physical thing; it is not a spiritual state, and, as a physical thing, it physically resides in our bodies; more specifically, it resides in our blood (in fact, there is good reason to understand that blood itself is the result of the fall and is not part of how man was created). This is why, throughout the entire Bible, blood and the shedding of blood is intricately connected with sin and the forgiveness of sin (Heb 9:22). This is also why Jesus' blood was precious, without defect or blemish (1 Pet 1:19)—since Jesus had no sin, there was no sinful nature residing physically in his blood, and therefore his blood was precious, pure, without spot, blemish, or defect.

It is the sinful nature that makes us mortal, making us subject to death (Rom 8:10). Throughout the Bible, only our bodies are ever described as being subject to death, described as being mortal; our spirits and our souls are never described as being mortal—only our physical bodies are mortal, subject to death. The reason for that is that sin, the sinful nature, resides physically in our flesh, in our blood. It is also for this reason that the sinful nature is repeatedly called "the flesh" (Rom 8:4–13;

Gal 5:13–24; 2 Pet 2:10, 18)—since our sinful nature resides in our blood, and since our blood imbues every cell of our flesh, it is therefore accurate to describe the sinful nature as "the flesh," for the sinful nature, by way of blood, inhabits our flesh.

Yet even though our bodies have sin residing within them, we still retain the full glory and holiness of God, for we are made in God's image and likeness (Gen 1:26) and, though fallen, we fully *retain* God's image and likeness (Gen 9:6).

Fallen humanity is a duality—the holiness and glory of God, which we have by virtue of being created in God's image and likeness, is now coexisting with sin. This in fact is why the Tree in Eden had the very specific name that it did—it was not called the "Tree of Death," or "Tree of Sin," but rather it was called the "Tree of the *Knowledge* of Good *and* Evil"—once Adam ate from that Tree, both God's holiness and glory *and* the sinful nature coexisted within him, and Adam would now intimately know them both. As Adam's physical descendants, we also now have both God's holiness and glory *and* the sinful nature coexisting within us, with our sinful nature residing in our flesh, in our blood. It is this coexistence of holiness and sin within us that is described by the Bible as a war between "flesh" and "spirit" (Rom 7:13–25; Gal 5:16–17).

GOD IS A REDEEMER

But God is a redeemer, and he will not abandon us, our bodies, his own creation, to destruction, and this is why there is a resurrection. The purpose of resurrection is to *remove* from our bodies what should not be there, the sinful nature, and that is exactly what resurrection accomplishes. In our resurrection, our sinful nature is removed from our bodies because we will *not* have blood in our resurrected bodies. Since the sinful nature resides in our blood, and since we will not have blood in our resurrected bodies, we will no longer have the sinful nature in our resurrected bodies, and so our bodies will be redeemed.

The fact that our resurrected bodies will not have blood is made clear in Scripture. We know, for a fact, that the resurrected Jesus is a "*flesh* and *bone*" man (Luke 24:39); we also know that we, in our resurrection, will be exactly like Jesus (1 John 3:2). As a result, since Jesus, in his resurrection, is a flesh-and-bone man, and since we will be exactly like him in our resurrection, we know, with certainty, that our resurrected bodies will also be flesh and bone. As a result, we know that *flesh* and *bone* can, and will, inherit the kingdom of God.

It is in that context that we read 1 Corinthians 15:50:

> I declare to you, brothers and sisters, that flesh and *blood cannot inherit the kingdom of God*, nor does the perishable inherit the imperishable. (NIV)

The Bible is absolutely clear—"flesh and *blood* cannot inherit the kingdom of God." We know, with certainty, that flesh and *bone* can, and will, inherit the kingdom of God (in fact the kingdom of God will be *ruled* by flesh and bone, since it will be ruled by Jesus Christ). As a result, since *flesh* can inherit the kingdom, and since *bone* can inherit the kingdom, we know that it is the *blood* that *cannot* inherit the kingdom. Why is that? It is because the sinful nature resides in the blood. As a result, in removing blood from the resurrected body, the sinful nature will no longer be present in our bodies.

As a result, we can understand that the purpose of the resurrection of humanity is to remove the sinful nature from our bodies, to remove from our bodies what should not be there. When we physically die, and our bodies are buried, we are buried with the corruption of the sinful nature in our bodies, but when we are resurrected, that sinful nature is removed from our bodies, and so we are raised incorruptible; when we physically die and our bodies are buried, we are buried with mortality, being made mortal as a result of the sinful nature within our bodies (Rom 8:10), but when we are resurrected that sinful nature and its mortality is removed from our bodies, and so we are raised immortal; upon our death, we are buried in the weakness of the sinful nature in our bodies, but when we are resurrected that weakness of the sinful nature in our bodies is removed and so we are raised in power (1 Cor 15:42–44).

The resurrection is God's redemption of our bodies. God redeems our bodies by removing the sinful nature from within it, so that upon our resurrection, our bodies, the exact same bodies that came from our mother's womb, will no longer have sin within them, for the sinful nature will be removed and our bodies will be completely free of sin and corruption. In our resurrection we will be exactly as was Adam before the fall, and as was Jesus Christ after his resurrection—sinless flesh-and-bone human beings (Gen 2:23; Luke 24:39).

All humanity will be resurrected, all believers and all non-believers, but believers are resurrected first. That resurrection happens with the opening of Seal 7.

THE RESURRECTION OF BELIEVERS

As God's redemption of humanity unfolds, it is the believers, Christians, who will be resurrected *first*, and then, much later, all non-believers will *also* be resurrected (Rev 20:11–15). The resurrection of believers happens *just before* Jesus descends to Earth at the Second Coming, during Seal 7. Upon being resurrected, *all* the resurrected believers will ascend into the sky to be with Jesus *before* he descends at the Second Coming and then, as Jesus descends to Earth at the Second Coming, all the resurrected believers *will descend and come to Earth with him*, and so the Lord "comes with all his holy ones" (1 Thess 3:13; Jude 14).

This resurrection of believers is also described as the wedding feast of the Bride and the Lamb, and it occurs *after* the Seal 6 fall of Babylon the Great, occurring with the opening of Seal 7.

> Let us rejoice and be glad
> and give him glory!

> For the wedding of the Lamb has come,
> and his bride has made herself ready.
> Fine linen, bright and clean,
> was given her to wear."
> (Fine linen stands for the righteous acts of God's holy people.)
> Then the angel said to me, "Write this: Blessed are those who are invited to the wedding supper of the Lamb!" And he added, "These are the true words of God." (Rev 19:7–9 NIV)

Revelation 19:7–9 is a declaration that is made *after* the fall of Babylon the Great, but *before* the Second Coming, with the Second Coming occurring at 19:11–21. The opening of Seal 7 results in the sounding of Trumpet 7, the last Trumpet, and it is at the sound of that last Trumpet that the resurrection of believers occurs, which is then followed by the Second Coming.

When Jesus finishes describing Seal 6 in Matthew 24, he immediately begins to describe Seal 7.

> Then will appear the sign of *the Son of Man* in *heaven*. And then all the peoples of the earth will mourn when they see *the Son of Man* coming *on the clouds* of heaven, with power and great glory. And he will send his angels *with a loud trumpet call*, and they *will gather his elect from the four winds*, from one end of the heavens to the other. (Matt 24:30–31 NIV)

We are told here that after Seal 6 Jesus will be seen in the earthly sky, on the clouds, but he does not yet descend to Earth. While he is in the sky, but before he descends, Jesus sends his angels to gather *all* "his elect"—this is the resurrection of believers and includes *both* the living *and* the dead elect.

Also, very importantly, Jesus tells us that this happens "with a loud trumpet call." What is this loud trumpet call? It is Trumpet 7, the last Trumpet of Revelation. This exact same event is described in 1 Corinthians.

> in a flash, in the twinkling of an eye, at *the last trumpet*. For *the trumpet will sound*, the *dead* will be *raised imperishable, and* we will be *changed*. (1 Cor 15:52 NIV)

This is also affirmed in 1 Thessalonians.

> For the Lord himself *will come down from heaven*, with a loud command, with the voice of the archangel and with *the trumpet call* of God, and the *dead in Christ* will *rise first*. After that, we *who are still alive* and are left *will be caught up* together with them *in the clouds* to *meet the Lord in the air*. (1 Thess 4:16–17 NIV)

All of these passages are describing exactly the same event, and all agree on the details. Here is what we know.

SEAL 7—THE RESURRECTION OF BELIEVERS

When Seal 7 is opened, Jesus returns to Earth for the Second Coming, but before he descends to Earth, Trumpet 7, the last Trumpet of Revelation, will sound (this is all in Seal 7). At the sounding of Trumpet 7, while Jesus is in the sky of the Earth, *all* the Christians who have ever lived *and died*, from Adam to that very day, will be *resurrected*—this is the "dead" who "rise first." Then, *after* the dead Christians are resurrected, the Christians who are *still alive* on Earth at that time will *also* be taken and *transformed* into their *resurrected* selves (i.e., the blood removed from their bodies, and so the perishable becomes "imperishable," 1 Cor 15:42-44). This is what 1 Corinthians 15:52 means when it tells us that we who remain (i.e., who are alive) "will be changed"—it is a description of the resurrection transformation of the *living* believers. *All* of this is a description of the *resurrection* of believers, and that event is also described as the wedding of the Bride and the Lamb (Rev 19:7-9).

In the resurrection of believers, all believers—all those who were resurrected from death and all those who were transformed while still alive—will rise, or be "caught up," into the air, into the clouds, where Jesus will be waiting—they will meet him and be with him in the sky (Matt 24:30; 1 Thess 4:17). Then, when *all* the resurrected believers meet Jesus in the earthly sky, *that* is when Jesus descends to Earth at the Second Coming, and *all* the resurrected believers *descend with him*, and so the Lord "comes with all his holy ones" (1 Thess 3:13; Jude 14).

These very same verses describing the resurrection of believers—1 Corinthians 15:52, 1 Thessalonians 4:16-17, together with Matthew 24:40-41—are invoked by John Darby to support his rapture teaching. As discussed previously, and affirmed here again, those verses do not support any such rapture teaching, not in in any way, shape, form, version, or variation of that teaching—those verses speak *only* of the resurrection of believers, which is the core foundational truth of the Christian faith.

This resurrection of all believers is also described as the "first resurrection" (Rev 20:4-6). In this Revelation 20 passage, the dead who were killed during the reign of the Beast for their faithfulness to Jesus are specifically referenced as being resurrected, which of course will be true. However, we know, with certainty, that those who were killed for their faith during the reign of the Beast are not the *only* ones who have died in Christ and who will be resurrected—we know that *all* who have died as Christians, not only those who died during the reign of the Beast, but all Christians who have ever lived and died throughout all of history, will be resurrected *at that time* (1 Thess 4:16; 1 Cor 15:52). First Corinthians 15:52 specifically tells us that "the dead" will be raised—not just some of the dead, but *all* the dead—and we know that this is referring *only* to the "dead in Christ," which is specifically affirmed in 1 Thessalonians 4:16. As a result, the specific Christians who died for Christ during the reign of the Beast are *included* with the "dead in Christ" of 1 Thessalonians 4:16, but Revelation 20:4-6 specifically highlights those specific Christians who died for Christ during the reign of the Beast since the entire book of Revelation is a description of the events of *that* time, and so the focus of Revelation 20:4–6 is on those who died *during* that time, during the events that have just been described.

When we apply 1 Corinthians 15:52 and 1 Thessalonians 4:16 in that same context, we get the full picture of the resurrection. That resurrection, the *first* resurrection, is the resurrection of *all* believers. The term "the rest of the dead" (Rev 20:5), which is referring to those who are *not* part of that first resurrection, is a reference specifically to all those who have died and who were *not* Christians—*those* dead, all *non-believers*, will *also* be resurrected, but only *after* the Lord Jesus has ruled on Earth for a thousand years—the resurrection of non-believers is a second resurrection. That second resurrection, and judgment, of non-believers is described specifically in Revelation 20:11–15, and it is described as occurring after the initial thousand-year reign of the Lord Jesus upon the Earth.

When Seal 7 is opened, Jesus returns to Earth, and waits in the sky. While he is in the earthly sky, Trumpet 7, the last Trumpet, is sounded, and with the sounding of that last Trumpet all the Christians who have ever lived and died are physically resurrected—their bodies, the same bodies that came from their mother's womb, will rise to life, but without the sinful nature and consequent blood, and so they will be raised immortal, imperishable, incorruptible, and powerful (1 Cor 15:50–54).

After the dead in Christ are resurrected first, *then* the *second part* of the *resurrection of believers* occurs. The second part of the resurrection of believers, which also occurs at the sounding of Trumpet 7, is all the living Christians who are still *alive* on the Earth at the time of the Second Coming being *transformed* into their resurrected selves, whereby the sinful nature, with its consequent blood, will be removed from their bodies, so that those *living* believers will also be raised and transformed as imperishable and powerful.

Then, upon that full resurrection, *all* the resurrected believers will rise into the earthly sky to meet Jesus—that will be the Bride uniting with the Bridegroom, which is described in the Bible as the wedding of the Bride and the Lamb. At that point, once all the resurrected believers meet Jesus in the air and are united with him in the clouds of the earthly sky, only *then* does Jesus descend to Earth, physically returning for his Second Coming, and *all the believers return with him*, as he leads the way.

It is important to understand that when Jesus descends to Earth at the Second Coming, all believers—dead and living—have been resurrected and have been gathered with Jesus in the air before he descends. That means that when Jesus descends to Earth, the *entire population remaining on Earth* will be all *non-believers*. This is very important to remember when we look at the judgment that follows the Second Coming—that judgment, the judgment of Jesus Christ upon the remaining humanity upon the Earth, will be *entirely* a judgment of non-believers.

20

SEAL 7—THE SECOND COMING

THE CULMINATION OF THE book of Revelation, and of the Christian faith, is the Second Coming. The Second Coming, the return and descent of the Lord Jesus Christ to Earth, occurs during Seal 7, after the resurrection of all believers. At the sounding of the last Trumpet, Trumpet 7, in Seal 7 (1 Cor 15:52; 1 Thess 4:16), all believers will have been resurrected and gathered to meet Jesus in the sky, in the clouds (Matt 24:31; 1 Thess 4:17), and then, as Jesus descends to Earth, all the resurrected believers, all of the "holy ones" who belong to Jesus Christ, will descend with him to Earth (1 Thess 3:13; Jude 14). Jesus will lead the way; the resurrected Christians will follow.

When Jesus descends, he does not come quietly, nor in secret; rather he comes with a "shout" (1 Thess 4:16 NKJV). Jesus will descend to Earth as the resurrected man that he is—an approximately six-foot-tall, flesh-and-bone (Luke 24:39; Eph 5:30) resurrected *man* (Acts 1:9–11). He will come upon the clouds, descending to Earth from the sky (Rev 1:7), and even though he is a normal-size man, when he descends the whole world will see him (Rev 1:7). Also, as Jesus descends to Earth, the Jews will finally recognize him as Messiah and mourn that they had previously rejected him (Zech 12:10).

When Jesus returns to Earth at the Second Coming, he will first touch land at the Mount of Olives, in the nation of Judah (modern-day Israel, Zech 14:4). When Jesus ascended to heaven, forty days after his resurrection, he ascended from the Mount of Olives (Acts 1:3, 9–12). The apostles watched him as he rose into the sky, where he was enveloped by a cloud as he continued to ascend (Acts 1:9). As they watched him ascend, two angels appeared to the apostles and told them that when Jesus returns, he will return in the same manner that he ascended (Acts 1:11). This means that Jesus will return from the sky and will return to the same location from which he ascended, the Mount of Olives.

This is further affirmed in Zechariah 14:3–4, which tells us that when Jesus returns at the Second Coming, his feet will stand on the Mount of Olives. As a result, we know that when Jesus returns at the Second Coming, he returns on the clouds, from the sky, with a shout, accompanied by all the resurrected believers, his holy ones, and he touches down at the Mount of Olives, the same place from which he ascended.

THE LAND WILL SPLIT

We are also told that when Jesus sets foot on the Mount of Olives at his return, the land at the Mount of Olives will split.

> And in that day His feet will stand on the Mount of Olives,
> Which faces Jerusalem on the east.
> And the Mount of Olives shall be split in two,
> From east to west,
> Making a very large valley;
> Half of the mountain shall move toward the north
> And half of it toward the south.
> Then you shall flee through My mountain valley,
> For the mountain valley shall reach to Azal.
> Yes, you shall flee
> As you fled from the earthquake
> In the days of Uzziah king of Judah.
> Thus *the Lord my God will come,*
> And *all the saints with You.* (Zech 14:4–5 NKJV)

When Jesus' foot touches down at the Mount of Olives, the Mount of Olives, which is near Jerusalem, will "be split in two," being split from east to west, resulting in a large valley—half of the mount will move north, half will move south, and the Jews who are there will flee into that valley for refuge and protection as Jesus' faces the armies of the world, and destroys them. Zechariah 14:5 also further affirms that when the LORD comes, all his saints (the resurrected Christians) come with him.

THE RIDER ON A WHITE HORSE

The description of Jesus' return at the Second Coming is given in Revelation 19:11–16.

> Now I saw heaven opened, and behold, a white horse. And He who sat on him was called Faithful and True, and in righteousness He judges and makes war. His eyes were like a flame of fire, and on His head were many crowns. He had a name written that no one knew except Himself. He was clothed with a robe dipped in blood, and His name is called The Word of God. And the armies in heaven, clothed in fine linen, white and clean, followed Him on white horses. Now out of His mouth goes a sharp sword, that with it He should strike the nations. And He Himself will rule them with a rod of iron. He Himself treads the winepress of the fierceness and wrath of Almighty God. And He has on

His robe and on His thigh a name written: KING OF KINGS AND LORD OF LORDS. (NKJV)

When Jesus appears in the sky at the Second Coming, he is described as riding a "white horse." He is also described as having eyes that "were like a flame of fire" and as wearing "many crowns." We are told that he had a "name written," presumably on himself, that no one but he himself knew, and that he was wearing a "robe dipped in blood." Armies followed him, with these armies being described as being "clothed in fine linen."

The description of the armies that followed him being clothed in fine white linen is yet another description of the resurrected Christians returning to Earth with Jesus, and we can understand that as follows. We are specifically told that it is Christians who, upon their resurrection, will be wearing white robes, which represents the "righteous acts of the saints" (Rev 7:13–17; 19:8). Since we know that all Christians will be resurrected prior to Jesus' descent to Earth at the Second Coming, and will then be caught up to meet Jesus in the air and return with him, and since we know that those resurrected Christians will be arrayed in white robes, and since Revelation 19:14 tells us that the armies returning with Jesus at his descent at the Second Coming are arrayed in white linen, we can conclude that the armies who descend with Jesus at the Second Coming are the same resurrected believers who were gathered to meet him in the sky and who return with him as he descends to Earth.

We are also told that a sharp double-edged sword is coming out of his mouth, and it is with that sword that Jesus will "strike the nations." We also know that the double-edged sword represents God's word (Heb 4:12). As a result, from this description of the double-edged sword coming from Jesus' mouth, we can conclude that Jesus will strike the nations with his spoken word—he will speak, and it will happen. This is affirmed in both Isaiah 11:4 and 2 Thessalonians 2:8.

> But with righteousness He shall judge the poor, And decide with equity for the meek of the earth; He shall **strike the earth with the rod of His mouth**, And **with the breath of His lips** He shall **slay the wicked**. (Isa 11:4 NKJV)

> And then the lawless one will be revealed, whom *the Lord will consume* with *the breath of His mouth* and destroy with the brightness of *His coming*. (2 Thess 2:8 NKJV)

Isaiah tells us that the Lord will "strike the Earth with the rod of his mouth," which seems an exact parallel to the Revelation 19 image of the two-edged sword coming out of Jesus' mouth. Then, related to that, we are told that "with the breath of his lips he shall slay the wicked." The phrase "breath of his lips" denotes speaking—as a result, we can know that it is with his spoken word that Jesus will slay the wicked.

Likewise, 2 Thessalonians tells us that at his coming Jesus will "consume" the "lawless one" (the Beast) "with the breath of his mouth." Again, the phrase "breath of his mouth" denotes speaking, which affirms again that it is by way of his spoken word that Jesus will accomplish these things. All of that is represented in Revelation 19:15 by the image of the two-edged sword that protrudes out of Jesus' mouth—the two-edged sword is his spoken word and is the power and authority of that word.

Jesus is also described as having written on his thigh the title "King of Kings and Lord of Lords." This title is a reference to both Jesus Christ and to all believers, for all believers will rule the Earth with Jesus Christ, reigning with him (Rev 20:4). The resurrected Christians will be the kings and the lords of the Earth, but Jesus will be *their* King and he will be *their* Lord. As a result, Jesus will literally be the "King of Kings and the Lord of Lords"—the resurrected Christians who are ruling the Earth with Christ are the kings and lords of whom Jesus is King and Lord.

At his Coming, Jesus is also described as treading the "winepress of the fierceness and wrath of Almighty God," which means that when he returns he comes as Judge, for all judgment belongs to the Son; the Father judges no one (John 5:22).

This image of the returning Jesus Christ in Revelation 19 is in great contrast to the image of Seal 1, the image of both a false Christianity *and* of the false Christ, the Beast, who is born as a human baby at the start of Seal 1. In that Seal 1 image, we see a poor imitation of the image of the returning Jesus Christ.

> And I looked, and behold, a white horse. He who sat on it had a bow; and a crown was given to him, and he went out conquering and to conquer. (Rev 6:2 NKJV)

Both the image of Seal 1 and the image of Jesus in 19:11–16 have a rider on a white horse. The Seal 1 image has a bow, but no arrows, while in Revelation 19 Jesus has a two-edged sword proceeding from his mouth. The Seal 1 image has a "crown" that "was given to him," while Jesus in Revelation 19 has "many crowns," and no one gave them to him. In addition, Jesus in Revelation 19 is wearing a "robe dripped in blood," and is named as "King of Kings and Lord of Lords," while the Seal 1 image has no such things. The Seal 1 image, which represents both the false Christianity and the coming the great apostasy of the church (Matt 24:4–5; 2 Thess 2:1–3; 1 Pet 4:17), *as well as* the birth of the Beast as a human baby, which occurs approximately nine months after Seal 1 is opened, is a poor imitation of the real Christ as represented in Revelation 19:11–16.

ARMAGEDDON

The Second Coming, Jesus' descent to Earth with the resurrected Christians, occurs in Seal 7, after the Tribulation of Seal 5 is over, and after the Seal 6 fall of Babylon the Great. The actual day of his descent will be 1,335 days *after* the Beast enthrones himself in the rebuilt temple, the act that is described as the "abomination of desolation" (Dan 12:12). The armies of the world had gathered to accomplish the destruction of

SEAL 7—THE SECOND COMING

Babylon the Great during Seal 6/Trumpet 6/Bowls 6 and 7 (Rev 9:13–16; 16:12–14). We are told in Revelation 16:14 that this *same* gathering of armies for the destruction of Babylon the Great is *also* a gathering of armies to fight against Jesus Christ at his Second Coming. As a result, we can conclude that after the fall of Babylon the Great, whose destruction was accomplished by the armies of the world, as stirred by God's will (Rev 17:16–17), those same armies will continue and gather both against Jerusalem (Zech 14:1–2) and at the valley of Megiddo, Har Megiddo, "Armageddon" (Rev 16:16). The armies that gather there will be the armies of the Beast (Dan 11:44–45) as well as the other armies of the world, including the army of two hundred million (Rev 9:16)—they will gather against Jerusalem and will also gather at the valley of Armageddon.

Armageddon is an actual place, an actual location in Judah (modern-day Israel). It is located approximately thirty kilometers southeast of Haifa and it is a vast plain, a place that can easily accommodate a huge military number, and it is the location to which the armies of the world will be gathered prior to Jesus' descent at the Second Coming.

WHAT HAPPENS AT JESUS' RETURN?

When Jesus returns to Earth at the Second Coming, with all the resurrected believers following him, he touches down on the Mount of Olives, which then splits in two, creating a great valley into which the Jews in Jerusalem will flee for refuge. Jesus then goes and confronts the world's armies at Armageddon, with the resurrected believers following him and witnessing his actions.

At Armageddon, the Beast will be there as head of the armies, and the False Prophet will be with him, and everyone there will have taken the mark of the Beast. We are very specifically told that it is at Armageddon that both the Beast and the False Prophet will be taken, captured, and "cast alive into the lake of fire" (commonly called "hell").

> And I saw the beast, the kings of the earth, and their armies, gathered together to make war against Him who sat on the horse and against His army. Then the beast was captured, and with him the false prophet who worked signs in his presence, by which he deceived those who received the mark of the beast and those who worshiped his image. These two were cast alive into the lake of fire burning with brimstone. And the rest were killed with the sword which proceeded from the mouth of Him who sat on the horse. And all the birds were filled with their flesh. (Rev 19:19–21 NKJV)

The Beast and the False Prophet will be the very first beings to ever have been cast into the Lake of Fire—no human being has ever been there; Satan has never been there; no fallen angelic being has ever been there. The Beast and the False Prophet will be the very *first* beings cast into the Lake of Fire, and that will happen at Armageddon.

After the Beast and the False Prophet are cast into the Lake of Fire, we are told that the rest of the gathered armies are "killed with the sword which proceeded from the mouth of him who sat on the horse." This is a reference to the double-edged sword that proceeds from the mouth of Jesus Christ—the armies of the world are destroyed at Armageddon, all at once, by the *word of power* spoken by Jesus Christ, the "breath of his mouth" (2 Thess 2:8).

WHAT DOES THEIR DESTRUCTION LOOK LIKE?

We know that those who are killed at Armageddon, which will be all the armies of the world gathered for battle against Jesus Christ, will be killed by the "breath" of Jesus' mouth, killed by his spoken word of power (Isa 11:4; 2 Thess 2:8). What will their destruction look like? We are given a clear description of exactly that in Zechariah.

> And this shall be the plague with which the Lord will strike all the people
> who fought
> against Jerusalem:
> Their flesh shall dissolve while they stand on their feet,
> Their eyes shall dissolve in their sockets,
> And their tongues shall dissolve in their mouths. (Zech 14:12 NKJV)

We are told that for those people who gathered to fight against Jerusalem in the day of the Lord's coming, "their flesh shall dissolve while they stand on their feet," and "their eyes shall dissolve" while still in their sockets, and "their tongues shall dissolve" while still in their mouths. The description seems clearly a representation of people melting on the spot, melting where they stand.

This is also a description of what it means to be "taken away" (Matt 24:39–41). Where John Darby, in his rapture teaching, teaches that to be "taken" at the Second Coming means to be rescued, Jesus, and Scripture, tells us that to be "taken" means to be utterly destroyed—that utter destruction, described as being "taken" at the Second Coming, is the same melting on the spot of Zechariah 14:12, a destruction accomplished by the breath of Jesus' mouth, by the power of his spoken word.

This is the Second Coming of the Lord Jesus Christ. He descends to Earth with all the resurrected believers, his Bride, who meet him in the earthly sky and who then follow him as he descends to Earth, witnessing his actions at his return. He touches down at the Mount of Olives, which then splits in two to create a valley into which the Jews at Jerusalem will flee for refuge. Jesus then confronts the world's armies at Armageddon, where both the Beast and the False Prophet are taken and thrown alive into the Lake of Fire, becoming the very first beings, ever, to be cast into hell. Jesus then destroys all the gathered armies at Armageddon with the breath of his mouth, by the power of his spoken word, whereupon the armies of the world dissolve on the spot and are utterly destroyed. At that point, the Lord Jesus Christ claims the dominion of Earth that he won upon his resurrection, the same dominion that God gave to Adam (Gen 1:26), and which Adam, upon his fall, gave to Satan (Luke 4:5–7), which same dominion was won back by Jesus Christ upon his resurrection and which is implemented by Jesus Christ at the Second Coming.

SATAN BOUND AND IMPRISONED

It is because Jesus takes back the dominion to the Earth at his Second Coming that one other great event happens at that same time—Satan himself is bound and imprisoned.

> Then I saw an angel coming down from heaven, having the key to the bottomless pit and a great chain in his hand. He laid hold of the dragon, that serpent of old, who is the Devil and Satan, and bound him for a thousand years; and he cast him into the bottomless pit, and shut him up, and set a seal on him, so that he should deceive the nations no more till the thousand years were finished. But after these things he must be released for a little while. (Rev 20:1–3 NKJV)

At the Second Coming, after the Beast and the False Prophet are taken and cast alive into the Lake of Fire, and after the armies of the world have been destroyed at Armageddon, Satan himself is then taken by an angel who comes down from heaven and who has the key to the Pit. The Pit is the place of imprisonment for the fallen angels, a place inside the Earth, and it was the original place to where the angels were thrown upon being cast out of heaven. That angel also has a great chain, and the angel takes Satan and binds him in the great chain and throws him into the Pit, the Abyss, inside the Earth. The angel then shuts the Pit, locks it up, and sets a seal on it so that Satan is bound and imprisoned for one thousand years, after which he will be released again upon the Earth.

As previously discussed, Satan, by being thrown into the Pit, is suffering the same fate as the "sons of god," the fallen angelic beings who went to the "daughters of men" in Genesis 6:2–4 and who fathered the Nephilim offspring. Those sons of God were subsequently bound and cast into the dark prison of the Pit (1 Pet 3:19–20; Jude 6–7). The fact that Satan now suffers the same fate as the previous fathers of the Nephilim is a further affirmation that Satan himself committed the same act of fathering an offspring with a human woman, in his case fathering the Beast, the seed of the serpent (Gen 3:15; Rev 20:2). It is very important to understand that even at that time Satan is *still not yet* in the Lake of Fire; he is *not* in hell—rather, he is imprisoned in the Pit, the Abyss, inside the Earth, from which he will later be released, to once again be free upon the Earth.

With Satan's imprisonment in the Pit, he will no longer have a presence in the world; rather, the world will be ruled by Jesus Christ. Upon his Second Coming, the

Lord Jesus Christ has reclaimed the dominion of the Earth and will now establish his kingdom upon it, ruling the Earth with his Bride, the resurrected church, comprised of *all* resurrected believers, all of whom descended to Earth with Jesus at his Coming.

With the armies who gathered against him now destroyed, with the Beast and False Prophet now cast into the Lake of Fire, and with Satan now bound and imprisoned, Seal 7 is finished and the Seven Seals are completed. Jesus will then take his seat in Jerusalem, in the rebuilt temple, in the holy of holies, and reign over the Earth as King and Lord, but first he will judge the remnant humanity that is still upon the Earth, the people who remain of the nations that went to war against him, a humanity comprised *entirely* of non-Christians, many of which did *not* take the mark of the Beast.

21

JUDGMENT AND THE KINGDOM

WHEN JESUS RETURNS TO Earth at the Second Coming, he will descend onto the Mount of Olives in Jerusalem. From there he goes to Armageddon to confront the armies of the Beast and of the world, where he destroys them. Upon the destruction of the armies, Jesus returns to Jerusalem where he will sit enthroned as King of the world (Zech 8:3; 14:16), reigning upon David's earthly throne in Jerusalem (Luke 1:32–33; Isa 9:7). It is almost certain that the location of his throne will be in the holy of holies of the rebuilt temple, which is why the abomination of desolation is the event that triggers the Tribulation, for with that act the Beast is usurping Jesus' own throne on Earth. When Jesus assumes the throne of David, in Jerusalem, he will then judge the remaining people of Earth.

JUDGING THE LIVING AND THE DEAD

The Creed of the church is very clear when it speaks of the Second Coming of the Lord Jesus Christ—when Jesus returns at the Second Coming, he will return "with glory" and he will "judge the living and the dead." The first dead that are judged are in fact the dead Christians, all of whom are judged to resurrection and to everlasting life, for those dead Christians are the first to rise (1 Thess 4:16). After that, the living Christians are judged, also to resurrection and to everlasting life (1 Thess 4:17). With those two judgments, Jesus is already judging the living and the dead, all in accordance with the Creed of the church.

After Jesus descends to Earth and destroys the Beast and the armies gathered against him at Armageddon, and after he is enthroned in Jerusalem, he then judges the rest of the living, which is all the *remaining non-Christians*, the people who remain of the nations that went to war against him.

> And it shall come to pass that *everyone who is left of all the nations which came against Jerusalem* shall go up from year to year to worship the King, the Lord of hosts, and to keep the Feast of Tabernacles. (Zech 14:16 NKJV)

The "everyone who is left" described in Zechariah 14:16 are *some* of the non-Christians who were judged at the Second Coming. Just as Matthew 24 gives us a detailed outline of the Seven Seals, in order, culminating in the Second Coming, so Matthew 25 continues that same narrative, giving us details of what the judgment of *the nations* will look like after Jesus returns.

> But when the Son of Man comes in His glory, and all the angels with Him, then He will sit on His glorious throne. And *all the nations* will be gathered before Him; and He will separate them from one another, just as the shepherd separates the sheep from the goats; and He will put the sheep on His right, but the goats on the left. "Then the King will say to those on His right, 'Come, you who are blessed of My Father, inherit the kingdom prepared for you from the foundation of the world. For I was hungry, and you gave Me something to eat; I was thirsty, and you gave Me something to drink; I was a stranger, and you invited Me in; naked, and you clothed Me; I was sick, and you visited Me; I was in prison, and you came to Me.' Then the righteous will answer Him, 'Lord, when did we see You hungry, and feed You, or thirsty, and give You something to drink? And when did we see You as a stranger, and invite You in, or naked, and clothe You? And when did we see You sick, or in prison, and come to You?' And the King will answer and say to them, 'Truly I say to you, to the extent that you did it for one of the least of these brothers or sisters of Mine, you did it for Me.' "Then He will also say to those on His left, 'Depart from Me, you accursed people, into the eternal fire which has been prepared for the devil and his angels; for I was hungry, and you gave Me nothing to eat; I was thirsty, and you gave Me nothing to drink; I was a stranger, and you did not invite Me in; naked, and you did not clothe Me; sick, and in prison, and you did not visit Me.' Then they themselves also will answer, 'Lord, when did we see You hungry, or thirsty, or as a stranger, or naked, or sick, or in prison, and did not take care of You?' Then He will answer them, 'Truly I say to you, to the extent that you did not do it for one of the least of these, you did not do it for Me, either.' These will go away into eternal punishment, but the righteous into eternal life." (Matt 25:31–46 NASB)

In Matthew 25:1–30, Jesus gives us two parables about people being prepared, or not prepared, for his Second Coming. These parables are given immediately *after* Jesus gives us the detailed outline of the Seven Seals in Matthew 24, and just *before* he continues to describe his judgment of the nations upon his return.

Matthew 25: 31 tells us that, upon his Second Coming, Jesus will sit enthroned in his glory. That throne will be the throne of David in Jerusalem, almost certainly located in the holy of holies of the rebuilt temple. We are then told that "all the nations" will be gathered before him, and he will judge the nations.

The nations referred to in Matthew 25:32 are the same nations as are described in Zechariah 14:16—these nations are *the remaining people* of the *nations* who were gathered for war against Jerusalem and against Jesus Christ at Armageddon. It is very important to remember that *all* of the people who remain *on Earth* are *non-Christians*, since *all* the Christians have already been resurrected, returning with Jesus at his Coming. The resurrected Christians are *not* among *any* who remain of the nations that gathered for war against Jerusalem or who gathered against Jesus. As the remaining people of the nations are gathered before Jesus for judgment, all the resurrected and immortal Christians are there with Jesus as he judges those people.

It is those remaining people, the ones who remain from the nations that gathered for war against him, that Jesus divides into two groups. One group of these non-Christians are called "sheep" and will be on his right-hand side, while the other group of non-Christians are called "goats" and will be on his left-hand side—and *all* of these are *non-Christians*. Jesus speaks to the non-Christians on his right-hand side and tells them to enter his kingdom, telling them that when he was hungry and thirsty, they fed him and gave him water; when he was a stranger and naked, they took him in and clothed him; when he was sick and in prison, they visited him and came to him. But, because all of those sheep on his right-hand side are not Christians, they have no idea what he is talking about, so they ask him "when" they did those things for him. Jesus answers them, with all the resurrected and immortal Christians standing with him and watching, that when they, the sheep, "did it to one of the least of *these* My brethren, you did it to Me." Who are the "least of *these*" that Jesus is referring to? Remember, the sheep on his right-hand side have no idea what he is taking about, since they are non-Christians, *but* all the resurrected Christians are there, standing with him, all now immortal and having returned with him at the Second Coming—it is to the *resurrected Christians* who are *there with him* that Jesus is referring to as the "least of *these*"—he is referring to the *least* of the resurrected Christians.

Also, since he is specifically judging the people who are still alive on the Earth after his Second Coming, when Jesus refers to the "least of *these*" he is in fact referring specifically to the Christians who have just come through the great persecution of the Beast during his three-and-a-half-year reign. When *those* Christians were being persecuted, persecuted by the Beast, the non-Christians at the time who did *not* take the mark of the Beast helped the persecuted Christians, just as some Germans in Nazi Germany helped persecuted Jews. Those non-Christians who did not take the mark of the Beast and who, during the time of the great persecution of the church by the Beast, helped the persecuted Christians—giving them food, drink, clothing them, visiting them—*they* are told by Jesus to enter into and inherit his kingdom.

Why do those non-Christians get to inherit the kingdom? It is in fact a fulfillment of Matthew 10:41–42.

He who receives a prophet in the name of a prophet shall receive a prophet's reward. And he who receives a righteous man in the name of a righteous man shall receive a righteous man's reward. And whoever gives one of these little ones only a cup of cold water in the name of a disciple, assuredly, I say to you, he shall by no means lose his reward. (NKJV)

Jesus tells us that anyone "who receives a *righteous* man," which, by extension, also means anyone who helps a righteous man, will receive the *same* reward as that righteous man. Likewise, anyone who gives "a cup of water" to a thirsting disciple (i.e., Christian) will be rewarded. The "cup of water" comment is almost identical to Jesus' words to the sheep at his right hand when he says to them, "I was thirsty and you gave me drink" (Matt 25:35)—since those sheep don't understand what he is talking about, Jesus explains to them that when they gave drink to any thirsting Christian, they gave it to him.

Also, the very clear reward of all Christians (who are all "righteous") is that they inherit God's kingdom; therefore, when someone helps a "righteous man" (a Christian), they will also get the "righteous man's reward." Since the reward of the righteous man (Christians) is to inherit the kingdom, then those people who, though they were non-Christians, helped Christians in their time of persecution, will also receive the reward of those Christians—they will get to inherit the kingdom, and they will inherit the kingdom as *mortal* human beings, while the Christians, all of whom are resurrected, will inherit it as *immortal* human beings. This is a profoundly beautiful thing, and a great witness to the love and mercy of God, who loves all people.

NOT EVERYONE RECEIVED THE MARK OF THE BEAST

In some translations we read that "every person on earth" who isn't a Christian gets the mark of the Beast and worships him. However, that is not true. The accurate translation, when describing those who worship the Beast and take his mark, is that people from "every tribe, tongue, and nation" will receive his mark.

> It was granted to him to make war with the saints and to overcome them. And authority was given him over *every tribe, tongue, and nation. All who dwell* on the earth will worship him, whose names have not been written in the Book of Life of the Lamb slain from the foundation of the world. (Rev 13:7–8 NKJV)

These same people are described again in Revelation 11.

> Then those from the *peoples, tribes, tongues, and nations* will see their dead bodies three-and-a-half days, and not allow their dead bodies to be put into graves. And *those who dwell on the earth* will rejoice over them, make merry, and send gifts to one another, because these two prophets tormented those who dwell on the earth. (Rev 11:9–10 NKJV)

A different group is referred to in the same way in Revelation 7, this time referring to Christians, the redeemed.

> After these things I looked, and behold, a great multitude which no one could number, *of all nations, tribes, peoples, and tongues*, standing before the throne and before the Lamb, clothed with white robes, with palm branches in their hands, (Rev 7:9 NKJV)

The phrase "every tribe, tongue, and nation" means people from *among* every tribe, tongue, and nation; it does not mean every single person on Earth.

Also, when reference is made in Revelation 13:8 to "all who dwell on the earth," that reference is *in the context of* people from every tribe, tongue, and nation and means those who dwell on the Earth who are *from* every tribe, tongue, and nation—it does not mean that all people on Earth will worship the Beast. The similar phrase "of all nations, tribes, peoples, and tongues" is use in Revelation 7:9 as a reference to the redeemed—the redeemed are also described as being "of all nations, tribes, peoples, and tongues"—this does *not* mean that *all* people on Earth are the redeemed, but rather it means that the redeemed *come from among* all nations, tribes, and tongues.

We know, with certainty, that the church is present on Earth through all the events of Revelation 6–19 (Matt 24:9; Rev 12:14–17), and so we can know that the phrase "of all nations, tribes, peoples, and tongues" does *not* mean every single person who dwells on Earth will worship the Beast, but rather it means that the people who worship the Beast and who take his mark will come from *among* all tribes, tongues, and nations—there will be many *non-Christians* during that time who will *not* take the mark of the Beast and who will, during the time of the Beast's persecution of Christians, *help* the persecuted church. *Those* are the people who, at that judgment of Matthew 25, are the sheep at the right hand of Jesus—they are the non-Christians who did not take the mark of the Beast and who helped the persecuted church. As a result of helping "a righteous man," those non-Christians get the "righteous man's reward"; they get to inherit the kingdom as *mortal, non-resurrected* human beings (and this is all further, and inarguably, affirmed in Isaiah 65:17–25).

The rest of the people that remain of the nations, those on Jesus' left-hand side, who are described as "goats," are the non-Christians who *did* take the mark of the Beast and who worshiped him. When Jesus tells them that when he was hungry, thirsty, naked, imprisoned, and sick, they did not help him, they too, like the "sheep" at his right hand, don't understand what he is talking about, since they, like the sheep, are all non-Christians, so Jesus explains it to them just as he explained it to the sheep at his right hand. All of *those* people will be sent to the Realm of the Dead to await their resurrection and subsequent judgment (Rev 20:11–15).

As a result, the inhabitants of Jesus' kingdom will be resurrected, immortal Christians (all Christians who have ever lived), *and mortal, non-resurrected* human beings, who will still age and die.

MORTAL INHABITANTS OF THE KINGDOM

This is all very clearly affirmed for us in Isaiah 65:17–25.

> "See, I will create
> new heavens and a new earth.
> The former things will not be remembered,
> nor will they come to mind.
> But be glad and rejoice forever
> in what I will create,
> for I will create Jerusalem to be a delight
> and its people a joy.
> I will rejoice over Jerusalem
> and take delight in my people;
> the sound of weeping and of crying
> will be heard in it no more.
>
> "Never again will there be in it
> an infant who lives but a few days,
> or an old man who does not live out his years;
> the *one who dies at a hundred*
> will be thought *a mere child*;
> the *one who fails to reach a hundred*
> will be *considered accursed*.
> They will build houses and dwell in them;
> they will plant vineyards and eat their fruit.
> No longer will they build houses and others live in them,
> or plant and others eat.
> For *as the days of a tree,*
> *so will be the days of my people*;
> my chosen ones *will long enjoy*
> *the work of their hands.*
> *They will not labor in vain,*
> nor *will they bear children* doomed to misfortune;
> for they will be a people blessed by the Lord,
> they *and their descendants* with them.
> Before they call I will answer;
> while they are still speaking I will hear.
> *The wolf and the lamb* will *feed together,*
> and *the lion* will *eat straw like the ox,*
> and dust will be the serpent's food.
> They will neither harm nor destroy
> on all my holy mountain,"
> says the Lord. (Isa 65:17–25 NIV)

This passage in Isaiah is describing a very unique time, a time that has never yet been upon Earth. This is describing a time when "the wolf and the lamb will feed together," and when "the lion will eat straw like the ox." The only time, ever, that the wolf and the lamb fed together (meaning they *both* ate plants) and the lion ate straw (plants) was in the time before Adam's fall, when God created the animals and gave them every green plant for food (Gen 1:30). It was only *after* Adam's fall, when Adam gave his God-given dominion to Satan, that animals began to kill and eat other animals, and plants became poisonous, for when Adam, upon his fall, gave the dominion of the Earth to Satan (Luke 4:5–7), the Earth and everything upon it came under the dominion of death (Heb 2:14).

How then, as described in Isaiah 65:17–25, are wolves and lions now eating plants again? It is because the dominion that Adam gave away to Satan was won back by Jesus Christ upon his resurrection. Upon the Second Coming, Jesus claims that dominion, and, as a result of the whole Earth now being again under the dominion of life, all animals will, for the first time since the fall of Adam, eat plants, as they were created to. As a result, we know, for a fact, that since Isaiah 65:17–25 is describing wolves lying down with lambs and lions eating plants, this is a description of the time *after* the Second Coming, after Jesus has taken back the dominion of the Earth and has instituted his kingdom.

It is in that context that we are told that, during that same time of Jesus' kingdom on Earth, if someone "dies at a hundred" years of age, they will be considered to have been only a "child," meaning they would have died so very young, which also means, by implication, that human lifespans will have been restored to what they were before the flood (Gen 5). However, we are also told that if, during that same time, someone dies *younger* than a hundred years of age, they "will be considered accursed." We know, for a fact, that Isaiah 65:17–25 is a description of Jesus' kingdom on Earth after his Second Coming. As a result, from these verses in Isaiah, we know, with certainty, that during Jesus' kingdom on Earth, after his Second Coming, *there will still be death and sin in the world*, and that the world will be populated, to some degree, by *mortal* people, people who are *not* resurrected, people who can still *sin* and people who can still *die*. That same kingdom will be ruled by Jesus, together with *all* the *resurrected* and *immortal* believers (Rev 20:4).

Since all Christians will have been resurrected and will therefore be *immortal*, then who are these people in that same kingdom who are *not* resurrected and who are *mortal*? They are the same non-Christians who did not take the mark of the Beast, the sheep at the right hand of Jesus when he judged the nations (Matt 25:33–40), and who received the righteous man's reward—mortal, non-resurrected non-Christians who inherit the kingdom.

We are also told that those same people who can sin and die, who are in Jesus' kingdom, will have children and descendants (Isa 65:23). This again is an affirmation that those are *mortal, non-resurrected* people.

In a further affirmation of the change of dominion from Satan to Jesus Christ, we are told that people will no longer "labor in vain" but will instead enjoy the fruit of their labor and will live in houses built with their own hands (Isa 65:22–23). This is in fact, finally, the breaking of the curse of Genesis 3:17–19, where God cursed all of man's toil as a result of the fall. That curse will be broken and removed at the Second Coming, for now the dominion of the Earth has been taken back by Jesus Christ, and now it is his kingdom that will reign on Earth, and it will be a blessed, joyful, and fruitful kingdom.

After Jesus is enthroned in Jerusalem and after he judges the nations, the resurrected, immortal Christians will rule the world with him, as kings and lords of whom Jesus himself is King and Lord, and the world will be populated by the non-Christians who did not take the mark of the Beast, who will also inherit the kingdom, receiving the righteous man's reward. They will live and work in joy and peace, and they will have children and the population of the world will grow, and Satan will remain imprisoned during that whole time, for a period of one thousand years. As a result of Satan's imprisonment, there will not be any temptation from the enemy to arouse the sinful nature, which nature will still be present in the non-resurrected mortal people of the kingdom, nor will there be the ceaseless onslaught of temptation by the world, for the world will be ruled by Jesus Christ, who will rule in power, love, holiness, and justice.

THE CHILDREN OF THAT KINGDOM

Throughout those initial years of Jesus' kingdom, the mortal humanity will live, work, and have children, and the world will be a place of joy, love, happiness, abundance, and prosperity. It is important to understand that the people who will be born *after* the Second Coming, who will be the children of that initial mortal humanity who inherited the kingdom, will know nothing of what the world was like *before* the Second Coming. They will certainly learn about it in school, but to those children it will be only stories, accounts and history that are read—they will have no *experience* of living in a world where Jesus was not King, and where there was an enemy that was free to tempt them. That time of joy, prosperity, happiness, and peace will last for a thousand years, during which entire time Jesus is King of the world, and the resurrected Christians rule with him, as lesser kings and lords. After one thousand years, Satan will be released from the prison of the Pit and will be allowed out upon the Earth again.

WHY IS SATAN RELEASED?

Why is Satan released from the Pit after one thousand years? Why was he not thrown into the Lake of Fire like the Beast and the False Prophet were? We can understand that as follows.

God has determined, and predestined, a specific number of people to be born, to be given the gift of life—the *entirety* of predestination is *only* that—being predestined to be *born* (Ps 69:28; Rom 11:25; Rev 3:5). There is a specific number of people who will be given the gift of life. It is also essential that each person have the opportunity to choose, of their own free will, whether they will choose for God or not. Satan was allowed to tempt Adam in regard to that choice, though with Adam, Satan conceived of a way to do that indirectly by way of Eve, setting up an indirect situation where Adam feared he might lose Eve, and so Adam chose Eve over obedience to God, rather than face the possibility of losing her and being alone again (Gen 2:18). This is also why, in regard to Jesus Christ, Satan was forced to tempt him directly, something he avoided with Adam. Being forced to tempt Jesus directly is something that Satan would have certainly argued was not fair, since it would not be the same situation as Adam in Eden, and so God accommodated that by allowing Satan to tempt Jesus only after he was put in a place of extreme physical weakness by fasting in the wilderness for forty days, and by allowing Satan to tempt him with anything, not just a temptation to transgress only one specific commandment, and Satan was also allowed to tempt Jesus three times—all of this so as to equalize the situation between Jesus Christ, the last Adam, and the first Adam. And so, with Jesus Christ, Satan must go to him *directly*, which he did, and he failed in his temptations (Matt 4:1–11).

Just as both Adam and Jesus Christ, and every other human being who has ever lived, had to face temptation and choose, likewise the children born during Jesus' kingdom must also face temptation by the enemy and choose. For the first thousand years of Jesus' kingdom on Earth, Satan is imprisoned in the Pit, the Abyss, inside the Earth (Rev 20:1–3), but then, after the thousand years are over, he is released and is free to tempt humanity, including all the people born during those one thousand years.

Why is Satan released after one thousand years? Why not after five hundred years? Or two thousand years? The only reasonable conclusion we can reach is that after the one thousand years all the people whom God has predestined to be born will have been born, and so the full number of humanity will have been reached, all the people whose names were written into the Book of Life, the book that records the names of all the people who will ever be born (Ps 69:28; Rom 11:25; Rev 3:5).

WHAT DOES SATAN DO UPON HIS RELEASE?

> Now when the thousand years have expired, *Satan will be released* from his prison and *will go out to deceive the nations* which are in the four corners of the earth, Gog and Magog, to *gather them together to battle*, whose number is as the sand of the sea. *They went up* on the breadth of the earth and *surrounded the camp of the saints* and *the beloved city*. And fire came down from God out of heaven and devoured them. The devil, who deceived them, was cast into the

lake of fire and brimstone where the beast and the false prophet are. And they will be tormented day and night forever and ever. (Rev 7:7–10 NKJV)

Upon his release from the prison of the Pit, the Abyss, Satan goes out to deceive the nations of Jesus' kingdom. We are not told how long that takes, but it will certainly take some amount of time—whether six months, one year, ten years, or a hundred years, we don't know, but Satan will certainly need some time to assess the world, to assess the nations and the people of the nations, and then calculate and create a plan as to how to deceive the nations and gather them for war.

Why would Satan do this? After being imprisoned for a thousand years, has he really not learned that he cannot succeed? We don't know why; all as we can conclude is that his nature is so utterly corrupted that he, himself, is deceived above all.

WHO IS DECEIVED?

Upon Satan's release from the Pit, who, among the mortal people of the world, would be deceived by Satan? It is almost certainly *not* the original mortals who inherited the kingdom—they all saw the Second Coming, and they all certainly would have believed in Jesus Christ upon being welcomed into Jesus' kingdom. But their children, born after the Second Coming, never witnessed any such thing—for those children, it was all stories, histories, and personal accounts from those who *were* there and who *did* witness those events.

Also, we are told in Isaiah 65:20 that of those mortals who inhabit Jesus' kingdom after the Second Coming, if any of them were to die at less than a hundred years of age, they would be considered "accursed" (and some translations translate that as "sinners").

When we put this together, we can conclude the following: after Satan's release from the prison of the Pit, it is the youngest generations of mortal people who will be primarily targeted and deceived by Satan, deceived to rebel against Jesus Christ. We can understand how that might unfold among the mortal humanity—except for that initial mortal generation who originally inherited the kingdom after the Second Coming, this would be a world of people who will have had no experience whatsoever of being tempted by either the world or the enemy; they would have no idea what such temptation would be like. They will be people whose entire lives have been lived under the rule of Jesus Christ, a resurrected, flesh-and-bone *man*, who rules as King over all the Earth. We can understand how, eventually, Satan would start to sow seeds of doubt in those younger generations, doubts as to: Is Jesus really who he says he is? Isn't he just a man, like you? Are the history books really telling you the truth? Why does he get to rule over you? We are not unaware of the devil and his tactics (Eph 6:11), and we know that Satan's strategies, generally, do not change. As a result, we can reasonably conclude that Satan will instill rebellion in the hearts of the younger generations.

As with all of Satan's strategies, they take time to unfold; they do not happen in an instant, and that will almost certainly be the case after his release from the Pit. Once Satan starts to sow seeds of doubt and whisper rebellion, it may take a few generations for that rebellion to grow, for the world will be an almost Edenic place of peace, joy, and prosperity, with nothing to rebel against (just as was heaven in regard to the angels—a perfect place with absolutely nothing to rebel against; but Satan found a way).

For whatever length of time that rebellion will fester, sooner or later it will come to fruition, and so every human being born during the time of Jesus' kingdom, born after the Second Coming, will, like every other human being who has ever lived, have to choose either faithfulness towards God or otherwise. Many will choose to rebel against the Lord Jesus Christ. Revelation 20:8 tells us that a great number of people from all over the world will gather as an army and march against Jerusalem, where Jesus is enthroned. Those people, having never lived through the Second Coming and so having no experience of Jesus' power, having only ever known his love and peace and joy, will intend, somehow, to remove Jesus from his throne. However, it is certain that during the entire time of their temptation by Satan, God himself would have been speaking truth to each of their hearts, so that they will clearly understand the foolishness of choosing against Jesus Christ, giving them time and opportunity to repent and to choose wisely and well. But their choice will be made, and for those who choose to go to war against Jesus Christ, fire will come down from the sky upon them as they surround Jerusalem for war, and it will be over in a moment. Those people who choose to go to war against Jesus Christ will be killed, in an instant. Their free-will choice will be a choice for death, while those of that generation who choose not to go to war against Jesus Christ choose life and remain forever in his kingdom.

With that final attempt by Satan at war against Jesus Christ, every human being who will have ever lived will have faced personal temptation to choose either for God or against him, and everyone's choice will have been made. The full number of people who were predestined to be born will have been reached.

SATAN THROWN INTO THE LAKE OF FIRE

It is then, after the final attempt of war against Jesus Christ, that Satan himself will be taken and, for the first time ever, thrown into the Lake of Fire, hell (Rev 20:10), where the Beast and the False Prophet still remained alive, after more than one thousand years.

Also, by implication, it is at that same time that all the rebel angels who had initially rebelled against God with Satan will also be thrown into the Lake of Fire, located inside the Earth, in the heart of the Earth, deep below the Realm of the Dead/Hades/Sheol, and deeper still than even the Pit, the Abyss.

THE GREAT WHITE THRONE

After Satan is finally cast into the Lake of Fire, a "great white throne" judgment is described.

> Then I saw a great white throne and Him who sat upon it, from whose presence earth and heaven fled, and no place was found for them. And I saw the dead, the great and the small, standing before the throne, and books were opened; and another book was opened, which is *the book of life*; and the dead were judged from the things which were written in the books, according to their deeds. And the sea gave up the dead who were in it, and Death and Hades gave up the dead who were in them; and they were judged, each one of them according to their deeds. Then Death and Hades were thrown into the lake of fire. This is the second death, the lake of fire. And if anyone's name was not found written in the book of life, he was thrown into the lake of fire. (Rev 20:11–15 NASB)

The one who sits upon the great white throne is the Judge, Jesus Christ (John 5:22). It is then that all the non-believers from all of history, from Adam's day to that very day, are resurrected and brought forth from the Realm of the Dead, where they have been waiting for judgment. Job specifically tells us that the Realm of the Dead, Hades, is "beneath the waters," that is, beneath the judgment waters of the *seas* and *oceans* (Job 26:5), this is why we are told, in Revelation 20:13, that the "sea" gave up its dead, and, in that same breath, that "death and Hades" delivered up the dead. This is in fact a description of the same event, for the Realm of the Dead, Hades, is located inside the Earth, *beneath* the floors of the seas, so when the "sea" gives up the dead, it is the same as the Realm of the Dead, Hades, giving up the dead, for, since Hades is located beneath the floors of the seas, both of those statements are a description of the Realm of the Dead giving up the dead to judgment.

The resurrection of non-believers is the second resurrection. As with the resurrection of believers, the resurrected body in that second resurrection will have the sinful nature removed, for the sinful nature is in the blood, and the blood is removed upon the resurrection (1 Cor 15:50). Those *resurrected non-believers* are then judged according to their works, rather than their faith, since they had no faith, and then, although it will break God's heart to do it (1 Tim 2:3–4), he will give them what they chose of their own free will—to be apart from him and have nothing to do with him. And so, for that reason alone, for the reason of honoring the free will choice that those people had made, those people will be cast into the Lake of Fire (Rev 20:15), though that is not God's will for them (1 Tim 2:3–4; 2 Pet 3:9).

We are also told that Hades, the Realm of the Dead, will be cast into the Lake of Fire. Remember that all of this is *inside the Earth*—the Realm of the Dead is inside the Earth; the Pit, or the Abyss, is deeper inside the Earth; while the Lake of Fire itself is at the very heart of the Earth, deepest down. So when Revelation 20:14 tells us that "death and Hades were cast into the lake of fire," we can understand it as those physical places, located inside the Earth, falling into, or collapsing down into, the Lake of Fire in the heart of the Earth.

It is exceedingly important to remember that all the resurrected non-believers will be in the Lake of Fire *without the sinful nature*, since the purpose of resurrection is to remove from our bodies what is not supposed to be there, the sinful nature. What will those people think, or come to understand, as they are in the Lake of Fire without the sinful nature to deceive them?

THE FIRE UPON THE EARTH

After the "great white throne" judgment, God will redeem this everlasting Earth (Mic 6:2), and he will redeem the *surface* of the Earth by *fire*.

> But they deliberately forget that long ago by God's word the heavens came into being and the earth was formed out of water and by water. By these waters also the world of that time was deluged and destroyed. By the same word *the present heavens and earth* are *reserved for fire*, being kept for *the day of judgment* and destruction of the ungodly. (2 Pet 3:5–7 NIV)

> But the day of the Lord will come like a thief. The heavens will disappear with a roar; *the elements will be destroyed by fire*, and *the earth and everything done in it* will be *laid bare*. Since everything will be destroyed in this way, what kind of people ought you to be? You ought to live holy and godly lives as you look forward to the day of God and speed its coming. That day will bring about **the destruction of the heavens by fire**, and *the elements will melt in the heat*. But in keeping with his promise *we are looking forward to a new heaven and a new earth*, where righteousness dwells. (2 Pet 3:10–13 NIV)

> their work will be shown for what it is, because the Day will bring it to light. It will be revealed with fire, and *the fire will test the quality of each person's work*. If what has been built *survives*, the builder will receive a reward. If it is burned up, the builder will suffer loss but yet will be saved—even though only as one escaping through the flames. (1 Cor 3:13–15 NIV)

Peter tells us that, just as the Earth had been previously destroyed by water in Noah's day (Gen 9:11), likewise, the Earth will be destroyed again, but this time by fire.

Where will this fire come from? Since Peter draws a parallel between the flood of Noah's day, and since Jesus also draws that same parallel (Matt 24:37–39), it is reasonable to conclude that looking at the source of the floodwaters of Noah's day can tell us something of the source of the fire to come.

The Bible describes for us very clearly the initial, and primary, source of the waters of the flood of Noah's day.

> In the six hundredth year of Noah's life, on the seventeenth day of the second month—on that day all *the springs of the great deep burst forth*, and the floodgates of the heavens were opened. And rain fell on the earth forty days and forty nights. (Gen 7:11–12 NIV)

The *initial* source of the water for the flood was from *inside the Earth*, described as the "springs of the great deep burst[ing] [or exploding] forth," and *then* it rained. The primary and initial source for the waters of the flood of Noah's day was from inside the Earth, which is also completely affirmed by Peter when he tells us that "the earth was formed out of water and by water" and by those *same* waters the world of Noah's day was destroyed (2 Pet 3:5–7).

As a result, since both Jesus and Peter draw a parallel between Noah's day and the Second Coming, and with Peter specifically paralleling the coming destruction of the surface of the Earth by fire with the previous destruction of the surface of the Earth by water, there is good reason to conclude that the source of the fire to come will, like the source of the waters of the flood, be from *inside* the Earth.

Since the Lake of Fire is located inside the Earth, in the very heart of the Earth, and since there is good reason to understand that the fire to come upon the Earth will itself come from within the Earth, is it possible that the fire to come upon the surface of the Earth will be the *same* fire as is in the Lake of Fire? When considering the purpose of the fire to come upon the Earth, that becomes a profound question.

THE PURPOSE OF THE FIRE

We are told very specifically the purpose of that fire to come, for we are told in 1 Corinthians 3:13–15 that there will be a fire coming upon the Earth that "will *test* the quality of each person's work"; that is, it will test the nature of everything accomplished by humanity. If one's work, one's accomplishment in life, was a work, or an accomplishment, unto God, that is, a work born out of a faithful heart towards him and done as a work unto him, that work will *survive* the fire. But if a work has been done for any other reason, for a selfish reason or as a work born of pride, or any reason that is not born of faithfulness to God and a true heart towards him, that work will *not* survive the fire but will be *burned up* by the fire.

The purpose of the fire is to *remove* those things of human accomplishment that are not unto God but *leave those that are*. It is very important to understand that *all* the human accomplishments done unto God will *remain* and will become the *culture* of God's everlasting kingdom on Earth.

The profound question then is this—since we know that the purpose of the fire that will come upon the Earth is to remove that which is not unto God but leave that which is, then, if the *nature* of that fire upon the Earth is the same as the *nature* of the fire of the Lake of Fire, what is the purpose of the Lake of Fire? Is the purpose of the Lake of Fire the same as the purpose of the fire to come upon the Earth—to remove that which is not unto God but leave that which is? If so, what then does that mean for the resurrected people who are in the Lake of Fire, who are there without the sinful nature? This is a colossal question.

Once the everlasting Earth comes through the fire, the curse of the oceans and the curse of darkness (Gen 1:2) are removed from the Earth, the everlasting Earth is redeemed, ready now to receive God's New Jerusalem, the home of God and his Bride on Earth.

22

THE NEW JERUSALEM

GOD IS NOT A destroyer; he is a redeemer. Too often, when talking about what follows the great white throne judgment of Revelation 20, people teach that God will then destroy his entire creation, including the Earth, and make a completely new creation, including a newly created Earth.

Why would God destroy his own creation? The usual answer is: because of sin. Why would God destroy his own creation because of sin? Is it because he's incapable of redeeming his creation? Is it because the corruption of sin, the corruption of the creature Satan, exceeds God's power of redemption, exceeds his holiness, is too great for God to deal with? This is all nonsense—if God were to indeed destroy his own creation because of sin, then he would be a worthless God, pitiful and pathetic, for it would mean that the creature Satan is greater than his Creator, that the corruption of the creature is greater than the Creator's power to redeem it. None of this is true. God is the Redeemer, and he *will* redeem his *entire* creation. God's redemption is not only the redemption of humanity, but also the redemption of the entire physical creation itself—the redemption of creation is *not* beyond God's capability, and he will accomplish it. After the great white throne judgment, after the fire consumes the Earth, removing that which was not done unto God but leaving that which was, God then *redeems* this *everlasting* Earth.

THE EVERLASTING EARTH

Throughout the Bible, there are three terms used to refer to the Earth:

1. the foundations of the Earth
2. the Earth
3. the world

These terms mean different things.

The term "foundations of the Earth" means, very specifically, the *planet* itself (1 Sam 2:8; Ps 104:5; Isa 48:13; Mic 6:2). We are also very specifically told that the "foundations of the Earth," the planet itself, last "forever."

> Hear, you mountains, the LORD's accusation; listen, you *everlasting foundations of the earth*. For the LORD has a case against his people; he is lodging a charge against Israel. (Mic 6:2 NIV)

> You who laid *the foundations of the earth, So that it should not be moved forever*, (Ps 104:5 NKJV)

The foundations of the Earth, the planet itself, is everlasting and will *never* cease to exist.

The term "the Earth" means the *surface* of the planet, the *land* upon the surface.

> Then God said, "Let the waters under the heavens be gathered together into one place, and let the dry land appear"; and it was so. And *God called the dry land Earth*, and the gathering together of the waters He called Seas. (Gen 1:9–10 NKJV)

> Thus I establish My covenant with you: Never again shall all flesh be cut off by the waters of the flood; never again shall there be a flood *to destroy the earth*. (Gen 9:11 NKJV)

God very specifically tells us, in Genesis 1:9–10, that it is the "dry land" upon the *surface* of the planet that he calls "Earth." He also tells us, in Genesis 9:11, that the flood of Noah's day *destroyed* the Earth—how can that be, since the Earth is still here and we are on it? It means only that the flood of Noah's day destroyed the *surface* of the planet; it destroyed the "dry land" upon it, *not* the planet itself. The term "Earth," by itself, *only* means the dry land upon the surface of the planet.

The term "the world" means everything that takes place *upon* the surface of the planet—people, humanity, civilization.

> For God so loved *the world* that He gave His only begotten Son, that whoever believes in Him should not perish but have everlasting life. (John 3:16 NKJV)

In Genesis 1:1, "In the beginning God created the heavens and the *earth*"—since we know that the term "Earth" means only the dry *land* upon the surface of the planet, we know that Genesis 1:1 is specifically telling us that God created dry, habitable land upon Earth, exactly as Isaiah 45:18 tells us. However, Hebrews 1:10 tells us,

> You, LORD, *in the beginning* laid *the foundation of the earth* (Heb 1:10 NKJV)

From these verses we can understand the creation of the Earth as follows. In Genesis 1:1, God created, first, the planet itself (the "foundations of the Earth," Heb 1:10), and, upon the surface of the planet, he created the dry, habitable land, "the Earth" (Gen 1:1). However, by Genesis 1:2 the Earth is a cursed and ruined waste, covered with the curse of the global ocean as well as the curse of darkness, all as a result of the rebel angels being cast down into the Earth, inside the Earth, into the Pit (Isa 14:12–15; Luke 10:18; Rev 12:9). God then begins to restore the cursed Earth to make it habitable again for man, beginning with "Let there be light" (Gen 1:3).

HEAVENS

Also, in Genesis 1:1, the word "heavens" is plural. Why is that? Just as there are three terms that describe the different aspects of the Earth, so there are three heavens.

> I know a man in Christ who fourteen years ago—whether in the body I do not know, or whether out of the body I do not know, God knows—such a one was caught up to the *third heaven*. (2 Cor 12:2 NKJV)

The "three heavens" are as follows—standing on the Earth and looking up, we see:

1. Heaven 1 – the earthly sky
2. Heaven 2 – beyond the sky, what we call "outer space," where the sun, moon, and stars reside
3. Heaven 3 – beyond the sky and space, the place where God established his throne, "heaven"

With that in mind, we turn to Revelation 21:1.

NEW HEAVEN AND NEW EARTH

> Then I saw "a new *heaven* and a new *earth*," for the first heaven and the first earth had passed away, and there was *no longer any sea*. (Rev 21:1 NIV)

Revelation 21 begins to describe the full redemption of God's creation, beginning with his redemption of "heaven" and Earth.

Why is the word "heaven" in Revelation 21:1 singular and *not* plural, as it is in Genesis 1:1? It is because the word "heaven" in Revelation 21:1 is speaking very specifically of only *one* of the three heavens; it is speaking *only* about the earthly *sky*.

Why does the sky need redeeming?

The reason that the earthly sky needs redeeming is because the earthly sky is where Satan had his base of operations.

> in which you once walked according to the course of this world, according to *the prince of the power of the air*, the spirit who now works in the sons of disobedience (Eph 2:2 NKJV)

> For we do not wrestle against flesh and blood, but against principalities, against powers, against the rulers of the darkness of this age, against *spiritual hosts of wickedness* in the *heavenly places*. (Eph 6:12 NKJV)

While Satan had dominion over the Earth, his base of operations was in the earthly sky; therefore the earthly sky needs redemption, and so it is redeemed by God in Revelation 21:1.

Also, the *surface* of the planet, the "Earth," is redeemed in Revelation 21:1, and this redemption is the result of the global fire that redeems the entire Earth, as well as redeeming the sky.

Also notice how, on that redeemed Earth, there is "no longer any sea"—the curse of Genesis 1:2, the curse of the seas and oceans, is finally lifted, as is also the curse of darkness of Genesis 1:2 (Rev 21:25; 22:3, 5). Finally, the entire Earth is now habitable again for man, as God had originally created it in Genesis 1:1 (Isa 45:18).

Also, notice how John says that he "*saw* a new heaven and a new earth"—this is a description of the redemption of the *existing* planet and sky, *not* a re-creation of something different; this is exclusively God's *redemption* of the everlasting Earth.

We also know that in addition to the full redemption of the everlasting Earth, and its sky, God is also redeeming his *entire* physical creation,

> For the *creation waits* in *eager expectation* for the *children of God* to be *revealed*. For the *creation was subjected to frustration*, not by its own choice, but by the will of the one who subjected it, in *hope that the creation itself will be liberated from its bondage* to *decay* and *brought into the freedom* and *glory* of *the children of God*. We know that *the whole creation* has been *groaning* as *in the pains of childbirth* right up to the present time. Not only so, but we ourselves, who have the firstfruits of the Spirit, groan inwardly as we wait eagerly for our adoption to sonship, the redemption of our bodies. (Rom 8:19–23 NIV)

Romans 8:19–23 is very clear—the very redemption of the physical creation is inextricably tied in with the redemption of humanity; God redeems us, humanity; he redeems Earth and sky; and he redeems his entire physical creation—God is a *redeemer*, not a destroyer.

GOD DWELLS WITH US

We are also told the following in Revelation 21:

> And I heard a loud voice from the throne saying, "Look! *God's dwelling place* is *now* among *the people*, and *he will dwell* with *them*. They will be his people, and God himself will be with them and be their God." (Rev 21:3 NIV)

It is profound to note the wording of this—it does *not* say that now "the people will dwell with God"; rather, we are told that God will come and that "*he* will dwell" with "the people," with *us*. We do not go to heaven; God leaves heaven, the physical place he created in Genesis 1:1, and comes to *Earth* to dwell *here* with us *forever*—Earth is the jewel of creation, and it is both *our* home and *God's* home, forever. God's everlasting kingdom is on Earth, not heaven, and Earth, not heaven, is the everlasting home of redeemed humanity. On this redeemed *Earth*, there will be no more death, and no more sorrow or pain (Rev 21:4).

THE NEW JERUSALEM

It is then that John is shown a great city, "coming down *out of heaven*," to *Earth*, the New Jerusalem.

> One of the seven angels who had the seven bowls full of the seven last plagues came and said to me, "Come, I will show you the bride, the wife of the Lamb." And he carried me away in the Spirit to a mountain great and high, and showed me *the Holy City, Jerusalem, coming down out of heaven from God*. It shone with the glory of God, and its brilliance was like that of a very precious jewel, like a jasper, clear as crystal. It had *a great, high wall* with *twelve gates*, and with twelve angels at the gates. On the gates were written the names of the twelve tribes of Israel. There were three gates on the east, three on the north, three on the south and three on the west. The wall of the city had *twelve foundations*, and on them were the names of the twelve apostles of the Lamb. The angel who talked with me had a measuring rod of gold to measure the city, its gates and its walls. The city was *laid out like a square*, as long as it was wide. He *measured the city* with the rod and found it to be 12,000 *stadia* [ca. 1400 miles] *in length*, and *as wide and high as it is long*. The angel *measured the wall* using human measurement, and it was 144 *cubits* [ca. 200 feet] *thick*. The wall was made of *jasper*, and the city of *pure gold*, as pure as glass. The *foundations of the city walls* were decorated with every kind of *precious stone*. The first foundation was jasper, the second sapphire, the third agate, the fourth emerald, the fifth onyx, the sixth ruby, the seventh chrysolite, the eighth beryl, the ninth topaz, the tenth turquoise, the eleventh jacinth, and the twelfth amethyst. The *twelve gates* were *twelve pearls*, each gate made of a single pearl. The *great street of the city* was of *gold*, as pure as transparent glass. I did *not see a temple in the city*, because *the Lord God Almighty* and *the Lamb* are its temple. The *city does not need the sun or the moon* to shine on it, for the glory of God gives it light, and the Lamb is its lamp. *The nations* will walk by its light, and the kings of the earth will bring their splendor into it. On no day will its gates ever be shut, for there will be no night there. The glory and honor of *the nations* will be brought into it. Nothing impure will ever enter it, nor will anyone who does what is shameful or deceitful, but only those whose names are written in the Lamb's book of life. (Rev 21:9–27 NIV)

> Then the angel showed me *the river* of *the water of life*, as clear as crystal, flowing *from the throne of God* and *of the Lamb* down *the middle of the great street of the city*. On each side of the river stood *the tree of life*, bearing *twelve crops of fruit*, yielding its fruit every month. And *the leaves* of the tree are for *the healing of the nations*. No longer will there be any curse. *The throne of God and of the Lamb will be in the city*, and his servants will serve him. They will see his face, and his name will be on their foreheads. *There will be no more night*. They will not need the light of a lamp or the light of the sun, for the Lord God will give them light. And they will reign for ever and ever. (Rev 22:1–5 NIV)

In John 14 Jesus tells us the following:

> My Father's house has many rooms; if that were not so, would I have told you that I am going there to *prepare* a *place* for you? And if I go and prepare a place for you, I will come back and take you to be with me that *you also may be where I am*. (John 14:2–3 NIV)

Jesus tells us that he is going to the Father, in heaven, and that while he is there, he will "prepare a place" for *us*, the church, his Bride. He says that he is doing this so that we, the church, can be with him where he is.

What is this place that Jesus prepared in heaven for his Bride? It is the New Jerusalem.

The New Jerusalem is most certainly a "place," and it is specifically described in Revelation 21:2 as being "prepared." It also described as being prepared "as a bride . . . for her husband." The city itself is *not* the Bride, for we know, with certainty, that the Bride is the church, and that the husband, the Bridegroom, is Jesus Christ, the Lamb (Eph 5:31–32; Rev 19:7, 21:9). To describe the New Jerusalem as being "as a bride" means only that the New Jerusalem is the place where the Bride, the church, will dwell. So the New Jerusalem is a place that has been prepared, in heaven, for the church. It then *leaves heaven* and comes down *to Earth* after the Second Coming, after Jesus himself has returned, to remain forever upon the Earth. As a result, *both* the Bridegroom, Jesus Christ, *and* the Bride, the church, will dwell *together* in the New Jerusalem on Earth, and so the Bride will be with Jesus where he is.

In every way, the New Jerusalem fulfills exactly what Jesus said he was going to do in regard to "preparing a place" for the church—the place that Jesus prepared in heaven for the church is the New Jerusalem, and that place, the New Jerusalem, *leaves* heaven and comes down *to Earth* to be the everlasting home of God and man *on Earth*.

Also note how utterly physical is the New Jerusalem—it is as physical as New York City, though made in heaven. The materials from which the New Jerusalem is made—gold, precious stones, pearls, gates, foundations—are all *physical materials from heaven*, and those materials are exactly as physical there as they are here on

Earth—heaven is exactly as physical as is the New Jerusalem, and so heaven is exactly as physical as is Earth.

GOD'S THRONE IS NOW ON EARTH

It is very important to note that the throne of God the Father, which he established (that is, brought into existence) in heaven in Genesis 1:1 (Pss 9:7; 93:2; 103:19), *also* leaves heaven and comes *to Earth*, to reside in the New Jerusalem, together with the throne of Jesus Christ (Rev 22:3).

Heaven was only the *temporary* place for God's throne; it was his base of operations while he made his creation and began to unfold his plan, which plan centered on Earth. Humanity was created by God to be his Bride, to be his companion, and man, God's companion, is *not* made from the dust of heaven; rather, we are made from the dust of the Earth (Gen 2:7). There is a reason for that—it is because we always and only belong to Earth, not to heaven. *Earth* is the center of God's creation; it is his jewel—that is why our bodies, and the flesh-and-bone body of Jesus Christ, the resurrected God Incarnate, are made from the created dust of this *Earth*. Our everlasting home, and God's everlasting home, is Earth, not heaven, and so the New Jerusalem leaves heaven and comes to Earth, to remain here forever, to be the home of both God and his Bride, the church, redeemed humanity.

THE LIVING WATER

We are told, in Revelation 22:1, that the "river of the water of life" flows in the New Jerusalem, flowing from the throne of the Father and the Son, here on Earth.

What is the "river of ... life"?

It is in fact the same as the "living water" spoken of by Jesus in John 4:10–14 and 7:37–39.

> On the last and greatest day of the festival, Jesus stood and said in a loud voice, "Let anyone who is thirsty come to me and drink. Whoever believes in me, as Scripture has said, *rivers of living water* will flow from within them." *By this he meant the Spirit*, whom those who believed in him were later to receive. Up to that time the Spirit had not been given, since Jesus had not yet been glorified. (John 7:37–39 NIV)

The Bible is very clear—the "living water," the River of Life that flows from the Father and the Son in the New Jerusalem, is the Holy Spirit. So we see that in the New Jerusalem, on Earth, is the Father and the Son, enthroned, and the Holy Spirit flowing from them—the entire Trinity is present in all their fullness here, on Earth, in the New Jerusalem, together with their companion and Bride, the church, redeemed humanity.

THE TREE OF LIFE

We are also told that, in the New Jerusalem, on either side of the River of Life, will be the Tree of Life (Rev 22:2). This is the exact same Tree of Life as in Genesis 2:9; 3:22, 24. That tree, since Genesis 3:24, has remained here on Earth but has been guarded by the cherubim with flaming swords so that no human being can find it and eat of its fruit. The reason for guarding that tree is because if anyone who has sin within them eats of the fruit of that tree, they will never die, but rather they will live forever in a state of permanent sin. It is for that reason that God drove Adam out of Eden—as an act of love and mercy, so that Adam, and all humanity, would not live forever in a state of sin, but could have redemption by way of resurrection (Gen 3:22).

After the New Jerusalem comes to Earth, then the cherubim who have been guarding the Tree of Life will step away from that tree and that tree will be available again, located in the New Jerusalem, on Earth, with broad branches, leaves, and fruit that will be found on both sides of the River of Life. We are told that the Tree of Life will bear twelve crops of different fruit, a new crop every month, and that its leaves "are for the healing of the nations" (Rev 22:2).

THE NATIONS

We are told, very clearly, that in the New Jerusalem, together with the redeemed humanity, there will still be "nations."

What does the term "nations" mean? Does it mean countries?

Throughout the Bible, what we today call "countries" are usually referred to as "kingdoms." However, when the Bible refers to "nations," it almost always refers to the divisions of humanity that happened at the tower of Babel (Gen 11:1–9). When God made division within humanity by way of the confusion of languages, as an act of love and mercy for humanity (Gen 11:6), simultaneous with that confusion of languages was the division of humanity according to physical features—skin colors, facial features, etc. Those physical divisions were in fact a mercy of God since, with the confusion of languages, when those initial people, who in an instant could no longer understand one another, would have been dismayed and filled with fear, then, when they would have seen themselves as also physically changed and then saw others with those same physical changes (for example, darker skin colors et al.), those people could then find each other and understand each other, and so the physical changes of humanity that accompanied the change of languages was an act of mercy upon humanity.

In our day, we call these physical differences among people "races," but that term, and that concept, does not exist in the Bible. There is only one "race" in the Bible—the race of "Adam," the race of humanity. The physical differences of skin color and facial features that we call "races" the Bible calls "nations."

It is in that context that we approach Revelation 22:2, where we are told that the leaves of the Tree of Life are for the "healing of the nations." What does that mean? What sort of "healing" will a resurrected, redeemed, sinless and immortal people need? The Bible doesn't elaborate, but we can know, for a certainty, that in the resurrection, all people will *retain* their physical differences, the physical differences of skin color, facial features, etc., and all will be perfect and glorious in those differences. The term "the healing of the nations" almost certainly refers to the healing of "division," but how that works in a redeemed humanity we cannot say. For some reason it will be necessary, and the leaves of the Tree of Life will accomplish that healing.

THEIR SMOKE GOES UP FOREVER

It is very important to remember that the Lake of Fire is inside the Earth, in the heart of the Earth. At the same time that the New Jerusalem and God's glorious kingdom is upon the *surface* of the magnificently redeemed Earth, there will be both people and fallen angels in the Lake of Fire, *inside* the Earth, and we are told that their smoke will rise up.

> And **the smoke** of their torment **ascends** forever and ever; and they have no rest day or night, who worship the beast and his image, and whoever receives the mark of his name. (Rev 14:11 NKJV)

This is a description of those in the Lake of Fire, and when it describes that smoke as "ascending," the implication is that it will rise *to be seen* upon the surface of the Earth.

This in fact is how the Bible ends—as you are standing upon your balcony of your home in the New Jerusalem, fully redeemed, and look out upon the glorious redeemed Earth, you look out and see, in the distance on the horizon, a plume of black smoke rising—the smoke from the Lake of Fire inside the Earth. As you walk the streets of the New Jerusalem, or upon the glorious nature of the redeemed Earth, deep beneath your feet will be people and fallen angels in the Lake of Fire.

That is the scene with which the Bible ends. Does any of that seem finished to you?

OUTSIDE THE CITY

We are told the following about those who are "outside" the New Jerusalem:

> Blessed are those who wash their robes, that they may have the right to the tree of life and may go through the gates into the city. Outside are the dogs, those who practice magic arts, the sexually immoral, the murderers, the idolaters and everyone who loves and practices falsehood. (Rev 22:14–15 NIV)

THE NEW JERUSALEM

> But the cowardly, the unbelieving, the vile, the murderers, the sexually immoral, those who practice magic arts, the idolaters and all liars—they will be consigned to the fiery lake of burning sulfur. This is the second death. (Rev 21:8 NIV)

We are told that outside of the New Jerusalem will be people who are described as "dogs," described as sexually immoral, practitioners of magic arts and falsehood, murderers and idolaters. Does this mean that those people will be living upon the *surface* of the redeemed Earth, outside of the New Jerusalem?

No, for Revelation 21:8 also speaks of those same people and tells us, very specifically, that they will be located in the Lake of Fire. Since the New Jerusalem is on the surface of the Earth, and since the Lake of Fire is inside the Earth, it is true to say that those people described in Revelation 22:14–15 are located outside the city—they *will* be outside the city, but not outside on the surface of the redeemed Earth, but rather *inside* the Earth, in the Lake of Fire.

THE AGES TO COME

It is in that context that we remember the words of the apostle Paul when he talks to us of the "ages to come" (Eph 2:7). How many "ages" will there be? Since we know that God is eternal, and we, resurrected humanity, as well as the Earth, are everlasting, we can understand that there will be an everlasting and continuous unfolding of "ages" to come.

What will God do in the "ages to come"? Will it involve those in the Lake of Fire? Whatever it is, it will be no less great than what he has done in this current age, and we, his Bride, will be there to watch him do it.

THE DOMINION OF JESUS CHRIST

In Genesis 1:26, God gave to Adam the dominion of the whole Earth. When Adam sinned, he gave that same dominion to Satan, which became a dominion of death (Luke 4:5–7; Heb 2:14). When Jesus lived and did not sin, and was then resurrected, he conquered both sin and death and, upon that conquest, he took back that same dominion that Adam had given away (John 12:31, 16:11). This is *why* there is a Second Coming—the Second Coming is Jesus Christ, the Second and Last Adam (1 Cor 15:45) returning to claim what is his own, the dominion of the Earth, and establishing his everlasting kingdom here, on Earth, together with the Father and the Holy Spirit, and with his Bride, all in the New Jerusalem. It is this establishing of his kingdom that is the "birth" that comes from the "birth pains" of the Seven Seals (Matt 24:8 NIV).

In regard to the dominion of Jesus Christ, 1 Corinthians 15:24 tells us something very profound—after Jesus has taken back all dominion and established God's everlasting kingdom here on Earth, Jesus, as King of the kingdom, will then *hand over* the kingdom and *all of its dominion*, to the Father.

> Then the end will come, when he **hands over the kingdom to God the Father** after he has destroyed all dominion, authority and power. (1 Cor 15:24 NIV)

The Son will give the dominion to the Father.

INVITATION AND WARNING

Just as the book of Revelation began with a blessing upon everyone who reads the words of the book aloud, so the book of Revelation ends with a warning.

> **I warn everyone** who hears the words of the prophecy of this scroll: If anyone adds anything to them, God will add to that person the plagues described in this scroll. And if anyone takes words away from this scroll of prophecy, God will take away from that person any share in the tree of life and in the Holy City, which are described in this scroll. (Rev 22:18–19 NIV)

Jesus warns us, very specifically, to not add anything to the words of his Revelation. He also warns us to not take away from the words of his Revelation. No other book in the Bible pronounces a blessing upon those who read the book, and no other book in the Bible gives a warning about adding or taking away from the words of the book. The book of Revelation is unique and exceedingly important, it is so important that it is the only book that pronounces blessing and gives warning—we are to take this seriously.

The book of Revelation ends, as always, with an invitation from God, from Jesus Christ, to all people to come and take the free gift of the water of life (Rev 22:17). God ends his Revelation with an invitation to his love.

23

THE BOOK OF REVELATION–A SUMMARY

THE BOOK OF REVELATION outlines, in detail, the return of Jesus Christ to claim the dominion of the Earth, a dominion he won back by living a sinless life. After living a sinless life, Jesus then took the sin of humanity upon himself while on the cross and brought that sin to conclusion and completion in his death, thereby breaking its power. He was then resurrected, and upon his resurrection the dominion to the Earth was now his. The Second Coming is the Lord Jesus Christ coming to claim what is his, and Revelation tells us how that will be accomplished.

The events of Revelation are colossal events, all yet to unfold, and the days and events of Revelation are the most prophesied days and events in the Bible. The book of Revelation is imbued with deep imagery and symbolism, but the Bible explains that imagery and those symbols for us, throughout the whole of Scripture, and, as with many other biblical truths, we need to just look at all of those Scriptures and put them together so as to see the whole picture.

The key to understanding the book of Revelation is that it goes back and forth in time as it outlines three timelines. The first timeline is the big-picture timeline, the overall timeline that encompasses the entirety of events, the timeline of the Seven Seals, which encompasses a period of forty years. The second timeline is the timeline of the Great Tribulation, all of which occurs in Seal 5, and is outlined by Trumpets 1–5. The third timeline is the final five months of the Great Tribulation, and is outlined by Bowls 1–5, all of which occur during Trumpet 5. Once the Great Tribulation is over, there is the thirty days of Seal 6, which includes Trumpet 6 and, as part of Trumpet 6, Bowls 6 and 7, which is the fall of Babylon the Great. Then the final Seal 7, which includes the final Trumpet 7, the last Trumpet and the resurrection of believers. Also included in Seal 7 is the actual Second Coming, the descent of Jesus to Earth with all of his resurrected church.

The other absolutely essential key to understanding Revelation is Matthew 24:3–31, for in that passage the Seven Seals are outlined for us, in order and in detail, by

Jesus Christ himself. It is only from Jesus' own words in Matthew 24 that we can know the timelines of Revelation, especially Seals 5 to 7. Matthew 24 is where the Judge explains to us the judgment to come.

One other very important point to remember is that there is no such thing as a rapture—the rapture is a false teaching invented by John Darby in the 1830s and has no biblical basis. The rapture teaching contradicts both Scripture and the Creed of the church—as a result of its contradiction of the Creed, the rapture teaching can be considered a modern heresy. The church remains on the Earth throughout the entirety of the events of Revelation.

Here is a summary of the events of Revelation, given chronologically, though in Revelation they are given across the three timelines, and as a result are not given chronologically. The scripture references for all of these events have already been given throughout the content of this book, and will not be repeated here, rather, this will just be an overview of the events, and for the actual details of those events, and the scripture references, refer to the content of this book where those events are discussed.

SUMMARY OF EVENTS OF REVELATION

The book of Revelation begins with the apostle John on the island of Patmos, where he sees the resurrected Jesus Christ and where he is told that he will be given a Revelation.

John is then told to write down seven letters, dictated to him by Jesus, that are to be addressed to the *angels* of seven churches, with those angels being the *protectors* of those churches. John writes those letters down, and later, after the Revelation is over, he sends those letters to those churches. In those letters Jesus tells each church what is good and strong about them, but also what is not good or strong and what they need to address and remedy. For two of the seven churches, he has nothing bad to say, only good, while for one church he has nothing good to say, only bad. In each case, for all seven churches, Jesus tells them to be prepared for what is about to come, to endure, to persevere, and, if they do, they will get rewards. The rewards that he lists are the rewards outlined in Revelation 21 and 22, rewards that come after the Second Coming. The seven churches have a number of issues that they must deal with, but two issues that come up repeatedly are the issues of sexual immorality and the occult.

John is then taken up to heaven where he sees twenty-four thrones with twenty-four elders seated upon the thrones. He also sees four living creatures, a great throne in the midst of those four living creatures, and he sees a great host of angels. The one who sits on the throne has a scroll in his hand, a scroll with Seven Seals, and there is no one in Creation who can open those Seven Seals, and John weeps over that fact. But then a Lamb comes to the throne, and the Lamb *can* open the Seven Seals. The Lamb then begins to open the Seals.

The judgment of Revelation begins with the opening of Seal 1, which is a judgment upon the church. During Seal 1 the church will forsake Jesus Christ and embrace false teachings, including teachings of sexual immorality and various degrees of the occult—this is the great apostasy spoken of by Paul. Also, it is in Seal 1 that the Beast is conceived as a human baby, which conception almost certainly occurs immediately upon the opening of Seal 1, with the Beast then being born during Seal 1, nine months later. Seal 1 lasts approximately thirty to thirty-two years or so.

Seal 2 is opened next, approximately thirty to thirty-two years after Seal 1, and results in Global war. After Seal 2 is opened, but still during the global war of Seal 2, Seal 3 is opened, bringing global famine. After Seal 3 is opened, but still during the events of Seal 2 and Seal 3, Seal 4 is opened, bringing global death from the war, from the famine and from disease and pestilence. One quarter of the human population dies during that time, as a result of Seals 2, 3 and 4.

Seals 2, 3 and 4 last until Seal 5 is opened. Seal 5 is opened thirty-three years after the opening of Seal 1, being opened when the Beast is thirty-three years old. Upon the opening of Seal 5, while the war, famine and death of Seals 2, 3 and 4 are ongoing, the Beast comes upon the world's stage and brings the global war to an end. He almost certainly comes to world prominence via the nation Babylon the Great. He makes a global peace covenant with all the nations of the world, and he ends the Global war. He also, as part of that peace covenant, brings and end to the global famine and the ensuing death. He is hailed as hero and saviour.

Soon after the Beast accomplishes the global peace, he will be "fake" assassinated before the eyes of the world, and his seeming mortal wounds will be to his right arm and to his right eye—he will not truly have been killed, but he will have *seemed* to die, and the world will mourn him greatly. However, soon after his "death," most likely three days later, he will be "alive," and will be seen by the whole world to be alive. As a result, he will be proclaimed as "Christ returned," the one who brought peace to the global war of Seal 2, a war which the world, and some Christians, will think was Armageddon. The "resurrection" of the Beast will be the convincing and inarguable proof to the world that the Beast is, in fact, Christ returned, and the world will be astonished, amazed and filled with wonder at his "resurrection."

At that same time, a great high profile Christian leader, though in truth a False Prophet, will point to the "resurrected" Beast and declare to the world that the Beast *is* Christ returned, and then this False Prophet will perform great miraculous signs, in full view of the world, to prove that his testimony about the Beast is true. People will believe the False Prophet and the world will proclaim the Beast as Christ returned.

The False Prophet will make a statue of the Beast, a statue that will be able to speak, and that statue will command all people to worship the statue or else be put to death. And people will worship the statue of the Beast, and thereby the Beast himself.

The False Prophet will then institute a new economy, an economy in which only those who worship the Beast can participate, and in order to show one's worship of the Beast, and thereby participate in that economy, people must receive the mark of the Beast—a "tattoo" of his name, the (stylized) number 666. They must place that mark on one of the two areas where the Beast received his "mortal" wounds—either on their right arm or on their forehead, above their right eye. The mark of the Beast is taken on the parts of the body where the Beast received his "death" wounds so as to commemorate the death of the Beast, to commemorate his sacrifice, the sacrifice of himself in bringing peace to the world, from which sacrifice he was "resurrected." The mark itself has nothing to do with being the means to buy or sell, rather it is only a mark that allows people to participate in the economy, with the actual buying and selling transactions being via whatever monetary means exist, as long as you have the mark so that you can participate in that economy. The mark says only "I belong."

Soon after the Beast's "resurrection," and as part of his global peace, the Beast will cause the Jews to begin to rebuild the temple, and so the Jews will hail him as Messiah. Muslims also will hail him as the Muslim saviour—people from all the nations of the world will hail the Beast as saviour.

As part of the Beast's global peace, the world will be divided into ten regions. Upon the Beast's "resurrection," the rulers of those ten regions will give the Beast their power, so that he will rule over the ten regions of the world. Three of those ten will reconsider and try to take back their power, but the Beast will forcefully subdue them and retain power, and so the Beast will be the ruler of the world. The nation Babylon the Great, a once-great Christian nation that turned its back on God in a spectacular way, and which will also be the greatest military and financial power on the planet, will be the Beast's initial power base. The Beast will be the King of the world for a total of three and a half years, and he will be worshiped as Christ returned.

During those three and a half years of the Beast's reign there will be Two Witnesses in Jerusalem exposing the Beast as a liar and as a false Christ. Those Two Witnesses will perform great miracles, and no one will be able to harm them—they will be God's voice of truth to the world during that time of great lies.

Simultaneous with the Two Witnesses, also during the three-and-a-half-year rule of the Beast, 144,000 people will be chosen, anointed and sent out by God into the whole world to preach the gospel to the whole of humanity—36,000 of those will be Jews, the remaining 108,000 will be, in the eyes of the world, Gentiles.

During that same three-and-a-half-year rule of the Beast, the church will be fully on the Earth, and the Beast will hunt the church, go to war against the church, persecute, kill and overcome the church (Matt 24:9). The church will refuse to worship the Beast and will, together with the Two Witnesses, declare the Beast to be a liar, a False Christ, but the church will be overcome by the Beast. When the world sees the Beast overcome the church, that will only be an even greater affirmation that the Beast is, in fact, Christ returned, and that the church, which is overcome by the Beast, is a false church, spreading only lies, for if that church was indeed the "true" church belonging to the "true" Christ, then how could the Beast overcome the church? The Beast's conquest of the church only further establishes him, to the world, as the "true" Christ.

The Book of Revelation–A Summary

During the Beast's three-and-a-half-year reign, there will be many people, non-Christians, who will *not* take the mark of the Beast and who, in fact, will *help* the persecuted church. As a result of the Two Witnesses in Jerusalem, and also as a result of the preaching of the 144,000, many people will believe and come to Christ.

At about three and a half years into the reign of the Beast, the rebuilding of the temple in Jerusalem will be completed. At that same time, the Beast will himself go to Jerusalem to confront the Two Witnesses. He will kill them, and their bodies will lie in the streets of Jerusalem for three and a half days, and the whole world, all those who belong to the Beast and who have taken his mark, will celebrate the death of the Two Witnesses and will exchange gifts with one another in that celebration. They will also even further honor and worship the Beast for, in killing the untouchable Witnesses, the Beast will accomplish what no one else could do. The Beast's killing of the Two Witnesses will only further establish him, to the world, as the "true" Christ.

After he kills the Two Witnesses, and while the world is in great celebration, the Beast, still in Jerusalem, will go to the rebuilt temple, where the Jews have only just begun to institute the daily sacrifice. When he gets there, the Beast will stop the daily sacrifice and go into the heart of the temple, going into the holy of holies. He will then set up, in the holy of holies, a throne for himself, and he will then seat himself upon that throne, in the holy of holies, proclaiming himself as Almighty God. That event is the abomination of desolation, and it is the event that marks the end of the Beast's reign and the beginning of the Great Tribulation.

Right after the Beast enthrones himself in the temple, and while the world is celebrating, a Voice will be heard from the sky, in Jerusalem, speaking to the bodies of the dead Witnesses which are lying in the streets of Jerusalem, telling them to rise and to come up. Then, in full view of the celebrating world, the Two Witnesses will be resurrected and will ascend to heaven. The world will see this and be terrified, and a great earthquake will strike Jerusalem, where the Beast will be sitting enthroned in the holy of holies, and 7,000 people will die, but the rest of the people in Jerusalem will believe and come to Christ.

It is then, at the mid-point of Seal 5, after the abomination of desolation, which is the Beast's enthroning of himself in the holy of holies of the rebuilt temple, that the Great Tribulation begins. This Tribulation upon the Earth will last for a total of three and a half years, the exact same length as was the reign of the Beast, and is unleashed by Trumpets 1 to 5, all of which are part of Seal 5. Those Trumpets bring great devastation to the Earth, but the church, during that same time, is protected in the wilderness, in a place of refuge, and kept from harm. The harm of that Tribulation falls only upon those who have the mark of the Beast and upon his kingdom.

Five months before the end of the Tribulation, Trumpet 5 will sound and will release Bowls 1 to 5, with one Bowl being poured upon the Earth every thirty days—all of this is still during Seal 5. The five Bowls bring even greater global devastation, much more frequent, and much more intense, than what came before, just as in birth pains. With the end of Bowl 5, the Great Tribulation is over, and Seal 6 is opened.

With the Earth devastated, but with the church protected, Seal 6 is opened and unleashes Trumpet 6, which in turn unleashes Bowls 6 and 7. The purpose of the events of Seal 6 is the destruction of the nation Babylon the Great, the Beast's initial power base. Seal 6 will last a total of thirty days, and armies will gather to militarily destroy Babylon the Great, with those armies to be led by the Beast himself. Babylon the Great falls with the end of Seal 6, 1,290 days after the abomination of desolation. With the end of Seal 6, and with the fall of Babylon the Great, the world is in darkness.

It is in that darkness that Seal 7 is opened. With the opening of Seal 7, Trumpet 7, the last Trumpet, sounds, and with its sounding *all* the Christians who have ever lived and died are resurrected, and rise into the sky to meet Jesus Christ, who has returned to Earth and who is waiting for them in the clouds, and so the resurrected believers will all gather with him before he descends to Earth. First, the dead Christians will be resurrected, and then the church who is still alive on Earth, and still protected, will be transformed into their resurrected selves, changed in the twinkling of an eye. All the resurrected believers then rise into the sky to meet Jesus, to gather with him there—this resurrection of the church and the subsequent gathering with Jesus Christ in the sky is referred to as the "wedding" of the Bride and the Lamb.

Once the whole church is resurrected and gathered in the sky with Jesus, then Jesus Christ, followed by the entire resurrected church, descends to Earth with a shout, descending to the Earth while the darkness of Seal 6 is still upon the Earth, and so he comes as a "thief in the night," as a "thief in the darkness." As he descends, the Lord Jesus Christ first touches the Earth on the Mount of Olives, exactly 1,335 days after the abomination of desolation. At his landing upon the Mount of Olives, the Mount of Olives splits in two to create a large valley into which the Jews of Jerusalem, and other non-Christians who are there and who did not take the mark of the Beast, will flee for refuge. From there Jesus goes to the valley of Armageddon, where the armies of the world are gathered to make war with him. He destroys them with a word, with the breath of his mouth, and they dissolve on the spot.

The Beast and the False Prophet however are taken alive and thrown into the Lake of Fire, the first beings ever to be cast into that Fire. Satan is then bound in chains by a great angel and thrown into the prison of the Pit, the Abyss, inside the Earth, to be bound for one thousand years.

Jesus then goes to the rebuilt temple, in Jerusalem, and takes his seat in the holy of holies, assuming the throne of David, where he sits as the King returned. With that event, Seal 7 is completed, and the Seven Seals are over.

After the Lord Jesus Crist is enthroned in Jerusalem, all the people who remain on Earth, the mortal, non-resurrected people who remain of the nations that went to war against Jesus at Armageddon, *all* of which are non-Christians, stand before Jesus in judgment. He divides those non-Christians into two groups—on his right is the group who did *not* take the mark of the Beast, and who helped Christians during the time of great persecution, they are called "sheep," and on his left are the people who *did* take the mark of the Beast, they are called "goats." The "sheep" are welcomed into the kingdom, where they will live, work and have children as mortal people, ruled over by the resurrected Christians and by Jesus Christ. The "goats" are killed and sent to the Realm of the Dead to await their resurrection and judgment.

For the next one thousand years, in the kingdom comprised of both immortal, resurrected Christians and mortal, non-resurrected people, there is peace, love, joy, fulfillment, children, families, work and harmony, all under the lordship of Jesus Christ. After one thousand years, Satan is released from the Pit and, over time, deceives the younger generations who were born during Jesus' reign and who did not know the world before his reign, and Satan deceives those people to go to war against Jesus Christ in Jerusalem. A great army gathers, from all over the world, to go to war against Jesus Christ in Jerusalem, and surrounds Jerusalem. But fire comes down from the sky and consumes them all, and there is no battle, and their rebellion is over. It is then that Satan is taken and cast into the Lake of Fire, along with *all* of the rest of the fallen angels who rebelled with him in heaven.

After that event there is the resurrection of all non-believers, who are raised to judgment, resurrected from the Realm of the Dead, where they have been awaiting judgment. The resurrected non-believers will be judged according to their works, since they had no faith. They will be given the reality of their free-will choice, which is the choice to be apart from God, and so will also be cast into the Lake of Fire. At that point, the now-empty Realm of the Dead, and also the Pit, both inside the Earth, collapse into the Lake of Fire, which itself is in the very heart of the Earth. It is then that a global fire is unleashed upon the Earth, almost certainly having its source from within the Earth, and that fire will consume everything on Earth that was *not* done unto God, but will *leave* everything that *was* done unto God, so that all that was done and made by humanity, done and made unto God, *will remain*, and will become part of the everlasting culture of God's kingdom. During that time, the fire will also burn the sky, so that both Earth and Sky are refined by the fire.

The result of the fire is that the everlasting Earth will be redeemed, as will the Sky, and so the redeemed Earth and Sky are described as a "new heaven and a new earth." In that redemption, the curse upon the Earth of the seas and oceans, as well as the curse of darkness, both elements present upon the Earth since Genesis 1:2, will be removed, so that there will now, finally, be no more curse upon the Earth.

At that time the New Jerusalem will descend to Earth from heaven, the place that Jesus prepared in heaven for his Bride. It comes to Earth, to remain on Earth forever, and with it comes the throne of God the Father and the throne of the Son, both of which are in the heart of the city, and Father and Son will sit enthroned, on *Earth*, in the New Jerusalem, with the Holy Spirit flowing out from them as the River of the Waters of Life, and the Bride, the church, God's Companion, will live in the New Jerusalem, on Earth, forever.

God's glorious kingdom and the New Jerusalem will now be upon the surface of the redeemed Earth, with God himself dwelling in the New Jerusalem on Earth, together with the redeemed humanity, but deep inside that same Earth, in the heart of the Earth, there remains the Lake of Fire, in which will be the whole humanity of non-believers as well as Satan and all the fallen angels, and their smoke will rise and be visible on the surface of the Earth.

These are the events of Revelation, outlined in chronological order.

A SUMMARY OF CHAPTERS

The actual book of Revelation is constantly going back and forth in time, and so the chronological events outlined above are not in fact conveyed in the book of Revelation as one chronological timeline, but as three timelines which go back and forth in time. The following is a brief chapter by chapter overview of the book of Revelation with a description as to how they fit into the chronological timeline.

Chapter 1

The Introduction, telling us that John is on Patmos and that Jesus Christ appears to him while he is there. Jesus tells John that he is to write down what he will see and hear.

Chapters 2 & 3

Jesus dictates to John seven letters to seven churches, with each letter addressed to the *angel* of the church, the protector of that church to which the letter is being sent. In each letter, Jesus describes what is good in that church and what is not good in that church and which therefore needs attention. For two of the seven churches Jesus has nothing bad to say, only good, for one church he has only bad to say, nothing good. He then tells the churches to prepare for what is to come and, if they persevere and endure through what is to come, they will receive rewards. The rewards that he lists are the rewards listed in Revelation 21 and 22, rewards that follow his Second Coming and the establishing of his kingdom on Earth.

Chapters 4 & 5

John is taken to heaven, where he sees twenty-four thrones, with twenty-four elders wearing crowns seated upon the thrones. He also sees four living creatures, a host of angels, and a great throne in the midst of all of that, with one seated upon the throne.

The one on the throne holds a scroll with Seven Seals, but no one in Creation can open the Seals. Then a Lamb appears, and the Lamb is the *only* one who can open the Seven Seals.

Chapter 6

This chapter lists the opening of Seals 1 to 6, which encompass a total of forty years—this is the big-picture timeline of Revelation. Seal 1 is the apostasy of the church and the birth of the Beast. Seal 2 is the Global War. Seal 3 is the Global famine. Seal 4 is the global death from the war, the famine and from disease—twenty-five percent of all humanity die from the war, famine and disease. Seals 1 to 4 encompass thirty-three years. Seal 5 is opened next and lasts for seven years and is when the Beast comes to power and rules for three and a half years, persecuting the church during that time. The Great Tribulation happens here, at the mid-point of Seal 5, and lasts for three and a half years. Seal 6 is darkness upon the Earth and is the gathering of armies and the fall of Babylon the Great. This is the chronology of the Seven Seals, all as exactly outlined by Jesus Christ in Matthew 24:3–29, and covering a period of forty years, from the opening of Seal 1 to the end of Seal 6. This is Timeline No. 1, the big, overall picture of the entire judgment, with the entirety of that judgment released by the Seven Seals.

Chapter 7

This now goes back in time to give us details on Seal 5. Seal 5 is when the Beast comes to power and during which he rules for three and a half years. Chapter 7 tells us of the 144,000 who will preach the gospel throughout the world in the first half of Seal 5, during the three-and-a-half-year reign of the Beast.

Chapter 8

Chapter 8:1–5 resumes where chapter 6 left off and describes only the *opening* of Seal 7. Once Seal 7 is opened, the action stops, with the description of what follows the opening of Seal 7 resuming in Revelation 19:6. The "peals of thunder, rumblings, flashes of lightning and an earthquake" is the punctuation that denotes that a new timeline will now begin to be outlined.

In chapter 8:6–13 the new timeline begins to be outlined. This is now going back in time to Seal 5, to the three-and-a-half-year Great Tribulation, which is described, in its entirety, by Trumpets 1 to 5. *All* of the Tribulation events, the events of Trumpets 1 to 5, occur during the second half of Seal 5. After Trumpet 4 is blown there is a pause, and an angel proclaims to the world that terrible things are about to follow.

Chapter 9

Describes Trumpets 5 and 6. We are told that Trumpet 5 lasts for five months, and Trumpet 6 describes the gathering of human armies. When Trumpet 5 is blown, it in fact unleashes the events of the Bowls, which are outlined later, and when Bowls 1 to 5 are poured, the Great Tribulation of Seal 5 is over. As events unfold, the opening of Seal 6 releases Trumpet 6, which in turn releases Bowls 6 and 7, resulting in the destruction of Babylon the Great.

Chapter 10

A scene in heaven, John is told by an angel that when Trumpet 7 is blown, "it will all be accomplished," and John is told to eat a little scroll and to continue to prophesy.

Chapter 11

We are now taken back in time, again to the first half of Seal 5, to the three-and-a-half-year reign of the Beast, the same timeframe of the 144,000 of chapter 7. Chapter 11 describes the Two Witnesses who will be on the Earth during the reign of the Beast, simultaneously with the 144,000, and the Witnesses will be exposing the Beast as a liar and as a false Christ. The Beast kills the Witnesses, in Jerusalem, and then the Witnesses are resurrected. Upon their resurrection, the Great Tribulation is unleashed.

We then go forward in time and resume with the action that follows Trumpet 6, which is the sounding of Trumpet 7, the last Trumpet. With the blowing of Trumpet 7 the angel announces that now the kingdom of the world becomes the kingdom of Jesus Christ. Trumpet 7, the last Trumpet, announces the resurrection of believers and the Second Coming. The action stops here, only to resume in Revelation 19:6. The "flashes of lightning, rumblings, peals of thunder, an earthquake and a severe hailstorm" is the punctuation that denotes that a new timeline will now begin to be outlined.

Chapter 12

Before the next timeline is outlined, we are again taken back in time, far back in time to the angelic rebellion, to the fall of Lucifer and of the rebel angels and are quickly taken to the birth of Jesus Christ and to his resurrection, followed by a description of the birth of the church. Upon the description of the birth of the church, we are taken far forward in time to the persecution of the church by the Beast in the first half of Seal 5, as well as the protection of the church during the Great Tribulation in the second half of Seal 5.

Chapter 13

Still back in time, this describes the Beast coming to power in Seal 5, telling us of his "death" and "resurrection" and that he is given global rule and authority by the dragon, and we are told that he persecutes, and overcomes, the church. We are also told of the second beast, the False Prophet, deceiving the world to worship the Beast, and instituting a new global economy, in which one can only participate if they receive the mark of the Beast.

Chapter 14

A behind the scenes look at events happening during the reign of the Beast in the first half of Seal 5, continuing to describe the fall of Babylon the Great and, symbolically, death during the Tribulation.

Chapter 15

The prelude to the outline of the next timeline, the timeline of the final five months of the Tribulation, with Bowls 1 to 5 being released by Trumpet 5, and then with Bowls 6 and 7 being released by Trumpet 6 to accomplish the fall of Babylon the Great.

Chapter 16

The outline of the next timeline—the Seven Bowls are poured, with Bowls 1 to 5 released by Trumpet 5, and encompassing the final five months of the three-and-a-half-year Tribulation. With the pouring of Bowl 5, the Great Tribulation is over. Bowls 6 and 7 are released with the sounding of Trumpet 6, which is itself released by Seal 6, and which results in the destruction of Babylon the Great and the ensuing darkness upon the Earth.

Chapter 17 & 18

Back in time, a description of the Seal 6/Trumpet 6/Bowls 6 and 7 destruction of Babylon the Great.

Chapter 19

The action of all three timelines—the action of Seal 7 and Trumpet 7, and the action which *follows* Bowl 7—resumes here, and from here on in, to the end of Revelation, it is now one chronological timeline. We are first given a description of the "wedding" of the Lamb, which is the resurrection of all believers, dead and living, who will be resurrected and then gathered to meet Jesus in the sky before he descends to Earth. This event precedes Jesus' descent to Earth.

Revelation 19:11 describes the Second Coming, where Jesus himself descends to Earth and destroys the armies gathered against him at Armageddon. The Beast and the False Prophet are taken and thrown alive into the Lake of Fire.

Chapter 20

Satan is taken and bound and cast into the prison of the Abyss, inside the Earth, to be imprisoned there for one thousand years, while Jesus and the resurrected church rule the Earth, the kingdom of the Lord Jesus Christ.

After one thousand years, Satan is released from the Abyss and deceives the nations to go to war against Jesus Christ in Jerusalem, but those armies are quickly destroyed. Satan is then taken and thrown into the Lake of Fire, and all the dead non-believers are resurrected and stand in judgment before Jesus Christ, judged according to their works, since they have no faith, and they will be cast into the Lake of Fire, according to their own free will choice. Death and Hades, the Realm of the Dead, also collapse into the Lake of Fire, in the heart of the Earth.

Chapter 21

The Earth and the Sky are redeemed, and the curse of seas and oceans is gone and the New Jerusalem descends down from heaven, onto Earth, and with it comes the throne of God the Father and of the Son, to remain here, on Earth, forever. The curse of darkness, the curse of night, is also gone. All the redeemed church lives in the New Jerusalem with the Father and the Son.

Chapter 22

A further description of the New Jerusalem, of God's throne in the city and of the Holy Spirit flowing from the throne of the Father and of the Son, flowing as the River of the Waters of Life, and with the Tree of Life in its midst.

The final chapter of Revelation ends with a warning to not add or take away any words from the prophecy, concluding with an invitation for all to "Come" and take the free gift of the water of life.

With that, the book of Revelation ends.

FINAL WORDS AND BLESSING

The book of Revelation ends with hope and redemption, but also on a very unfinished note, for deep within the same redeemed Earth of God's everlasting kingdom, where sits the New Jerusalem and where live all the redeemed, is the Lake of Fire, with a resurrected humanity alive in that fire, together with Satan and all the fallen angelic beings. The ending scene of Revelation tells us that there is more to come, and what is to come will unfold in the "ages to come" (Eph 2:7).

Throughout the Bible, the major symbols and imagery of Revelation—beasts, prostitutes, Babylon—are explained for us, so that, when we encounter them in Revelation, we can understand them.

In addition to that, Jesus himself explains for us the Seven Seals of Revelation, in order and in detail, in Matthew 24:3–31, and it is his explanation that enables us to know, with certainty, the chronology of many of the key events of Revelation. It is essential to understand that the Seven Seals are the entirety of the events that precede the Second Coming, with the Trumpets and Bowls being only details of the final three Seals. The Seven Seals, together, encompass a period of forty years, with the entire three-and-a-half-year reign of the Beast as well as the entire three-and-a-half-year Tribulation occurring during Seal 5. The Seven Seals are, as Jesus describes them in Matthew 24, "birth pains," for they culminate in the "birth" of God's kingdom on Earth, to be established by Jesus at his Second Coming.

With all of this in mind, the events of Revelation are understandable, and they are profound. We can understand the events of Revelation because God has shown us how to understand them, understanding them, and the entirety of the book of Revelation, from God's own Scripture, which speaks to every aspect of Revelation. One of the very key parts of Scripture that speaks to the events outlined in Revelation is the book of Daniel, to which Jesus himself refers in Matthew 24:15. God has not left us to flounder in our attempts to understand Revelation, rather he has given us everything we need to understand it.

As the book of Revelation itself begins with a blessing upon all those who read its words aloud, so I end this book with a blessing upon all those who study Revelation, a blessing of insight and understanding, a blessing of hope and wonder, a blessing of awe and amazement at God, at his love and his redemption.

www.ingramcontent.com/pod-product-compliance
Lightning Source LLC
Chambersburg PA
CBHW081148290426
44108CB00018B/2473